Education and Federalism in India

Education and Federalism in India

M.R. Kolhatkar

RAWAT PUBLICATIONS
Jaipur • New Delhi • Bangalore • Hyderabad • Guwahati

ISBN 978-81-316-0522-6

Published by
Prem Rawat for **Rawat Publications**
Satyam Apts, Sector 3, Jawahar Nagar, Jaipur 302 004 (India)
Phone: 0141 265 1748 / 7006 Fax: 0141 265 1748
E-mail: info@rawatbooks.com
Website: www.rawatbooks.com

New Delhi Office
4858/24, Ansari Road, Daryaganj, New Delhi 110 002
Phone: 011 2326 3290

Also at *Bangalore, Hyderabad* and *Guwahati*

Typeset by Rawat Computers, Jaipur
Printed at Nice Printing Press, New Delhi

Contents

List of Table and Boxes

List of Tables

List of Boxes

Acronyms and Abbreviations

AE	Adult Education
AEC	Adult Education Centre
AICTE	All-India Council for Technical Education
AIIMS	All-India Institute of Medical Sciences
AISES	All-India School Education Survey
AIU	Association of Indian Universities
ARC	Administrative Reforms Commission
Art.	Article of Constitution
AMU	Aligarh Muslim University
ASIST	Assistance for Strengthening of Infrastructure of Science & Technology
AYUSH	Ayurveda, Unani, Siddha and Homoeopathy
BHU	Banaras Hindu University
BITS	Birla Institute of Technology & Science
BPU	Bureau for Promotion of Urdu
CABE	Central Advisory Board of Education
CAS	Centre for Advanced Study
CAT	Common Admission Test
CBSE	Central Board of Secondary Education
CCE	Continuous & Comprehensive Evaluation
CDC	Curriculum Development Centre
CDP	Community Development Project
CE	Continuing Education
CEC	Continuing Education Centre
CHD	Central Hindi Directorate
CIFE	Central Institute of Fishery Education
CIEFL	Central Institute of English & Foreign Languages
CIET	Central Institute of Educational Technology
CIIL	Central Institute of Indian Languages
CISCE	Council for Indian School Certificate Examination
CIVE	Central Institute for Vocational Education

CLASS	Computer Literacy & Studies in School
COBSE	Council of Boards of Secondary Education
COL	Commonwealth of Learning
COSIST	Scheme of Strengthening of Infrastructural Facilities in Science & Technology
CPWD	Central Public Works Department
CSIR	Council for Scientific and Industrial Research
CSTT	Commission for Scientific and Technological Terminology
CTE	College of Teacher Education
CU	Central University
CVCP	Committee of Vice-Chancellors and Principals
DA	Dearness Allowance
DAE	Directorate of Adult Education/Department of Atomic Energy
DBT	Department of Bio-Technology
DEI	Distance Education Institute
DEC	Distance Education Council
DEEL	Department of Elementary Education and Literacy
DIET	District Institute of Education & Training
DONER	Development of North-Eastern Region (Department or Ministry for)
DOS	Department of Space
DPEP	District Primary Education Programme
DRDO	Defence Research & Development Organization
DU	Deemed University/Delhi University
DWCD	Department of Woman and Child Development
DHE	Department of Higher Education
EAI	Eradication of Adult Illiteracy
EB	Educationally Backward
EC	European Commission
ECCE	Early Childhood Care & Education
EE	Elementary Education
EFA	Education for All
EGS	Education Guarantee Scheme/Employment Guarantee Scheme
ESTD	Established
FRI	Forest Research Institute

FYP	Five-Year Plan
GATS	General Agreement for Trade in Services
GER	Gross Enrolment Ratio
HEIs	Higher Education Institutions/s
HC	High Court
IAMR	Institute of Applied Manpower Research
IARI	Indian Agricultural Research Institute
IASE	Institute of Advanced Study in Education
ICDS	Integrated Child Development Services
ICFRE	Indian Council for Forestry Research & Education
ICHR	Indian Council of Historical Research
ICMR	Indian Council of Medical Research
ICPR	Indian Council of Philosophical Research
ICSSR	Indian Council of Social Science Research
ICT	Information & Communication Technology
IES	Indian Education Service
IIM	Indian Institute of Management
IIT	Indian Institute of Technology
IIS	Indian Institute of Science
IIIT/M	Indian Institute of Information Technology & Management
IIEP	International Institute of Educational Planning
IGNOU	Indira Gandhi National Open University
ILO	International Labour Organization
IMA	Indian Management Association/Medical Association
INFLIBNET	Information and Library Network
INI	Institute of National Importance
ISC	Inter-State Council
ISI	Indian Statistical Institute
ISM	Indian School of Mines
ISMH	Indian Systems of Medicine & Homoeopathy
ISRO	Indian Space Research Organization
ITI	Industrial Training Institute
IUB	Inter-University Board
IVRI	Indian Veterinary Research Institute
JRF	Junior Research Fellowship

JNU	Jawaharlal Nehru University
JNV	Jawahalal Navodaya Vidyalayas
KHS	Kendriya Hindi Sansthan
KOU	Kota Open University
KV/S	Kendriya Vidyalaya/Samiti
LCI	Law Commission of India
MDM	Mid-day Meal
MNP	Minimum Needs Programme
MoA	Memorandum of Association
MoU	Memorandum of Understanding
MTA	Mid-Term Appraisal (of Five-Year Plan)
NAB	National Accreditation Board
NAAC	National Assessment & Accreditation Council
NBT	National Book Trust
NCERT	National Council for Educational Research & Training
NCHE	National Council for Higher Education
NCOS	National Consortium for Open Schooling
NCPSL	National Council for Promotion of Sindhi Language
NCPUL	National Council for Promotion of Urdu Language
NCRI	National Council for Rural Institutes
NCTE	National Council for Teacher Education
NDA-I	National Democratic Alliance (Government-I) (2004–2009)
NDA-II	National Democratic Alliance (Government-II) (2009 onwards).
NDC	National Development Council
NDRI	National Dairy Research Institute
NEHU	North-Eastern Hill University
NER	North-Eastern Regions
NERIST	North-Eastern Regional Institute of Science & Technology
NET	National Eligibility Test
NF	National Front (Government)
NGO	Non-governmental Organization
NIAE	National Institute of Adult Education

NIEPA	National Institute of Educational Planning & Administration
NLMA	National Literacy Mission Authority
NIC	National Informatics Centre/National Integration Council
NIOS	National Institute of Open Schooling
NIPER	National Institute of Pharmaceutical Education & Research
NITTR	National Institute of Technical Teachers' Training & Research
NITIE	National Institute of Training in Industrial Engineering
NIT	National Institute of Technology
NPE	National Policy on Education
NPEGEL	National Programme for Education of Girls at Elementary Level
NUEPA	National University for Educational Planning & Administration
NV	Navodaya Vidyalaya
NVS	Navodaya Vidyalaya Samiti
OS	Open School(ing)
OU	Open University
PC	Planning Commission
PG	Post-Graduate
PGIMER	Post-Graduate Institute of Medical Education & Research
PoA	Programme of Action
PTA	Parent-Teacher Association
QIP	Quality Improvement Programme
R&D	Research & Development
REC	Regional Engineering College
RFLP	Rural Functional Literacy Project
RIE	Regional Institute of Education
RRC	Regional Resource Centre
S	Section (of Act, Bill etc.)
SAARC	South Asian Association for Regional Cooperation
SAU	State Agricultural University
SC	Supreme Court
SCs	Scheduled Castes
SCERT	State Council for Educational Research & Training

SCHE	State Council for Higher Education
SCTIMST	Sree Chitra Tirunal Institute of Medical Science & Technology
SCVE	State Council for Vocational Education
SIE	State Institute of Education
SIET	State Institute of Educational Technology
SLIET	Sant Longowal Institute of Engineering & Technology
SLM	Self-Learning Material
SLMA	State Literacy Mission Authority
SPA	School of Planning & Architecture
SPOA	State Programme of Action
SRC	State Resource Centre
SSA	Sarva Shiksha Abhiyan
STs	Scheduled Tribes
SUPW	Socially Useful Productive Work
TA	Travelling Allowance
TE-QIP	Technical Education-Quality Improvement Programme
TLC	Total Literacy Campaign
TLE	Teaching Learning Equipment
TTTI	Technical Teachers Training Institute
UEE	Universalization of Elementary Education
UF	United Front (Government)
UG	Under-Graduate
UGC	University Grants Commission (India)/University Grants Committee (UK)
UN/O	United Nations/Organization
UNDP	United Nations Development Programme
UNESCO	United Nations Educational, Scientific & Cultural Organization
UNFPA	United Nations Population Fund
UNICEF	United Nations Children Fund
UNFEM	United Nations Programme for Women
UPA	United Progressive Alliance (Government)
UPE	Universalization of Primary Education
UT	Union Territory
VO	Voluntary Organization
WTO	World Trade Organization
VE/P	Vocational Education/Programme
ZC	Zonal Council

Abbreviations used for widely cited Reports

1. **ARC Report (Main):** Report of Administrative Reforms Commission on ....(Subject). (Government of India, Ministry of Home Affairs, New Delhi, 1969–71).
2. **Dar Commission Report:** Report of Linguistic Provinces Commission of the Constituent Assembly (Chairman: Justice Dar).
3. **Gajendragadkar Report:** Report of the Committee on Governance of Universities and Colleges, Part I – Governance of Universities (UGC, New Delhi 1971).
4. **Gnanam Report:** Report of the UGC Committee: Towards New Educational Management (UGC, New Delhi 1990).
5. **Hartog Report:** Auxiliary Committee Report on Review of Growth of Education in British India: Interim Report of the Indian Statutory Commission (Government of India, Calcutta, September, 1929).
6. **Janardhan Reddy Report:** Report of CABE Committee on Policy (Ministry of HRD/Department of Education, Government of India, New Delhi, January 1992).
7. **Jha Report:** Report of the Review Committee on the UGC (Ministry of Education and Social Welfare, Government of India, New Delhi, 1977).
8. **JVP Report:** Report of the Congress Party in Constituent Assembly on Dar Commission Report [Known after three Members: Jawaharlal (Nehru), Vallabhabhai (Patel) and Pattabhi (Sitaramayya), then President of the Congress].
9. **Kothari Report:** Report of the Education Commission 1964–66 (Ministry of Education, Government of India, New Delhi, 1966) (NCERT Reprint, 1970).
10. **Madhuri Shah Report:** Report of the Committee to Enquire into the Working of the Central Universities (UGC, New Delhi, 1983) [Chairman: Dr Mrs Madhuri R. Shah, then Chairman of UGC].
11. **Madhuri Shah Task Force Report:** Report of the Task Force on Working of NCERT (New Delhi, 1984) [Chairperson: Dr Mrs Madhuri R. Shah, former Chairman of UGC].
12. **Model Act Report:** Report of the UGC Committee on Model Act for Universities (UGC, New Delhi, 1964) [Chairman: Prof. D.S. Kothari].
13. **Montford Report:** Report on Indian Constitutional Reforms (HMSO, London, 1918).

14. **Mudaliar Report:** Report of the Secondary Education Commission (Government of India, New Delhi, September, 1953).
15. **The Muddiman Report:** Report of the Reforms Enquiry Committee (Calcutta: Government of India, Central Publication Branch, 1929) [Chairman: Sir Alexander Muddiman].
16. **Nagchaudhuri Report:** Report of Review of NCERT (Government of India, 1969).
17. **NPE 1968:** National Policy of Education 1968 (Ministry of Education, Government of India, New Delhi, 1968).
18. **NPE 1986:** National Policy of Education 1986.
19. **NPE 1986/92:** National Policy of Education 1986 as modified in 1992 (Ministry of Education, Government of India, New Delhi, 1992).
20. **PoA 1986:** Programme of Action, 1986 (Ministry of Education, Government of India, New Delhi, 1986).
21. **PoA 1992:** Programme of Action, 1992 (Ministry of Education, Government of India, New Delhi, 1992).
22. **Punchchi Commission Report:** Report of the Commission on Centre-State Relations [Chairman: Justice M.M. Punchchi, 2010].
23. **Radhakrishnan Report:** Report of University Education Commission (Ministry of Education, Government of India, New Delhi, 1949, Reprint 1983) [Chairman: Dr S. Radhakrishnan].
24. **Rajamannar Report:** Report of the Centre-State Relations Inquiry Committee (Government of Tamil Nadu, Madras 1971).
25. **Ramamurti Report:** Report of the Committee for Review of NPE 1986 – Final Report (New Delhi, December, 1990). (Entitled: "Toward a More Humane and Enlightened Society").
26. **Robbins Report:** Report of the Committee on Higher Education, (HMSO, London, 1963) [Chairman: Lord Lionel Robbins].
27. **Sachar Report:** Report of Prime Minister's High Level Committee on Social, Economic and Educational Status of the Muslim Community in India (Cabinet Secretariat, Government of India, November, 2006).
28. **Sarkaria Report:** Report of the Commission on Centre-State Relations, Vol.I & II (Government of India, New Delhi 1988).
29. **Sadler Report:** Report of Calcutta University Commission (Manager, Government Press, Calcutta, 1919). [Chairman: Prof. Michael Sadler].

30. **Sapru Report:** Report of the Committee of Members of Parliament on Higher Education (Ministry of Education, Government of India, 1964).
31. **Sargent Report/Plan:** Educational Development in India: Report by CABE (Government of India, New Delhi, 1944, Reprint 1964) [Chairman: Sir John Sargent].
32. **Simon Report:** Report of the Indian Statutory Commission, Vol. I & II (Government of India, Calcutta 1930).
33. **Soneri Report:** Report of CABE Committee on Gnanam Committee Report. (1992, Mimeo). [Chairman: Karsandas Soneri, Education Minister, Gujarat].
34. **SRC Report:** States Reorganization Commission Report (Government of India, New Delhi 1955).
35. **Venkatachaliah Report, Vol. I:** Report of the National Commission to Review the Working of the Constitution of India (or NCRWC), New Delhi, Universal Book Publishers, 2002).

Preface and Acknowledgement

This is a revised and updated version of my Ph.D. thesis on a related theme.

In the US all political discourse begins and ends with federalism. In India, federalism became a live issue in the 1980s when Indira Gandhi was compelled to constitute Sarkaria Commission on Centre-State Relations. Sarkaria Report is indeed a magnum opus of federalism in India. The Supreme Court in its Bommai judgment (1994) recognized federalism as part of the basic structure of the Constitution. Education is an instrumentality of human resource development and their interrelationship is a challenging theme. No apology is needed for attempting this theme.

Since the thesis was submitted in July 2006 and in view of the lapse of time of about three-and-a-half years, I have tried to update it as to the facts. Fortunately, I was able even to refer to the successor report to Sarkaria, viz., Punchchi Commission Report, submitted to government in April 2010.

First of all, I wish to place on record my thanks to late Prof. Amrik Singh, the doyen of Indian scholars on education. He was kind enough to go through my original thesis during his visit to Mumbai and had encouraged me to publish it. It is a matter of profound regret that he is no more to peruse it.

Next, I wish to thank Dr. Vijay Khole, former Vice-Chancellor of the Mumbai University for providing me with certain physical facilities in the Fort Library of the University.

I am also grateful to Shri Pranit Rawat of Rawat Publications, who readily agreed to publish the revised thesis under his imprint.

I wish to thank Shri Anil Lele who, as in the past, typed and retyped several versions of chapters. That he could decipher my handwriting and various signs and symbols is a tribute to his unique skills, good humour and willingness to act beyond call of duty.

As in the past, I have drawn on the resources of the Fort and Kalina Libraries of the University of Mumbai and Asiatic Society Library and the

IIPA Library, Mumbai. At the Fort Library, in particular, I am thankful to Mrs. Tilaka Joseph and her successor Ms. Anjali Kale and their staff-cum-sorority including, in particular, Ms. Varsha Deodhar for supplying me with books as and when required.

Lastly, I could not have completed this venture but for the whole hearted and unstinted support and latitude extended to me by my wife Mrs. Sushama and my daughter Ms. Uttara.

Needless to add, I am alone responsible for the way the final output in the form of revised and updated thesis has emerged.

Part I

Introduction

1 The Dynamics of Education and Federalism

The main aim of the present study is to consider the interrelationship between education and federalism as a political system, and specifically to explore the impact of federalism on education. In this introductory chapter, the objectives and role of education in modern societies with special reference to India are examined and thereafter the significance of federalism as a political system is described. The justification for such a joint study is that federalism and education have a symbiotic relationship in the sense of mutually advantageous association, arising from the principle of subsidiarity, according to which in a multi-level political structure (like federalism) the jurisdictional competence should follow the principle of need and efficiency.[1] Under most federal systems,[2] education tends to be a state subject but the State Governments may, on the one hand, devolve primary education to the district level and may, on the other, look up to the central level for financial assistance for tertiary education and research.

Education is a multi-stage (primary, secondary and tertiary stages) and diversified process (tertiary education has several branches like general, technical, teacher, agricultural and medical education and the school curriculum has a variety of aspects like vocational, aesthetic etc. depending on the interface of education with the world of work and with the world of art). It is, therefore, proposed first to deal with the stages and diversity of education and with the changing perspectives on education in modern times and thereafter to introduce the topic of federalism as a preliminary to its detailed treatment.

Stages of Education

The stages of education, their objectives and curricula are briefly set out in Table 1.1.

Table 1.1

Stages of Education, Objectives and Curricula

	Stage of Education	*Objectives and Curricula*
1.	Pre-primary (Age Group 3–6), also called Early Childhood Care & Education (ECCE)	Physical, emotional and intellectual development of children through a variety of methods including play.[3]
2.	Primary (a) Lower primary: Classes I–V (b) Upper primary or middle: Classes VI–VIII	1. To impart skills of literacy (reading and writing with understanding) and numeracy (i.e., computation) through the medium of mother tongue. 2. To prepare individuals to be responsible and useful citizens through study of science, history, geography and civics. 3. Introduction of second language, mostly English
3.	Secondary Education (a) Lower secondary: Classes IX–X (b) Higher secondary: Classes XI–XII	1. Training of character for development of democratic citizenship. 2. Improvement of practical and vocational efficiency. 3. Development of literary, artistic and cultural interests for development of personality. 4. Training for leadership.[4] The curriculum would consist of four major areas: language, mathematics, science and social sciences at an advanced level as clarified in the National Curriculum Framework.[5]
4.	Tertiary Education (a) Diploma level, e.g., polytechnics in technical education (b) Degree level (three years after HSC) (c) Postgraduate level (two years after degree) in general education	The objectives of tertiary education may be derived from those of universities which are: (i) To develop the power of the mind and cultivate right interests, attitudes and moral and intellectual values. (ii) Training for world of work including professions like agriculture, engineering, management, teaching, science and technology etc. (iii) Impart a sense of social purpose.
5.	Research – leading to the degree of Ph.D. (three to five years after postgraduate degree)	(i) To seek and cultivate new knowledge, to engage vigorously and fearlessly in the pursuit of truth and to interpret old knowledge and beliefs in the light of new needs and discoveries. (ii) The above should result in contributions to peer-reviewed journals and application for and award of patents.

Cont'd...

...Cont'd

6.	Adult education – expanded to include life-long education since the Faure Report	This has a practical aspect and an idealistic aspect. In practical terms, it includes: 1. Functional literacy at the minimum for those who missed primary education. 2. Mandatory continuing education (MCE) for professionals in higher education. 3. Imparting of skills for re-employment in post-industrial risk society. In terms of Faure Report, it has: (a) A vertical aspect (education should occur throughout life). (b) A horizontal aspect (promotion of education through non-formal aspects, e.g., media). (c) Democratization aspect which involves removal of barriers that impede access to education and involvement of learners in the design of and management of education. (d) Creation of a learning society as envisaged by Faure Report.

Sources: 1. Report of Education Commission (1966).
2. Report of the Secondary Education Commission (1955).
3. John Holford, *International Perspectives on Life-long Learning* (1999).
4. Report of Faure Commission on Learning To Be (1972).

Diversity and Differentiation in Education

As observed by Faure Commission,[6] the physical, intellectual, emotional and ethical integration of the individual into a complete man is the fundamental aim of education. Education aims not only at cognitive development but also at aesthetic cultivation and prepares man for the world of work. Hence, the division of the academic curriculum into four basic subjects, viz., languages, mathematics, science and social sciences. These are sub-divided further. Language may be taken to stand for humanistic disciplines which include literature, philosophy and history. Science is applied to practical life by way of technology and has been sub-divided into physics, chemistry and biology which have proliferated further. Social sciences are sub-divided into sociology, psychology, political science and public administration and economics, of which the last mentioned discipline now appears to rule the world.

Apart from curricular diversity, there is education for cultivation of senses (aesthetics), of body (sports and physical education), education for adjustment to political life (citizenship education) and education for preparing a citizen for earning livelihood (vocational education).

Higher education finds diversification in the branches of medicine and allied disciplines (nursing, pharmacy, physiotherapy), legal education, teacher education, agricultural and veterinary education, engineering and management education etc.

Likewise, modern education is characterized by institutional differentiation which is particularly salient at higher education stage. We have a variety of colleges and universities. The World Bank Report on Higher Education and Society[7] has distinguished between horizontal and vertical differentiation. Vertical differentiation is manifested in juxtaposition of traditional research university with polytechnics, professional schools, institutions that grant degrees but do not conduct research and community colleges. Horizontal differentiation is seen at work in the co-existence of for-profit colleges and universities with philanthropic and public institutions. Distance learning institutions like open schools and open universities have both vertical and horizontal features.

The Changing Perceptions of Education

Role of Cultural Transmission and Socialization

It would thus be seen that education is a complex phenomenon extending from pre-primary education through primary and secondary education and to tertiary education and research. The perceptions about the role of education have undergone substantial changes over the last three centuries extending from the Enlightenment Europe of the 18th century to the beginning of the 21st century, thanks to socio-economic changes brought about by Democratic Revolutions (in France and USA), Industrial Revolution in England, followed by urbanization, two World Wars, the Russian Revolution in the inter-war period and decolonization after World War II, and the role played by international organizations like the UNESCO and the World Bank in recent years. In the 18th century western Europe, mass education at primary level was regarded as a public service to be provided to its citizens by the newly emerging nation-state on a free and compulsory basis. The European colonial powers transplanted to their colonies (including India) the modern system of education. In India the call for mass primary education and adult literacy was first raised by Keshab Chandra Sen of Brahmo Samaj in the 1870s in Bengal and the same was taken up by Gopal Krishna Gokhale in the Central Legislature of Imperial Government in 1911. However, India was slow to awake to the importance of pre-primary education for sustainability of mass primary education. In this connection, the following observations of Education Commission are significant:

> These, i.e., pre-primary schools attempted to compensate for the unsatisfactory home environment of children from slum areas or poor families … Modern researches have shown that the years between three and ten are

> of the greatest significance in the child's physical, emotional and intellectual development. It has also been found that children who have been to a pre-primary school show better progress at the primary stage and help in reducing wastage and stagnation (para 7.04 of Kothari Report).

The new research after Kothari Report has, if anything, underlined the importance of early childhood care and education (ECCE). It shows that the period 0–6 years is the most critical period in the development of the child when his/her capabilities (health, nutrition, learning abilities etc.) are largely determined. For example, this is the time when 90 per cent of the brain develops and when the nutritional status of Indian children deteriorates in an irreversible way.[8]

Prior to World War II, education was regarded as a sub-system of social system which performs through schooling the function of cultural transmission and socialization.[9]

Education as the Master Determinant of Development

After World War II, education came to be viewed as a master determinant of all aspects of change mainly due to the first wave of decolonization in which leaders of nationalist movements were the products of formal western educational institutions. This perceived role of education in the development process of the developing countries was reinforced within the western societies themselves by the domination of their economy by institutions of research and technological innovation.[10] The existence of the Communist bloc of the countries led by the Soviet Union, the new name for Russia after the Russian Revolution, and its Eastern European satellites as well as the post-World War II revolutionary China, which was technically a member of the Communist bloc, helped to reinforce the role of education in development. The existence of an international organization (i.e., UNESCO) devoted *inter alia* to the promotion of education, and of multilateral development banks (IBRD or World Bank, Asian Bank, African Bank and Inter-American Bank) has influenced national policies for spread of education. Thus, India's Constitution has incorporated the goal of universalization of elementary education by 1960 but as will be seen in the following pages, the stress in Five-Year Plans in the heyday of central planning was on secondary and higher education, especially technical education. In this background, UNESCO encouraged developing member-states to draw up ambitious plans for universalization of primary education and for eradication of illiteracy. Thus, the "Karachi Plan" drawn up for the period 1960–70, envisaged achievement of the above target in Asian countries including India by raising education expenditure to 5.43 per cent of the GNP. This is the background of the target fixed by Kothari Commission of investment of 6 per cent of GNP in education, the bulk of the increase being accounted for substantial increase in the outlays for elementary education and adult literacy. During this period, the World Bank also focused on financing physical infrastructure in developing countries. The decade of 1960–70 however ended with a disillusionment about the role of education. This was due to a complex interplay among social, political and economic factors which may be analysed in terms of political development theory of James S. Coleman.

Education has no doubt a big role to play in development, but the relationship between education and development is not simple and straightforward. There are both positive and negative fallouts as development proceeds. Formal education was a decisive factor in the political socialization process in the US, but the later studies indicated that the influence of education upon political attitudes was more complicated. According to Robert E. Lane, as quoted by Coleman,[11] the longer a student stays in college, the more he or she expresses cynical views on politics and a disinclination to take part in civic or political affairs. Lord Bryce, speaking of Latin America, observed that education if it does not make men good citizens, makes it at least easier for them to become so. Lord Bryce's conclusion was reformulated by Seymour M. Lipset as below: "If we cannot say that a 'high' level of education is a sufficient condition for democracy, the available evidence does suggest that it comes close to being a necessary condition in the modern world."[12]

Developing countries, unlike the developed western countries, are characterized by the continued primacy of the family in socializing the vast mass of population residing in rural areas. This is due to limited social mobilization, weak penetration by the national government, discontinuities in the communication systems and the absence of mass education. Also, these countries are characterized by a very high degree of cultural fragmentation in terms of major political culture discontinuities among traditional authority systems of different ethnic groups (in countries like India, cultural fragmentation may be attributed to the immense cultural diversity as between Hindus and Muslims, Sikhs, Christians, Parsees etc.). But precisely because of this, since developing countries are engaged in the task of nation-building, the national elite in the new states expect the educational system to bear a much heavier load of socialization. Further, there is absence of other, i.e., non-educational non-family socializing agencies, viz., absence of associational life in the form of clubs, fraternities etc.; in other words, there is absence of what is now also called social capital.[13] Thus, the formal education system does carry a heavier load of socialization.

Moreover, the objective of an educational system in all societies being to inculcate in youth attitudes that would support the society in which they live by way either of citizenship training or indoctrination or manipulation of curriculum content, the national elite in developing countries tend to formulate and enforce a national curriculum comprising not only subject mix (e.g., emphasis on science and technology content, rather than humanistic literary content), but also specific values (e.g., secularism). This may involve the way the history of the past is projected in history textbooks in countries like India where the history textbooks for medieval or Mughal period of history could be perceived to promote either secularism (good) or communalism (bad) depending on the approach. In federal settings, states (or sub-units) may be legally in charge of school education, but the federal government may choose to commission and prescribe model textbooks for the whole country or may launch on a project of scrutinizing history textbooks prescribed by opposition ruled State Governments in the name of national integration.

Additionally, the effect of the environment or 'culture' of the school is important in the formulation of political attitudes and mentalities. In the developing countries, the schools may be expected to reinforce achievement orientation and elitism since school lessons are formal – abstract and strictly cognitive. And, since schools are isolated, they tend to deepen the gap between the elite and the mass.

In regard to the role of education in political recruitment, Coleman has pointed out that in most developing countries, there is a tight fit between education and occupational mobility, but since opportunities for promotion are limited, four problems arise: (1) anti-intellectual tendencies get strengthened in post-independence period, (2) there is a tension between incumbent political elites and new bureaucracies and technical cadres, (3) the second-generation aspirants tend to have restricted political mobility, and (4) the unemployed school leavers have an anomic potential. Hence, the original presumptive monopoly of the educated minority in the political arenas gets reduced and political power gravitates toward persons of lower educational attainments who command local power hierarchies. Most importantly, introduction of 'mass' primary education leads to a vast increase in the number of unemployed and underemployed school leavers.

Lastly, formal education by initially perpetuating an elite-mass gap and intensifying divisions among different ethnic, regional and parochial groups may, in the short run, be dysfunctional to political unification. By the operation of the law of unequal development advantage, children of persons in the upper social stratum have greater access to higher education and areas more richly endowed by nature may attract investment more readily. Thus inequalities are exacerbated unless egalitarian political policies are followed. We have, therefore, an equality-capacity dilemma. Short-run inequality maximizes capacity by way of educational expansion devoted to producing high-level manpower, preferential recruitment from groups having the requisite skills or preferential allocation of development funds for the quicker and more substantial returns.[14]

The role of teachers as intellectuals needs to be particularly noted. In colonial societies, teaching (apart from law) was the only profession practically open to subject low class population. As a result, it attracted many people of high ability and energy who would otherwise enter more highly placed professions. As elite they are mid-way between lower classes and lower levels of the professional class which creates among them a personal dissatisfaction with their position. Since they played an active part in the struggle for independence, many of them became legislators and ministers in the immediate post-colonial period. Moreover, they were geographically dispersed with some of them being regarded as prestigious persons in rural communities. They were among the most predisposed, available and qualified elite categories to participate in political life. But, with the introduction of mass education, the teacher's status tends to suffer a relative decline. This progressive devaluation, coupled with their diminished prestige and the loss of their own sense of self-esteem, is an element in a 'deflation syndrome' leading to a political apathy and alienation.[15]

One of the most pervasive problems of inter-elite relationship in developing countries is general discontinuity at two points of tension: (1) the gap between traditional elite and the first wave of modern educated elites, and (2) division between the latter and the succeeding generation of better educated and professionally more qualified persons. This discontinuity also accounts for the schizoid character (simultaneous anti-traditionalism and anti-intellectualism) of the outlook of many of the incumbent groups. It is an important element in the phenomenon of 'student indiscipline'.[16]

Where alternative channels of mobility do not exist (e.g., absence of a vigorous and expanding private sector which can absorb the new products of expanding university system), a politically dysfunctional intellectual proletariat is likely to appear.[17] In India, where a policy of centrally planned socio-economic development was followed with its inevitable licence-permit raj and repression of opportunities for large private sector expansion, this is what appears to have happened.

The World Crisis in Education: The Educational Disjuncture, 1965–68

James Coleman was a political sociologist of the political development perspective who took a macro-view of role of education in the mid-sixties. By that time, a crisis had overtaken education sector world wide which might be called a crisis of growing maladjustment between educational situation and its curricular, employment, equalitarian and development goals. Pragmatically, it was an employment and financial crisis. The educated population had outstripped the capacity of the system to absorb them and the politicians were not willing to put more money into education whose credibility as a development agent was in question. This was described at length by Philip H. Coombs, in 1968, who took a fresh look at it in 1985.[18] The world education crisis of 1968 involving a lack of economic growth and a certain ambivalence about the role of education in development, may be called, following Nivedita Menon and Aditya Nigam as a ruptural educational moment,[19] when the following events of great educational significance took place, nationally and internationally: (1) The Education Commission reported in 1966 leading to the Committee of MPs on Educational Policy which resulted in a rather disappointing NPE 1968, (2) Plan Holidays of the years 1966–69, and (3) Student Rebellion in France 1968, which spread to Europe and to the US. In India, in the political sphere, Congress lost power in 1967 General Elections in most states and Indira Gandhi split the Congress party in 1969. In Indian agriculture, these years coincided with the Agricultural Revolution based on hybrid varieties of seeds in wheat and maize crops but it was only in retrospect that the significance of these developments for the revolution in agricultural productivity was realized. This rupture in educational development, however contained within it seeds of revival of interest in another facet of education, viz., economics of education as against the political sociology of development of James Coleman, so far referred to.

Education as Investment

In fact, James Coleman was the lead author of the much publicized Coleman Commission Report published by the US government which found that socio-economic factors are more important than school variables in explaining regional and racial differences.[20] Such negative findings led to the revival of interest in the earlier work of Schultz and Dension[21] that education contributes directly to the growth of national income by improving the skills and productive capacities of the labour force. Further work in this area underlines the fact that the production function in education, i.e., the process by which inputs are converted into outputs, is far more complex and includes many variables. If both formal and non-formal education ('on-the-job' training, indirect efforts of education and links of education with cognate sectors of development like health and fertility) are considered, the correlation between economic growth and human resource development as measured by literacy and life expectancy is confirmed.[22]

One can also notice that there is a parallel transformation of paradigm of both education and economic development. In the sphere of educational thought, the Faure Report of UNESCO in 1972 marked the transition from the view of education as formal schooling to its new view as *learning* (lasting change in knowledge, skills and attitudes which is the result of experience rather than maturation) and education as a life-long process spanning all the years – infancy to end of life. Marking a further advance, the Delors Report of UNESCO in 1996,[23] identified four pillars of learning, viz., (a) learning to know (learning to learn), (b) learning to do (vocational needs), (c) learning to live together (social aspect), and (d) learning to be (life-long learning) which was emphasized by the earlier (1972) Faure Report.

This transformation in the paradigm of education as investment in human resource development and its extended definition to include lifelong education ran parallel to the paradigm shift in the view of economic development as an increase in per capita income to its view as the process of human development in terms of building up human capacities and creating human opportunities for exercise of those capacities in all compartments of human development, viz., equity, sustainability, productivity and empowerment. A Human Development Index (HDI) is being computed by the UNDP since 1990, which is an amalgam of three components including mean year of schooling and expectancy of life at birth whose role was underlined in the 1980 research of Hicks. The wide dissemination of annual Human Development Reports by the UNDP and the incentives provided by the UNDP to various countries including India has resulted in a crop of many useful Human Development Reports for India (by the Planning Commission) and by various states of India creating a new awareness of the role of education sector in the development process.

1980s: The Dichotomy between Primary and Higher Education

1970s were marked by turbulence, both nationally and internationally. Nationally, they were the years of Indo-Pak war of 1971 leading to liberation of Bangladesh, inflationary pressures due to the rise of petroleum prices and the political instability due to the Emergency (1975–77) followed by the short-lived Janata government (1977–79). Internationally, it was marked by the international financial problems associated with the abandonment by the US of fixed exchange rate policy, the Gulf War and the rise of petroleum prices and the Islamic Revolution in Iran. This was not a period conducive to new policy initiatives. The UNESCO appeared to be preoccupied by the problems of the New International Information Order and the World Bank had become active in areas of rural development and poverty alleviation under its new President MacNamara. In the 1980s, the World Bank, influenced by rate of return analysis in labour economics, which appear to show that both private and social rates of return on primary education were higher than corresponding rates of return for higher education decided that its lending strategy should emphasize primary education relegating higher education to a relatively minor place in its development agenda. International donors and leaders (including not only World Bank but also UNDP, UNICEF etc.) also felt justified in this policy by the obvious gains in social equity associated with such a strategy as highlighted and endorsed by the Jomtien Declaration on Education for All at the beginning of the year 1990.

1990s Onwards: Emphasis on the Role of Education at All Stages

1990s have seen a resurgence both in the advocacy and scholarship for education as an integrated whole. The World Conference on Education for All held at Jomtien in Thailand in 1990 under the auspices of a consortium of international agencies, affirmed the commitment of the global community to achieve basic learning needs of all the relevant age groups. The Jomtien Conference was paralleled by the adoption of a World Charter for Children under the impetus of the UNICEF which emphasized Early Childhood Care and Education (ECCE) component. The adoption by the UNESCO in 1998 of a World Declaration on Higher Education was paralleled by the World Bank Task Force's Report (2000) on "Higher Education in Developing Countries: Perils and the Promise". The emphasis of the World Bank on primary education and vocational education in the 1980s and 1990s has been followed by the World Bank's recent report on Tertiary Education (2002), which has underlined the linkages between tertiary education and other levels of education through training of teachers, curriculum design and educational research, thereby highlighting the potential of tertiary education to stimulate a 'virtuous circle' of capacity building.[24] The World Bank's subsequent report on school education has completed the gamut of all stages of education.[25] Delors Report, while dealing with the four pillars of learning, identified learning to live together, which really means learning to live with others as one of the major issues in education in today's world which is characterized by group conflict. This pillar of learning is particularly relevant in India which is characterized by an immense diversity of languages, religions and regions.

Enter Federalism

Since human development is facilitated by democratic institutions and practices in the form of availability and enforcement of human rights, decentralization of government institutions and participatory processes since diversity is accommodated by a federal polity as possessed by India and since 1950, Federalism would appear to provide an ideal ground for the study of evolution of education in the post-Independence period. This would appear to provide an ideal point of entry for consideration of federalism as a political system.

The Morphology of Federalism

A federal government is distinguished from a unitary government by the division of powers between at least two levels of government (general and regional), each within its sphere, coordinate and independent.[26] Although, the federal revolution expected by a distinguished American scholar of federalism, Daniel P. Elazar[27] to sweep the world did not materialize and the world actually saw the break-up, successively, of the Soviet Union and Yugoslavia in East Europe, the fact remains, as noted by a veteran observer of the federal scene that some 40 per cent of the world's population encompassing a total of about 480 federated states now live in countries that can be considered to be federations.[28]

If the UK was the classical unitary state, the USA was the classical federal state. Alexis de Tocqueville, the distinguished French statesman, observed in 1838, that the American form of government rests "in truth upon a wholly novel theory which may be considered as a great discovery in modern political science." The American polity is characterized by a set of interlocking principles, each dependent on the other, the whole set forming a system.[29] Broadly, the American Constitution combines the two distinct principles of the distribution of powers and the separation of powers and institutions and backstops this combination with supportive subsidiary principles. It recognizes two levels (the federal and the state) for distribution of powers with the residuary powers belonging to the states. Local governments remain subordinate to the states but the tendency of the federal government to deal directly with the local governments has given rise to the terminology of IGR (inter-governmental relations). Traditionally, the legislature, the executive and the judiciary are regarded as the triad of great powers. The separation especially of the legislature and the executive results in the presidential-congressional form of government in the US as against the fusion of these powers in the UK which gives rise to the cabinet-parliamentary form. The UK system of fusion also prevails in Canada and Australia, which are federations.

In the US, the separation of powers, which operates at both the federal and state levels, is maintained through the system of checks and balances, implying that each power exercises a check over the other resulting in a balanced constitution and curbing the executive branch of Government. Thus, the President can veto a Congressional Bill, and the Senate, the upper house of the American Congress, can decline to confirm the appointments to posts made by the President. The Congressional Committees exercise supervision over the executive branch in all departments of government. The Public Accounts Committee and Estimates Committee of the British parliamentary type are no patch on the Congressional Committees in the US, which wield enormous clout in various fields including in financial matters. The separation of powers is sustained by the separation of institutions.

The superior judiciary occupies a unique position in the American Constitution. By dint of the principle of judicial review, the courts have a special role, not only interpreting laws but defending the constitutional separation and distribution of powers. Judicial review not specifically provided for in the US Constitution, became accepted wisdom with the American Supreme Court's decision in *Marbury vs. Madison* (1803), holding that the Supreme Court can pronounce on the constitutionality of the action of the President/Governors or legislation by the federal state legislatures.

The next structural principle is commitment to *triple-E* senate or the second chamber, meaning that the senate is an elected one, represents the states equally, and has powers equal to those of the House of Representatives. Incidentally, the American Senate was an indirectly elected one till 1913. As a result, the eight smallest states of the USA with a combined population of about 5 million people, each returns the same number of senators (two) as California with its 31 million inhabitants.[30]

The principle of limited government is embodied in the Tenth Amendment of the Constitution which provided that the powers not delegated to the US by the Constitution, nor prohibited by it to the states, are reserved to the states respectively, or to the people. This implies firstly, that the residuary constitutional power rests with the State Government and secondly, that the sovereignty vests with the people. This principle stands in opposition to the British system of triple sovereignty under which the sovereignty vested partly with the Crown, partly with the Parliament and for a brief while with the people, when they exercised their right to vote. The rationale for this principle was the intention of the founding fathers of the American Constitution to make a break from a feudal system.

As pointed out by Wheare,[31] the federal principle additionally requires that in all that concerns the division of authority between governments, the Constitution must be supreme. Lastly, a principle which is not incorporated in the Constitution but which has evolved logically from the principle of dispersal of authority is that the political parties are primarily state-based.[32]

India: A Quasi-Federation?

K.C. Wheare distinguished between a federal constitution and a federal government and held that the US, Switzerland and Australia are examples of countries with federal constitutions, and federal governments, that the Canadian Constitution is quasi-federal in law but predominantly federal in practice and so far as India is concerned, both its constitution and the government were quasi-federal.[33] The grounds for his judgment on India were as below:

1. Powers in the Union List and Concurrent List cover almost all subjects of importance and subjects in the State List tend to be of

subordinate concern. In other words, the states do not have coordinate authority.

2. Significant powers of intervention in the affairs of the states are given by the Constitution to the Union Government or Parliament:
   (i) The Parliament may increase or diminish the area of any state and may alter the boundaries or name of any state, but the consent of the state legislature is not required for such action.
   (ii) Important Emergency provisions enable Union Government to convert Union (federation) into a unitary State, in case of threat to security of the federation by war, external aggression or internal disturbance.
   (iii) Existence of power to impose President's rule in the states in case of alleged violation of constitutional provisions by states.
   (iv) Similar powers of intervention or powers of issuing directions. (Note: K.C. Wheare could have pointed out that the Indian Parliament can encroach on states' legislative field not only during Emergency (Art. 350), but also during normal times, e.g., Art. 249 of the Indian Constitution which empowers Parliament to legislate on state list matters in national interest or power of Parliament under Art. 252 to legislate on State List matters by the consent of states).

As for constitutional practice or government, Wheare notes that powers of reorganization of states were in fact exercised and concedes that these changes were the result of strong regional pressures and were not imposed by the central authority on its own volition. He notes that President's rule was imposed in Assam in 1958 and in Kerala in 1959. (He was writing in 1963.) He concedes that it is difficult to assess the position but, the reasonable conclusion is that both the constitution and the government in India were quasi-federal. Finally, this appears to have escaped notice of many scholars, he observes, that a quasi-federal system may well be more appropriate for India.

The judgment of Wheare on Canada and Australia, which have combined the parliamentary form of government with a federal constitution, is particularly relevant. He notes about Australia (estd., 1900) that both levels of government are sovereign and coordinate in their respective spheres, but that Australia has the additional merit, not possessed by the US, of the qualifier 'federal' (common wealth) expressly occurring in its Constitution. As for Canada (established much earlier in 1867), he holds its constitution to be quasi-federal because of the following features:

- Federal (Dominion) government's powers to disallow any Provincial Act.
- The federal government's power to appoint Lieutenant-Governors of provinces. It can instruct the Lieutenant-Governor to withhold

assent from provincial bills and to reserve them for consideration of the federal executive, which may veto the same.

- Appointments to all important judicial posts are in the hands of the Federal Government.

Wheare notes that in practice the power of disallowance has been used sparingly, but still it has been used not only in *ultra vires* cases (which could be within the purview of courts), but also in matters of policy. He notes that the power of veto has been similarly used to destroy provincial bills. But, Wheare feels that the Dominion executive is careful not to use these powers frequently. He also observes that by constitutional customs, Lieutenant-Governors appointed by the Dominion follow the convention of the cabinet system, viz., to appoint only such ministers as can command a majority in the provincial legislature. The Dominion executive has used powers of judicial appointments with discretion and has not attempted to pack the courts with partisans, opposed to provincial powers. Wheare concludes that Canada is predominantly federal in practice.

Combining Federalism with Parliamentary System: Structural Aspects

Canada was the first country to combine federalism with parliamentary system. As is well known, in the parliamentary system the executive is directly responsible to the democratically elected legislature, which is itself periodically accountable to the electorate through the electoral process. Since the executive is primarily responsible to the first chamber, this, in practice, involves devaluation of the second chamber. The second chamber, at the federal level, is regarded as essential as representing, in some sense, the provinces. At the state level, the second chamber was at one stage perceived to be redundant. In India, legislative councils have powers to recommend abolition of second chambers and only five states have them, though the latest tendency is to revive them where they have been abolished (e.g., Andhra Pradesh and more recently Tamil Nadu, where the Act received Presidential assent in May 2010). AIDMK government which replaced DMK government after elections in May 2011 has, however, a different perspective in the matter.

Canada and India share another feature. Unlike in the US where a few areas are reserved exclusively for federal jurisdiction, with the areas of exclusive state jurisdiction being left unlisted, in Canada and India, there are three enumerated lists, viz., the federal (central), the Provincial (state) and the Concurrent. In both India and Canada, the formal allocation of powers to the federal Parliament is considerably greater. In Canada, this has checked the tendency of the courts to use the doctrine of implied powers to expand progressively the scope of federal powers and thus, protected the use of provincial powers.

In most federations, the federal form is adopted to accommodate diversity. The US and Australia have fundamentally monolingual and mono-cultural societies. In their case, the federal form of government is historically rooted (states and colonies coming together) with the size of the territories dictating a federal form.

India and Canada are, however, different. They have fundamental linguistic, ethnic, religious, cultural and social differences and have experienced greater difficulty in generating internal cohesion. There is this difference however that India's diversity is multi-pronged, whereas the Canadian diversity is essentially bi-polar (francophone vs. anglo-phone speakers). Two strategies to tackle the problems of internal cohesion are: (1) use of quasi-unitary powers, and (2) provision of opportunities for self-government and distinctiveness. India is required to wield both these strategies whereas in Canada, the use of quasi-unitary powers has fallen into disuse.

The adoption of the parliamentary form also affects the operation of fiscal federalism. In both Canada and India, it is the cabinet and the ministry of finance which control the purse-strings with the difference that in India, the ministry of finance shares its powers with the Planning Commission, in the matter of allocation of plan outlays.

Both in India and Canada, the provincial heads are appointed by the federal executives, who have the powers of withholding assent to the provincial bills and reserving them for the assent of the federal Government. In the American system, of course, the Governors are directly elected and serve as fixed-term executives at the state level.

Combining Federalism with Parliamentary System: Party System

However, the parliamentary system more significantly has an impact on (a) the role and operation of parties because of the need for party discipline required to ensure the stability of the executive, and (b) inter-governmental relations, predominantly involving interactions between the executive and the bureaucracy, giving rise to the executive federalism.[34]

The parliamentary system assumes a two-party system with an official 'opposition'. In Canada and India, new political parties have developed at the state or regional level but, the assumption of a two-party system dies hard. This worked quite well in India, when the Congress system[35] was prevalent. When it began to disintegrate in 1967, it led to the emergence, in the post-Emergency period, of groupings of parties mostly regionally based which ran coalition governments (Janata 1977–79 NF 1989–91, UF 1996–98 and NDA 1999–2004). (The sympathy wave elections in 1980 and 1984 held the appearance of the phenomenon in check in the period 1980–89.)

The concentration of powers in the cabinet in the parliamentary government, especially in the matter of appointment to various posts, not only in the Central Government but to posts which have federal significance (e.g., in India – Election Commissioners, Central Vigilance Commissioner, Comptroller and Auditor General of India, Director, CBI) can conceivably lead to abuse of powers. The potential for abuse is greater when the Prime Minister tends to act as a President in the sense of a supreme leader, who does not care much for his Cabinet (as happened in the case of Indira Gandhi). In India, the trend has grown of making such appointments on the recommendation of a committee which may comprise, *inter alia* the Speaker of the Lok Sabha and the leader of the opposition.

In India, little thought has been given to the modification of the composition of the Rajya Sabha. An entrenched provision of the Constitution [(Art. 249) which provides that in the event of Rajya Sabha declaring by two third majority that it is necessary or expedient in national interest that Parliament should pass a law on a subject on State List; however, subject to the condition that such a law remain in force only for one year], does underline the fact that the fathers of the Constitution recognized the federal role of the Rajya Sabha, but recent trends indicate that the Rajya Sabha may gradually lose its character as a second chamber representing federalism. Thus, the domiciliary qualification for election to the Rajya Sabha has recently been done away with by an amendment to the Representation of the Peoples Act 1951 effective August 2003 and a writ petition questioning the constitutionality of the same was dismissed by the Supreme Court vide Kuldip Nayar vs. Union of India (2006) AIR SCW 4408. Even earlier, the domiciliary restrictions could easily be flouted by the candidates adopting a temporary address in the respective states.

Thanks to judicial interpretation and the operation of the Commonwealth Grants Commission, Australia has become more centralized and the dependence of the states on the Central (Commonwealth) government has increased. There is a growing sense of national consciousness which has transcended the traditional state loyalties and compels the people to look up to the Commonwealth rather than to states for a solution of their manifold problems.[36] The party system has undermined the role of the Senate as a second chamber and as in the US, the party system has tended to be region-based except for the persistence of the Labour Party at the national level.

Precedents for the Study

Foreign studies examining the role of federalism vis-à-vis the functional area of education are scanty. In the USA, Hollis P. Allen's study[37] appears to have been followed by Bobbit-Rozenzweig's study.[38] In Canada, there is ample literature on Canada's own brand of "Executive Federalism", a term coined by Donald V. Smiley.[39] Grant P. Harman-edited study of Australian federalism and education is valuable but dated.[40]

Recently, a trend is seen of comparative studies in federalism between India and Canada/Australia. Rekha Saksena made a comparative study of Canadian First Ministers' Conference (FMC) and Indian NDC/ISC (2006), but does not refer to education.[41] The comparative study of Indian and Australian Federalism edited by Ian Copland and John Rickard (1998), focuses on constitutional, financial and political issues.[42] Broadly, it may be stated that while the Canadian experience is relevant in the political study of Indian federalism, Australian experience with its Schools Commission and the federal organizations in higher education is relevant for the education sector in the Indian brand of federalism.

There are some limited studies relating to social sector policies including education policy, but without a focus on federalism. S.P. Singh has dealt with centre-state relations in agricultural education and research up to 1966.[43] Meera Chatterji looked at the evolution of health policy in India up to 1990,[44] and H.W. Bjorkman and Kuldeep Mathur, in a jointly authored comparative volume dealing with the Netherlands and India, examined the technocratic hypothesis as applicable to the Indian education policy.[45]

So far as studies directly bearing on federalism and education are concerned, Anirudh Prasad[46] and Chandra Pal[47] have written on the subject from the legal angle and Santosh Agrawal has examined the 'three language formula' as an educational curricular problem.[48] The following five titles study the subject of federalism and education in India from a politico-administrative angle:

1. Abu Baker: *The Union and the States in Education* (1976).[49]
2. Sharada Rath: *Centre-State Relations in the Field of Social Services 1950–1970*(1978).[50]
3. Marina Pinto: *Federalism and Higher Education: The Indian Experience* (1982).[51]
4. Narasingha Rai: *Centre-State Relations in the Field of Education* (1990).[52]
5. Mahatab Giri: *Centre State Relations in Higher Education with Reference to Andhra Pradesh* (1992).[53]

While Sharada Rath deals with planning and financing of various social services including education with comparisons drawn with the USA, Australia and Canada for the period 1950–70, Narasingha Rai focuses on the same areas for a slightly longer period (1950–75) and with comparisons drawn from four countries including the USSR. The focus of

Mahatab Giri, is on the colleges and universities in Andhra Pradesh with special reference to the Osmania University. Though published in 1992 and though referring to the NPE 1986, its data do not go beyond 1982–83.

Books by Abu Baker, an educationist and Marina Pinto, a political scientist are particularly notable. In his book, Abu Baker deals with planning and financing and consultative machinery covering NDC, CABE and the Conference of State Education Ministers. His recommendation is that education should be made a concurrent subject, thus making de jure what is a de facto situation. In her book, Marina Pinto focuses on higher education, particularly UGC and also covers other bodies like the AICTE, ICSSR, and CSIR etc. Her suggestion is to establish regional offices of UGC to satisfactorily resolve the triangular relationship between the UGC, State Governments and State Universities. Almost all the authors work within the framework of cooperative federalism in the sense postulated by A.H. Birch.[54] According to A.H. Birch, this involves (1) the practice of administrative cooperation between general and regional governments, (2) partial dependence of regional governments upon payments from general governments, and (3) general governments promoting developments in regional matters by the use of conditional grants.

Special Features of the Study

The present study deals with centre-state relations in the field of education in India during the last 60 years (1950–2010), i.e., broadly from the time of adoption of the Constitution till the first decade of the twenty-first century. Secondly, a sharp distinction has been made between fora and organizations, the former being either inter-governmental or sectoral consultative platforms without a permanent secretariat (e.g., NDC, CABE, Education Ministers' Conferences, Central Health Council) and the latter being quasi-autonomous governmental organizations (e.g., UGC, NCERT, MCI, ICAR) with their own staff and independent corporate status. The latter generally operate at the central level though they may also have state level formations or regional offices. Particular note may be made of detailed treatment of CABE as a sectoral Inter-State Council, which has tended to be omitted in mainstream literature on federalism. A comprehensive enumeration and tabulation of participatory features of twenty-eight coordinating organizations is a novel feature. Thirdly, a distinction is made between central organizations and all-India organizations. Fourthly, organizations in school education like NCERT, NIEPA, CBSE, NIOS and NCTE have been dealt with, in addition to the organizations in higher general education (the latter alone are covered in the available literature on the subject). Fifthly, the scope of the study extends beyond the organizations of the

Ministry of Education as is necessitated by the demands of the subject. Sixthly, the role of the Planning Commission as a federal body, which plans not only for the centre but also for the states and which is ideally positioned to provide an umbrella for a super-coordinator involving both horizontal and vertical coordination in the field of education is highlighted. Seventhly, the study contextualizes various official reports, policies and projects that bear witness to the dialectical and dynamic relationship between education and federalism.

To the best of author's knowledge, this is the first elaborate, comprehensive, detailed and up-to-date study of the subject of interrelationship between federalism and education in the Indian context highlighting the role of coordinating and standard-setting bodies in all areas of education from pre-primary to research.

Methodology

The study is presented in a descriptive-cum-analytical frame against a relevant historical backdrop on the basis of aggregate analysis. A special feature of the study is that it has benefited from the researcher's experience in government service as an "actor-observer", a term popularized by Yehezkol Dror,[55] an authority on public policy. Any actor-observer of the government scene in India is constrained by government conduct rules, relating to confidentiality; however, while strictly remaining within the confines of public documents supplemented by press reports for the study, the researcher's involvement in governmental affairs in the education sector with its resultant insight in various matters has been utilized to the fullest extent.

The study relies heavily on primary sources including not only reports of important official committees and commissions but also annual reports of respective organizations as presented to Parliament. Moreover, it draws on material generated by all the three branches of government, viz., (a) the Executive (Government Departments/Organizations), (b) the Legislature (Parliamentary Committee Reports), and (c) the Judiciary (relevant High Court and Supreme Court judgments). It also draws upon reports of international organizations like UNESCO, UNDP, World Bank etc., apart from relevant secondary sources. The unstructured interviews with a few educationists have added value to the study.

Indian federalism is *sui generis* and has endured for sixty years, owing to special factors, as observed by J. Dasgupta.[56] Education as a subject is primarily a state one but in the period under discussion, it underwent massive centralization which gave rise to countervailing forces. This study deals with the forces at work, which aided this centralization in all the stages of education and in a variety of coordinating organizations and the resultant situation. This necessitates the study of various constitutional functionaries, policies followed by the Central and State Governments and mechanisms and modalities of both types of forces. The study is an attempt to weave all these factors together culminating in an 'overview' which sets out some new angles of the theme in the times to come.

Chapter Scheme

This introduction is followed by Part II comprising three chapters, sketching how Indian federalism has been shaped from 1947 to 2010. Chapter two gives the background of proto-federalism (dyarchy and provincial autonomy) in the inter-war years and the historical significance of linguistic diversity in India which makes the role of language policy in India highly significant. The third chapter deals with the linguistic-cum-tribal based reconstruction of federal polity in India and then describes how the constitutional scheme of language policy unraveled. The fourth chapter traces the journey of education from being a state subject to concurrent subject and ineffectiveness of this provision shows how states continue to prevail in education. It also points out how the Supreme Court of India took time to come to terms with the fact of federalism.

The third part is the core of the book, dealing as it does with the impact of federalism on education sector. After detailing colonial roots of education and describing how educational planning provides the federal framework for educational financing and policy making including the operation of the Central Advisory Board of Education (CABE), I successively deal with four important stages, viz., (1) Elementary Education and Literacy, (2) Secondary and Higher Secondary Education, (3) Higher Education to which two chapters are devoted, and (4) Technical and Professional Education followed by research. As higher education has to cope with the new trend toward globalization I deal with reform proposals, viz., Report of National Knowledge Commission, Report of Yashpal Committee, an alternative proposal for National Council for Higher Education and the proposal to regulate foreign universities.

The concluding part/chapter is devoted to overview and prospects. It first of all summarizes the argument of earlier thirteen chapters. Thereafter, it reviews the state of Indian federalism at the start of 2010. The focus of the remaining chapter is on devising a new federal mechanism to enable Indian federalism to face challenges of education in the post-2010 period.

Notes

1. M.A. Fazal, "Subsidiarity Principle in European Union", *Journal of Indian Law Institute*, (July-September, 1996): 311–330.

2. K.C. Wheare, the great authority on federalism defines the federal principle to mean the method of dividing powers so that the *general* and *regional* governments are each, within a sphere, coordinate and independent. (Idem: *Federal Government,* Oxford University Press, 4th Edition, 1963, 10). (In this study, I would uniformly follow the Indian usage of Central to mean general government and State to mean regional governments for the sake of uniformity and also because the term regional has many other connotations).
3. *The Report of Education Commission* (para 7.03) sets out the objectives of pre-primary education at length as below:

   To develop in the child good health habits and to build up basic skills necessary for personal adjustment, such as dressing, toilet habits, eating, washing, cleaning, etc.;

   To develop desirable social attitudes and manners, and to encourage healthy group participation, making the child sensitive to the rights and privileges of others;

   To develop emotional maturity by guiding the child to express, understand, accept and control his feelings and emotions;

   To encourage aesthetic appreciation;

   To stimulate the beginnings of intellectual curiosity concerning the environment and to help him understand the world in which he lives, and to foster new interest through opportunities to explore, investigate and experiment;

   To encourage independence and creativity by providing the child with sufficient opportunities for self-expression;

   To develop the child's ability to express his thoughts and feelings in fluent, correct and clear speech; and

   To develop in the child a good physique, adequate muscular coordination and basic motor skills.
4. *The Report of Secondary Education Commission* (p. 23). The more detailed formulation of the SEC is as below:
   (i) The training of character to fit the students to participate creatively as citizens in the emerging democratic order;
   (ii) The improvement of their practical and vocational efficiency so that they may play their part in building up the economic prosperity of their country;
   (iii) Development of their literary, artistic and cultural interests, which are necessary for self-expression and for the full development of the human development without which a ... National culture cannot come into being.
5. *National Curriculum Framework* (New Delhi: NCERT, 2005).
6. *Faure Commission Report*, 156.

7. *Report of World Bank Task Force on Higher Education and Society* (Washington DC, 2000), 28–29.
8. Shanti Ghosh as quoted by Jean Dre'ze (*EPW*, 26th August, 2006): 3710.
9. Burton R. Clerk et al., "Education", in David Sills (Ed.), *International Encyclopaedia of Social Sciences*, Vol. 4 (London: Macmillan & Co., 1967), 509–516.
10. James S. Coleman (Ed.), *Education and Political Development* (Princeton, N. Jersey: Princeton University Press, 1965), 3–5.
11. Coleman, op. cit., 19.
12. Coleman, op. cit., 20.
13. Robert D. Putnam, *Making Democracy Work: Civic Traditions in Modern Italy* (Princeton: Princeton University Press, 1993).
14. Coleman, op. cit., 32.
15. Coleman, op. cit., 369.
16. Coleman, op. cit., 358.
17. Coleman, op. cit., 231.
18. Philip H. Coombs, *The World Educational Crisis: A System Analysis* (New York: Oxford University Press, 1968) and Idem. *The World Crisis in Education: The View from the Eighties* (New York: Oxford University Press, 1985).
19. Nivedita Menon and Aditya Nigam, *Power and Contestation: India Since 1989* (Hyderabad: Orient Longman, 2008), 35.
20. James S. Coleman et al., *Equality of Educational Opportunity* (Washington DC: US Government Printing Office, 1966).
21. (a) T.W. Shultz, "Education and Economic Growth", in *Social Forces Influencing American Education*, ed. N.B. Henry, (Chicago: National Society for the Study of Education, University of Chicago Press, 1961). (b) E.F. Denison, *The Sources of Economic Growth in the US and the Alternative before US* (New York: Committee for Economic Development, 1962).
22. George Psacharopoulos and Maureen Woodhall, *Education for Development: An Analysis of Investment Choices* (New York: Oxford University Press, 1985).
23. *Education for the 21st Century* (Paris: UNESCO, 1996) (Chairman: Jacques Delors).
24. *Constructing Knowledge Societies: New Challenges for Tertiary Education,* (Washington DC: The World Bank, 2002).
25. *Expanding Opportunities and Building Competencies for Young People: A New Agenda for Secondary Education* (Washington DC: The World Bank, 2005).
26. Vide Footnote 2 supra.
27. Daniel J. Elazar, *Exploring Federalism* (Alabama: The University of Alabama Press, 1987).

28. Ronald L. Watts in Anwar Shah et al. (Eds.), *Conference Record of the Fourth International Conference on Federalism* (New Delhi: Inter-State Council, 2007).
29. Douglas Verney, "Are all Federations Federal? The US, Canada and India", in Balveer Arora and Douglas Verney (Eds.), *Multiple Identities in Single States* (New Delhi: Konark Publishers, 1985): 19–59.
30. Douglas Verney, "India in Search of a New Regime", in Francine R. Frankel et al. (Eds.), *Transforming India: Social and Political Dynamics of Democracy* (New Delhi: Oxford University Press, 2000).
31. Vide reference in Footnote 2.
32. Vide reference in Footnote 29.
33. Vide reference in Footnote 2.
34. Ronald Watts (1995), "Parliamentary Federations: Canada and India", in Balveer Arora and Douglas Verney (Eds.), *Multiple Identities in Single States* (New Delhi: Konark Publishers, 1989), 60–70.
35. Rajani Kothari, "The Congress 'System' in India", in Hasan Zoya (Ed.), *Parties and Party Politics in India* (Oxford: Oxford University Press, 2002) (originally published in *Asian Survey* in 1963).
36. S.P. Aiyar, *Federalism and Social Change* (Bombay: Asia Publishing, 1961).
37. Hollis P. Allen, *Federal Government in Education* (New York: Princeton Hill Book Co., 1950).
38. Bobbit-Rozenzweig's, *Federal Intervention in Higher Education* (USA, 1962).
39. Donald V. Smiley, *The Federal Condition in Canada* (Toronto: McGraw Hill Press Ltd., 1987).
40. G. Harman and D. Smart, *Federal Intervention in Australian Education: Past, Present and Future* (Melbourne: Georgia House, 1987).
41. Rekha Saxena, *Situating Federalism: Mechanisms of Inter-Governmental Relations in Canada and India* (New Delhi: Manohar, 2006).
42. Ian Copland and John Rickard (Eds.), *Federalism: Studies in Indian and Australian Federalism* (New Delhi: Manohar, 1998).
43. S.P. Singh, *Centre-State Relations in Agricultural Development* (New Delhi: Vikas, 1973).
44. Meera Chatterjee, *Reaching Health For All* (New Delhi: Oxford University Press, 1997).
45. H.W. Bjorkman and Kuldeep Mathur, *Policy, Technocracy and Development: Human Capital Policies in the Netherlands and India* (New Delhi: Manohar, 2002).
46. Anirudh Prasad, *Centre-State Powers under Indian Federalism* (New Delhi: Deep & Deep Publishers, 1981).
47. Chandra Pal, *Centre-State Relations and Comparative Federalism* (New Delhi: Deep & Deep Publishers, 1993).

48. Santosh Agrawal, *Three Language Formula: An Educational Problem* (New Delhi: Gian Publishers, 1991).
49. Published by Shabda Prakashan, Hyderabad.
50. Published by Oriental Publishers & Distributors, New Delhi.
51. Published by Orient Longman, Bombay.
52. Published by Atmaram & Sons, New Delhi.
53. Published by Narottam Book Centre, New Delhi.
54. A.H. Birch, *Federalism, Finance and Social Legislation in Canada, Australia and the US* (Oxford: Clarendon Press, 1955).
55. Vide "Introduction" in Yehezkol Dror, *Public Policy Making Re-examined* (USA, New Brunswick: Transaction Publishers, 3rd Printing 1983; 1st edition 1968): Dror states that the role of actor-observer is quite different in intensity and reality from involvement as 'participant observer' as a deliberate research method. According to him, social science studies from the outside do not penetrate into the realities of central high level decision making and are required to be supplemented by alternative approaches including actor-observation.
56. Jyotirindra Dasgupta, observes: ... "the reconstructive opportunities incorporated in the constitutional design of federalism in India when treated in the context of the operation of democratic participation can reasonably account for the durability of Indian federal institutions." Vide "India's Federal Design and Multi-cultural National Construction", in Atul Kohli (Ed.), *The Success of India's Democracy* (New Delhi: Cambridge University Press, 2000), 49–77.

Part II

Shaping up of Indian Federalism

2 Indian Proto-Federalism and Its Historical-Linguistic Base

Federal Idea in India

S.P. Aiyar has eruditely dealt with the genesis and persistence of the federal idea in India in the years leading to Independence and Constitution making.[1] Firstly, the federal system in India was formed not by the coming together of independent states but by the gradual devolution of autonomy on the provinces (Aiyar, 16). Secondly, the first foundations of the Indian political system as it now exists, were laid in the Round Table Conference (1930–31) where it was considered that federalism was a political solution of India's problem (Aiyar, 12), which was two-fold. Firstly, the problem of coming to terms with the Indian states in an organic federal unity and secondly the need to safeguard the rights of minorities especially the Muslim community (Aiyar, 10–11). Thirdly, the Government of India Act, 1935 was a landmark in the evolution of the federal idea in India (Aiyar, 16), though being highly centralized, it was not to the liking of the Muslim community as then represented by the Muslim League led by M.A. Jinnah. The Cabinet Mission Plan tried to deal with the concerns of the Muslim community, but with Independence Act involving partition and with Sardar Patel as Home Minister successfully dealing with what was earlier the problem of the Indian states, a new situation had arisen. The earlier rationale for the federal idea no longer held. According to S.P. Aiyar, the only reason federalism found a place in the Constitution was that Gandhiji had given his consent to it through the Gandhi-Irwin Pact (Aiyar, 12 and 18), and the framers of the Constitution had played the role of synthesizers by striking a compromise (Aiyar, 33).

S.P. Aiyar's insights, valuable as they are, need to be broadened and deepened in three respects. Firstly, he gives the entire credit for the structural features of Indian federalism to the 1935 Act, and is less than fair to the role of the deliberations of Montford Report and the working of Dyarchy (based on the Montford Report) in the period 1920–1936. Secondly, the spell of experience in office of the provincial leaders of Congress in the government in the period 1937–39 played its role in clinching the matter in favour of a federation.[2] Thirdly, the growth of linguistic regionalism which began to be manifested in the constitutional politics in India, e.g., with the demand first voiced in 1894 for the formation of a separate Hindi-speaking state of Bihar and which persisted right up to the crucial period of 1947–50 in the subdued desire for enumeration of linguistically reorganized states in the schedule of the Constitution needs to be taken note of. The language problem has manifested itself not only by the claim of language to be the basis of formation of constituent states of India but also in the rival claims of English, Hindi and Hindustani to be the official language of the Indian Federation and also in the opposition from the Tamil-speaking Madras state to Hindi as official language. As the language is not only a means of communication but also medium of instruction in schools and colleges, the language issue has a peculiar resonance in any discussion of education and federalism in India. Accordingly, it is proposed to deal with the following aspects in the shaping of Indian federalism:

- From Dyarchy-Provincial Autonomy to the Constitution of Independent India.
- The Issue of Provincial Reorganization till Independence.
- The Language Problem in India till 1947 (including Official Language Problem).

From Dyarchy-Provincial Autonomy to the Constitution of India (1919–1950)

As pointed out by S. Gopal,[3] in the inter-war period, Dyarchy was a term of abuse and K.R. Bombwall's initial assessment was that it was a colossal failure, though later on he revised his view and called it as federalism in embryo.[4] (For factual studies of Dyarchy, please see the footnote.[5]) It is argued in this study that it was the Government of India Act, 1919, based on the momentous Montford Reforms, establishing the Dyarchy and followed logically by provincial autonomy (1937–47), which marked the beginning of what may be called proto-federalism in India with its twin structural features of division of powers and of finances between two levels of government.

The possibility of a federal India was *officially* broached by Lord Hardinge in his well-known Despatch of 25th August 1911 proposing reunification of Bengal and shifting the capital of India from Calcutta to Delhi.[6] Edwin Montague, Secretary of State for India, was not only associated with the enunciation of the well-known British policy statement of 20th August 1917 about progressive realization in India of responsible government but was formally the joint author of a genuinely liberal and much underestimated document of India's constitutional history, Montague-Chelmsford (Montford) Report 1918, which was the basis of the 1919 Act establishing the Dyarchy. (Montague's personal papers show that he was the real author of the Report.)

Dyarchy itself is not a term used in Montford Report, but its use was popularized by Lionel Curtis, the author of a book of that name.[7] Gerald Studdard-Kennedy has called Lionel Curtis as an eccentric but influential constitutional journeyman.[8] In the face of intense opposition in official circles for grant of responsible government to Indians even at the provincial level, the model of Dyarchy represented a half-way house in which the provincial subjects were divided between the 'transferred' and 'reserved', of which the former would be in the sphere of ministerial responsibility. It was envisaged that gradually, the list of the reserved subjects would be diminished till the category was abolished. The executive government of the provinces was to be in two parts (hence the term Dyarchy), ministers dealing with the "transferred" subjects and the officers dealing with the reserved subjects, the two parts being coordinated by the Provincial Governors.[9]

It was to the credit of the authors of the report that they recognized that transfer of powers and functions to the provincial level pre-supposed separation of resources of the Central Government from those of the provinces[10] and, therefore, replacement of the system of "divided heads of revenue" prevalent since 1882–83 under which provinces were given a fixed percentage of certain imperial taxes, like forests, excise, income tax, stamps, registration and land revenue. Under Dyarchy, the provinces were allocated distinct heads of revenue. The Centre retained the income tax while the provinces were given land revenue (closely connected with rural administration), liquor excise (already given to Bengal, Bombay and Assam), judicial stamps and irrigation receipts. The provinces could fix the rate of tax on all the provincial heads mentioned and a few others including taxes on amusements, betting and succession duties. On the other hand, the provinces had to pay for famine relief and protective irrigation works. This scheme left the Central Government with recurring deficits and the provincial 'contributions' were fixed by the Meston Settlement of 1920, based partly on past contributions, capacity to pay, population etc. The Meston award also provincialised general stamps revenue. The 1935 Act made no radical changes in the division of sources of revenue or power of taxation between the Centre and the provinces. Instead, it was decided that proceeds of certain central taxes such as income tax and export duties could be divided between the centre and the provinces.[11] This scheme continued till the Constitution of 1950 with its innovation of the five-yearly Finance Commission. Thus, Dyarchy ushered in fiscal federalism as well as division of powers, which are the two essential features of a federal system. The Montford Report was also aware of the need for revising what it called the *political geography* of the country along the linguistic or racial lines. It observed that "it is a strong argument in favour of linguistic or racial units of government that by making it possible to conduct the business of legislation in the vernacular, they would contribute to draw into the political arena of public affairs men who were not acquainted with English," but the report preferred the process of revision to follow constitutional reform (para 246 of Report). It envisaged eventual transfer of responsibility at the central level also within a federal framework. The Report observed prophetically: "Our conception of the eventual future of India is a sisterhood of states, self-governing in all matters of purely local or provincial interest over which would preside a Central Government increasingly representative of and responsible to the people of all of them."[12] It is good to remember that Montford Report/Reforms were initially welcomed by the nationalists but came to be vilified in reaction to the Rowlatt Acts and the tragedy of Jallianwala Bagh. Dyarchy might have been ill-starred but its significance as harbinger of Indian proto-federation needs to be recognised. As pointed out by D.A. Low,[13] the decision to contest elections in 1936 under the Government of India Act, 1935 and to accept office in 1937 was taken by the Congress leaders after having watched the 1919 Act in operation. Dyarchy can thus be said to have well and truly laid the foundation of British-province based federalism, leading to provincial autonomy. V.P. Menon has underlined the fact that the Devolution Rules under the 1919 Act remained in force in respect of the provincial governments right up to 1937 and in respect of the Government of India right up to 1947.[14]

Provincial Autonomy (1937–1947)

The provincial autonomy, recommended by the Statutory Commission, endorsed by the Round Table Conferences, confirmed by the report of the Joint Parliamentary Committee (1933–34) and inaugurated by the 1935 Act from 1st April 1937 was a natural but limited extension of Dyarchy, limited because its main novelty, the All-India Federation, embodying the principle of Dyarchy at the Centre was not enforced. Dr B.R. Ambedkar severely criticized the disparity in the position of British India and the Indian states under the federation, the latter enjoying many benefits and many exemptions, which were denied to British India particularly so in the matter of taxation.[15] K.C. Wheare, the international authority on federalism, doubted the viability of the projected federation of the 1935 Act on the ground that constituent units of a federation must have similar political institutions, that the authoritarian or oligarchic institutions and democratic institutions cannot be combined and that it would have been particularly difficult to create a union between (princely) states and (British) provinces of India as envisaged under the Act. He noted that

Indian leaders, before inaugurating the Union, established by the 1950 Constitution, took steps to promote homogeneity in the institutions of the component states, a clear reference to India's wisdom in integration of the princely states.[16] Scholars and historians like R.J. Moore have rightly called the federation of 1935 as a 'paper federation'.[17]

The active innovations of the Government of India Act, 1935, as to the topic of the division of functions, were two-fold. Firstly, the division of functions was statutorily entrenched by being incorporated in the Schedule of the Act rather than being part of the (Devolution) Rules as earlier. Secondly, a third list, viz., the Concurrent List was added to the pre-existing Central and Provincial Lists. The significance of the Concurrent List was two-fold. Firstly, it put an end to the loose concurrency operating in practice for all subjects. To quote the Joint Committee, "At present, the Central legislature has the legal power to legislate on any subject even though it be classified by rules under the Government of India Act as a provincial subject and a provincial legislature can similarly legislate for its own territory on any subject even though it be classified as a Central subject, so long as assent of Governor-General was obtained".[18] Secondly, the Joint Committee set out the rationale of the Concurrent List which is valid even in the 21st century and has been quoted with approval by P.M. Bakshi in his paper prepared for the use of the Venkatachaliah Commission Report.[19] To quote: "Experience has shown, both in India and elsewhere, that there are certain matters which cannot be allocated exclusively either to a Central or a Provincial legislature and for which ... it is equally necessary that the Central legislature should have a legislative jurisdiction to enable it (i) in some cases to secure uniformity in the main principles of law throughout the country, (ii) in others, to guide and encourage provincial efforts, and (iii) in others again to provide remedies for mischiefs arising in the provincial sphere but extending or liable to extend beyond the boundaries of a single province. Instances of the first are provided by the subject matter of the great Indian Codes, of the second by such matters as labour legislation and of the third by legislation for the prevention and control of epidemic diseases."[20]

Elsewhere, the Joint Committee has made it clear that while the Concurrent List gives the power to the Centre to coordinate and unify regulations, the subjects themselves are essentially provincial in character and will be administered by the provinces and mainly in accordance with provincial policy. However, the normal rule must be that in case of conflict between a Central and a Provincial Act in the concurrent field, the former must prevail.[21] It may be noted that the Concurrent List under 1935 Act was in two parts. Part I consisted of 25 entries which mainly related to the legal system and courts, legal, medical and other professions, newspapers, books and printing press etc. Part II consisted of 11 entries, mostly relating to labour laws, electricity, shipping, cinema, films etc. Under 126(2) of the 1935 Act, the executive authority of the federation extended to the giving of directions to a province as to the carrying into execution of any federal legislation which related to Part II of the Concurrent List. Non-compliance of the directions could be followed by the issuance of Governor-General's orders to the Governors. In other words, provinces were agents of the Government of India in respect of subjects in Part II of the Concurrent List. Such a classification is absent in the Constitution.

Thus, the constitutional reforms of the inter-war period accepted the two basic principles of federalism, viz., division of powers and division of revenue heads. These were incorporated in the Seventh Schedule of free India's Constitution with its three-fold lists (Central, State and Concurrent). It only required the coping stone of the Finance Commission to make the operation of division of heads smooth and sustainable. As noted, the Montford Report had also hinted at the post-reform revision of the political geography of India.

The Issue of Provincial Reorganization till Independence

The British government was aware of the need for provincial reorganization and language as a plausible basis for the same at least since the time of Curzon, but while the bureaucracy could make proposals for minor adjustments, the imperial interest was to ensure that there was no consolidation of groups which were considered as centres of disaffection against the Empire, e.g., Bengalis, Marathas and among them the Chitpavan Brahmins who were anathema to the ruling class. Thus, when the Nizam of Hyderabad was compelled to cede to the British Berar districts which were Marathi speaking they were merged with Hindi-speaking Central Provinces. In 1901, Sir Andrew Frazer, Lt. Governor of the Central Provinces proposed transfer of Oriya-speaking Sambalpur district to the Orissa division of Bengal on the ground of administrative convenience. The proposal ended with the imperial decision to partition Bengal into: (a) East Bengal and Assam, and (b) Bengal, with a view to disperse revolutionary element. The original proposal about transfer of Sambalpur to Orissa, however, did not materialize. The partition of Bengal became a fait accompli in 1905 and was undone in 1911, not so much because of the agitation against partition but because of the imperial need for curbing the revolutionary activities and the ascent to power in the UK, of the Liberal Government which had earlier given the boon of Morley-Minto Reforms, 1909.

Lord Hardinge not only broached the subject of federalism, but can also be said to have supported linguistic units as the basic autonomous units of federalism in the dispatch of 25th August 1911, earlier referred to which was later on published under the heading of "Coronation Durbar Despatch". He mentioned the cry of Bihar for Biharis and when the partition of Bengal was annulled, the foundation for eventual formation of unilingual states of Assam, Bihar and Orissa was laid. In particular, the case of Orissa was exemplary, thanks to the support of Simon Commission (1930) based on the report of its sub-committee chaired by Clement Attlee (future PM of Great Britain) and thanks further to the subsequent Orissa Committee (O'Donnell Committee), a unilingual state of Orissa came into existence in 1936 which also meant simultaneous creation of a unilingual Bihar. It needs to be remembered however, that Assam and Orissa were small units and their creation was not considered to pose a threat to the imperial interests.

Ashis Banerjee[22] has underlined the significance of the year 1906 which saw, on the one hand, the partition of Bengal and led to the politicization of the consciousness among the indigenous elite of the latent linguistic sub-nationalism and on the other the formation of the Muslim League in 1906 symbolizing another aspect of identity expression which eventually resulted in the partition of India in 1947 which, therefore, became the year in which the spectre of anarchy predisposed Indian leadership to oppose any idea of a schedule to the Constitution recognizing linguistic regions.

There was no doubt constitutional-legal effort to persuade the colonial government to form linguistic provinces as seen *inter alia* in the Council resolution of Mahesh Narayan Singh in 1894 for formation of separate Bihar province. Ashis Banerjee has also pointed out that Home Rule League seems to have been the first to take a principled position on adopting linguistic principle as determining the provincial delimitations. It is, of course, conventional wisdom that Gandhiji persuaded the Congress party to reorganize all its units along linguistic lines in 1920. The question, however, is whether linguistic units were conceived as constituents of a federal polity or a unitary one. Again, Ashis Banerjee points out that on a closer reading of the supplementary report of the Nehru Committee (1928), it appears that the sentiment was in favour of as close a union as possible.

The fact that the Congress leadership was opposed to linguistic reorganization in 1947–50, but still had to concede the demand underlines the linguistic urges of the people. These linguistic urges had deep historical roots and the same are traced in the next section, because identities other than linguistic (e.g., religion, caste) and various ideological currents like orientalism, vernacularism, evangelism etc., were also implicated in the course of events. A separate section is devoted to official language problem.

The Language Problem

Earlier, scholars like N.C. Roy who have written on federalism and linguistic states,[23] have traced the growth of linguistic diversity in India going back to the ancient historical period tracing the development of Sanskrit, Prakrits, Apabhransha, the rise of modern Indian languages from the 12th century onwards and the growth of literature therein through the activities of Bhakti saints in respective regional dialects. The impetus given by the British rule to the development of prose literature has also been noted. More recently, S.H. Patil has brought the account up-to-date.[24] I have tried to make use of the latest research which is necessarily interdisciplinary to give an account of the growth of linguistic regionalism in India.

Since the time of Warren Hastings, the Governor-General of India, the study of Indian languages was encouraged through various institutions like (a) the Asiatic Society, Calcutta (estd. 1784), which promoted scientific study of Asia through the issuance of Society's well-known journal, and (b) the founding by Wellesley of the College of Fort William in 1800 at Calcutta, for education of civil servants. Sir William Jones, a judge in the employment of East India Company, propounded in 1786 his well-known "Indo-European Hypothesis" in his third address before the Asiatic Society. This hypothesis suggested that Sanskrit belonged to the Indo-European language family and was more ancient than Greek and Latin. This dignified the status of Sanskrit as an ancient and rich classical language from which were derived not only the modern Indian vernaculars but which was a precursor of Greek and Latin from which modern European languages were derived. The labours of the Asiatic Society and of the Fort William College virtually led to a Renaissance of Indian learning. Not only the study of Sanskrit but of all vernaculars including Hindi, Urdu, Bengali etc., was encouraged. Although, the College of Fort William declined from 1830 onwards and closed in 1854, its work can be said to have been continued by the modern universities which came into existence from 1857 onwards. Asiatic Society promoted the study of Indology, which included the study of Hinduism, Buddhism, Indian archaeology and related disciplines. It is fashionable nowadays to disparage such studies as part of an "Orientalist" discourse of dominance vide Edward Said,[25] but as pointed out by Thomas Trautmann and O.P. Kejariwal, one needs to recognize the value of orientalist scholarship irrespective of Foucault's discourse of power/knowledge which is the point of departure for Edward Said.

One aspect of the oriental scholarship which is little noticed in the literature on language development is the existence of the Madras School of Orientalism associated with the College of Fort St. George at Madras, established in 1812 to which is attributed the Dravidian proof of 1816, associated with the civil servant scholar F.W. Ellis, to the effect that the four major South Indian languages, Tamil, Telugu, Kannada and Malayalam belonged not to the Indo-European but to the Dravidian family of languages. These ideas were further developed by missionary scholars like Robert Caldwell and their political impact is examined separately. So, today, India is regarded as having languages belonging to five linguistic families, viz., Indo-European, Dravidian, Austric, Tibeto-Burman and Andamanese.[26]

Consequent upon the labours of the College of Fort Williams and Fort St. George, growth of printed books in the vernaculars (now called regional languages) was promoted and this is the beginning of sub-national consciousness in the linguistic regions of India. As observed by Benedict Anderson,[27] nations are imagined communities and in the 19th century India as in western Europe much earlier, it was "print capitalism" which made it possible for rapidly growing number of people to think about themselves and to relate themselves to others in new ways. Anderson observes that the print languages laid the basis for national consciousness in a variety of ways. Firstly, they created unified fields of exchange and communication below English, which was the rulers' language. Secondly, print capitalism gave a new fixity to language which in the long run helped to build the image of antiquity which is central to the subjective idea of the nation. Thirdly, print capitalism created language of power of a kind different from dialects.

In India, the western-inspired growth of printing and publishing is traced at length by B.S. Kesavan in his multi-volume book,[28] which he has sub-titled as "a story of cultural reawakening". He has pointed out how printing in India originated in South India and how it came to flourish in Bengal and then spread to other regions of India. Printing facilitated not only books of a comparatively great value but also journalism. This is traced in the second volume of the report of the Press Commission.[29] It is now acknowledged that the thesis of print capitalism as the basis of nationalism, which is based on Elizabeth Eisenstein's scholarly work,[30] cannot be directly applied to colonial situation in India. Elizabeth Eisenstein identified increased dissemination, standardization and fixity as the main features of the print culture. But, in India, with its orality and high illiteracy, any type of revolutionary transformation was out of the question. Book trade was underdeveloped and there was dearth of good material for printed books. However, regional language journalism did play a more prominent role in the diffusion of public knowledge, in generating critical opinion and in shaping Indian nationalism.[31] According to Stuart Blackburn,[32] the change produced by print appears more innovative than revolutionary. There were new literary practices – translation, inter-lingual dictionaries and grammar and script reform and modern discursive prose. Also, a shift was encouraged from memorization to reference, especially through alphabetization which was stimulated by printing.

The subject of how regional linguistic identity was established and came to efflorescence in various linguistic regions of India, but without entering into rivalry with the larger Indian nationalism except perhaps in Tamil Nadu is a fascinating one, but unfortunately has not been studied in depth, especially because it involves a very difficult type of interdisciplinary and inter-linguistic study in a comparative framework. Such studies had been conducted in Bengal under the rubric 'Renaissance Studies' but the fact of the matter is that there was a double renaissance almost in every province, the first renaissance instigated by indology and the second renaissance instigated by European knowledge through English. Moreover, the course of events was not smooth but was full of conflicts. There was a state of disagreement between Christianity and Hinduism/Islam. Moreover, there was conflict not only between English and regional languages, but also between two regional languages. Thus, both Assam and Orissa had to put up with hegemony of Bengali language but this was a passing phase. Generally, the phases of this development comprised of:

1. Missionary effort to standardize regional languages through publication of dictionaries and grammars.
2. Growth of Anglo-Indian press.
3. Growth of indigenous press.
4. Growth of public sphere/associations.
5. Growth of regional language literature including the novel which is regarded as the soul of a nation.

   In this connection, Meenakshi Mukherjee[33] has put the whole matter concisely in following words: "within about 25 years after the passing of the Education Minutes of 1835, which made English the official language of higher education in India, the new narrative form called the novel began to appear first in Bangla and Marathi to be followed thereafter in Hindi, Urdu, Tamil and Malayalam. By the end of the century, the novel became the most popular form of print medium entertainment in at least eight major languages of the country".
6. Penetration of vernaculars in the secondary school curriculum (since it was axiomatic that pragmatic vernacularism would assure instruction of primary education through the regional languages).

7. Growth of higher education institutions in the respective regions.

In the footnote is given a suggestive list of books which seek to grapple with the problem of growth of regional linguistic cultures.

The Official Language Problem

It is well settled that at the time of the Muslim invasion, Sanskrit was the lingua franca of India. This is established both from linguistic and inscriptional evidence.[34] With the advent of the Muslim rule, Persian influenced by Arabic, which was important from religious point of view, became the official language but Persian did not supersede Sanskrit entirely. Sanskrit continued to be used for inscriptions and to produce creative literature in philosophy, theory of literature etc. There is evidence of co-existence of Sanskrit as a prestigious language with regional languages. Sanskrit was also a cosmopolitan language because it had spread to what is called Greater India comprising Indo-China (Vietnam, Cambodia, Laos) and Indonesia.[35]

With the advent of the British, a new foreign language, English, arrived on the scene. But, the East India Company, which was geared to maximize its profits from trade was slow to introduce English in the official transactions. In December 1798, the Governor-General at Calcutta issued a notification that from 1st January 1798, no civil servant could be appointed until he had passed an examination in the laws and regulations and in the two languages of Persian and Hindustani which, according to Gilchrist, had three styles, viz., the High Court or Persian style, the middle Hindustani style and the vulgar or Hinduwee style. Thus, Hindi as well as Urdu was comprised in Hindustani. The institutionalization of Hindustani and Hindi as two autonomous entities came about with the establishment of Fort William College in 1800.

1837 was a landmark year for the purpose of the official language. From 4th September 1837, the Governor-General empowered the Supreme Court and local governments to substitute vernacular languages of the country for the Persian in legal proceedings and proceedings relating to revenue. As a result, regional languages came into their own, except in Punjab, North-West Province and Bihar. This was because the official policy was ambiguous regarding the 'character' or the script. Hence, Hindustani in Perso-Arabic script continued to be the court/revenue language, in the North-Western Province and in Bihar. But, there was grass root as well as official support for Hindi in Devanagari script. In Bihar, the Persianized Urdu was replaced by Hindi in 1872, under orders of Sir George Campbell, Lt. Governor of Bihar, but in the North-Western Province there was opposition both from Anglo-Indian Press (pioneer of Allahabad, estd. 1865) and from the Muslim community led by the

Aligarh gentry (represented by Syed Ahmed Khan). Rajendralal Mitra in 1864 in a scholarly article and Babu Shivprasad in 1866 in a memorandum, supported the cause of Hindi but to no avail. The Hunter Commission of 1882, from which a lot was expected was a disappointment. There was a large-scale mobilization and a mammoth petition by Pandit Madan Mohan Malaviya in 1893 which bore fruit and in 1900 the use of Nagari characters in the courts which meant Hindi in Devanagari script was permitted by the Lt. Governor Sir A.P. McDonnell.[36]

Macaulay's Minute of 1835 had a bearing on the use of English language for spread of European knowledge in high schools, colleges and universities and also in higher judiciary and council politics.

The indigenous leaders like Keshab Chandra Sen and Swami Dayanand of Arya Samaj had identified Hindi in Nagari script as the future national language of India, but Gandhiji's insistence on Hindustani in the context of his programme of Hindu-Muslim unity tilted the scales in its favour in the inter-war period, though it did not affect the indigenous efforts for the spread of Hindi as for example through Dakshin Bharat Hindi Prachar Sabha of Madras and other regional institutions. In 1947, therefore, there was no doubt that in future independent India, Hindi in some form and English would be languages of power. Sanskrit was a language of prestige and regional vernaculars had already been introduced as languages of instruction in secondary schools. The position of princely states varied but except in Hyderabad and J&K where Urdu was recognized as the official language, the situation was similar to that in the rest of British India.

Roots of Asymmetry of Tamil[37]

The Tamil language did have its renaissance which was, however, accompanied by the claim of the language to antiquity and to classical status. Unfortunately, the technical study of linguistic families which was dominated in South India and particularly in Madras Presidency by Christian missionaries like Robert Caldwell became mixed up with north-south ideology in the political discourse at the end of the 19th century and beginning of 20th century. It became the basis of Brahmin/non-Brahmin differences and consequently of Backward Class Movement, thus entering the political discourse. Nicholas Dirk thinks that Caldwell's anti-Brahminism played a role in this formation as shown in Caldwell's sketch of Tinnevelly Shanars. According to Nilkanth Shastri, Caldwell's use of Brahmins as synonymous with Aryans in his scientific work may be said to provide the basis in modern times of the simplistic equation of Aryans = Brahmins = Sanskrit = North = Hindi, which was at the root of much social and political trouble in the years to come.

In Madras, Hindi with its identification with Sanskrit/North/Aryans faced opposition from 1937 onwards when the Congress government's attempt to introduce compulsory study of Hindi in schools was thwarted by Self-Help Group of Dravida Kazagam as well as by Congressmen sympathetic to the cause of Tamil.[38]

Notes

1. S.P. Aiyar, "The Federal Idea in India", in S.P. Aiyar and Usha Mehta (Eds.), *Essays on Indian Federalism* (Bombay: Allied Publishers, 1965), 1–33.
2. D.A. Low, *Britain and Indian Nationalism* (Cambridge: Cambridge University Press, 1997).
3. S. Gopal, *The Vice-Royalty of Lord Irwin* (New Delhi: Oxford University Press, 1957), 2–4.
4. K.R. Bombwall, *Indian Politics and Government* (New Delhi: Atmaram & Sons, 1951), 171–175. Idem, *Foundation of Indian Federalism* (Bombay: Asia Publishing House, 1967).
5. K.M. Panikkar, *Working of Dyarchy in India, 1919–1927* (Bombay: D.B. Taraporevala Sons & Co., 1928); A. Appadorai, *Dyarchy in Practice* (London: Longmans, Green & Company, 1937); M.R. Masani, *India's Constitution at Work* (Bombay: Allied Publishers, 1940).
6. P. Mukherji, *Indian Constitutional Documents (1600–1918)*, Vol. II, (Calcutta/Simla: Thacker, Spink & Co., 1918), 454.
7. Lionel Curtis, *Dyarchy* (Oxford: Clarendon Press, 1920).
8. Gerald Studdert-Kennedy, *Province and the Raj* (New Delhi: Sage, 1998), 167–187.
9. Montford Report, 2.18.
10. Montford Report, 2.00.
11. On the Financial Scheme of Dyarchy/Provincial Autonomy, see generally: B.R. Ambedkar, *The Evolution of Provincial Finance in British India: A Study in the Provincial Decentralization of Fiscal Finance* (London, P.S. King & Sons Ltd., 1925) and Dharma Kumar, *Cambridge Economic History of India* Vol. II, (New Delhi: Orient Longman, 1992), 904–944.
12. Montford Report, 3.49.
13. Vide Footnote 2.
14. V.P. Menon, *Montague-Chelmsford Reforms* (Bombay: Bharatiya Vidya Bhavan, 1965).
15. B.R. Ambedkar, *Federation vs. Freedom* (Poona: Gokhale Institute of Politics and Economics, 1939), 142–143.
16. K.C. Wheare (1963), 46.
17. R.J. Moore, "The Making of India's Paper Federation", in C.H. Phillips and Mary Wain Wright (Eds.), *The Partition of India: Policies and Perspectives* (London: George, Allen & Unwin, 1970), 54–85.

18. Report of the Joint Committee on Indian Constitutional Reforms, Vol. I, Part I, (London, 1934), Paras 228 to 242.
19. Vide Venkatachaliah Report, Vol. II, Book 3: 1249–1257.
20. Report of the Joint Committee: para 51.
21. Report of the Joint Committee: para 233.
22. Ashis Banerjee, "The Ideology and Politics of India's National Identity", in Zoya Hasan et al. (Eds.), *The State, Political Process and Identity* (New Delhi: Sage Publications, 1983), 283–296.
23. Naresh Chandra, *Federalism and Linguistic States* (Calcutta: Firma K.L. Mukhopadhyaya, 1962), 143–153.
24. S.H. Patil, *Changing Bases of Federal Units in India*, Vol. II, (New Delhi: Mohit Publications, 2006).
25. Edward Said, *Orientalism* (London: Penguin, 1978).
26. This account is based on the following authorities: (i) Thomas R. Trautmann, *Aryans and British India* (Berkeley: University of California Press, 1997). (ii) Idem, *Languages and Nations: The Dravidian Proof in Colonial Madras* (Berkeley & Los Angeles: The University of California Press, 2006). (iii) David Kopf, *British Orientalism and the Bengal Renaissance: The Dynamics of Indian Modernization 1773–1835* (Berkeley: University of California Press, 1969). (iv) O.P. Kejariwal, *The Asiatic Society of Bengal: The Discovery of India's Past 1784–1838* (New Delhi: Oxford University Press, 1988). (v) Anvita Abbi, "Vanishing Diversities and Submerging Identities: An Indian Case", in Asha Sarangi (Ed.), *Language and Politics in India* (New Delhi: Oxford University Press, 2009), 299–311.
27. Anderson Benedict, *Imagined Communities: Reflections on the Origin and Spread of Nationalism* (London, New York: Verso, 1983, 2nd ed., 1991), 36 and 46.
28. B.S. Kesavan, *History of Printing and Publishing in India: A Story of Cultural Re-awakening*,

    Vol. I: *South Indian Origins of Printing and Its efflorescence in Bengal*.

    Vol. II: *Origins of Printing and Publishing in Karnataka, Andhra and Kerala*.

    Vol. III: *Origins of Printing and Publishing in the Hindi Heartland* (New Delhi: National Book Trust, 1985, 1988, 1993).
29. J. Natarajan, *History of Indian Journalism: Part II of the Report of the Press Commission* (New Delhi: Publication Division, Ministry of Information and Broadcasting, August 1955).
30. Elizabeth Eisenstein, *The Printing Press as an Agent of Change*, 2 Volumes, (Cambridge: Cambridge University Press, 1978).
31. Stark Ulrik, *An Empire of Books: The Naval Kishore Press and the Diffusion of the Printed Word in Colonial India* (New Delhi: Permanent Black, 2007), 5–6.
32. Stuart Blackburn, *Print, Folklore and Nationalism in Colonial South India* (New Delhi: Permanent Black, 2003), 1–25.

33. Meenakshi Mukherjee, *Realism and Reality: The Novel and Society in India* (Delhi: Oxford University Press, 1985); idem, *The Perishable Empire: Essays in Indian Writing in English* (New Delhi: Oxford University Press, 2003); Alok Bhatt and Sudhir Chandra (Eds.), *Indian Responses to Colonialism in the 19th Century* (New Delhi: Sterling Publishers, 1993); Sudhir Chandra, "Regional Consciousness in 19th Century India: A Preliminary Note", *EPW*, 7th August 1982; Nivedita Mohanty, *Orissa Nationalism: Quest for United Orissa 1866–1936* (Delhi: Manohar, 1982); K.V. Narayan Rao, *The Emergence of Andhra Pradesh* (Bombay: Popular Prakashan, 1973); Amalendu Guha, *From Plunder Raj to Swaraj* (New Delhi: ICHR, 1977); G. Phukon, *Assam's Attitude to Federalism* (New Delhi: Sterling, 1984); D.M. Muthanna, *History of Modern Karnataka* (Delhi: Sterling, 1980); Re. Bengal renaissance, see A.K. Majumdar, *British Paramountcy and Indian Renaissance* (Bombay: Bharatiya Vidya Bhavan, 2nd ed., 1981); Atulchandra Gupta (Ed.), *Studies in Bengal Renaissance* (Jadavpur: National Council of Education, 1958); and the latest study by Subrata Dasgupta, *The Bengal Renaissance: Identity and Creativity from Ram Mohan Roy to Rabindranath Tagore* (New Delhi: Permanent Black, 2007). For Maharashtra see: Veena Naregal, *Language Politics, Elites and the Public Sphere: western India under Colonialism* (Delhi: Permanent Black, 2001).
34. M.M. Deshpande, *Sanskrit and Prakrit Bhasha* (Marathi) (Pune: Shubhada Saraswat, 1995).
35. Pollock Sheldon, *The Language of Gods in the World of Men: Sanskrit Culture and Power in Pre-Modern India* (New Delhi: Permanent Black, 2006).
36. See following references: Vasudha Dalmia, *The Nationalization of Hindu Tradition* (New Delhi: Oxford University Press, 1996). Tariq Rahman, *Language and Politics in Pakistan* (Karachi: Oxford University Press, 1998); Paul Brass, *Language, Politics and Religion in North India* (Cambridge: Cambridge University Press, 1974).
37. See the following select literature: Eugene F. Irschik, *Politics and Social Conflict in South India* (Bombay, Oxford University Press, 1969), 275–311.

    R.E. Usher, "The Tamil Renaissance and the Beginnings of Tamil Novel", in T.W. Clark, *The Novel in India* (London: Allen & Unwin, 1970), 179–204.

    Thomas R. Trautmann, *Languages and Nations: The Dravidian Proof in Colonial Madras* (Berkeley and Los Angeles: The University of California Press, 2006).

    K.A. Nilkanth Sastri, *Cultural Contacts between Aryans and Dravidians* (Bombay: Manaktala, 1967).
38. L.S. Saraswathi, "The Medium of Instruction in Tamil Nadu", in P.R. Panchamukhi (Ed.), *Studies in Educational Reforms in India*, Vol. IV, (Bombay: Himalaya Publishing Co., 1989), 1–59.

3 Reconstruction of Indian Federalism and the Role of Language Policy

Federalism has been described by Ivo D. Duchacek as the territorial dimension of politics. The same author has pointed out that India successfully passes most of the ten criteria/tests for federalism proposed by him (see Box 3.1) except the indestructibility of the component states and that most federations are subject to federal asymmetry which can be exacerbated by multilingualism as in the case of India.[1]

Box 3.1

The Ten Yardsticks of Federalism

1. Exclusive control by central authority over foreign relations and defence.
2. Immunity of federal union against secession.
3. Independent sphere of central authority.
4. Sharing of the ultimate control over amending the federal constitution.
5. Indestructible identity and autonomy of constituent units.
6. Residual and significant powers for constituent units.
7. Bicamerialism and equal representation of union and states.
8. Two sets of courts.
9. Existence of a Supreme Court to interpret the Constitution and settle inter-state disputes.
10. Clear and unambiguous territorial division of authority.

Source: Ivo D. Duchacek (1970), op. cit., pp. 188–275, but especially p. 207.

In the present chapter, an attempt is made to historically contextualize the territorial reorganization and language policy and planning in India. It would be shown that state reorganization has rationalized the Indian federalism but a lack of cohesion in the approach to reorganization and particularly the failure to have a fresh look at the continuation of Article 3 of the Constitution of India, coupled with deficiencies of planning in the implementation of language policy have intensified the asymmetry of Indian federalism necessitating a greater centralization of the polity which in turn have impacted education sector in which language both as a subject and as a medium of instruction plays a crucial role.

Considering that both the colonial government and the freedom fighters had independently accepted the need for provincial reorganization prior to 1947, it should have been supposed that the matter would be quickly settled in the post-1947 period. As a matter of fact, there was great resistance to the reorganization especially based on the linguistic principle. This was articulated by the Dar Commission Report of the Constituent Assembly, which was asked to go into the question of formation of the provinces of Andhra, Kerala, Karnataka and Maharashtra.[2] The Commission held that the formation of linguistic provinces was not in the larger interests of the Indian nation. The Dar Commission Report was only slightly moderated in favour of formation of Andhra by the JVP Report of the Congress party.[3] The Dar Commission Report appears to be less balanced than the subsequent SRC Report but its reference to the integration of Indian states as a pre-condition for "reformation" of Indian provinces was quite valid. The story of states reorganization has been dealt with at length by Joan Bondurant[4] and others and need not be repeated.

Stages of Federal Reconstruction

The successive stages of the federal reconstruction are considered chronologically in the following paragraphs:

Federal Consolidation Ahead of the Constitution

Even before India attained independence, the State Department of the Central Government, under the administrative leadership of V.P. Menon and political stewardship of Sardar Patel, subsequently hailed as the Bismarck of the unified Indian polity, had initiated the process of integration of 550 or so princely states of India. This process gathered momentum after Mountbatten became the Governor-General, who helped along the process pointing out that the princely states, after the lapse of British paramountcy over the Indian sub-continent had to make peace with the upcoming Indian Dominion. By the 15th August 1947, all but the three states of Junagadh, Jammu & Kashmir and Hyderabad had acceded to the Indian Dominion. Sardar Patel and the Congress party were working in parallel, cleverly using the threat of popular protest to make the princes fall in line. After the princely states had acceded, they were asked to integrate, i.e., dissolve their states and merge with the proposed Union of India. In exchange, they were given privy purses and allowed to retain their titles. Post-independence, the problems of the three outstanding states were tackled – Hyderabad by police action, Junagarh by people's action and J&K by a belated Treaty of Accession (October, 1947) which was the beginning of a constitutionally embedded asymmetry in the emerging Indian federal nation-state. But, as noted by Ramchandra Guha,[5] the dissolution of over 500 autonomous and sometimes ancient chiefdoms into fourteen new autonomous units of India was, by any reckoning, a stupendous achievement which had been brought about by wisdom, foresight, hard work and not a little intrigue.

There is one oft neglected dimension of integration of the princely states which is noted by the States Reorganization Commission (SRC). About 216 princely states having a population of 19 million had been merged with the contiguous British provinces, e.g., the southern Maratha states in the then Bombay Presidency mainly on the basis of geographical contiguity-cum-linguistic affinity. Thus, the process of linguistic reorganization had been set in motion even before the inauguration of the Indian Constitution.

Constitution sans Federalism (26th January 1950)

The term 'federalism' did not figure in the Constitution of India. The mind of the founding fathers was greatly affected, as noted by Mohit Bhattacharya,[6] by the consequences of partition which, striking at the root of Congress party's platform of Hindu-Muslim unity essentially was an ethno-federal disjuncture with territorial implications. "What loomed large at that moment of crisis was not federation but national integration. The historic freedom movement was directed both towards emancipation and nation-building. With the acquisition of independence, what remained to be solved was integrated nation-building." The centralized parliamentary federalism of the Indian Constitution was the result. The Congress leadership generally hated the term 'federalism' because it was associated with the Government of India Act, 1935 which envisaged federation between British provinces and the Indian princely states, which the Congress leadership regarded as puppet regimes of the colonial power. Hence, the Constitution avoids the term 'Federation' and uses the term 'Union of States' (Article 1 of the Constitution). Article 3 of the Constitution providing for the formation of new states and alteration of area, boundaries or names of the existing states is the modified mirror image of section 290 of the 1935 Act and poses a challenge to India's claim to being called a real federal polity as noted in the beginning of the chapter. Incidentally, the most commonly used politico-administrative term for federalism in India is centre-state relations which amount to narrowing down the significance of the term, which also includes state-state relations and several other dimensions including the Panchayati Raj, the third tier of federalism.

Granville Austin's treatment of provisions regarding federalism[7] shows that there was a relative absence of conflict between 'centralizers' and 'provincialists' in the Constituent Assembly and he surmises that the Constituent Assembly was perhaps the first constituent body to embrace from the start what A.H. Birch[8] has called cooperative federalism. Schedule I of the Constitution enumerated the constituent states in India in four parts: (A) British provinces (9); (B) Princely states or groups of them (9); (C) Commissioner's provinces of which eight represented princely states; and (D) Andaman & Nicobar Islands.

Constitutional Entrenchment of Asymmetry: Article 370 of the Constitution

Article 370 of the Constitution entitled "Temporary Provisions with Respect to the State of J&K" shows how the Constitution makers were sagacious enough to realize that special cases need special provisions. J&K acceded to India on 27th October 1947 under an instrument of accession by which only three subjects (external affairs, defence and communications) were surrendered to the Union. Article 370 empowers the President to define the constitutional relationship of the state in consultation with the state in relation to the matters enumerated in the instrument of accession and with the concurrence of the State Government in all other matters. The state of J&K was left out of the purview of the SRC. J&K, alone among the states, has its own Constitution which came into force on 26th January 1957 with residuary powers vested with the state. Its official language is Urdu, not Kashmiri, which is spoken in the valley and is an Eighth Schedule language, nor Hindi or Dogri, which are spoken in Jammu. The jurisdiction of the Union Parliament was restricted initially to foreign affairs, defence and communication with the state legislature supreme in all other matters. The gradual extension of the other provisions of the Indian Constitution with concurrence of the state legislature has somewhat modified this initial arrangement. However, the procedure of obtaining concurrence of the State Government during the Governor's rule has been impugned. After the death of its charismatic leader Shaikh Abdullah on 7th September 1982, the state has experienced recurrent political instability and central intervention. Since 1989, the demand for autonomy has become strong. Some of the problems in J&K were due to the suspicion that elections to state assembly were not free and fair. But with this grievance addressed by the Election Commission in two successive general elections held in 2004 and 2009 and with the restoration of democratic political process, some solution to J&K situation which is a real challenge to the Indian federalism may not be difficult.

Post-Constitution Reorganization

The territorial reorganization of India has taken place in several sequential but overlapping phases which may be identified as below:

(a) *The phase of linguistic reorganization of Parts A, B and C states in the period 1953–1966*. In the first part of this phase, firstly, a unilingual state of Andhra carved out of Madras province was formed with effect from 1st October 1953. In the second part of the phase the SRC was appointed and its report was discussed, a communiqué incorporating a consensus was issued and then the States Reorganization Act was passed in 1956, in terms of which most linguistically reorganized states as now existing came into existence as on 1st November 1956. In the third and fourth parts of the phase, Maharashtra/Gujarat were formed on 1st May 1960 and Punjab/Haryana were formed in 1966. As a result, the categorization of the states into Part 'A', 'B' and 'C' states was abolished. Part 'C' states and Part 'D' territories were, with some changes, classified as Union Territories and the institution of the Rajpramukh, i.e., a former prince acting as Governor was abolished. Linguistic reorganization can be aptly characterized as a *silent democratic revolution* which completed the work of integration of princely states, ended feudal regimes, rationalized administration and brought the states closer to the people consequent on the business of the states being conducted in the people's language. W.H. Morris Jones[9] has rightly remarked: "States reorganization is best regarded as clearing the ground for national integration. The newly fashioned units have a self-conscious coherence and pride but they are willing, thus equipped, to do business with the Centre, to work as part of a whole that is India".

(b) *The phase of liberation and integration of non-British foreign possessions* (Portuguese and French) and the decision to retain their identity, which is one factor in the phenomenon of multiple Union Territories.

(c) *The phase of reorganization of the tribal areas in the North-East* (1962–1987) as a result of which, what were essentially hill tribal districts in Assam, were constituted into separate states of Nagaland, Meghalaya, Mizoram and Arunachal Pradesh, the last two graduating from the status of Union Territory to state. Manipur and Tripura, the adjoining princely states with tribal concentration, also became separate states. Sikkim in the north-east was added by accession in 1975.

(d) *The phase of reorganization in the hilly north and tribal Central India* as a result of which three new states – Uttaranchal, since renamed Uttarakhand (separated from UP), Jharkhand (separated from Bihar) and Chattisgarh (separated from MP) have come into being in 2000. The simultaneous creation of the three states was a matter of political bargaining. BJP was interested in the creation of Uttaranchal where there was agitation against reservation for backward classes, especially SCs and OBCs. There was a long pending popular agitation for Jharkhand which Lalu Prasad Yadav, then Chief Minister of Bihar initially opposed. His opposition was, however, softened by behind the scene bargaining as a result of which not only Jharkhand but also Chattisgarh, a tribal region of Madhya Pradesh with Bastar as its central region were made into separate states.

The four rules of Paul R. Brass[10] regarding states reorganization sum up high policy of the Nehru era which was generally followed by his successors. These are summarized in Box 3.2.

Box 3.2

Brass Rules of States Reorganization

1. Non-recognition of groups which made secessionist demands, e.g., Nagas, Mizos, Khalistanis and Kashmiri secessionists.
2. Non-accommodation of regional demands based upon religious differences (Punjab treated as a Punjabi-speaking state rather than as a Sikh state).
3. Not conceding demands for creation of separate linguistic states on the objective ground that a distinctive language was the predominant spoken language in a particular state, e.g., demand for a separate province for speakers of Maithili.
4. In multi-lingual states demand for reorganization would need to be supported by both the linguistic groups – hence the delay in reorganization of Bombay and Punjab.

Source: Paul Brass (1994), *The Politics of India since Independence*, pp. 170–172.

According to Paul Brass (1994), the application of these rules led to the recognition of the dominance of some language groups and not others in major regions of the country. His other observation that in the north, the religion is the first line of cleavage unlike in the south where language is the division factor, no doubt applies to the cases of Jammu & Kashmir, the Punjab and the three north-eastern states of Nagaland, Meghalaya and Mizoram, but the case of Goa in the south, where Christianity was a decisive factor in the formation of a separate Goa state, would show that his picture of the north-south divide in this area needs to be qualified.

Asymmetrical Features in the North-East

The resultant Indian federalism is also marked by asymmetry in the sense of Duchacek[11] (disparities among units in terms of size, population and wealth etc. or in other extra-constitutional factors or power ingredients). The concept of constitutionally entrenched special status was extended to the north-east, beginning with Nagaland when the Government of India entered into an agreement with the leaders of the Naga Peoples' Convention in July 1960 to form a separate state of Nagaland which came into existence in 1963. The Constitution was amended vide the 13th amendment, to provide under Article 371A that Acts of Parliament would not apply to the Nagas, unless so decided by the Nagaland Legislature with regard to: (a) religious/social practices of the Nagas, (b) Naga customary laws and procedures, (c) administration of civil and criminal justice involving decisions according to Naga customary laws, and (d) ownership and transfer of land and its resources. This set the pattern for incorporation of similar asymmetrical features in the north-eastern states by way of Article 371B regarding Assam, 371C in respect of Manipur, 371F concerning Sikkim, 371G relative to Mizoram and 371H applying to Arunachal Pradesh. Schedule VI relating to administration of tribal areas in Assam, Meghalaya, Tripura and Mizoram was also amended as part of the reorganization of the north-east.

Union Territories and Asymmetry

As observed by the Study Group of the ARC,[12] any study of the Union Territories (UTs) is in fact a study of the territorial administration by the Central Government. UTs have their origin in the backward tracts or scheduled districts whose existence was recognised since the British times vide Scheduled Districts Act, 1874. In 1950, Andaman & Nicobar Islands was the only UT in India tentatively categorized as a Part 'D' state. In 2010, India has seven UTs, including not only the Andaman & Nicobar Islands, but also Delhi (the Union Capital), Lakshadweep (formerly Laccadive, Minicoy and Amindivi Islands), Daman, Diu and Dadra Nagar Haveli (Portuguese possessions, not part of Goa state), Pondicherry since renamed Puducherry (French possession, which includes three separate enclaves in Tamil Nadu, Andhra Pradesh and Kerala) and Chandigarh. The States Reorganization Commission (SRC) had noted excessive dependence of Part 'C' states on the centre and had categorically recommended merger of most of them with neighbouring states except Delhi and Andaman & Nicobar Islands. The Central Government's approach to the UTs however appears to have undergone a sea change in 1962. The 14th amendment to the Constitution in December 1962 introduced a new Art. 239A providing for creation of local legislatures/councils of ministers for certain territories in terms of which Union Territories Government Act, 1963 was passed which holds the field at present. By the Constitution (69th Amendment) Act, 1991, Delhi UT was renamed National Capital Region and was given a legislature and a Council of Ministers.

Although the two UTs of Delhi and Puducherry have trappings of assemblies and cabinets, all UTs are, in effect, centrally controlled areas. They are administered by an administrator on behalf of the President and, in the case of Delhi and Puducherry, it is the Lieutenant-Governors who have the control over public order, police and land subjects. Irrespective of existence of assemblies, not only has the Union Parliament plenary power to legislate for them in respect of any entry in all the three lists of Schedule VII, but the President may also make regulations for the peace, progress and good governance of all UTs except Chandigarh, Delhi and Puducherry. The President, moreover, can issue ordinances for the UTs and the administrator can issue ordinances for the UTs of Delhi and Puducherry when their legislative assemblies are not in session. The continued prevalence of a large number of UTs in spite of the weighty recommendations of the SRC marks a facet of the centralization of authority in the Central Government which is partly due to vested interests of local areas and their MPs. The Sarkaria Commission considered it imperative that powers analogous to those of a State Government in all legislative, financial and administrative matters should be delegated to UT administration.[13] However, the Union Government in its reply observed that UTs do not stand on the same footing as the states, since the Union Government is responsible for proper administration in the UTs. This is a strong proof of the Union Government's real role vis-à-vis the UTs. It may also be noted that retention of Diu and Daman as UTs (instead of their merger with the neighbouring Gujarat) was a result of a referendum held in 1970 when Goa opted for the status of UT (and in due course, became a state).

Planning-based Asymmetry

Since 1950, India has adopted the strategy of central socio-economic planning for which the Planning Commission was set up, which formulates, finances, implements and reviews Five-Year Plans with the help of the states and UTs under the supervision of the National Development Council which is a non-statutory Inter-State Council embodying the idea of cooperative federalism. As noted by the Sarkaria Commission, central assistance to state plans was initially in the form of assistance for specific projects and programmes. Since the Fourth Five-Year Plan, in place of different schematic patterns, central assistance is given in the form of block loans (70%) and block grants (30%). However, there are ten special category states (all north-eastern states including Assam, a total of eight states) plus Himachal Pradesh and J&K to which a liberal pattern of 90 per cent grant and 10 per cent loan is applied.[14] Thus, economic weakness entailed by backwardness introduces another dimension of asymmetry in the Indian federal set-up.

The end-product of federal evolution has meant substantial rationalization of federal territory. It has, however, involved making compromises not only with linguistic but also with religious and tribal communities, as in the Punjab and the north-east, and historically entrenched parochial groups as in the case of UTs. The resultant Indian federation at the start of the 21st century (in 2010) presents a patchwork quilt of twenty-eight states, in addition to seven UTs, the latter controlled by the Central Government in toto, characterized by asymmetry. A summary of asymmetrical features of the Indian federalism is presented in Box 3.3.

Box 3.3

Summary of Asymmetrical Features of the Indian Federalism

(1) J&K	Art 370 of the Constitution
(2) North-Eastern States	Art 371–A,B,C,E,G,H and Schedule VI
(3) Union Territories	Art 239–241 of the Constitution
(4) Special Category States (Assam, Nagaland, Tripura, Mizoram, Meghalaya, Manipur, Sikkim, Arunachal Pradesh, Himachal Pradesh and Jammu & Kashmir)	Schedule VII – List Three – Entry 20: Economic and Special Planning Planning Commission's Financing Pattern in terms of loan-grant share from 1969 onwards
(5) Exemption of Tamil Nadu from Official Language Rules 1976	Historical reasons
(6) Role of President of India and Governors of States vis-á-vis Central and State Universities respectively	(Art 74 and Art. 169 and 200 of the Constitution)

Source: Compiled by author. For discussion of Sr. No. 5, see p. 62 or Sr. No. 6, p. 221.

Cooperative Federalism in Action: The Evolution of Inter-Governmental Relations in India

Immediately after the inception of the planning era, referred to in the preceding paragraph, centre-state bodies like Bhakra Nangal Central Board and Damodar Valley Corporation were set up, both dealing with major irrigation projects involving inter-state cooperation under the leadership of the Central Government. The former covered the states of Punjab and Rajasthan and the latter the states of West Bengal and Bihar. Both appeared to have the example of Tennesse Valley Authority in the US. Marcus Franda has reviewed the functioning of the DVA as part of Indian federalism.[15]

However, apart from these incidental functional bodies, a conscious effort to promote inter-state cooperation to guard against the narrow linguistic loyalties was made consequent on the reorganization of the states through two novel inter-state organizations, viz., Zonal Councils and the North-Eastern Council, the latter of which was a particular example of a Zonal Council in the case of the north-east.

In December 1955, when the Lok Sabha had begun to consider the SRC report, the Prime Minister proposed that following the reorganization of states, India should be divided into four or five larger divisions in each of which could be established an advisory zonal council to develop the habit of cooperative working. The idea was well received and in the communique of Government of India on the SRC issued on 16th January 1956, the government proposed to establish these councils simultaneously with the creation of the new states to deal with the matters of common concern.[16] It is significant to note that these councils not only became part of the SR Act of 1956, but began to function almost immediately, viz., from April 1957, underlining the Central Government's seriousness in the matter. Their functions covered all matters of common interest in the form of *socio-economic planning, border disputes, linguistic minorities, inter-state transport* and *manpower and technical education*. Union Home Minister was ex-officio chairman of the Zonal Councils and the respective CMs were members. There were five zonal councils. Initially great hopes were set on these new bodies but gradually, they became routinized. The Sarkaria Commission noted that initial enthusiasm after the formation of the zonal councils had subsided gradually, and in particular that during the prevalence of single party rule, there was no incentive for availing of the forum. Moreover, absence of an independent secretariat was a handicap. It recommended reactivation of zonal councils under Article 263 as zonal arms of the Inter-State Council. It wanted the zonal councils to be the first level for discussing most of the regional and inter-state issues and their meetings to be held at least twice a year.[17]

As pointed out by Balveer Arora,[18] the centrally established and controlled institutions for *multi-state executive federalism* have an inherent limitation of absence of roots in the processes of electoral democracy and they have failed except in the north-east where the North-Eastern Council (NEC) created by an Act of Parliament (1971) is perceived to augment collective bargaining power of small north-eastern states. In a review of the work of this Council till 1985, it was pronounced to be a success, by V. Venkat Rao.[19] However, a closer look at its composition, (it includes both the Governors and the chief ministers of north-eastern states and nominee officers of central ministries of Finance, Planning, Home Affairs and Defence), and a review of its working up-to-date, brings out clearly that it is essentially a centrally controlled body. In October 1996, the Government of India decided that each department should earmark and spend at least 10 per cent of gross budgetary support of the plan for specific development programme of the north-east region which accounts for 7.7 per cent of geographical area and 4 per cent of population of the country. In 2002, the Department of North-Eastern Region (DONER) was set up which was duly promoted to be a ministry in 2004. Minister for DONER would be chairman of North-East Council in place of a senior Governor, as was the practice earlier. This amounts to centralization no doubt, but it is required by the need of holding the north-eastern states together with the Indian federation, considering that Indian federal nation-state is, in the words of Alfred Stepan, a "holding together" polity.[20] There is, moreover, the precedent of the Union Home Minister, being the chairman of zonal councils.

Intra-State Regional Boards

Related institutional innovations also indicative of the federal asymmetry are regional committees/councils/boards set up in terms of Art. 371(2).[21] This Art. in its present form provides only for special development boards in Maharashtra and Gujarat. Earlier, it also provided for a regional committee for Andhra Pradesh but the same was replaced in 1967 by a different arrangement vide Article 371D. Earlier, regional committees were also set up in the Punjab for Hindi-speaking and Punjabi-speaking districts with special powers for Governors. These were functional committees and/or integral part of electoral process but they turned out to be transitional committees. With the formation of Punjab and Haryana as separate states, they lost their relevance. At present, such regional development boards are functioning only in Maharashtra in relation to Vidarbha, Marathwada, Konkan and the rest of Maharashtra. The validity of the boards expired at the end of April 2010 and newspaper reports indicate that the ruling Congress-NCP Democratic Front government in Maharashtra has decided to recommend extension of the boards for a further period of five years. A special feature of such development boards/regional committees is that the Governor enjoys wide powers, to issue directions to the State Government for allocation of funds for development.

Inter-State Council under Article 263 of the Constitution

Article 263 provides for setting up of an Inter-State Council (ISC) by the President for (a) inquiring into and advising upon inter-state disputes, (b) investigating or discussing subjects of common interest to the union and/or states, and (c) making recommendations for better coordination of policy and action with respect to a subject. The ARC (1969) had recommended setting up of the ISC for a period of two years, but no action was taken. The Sarkaria Commission recommended setting up of an ISC re-named Inter-Governmental Council (IGC), on a long-term basis. As observed by the Sarkaria Commission,[22] ISC has basically investigative, deliberative and recommendatory duties, being an advisory and consensus seeking body. It was noted by the Commission that the National Development Council (NDC) which was set up by the Planning Commission in 1952, under chairmanship of the Prime Minister and comprising the CMs of all the states was, in essence, an ISC though it was set up by an executive order and not under Article 263. The Commission recommended the re-constitution of the NDC under Article 263 and its renaming as National Economic Development Council (NEDC). The Commission also noted existence of sectoral ISCs in the three spheres of health, local self-government and sales tax. Surprisingly, it did not take note of the existence since prior to independence of such a body in the education sector called CABE (Central Advisory Board of Education), which is dealt with in the chapter on Educational Planning ahead.

The Congress government which had appointed the Sarkaria Commission ignored the Commission's recommendations in regard to IGC, NEDC and zonal councils. It was during the UF regime led by V.P. Singh as PM that ISC (not IGC) came to be set up in 1990 with administrative support provided by the ISC secretariat under the Ministry of Home Affairs. Its first secretary was a former Cabinet Secretary, indicating the importance attached to the organization by the UF government.

Rekha Saxena, who has studied both the ISC and the NDC as inter-governmental bodies, had earlier assessed NDC as a success and termed ISC as a 'monumental failure'.[23] She has subsequently modified her judgement to hold that both the NDC and the ISC have emerged as two apex inter-governmental mechanisms of great importance, but neither is as effective as the First Ministers' Conference in Canada which is a premier example of a body embodying executive federalism.[24] However, another scholar holds that in a federal system that features growing inter-jurisdictional competition among the states, it is unlikely that states would acquiesce to central regulations that may jeopardize a foreign investor's decision to invest in a given state.[25] M.P. Singh is inclined to agree with Rekha Saxena on following grounds: (a) the tendency towards increased federalization in the economic polity, (b) statutory regulating authorities are quasi-judicial bodies, and (c) states in India are not as autonomous or resourceful as in Canada and there is always a scope for bodies like the ISC.[26]

The question remains whether the ISC would be a functional body irrespective of the regime. It is noted that the ISC met only when the non-Congress governments were in power (UF, NF and NDA). Somehow, the Congress-dominated regimes have relied on the NDC and not convened meetings of the ISC (e.g., UPA-I and UPA-II). ISC has been however, kept busy in providing secretarial support to events or Commissions. This would be considered in the concluding chapter.

The Role of Language Policy

The Official Language of Independent India and Its Implications for Federalism

The issues involved in the constitutional settlement as to the official language of the Union need to be understood before we consider what followed. These issues were settled as part of what was known as the Munshi-Ayyangar formula,[27] and are listed below:

(i) *The identity of the official language and its script:* In the inter-war period, the official policy of the Congress which was largely influenced by Gandhiji was to support Hindi-Hindustani with two optional scripts – Devanagari and Perso-Arabic. It was clearly understood that the former's vocabulary was drawn from Sanskrit and the latter's from Persian – Arabic. The former was Hindi proper and the latter was indistinguishable from Urdu. However, consequent on partition and with Pakistan adopting Urdu as its official language, it was difficult for official leadership of the Congress to continue its support for Hindustani/Urdu as the official language. Still, there was attachment to the term Hindustani. There was a strong lobby within the Congress party for Hindi in Devanagari script whose moderate face was K.M. Munshi and whose extremist face was P.D. Tandon. It is significant to note that Munshi succeeded Gandhiji as the President of the Hindi Sahitya Sammelan, Allahabad, a position which Gandhiji vacated in 1945 because of the difference of opinion with the Sammelan authorities on the twin issues of vocabulary and the script.[28] Munshi played a leading role in the constitutional settlement. There was a consensus over identification of Hindi in Devanagari script as official language. There was, of course, opposition to Hindi from the South. However, at the stage of Constitution making, the South was some how persuaded to accept Hindi in Devanagari script as official language as an independent country could not afford to have a foreign language as its official language. Urdu was included in the Eighth Schedule of the Constitution, but English was not. The 'term' Hindustani was referred to in Article 351 which deals with the subject of development of the Hindi language,[29] but it was not a scheduled language.

(ii) *The form of numerals:* The supporters of Hindi were keen to adopt Devanagari, which is known as Arabic form of numerals. But the South side took its stand on international form of numerals and it was so provided in the Constitution.

(iii) The South wanted English to be continued as a transitional language for a much longer period but a compromise was struck by providing for its use for fifteen years beyond 1950. However, it was also provided that the question of progressive use of Hindi may be decided by the Commissions to be appointed at intervals of five and ten years respectively. The

Commissions were to have due regard to (a) the industrial, cultural and scientific advance of the country, and (b) just claims/interests of non-Hindi speaking areas in regard to public services. The Commissions' reports were to be considered by a Parliamentary Committee.

(iv) English was to be the language of the Supreme Court/High Courts and for Acts and Bills etc., but the Governor of the state with the previous consent of the President could authorize the use of Hindi or any other language.

(v) Articles 345 to 347 dealt with regional languages which were listed in the Eighth Schedule and it was understood that they were to be the official languages in the respective states.

(vi) *The federal official language was to be the language of inter-state communication:* Since any discussion on language provisions tended to involve acrimonious debates and controversies, the same were taken up for discussion towards the fag end of the Constituent Assembly debates. The Munshi-Ayyangar formula was discussed in the party meetings in August 1949 and the final decision was taken on 2nd September 1949. The discussion in the Constituent Assembly was started on 12th September 1949 and concluded on 14th September.[30] The formula was carried unanimously. Inclusion of Sanskrit as a scheduled language was decided at the last minute. In spite of the fact that decision regarding Hindi as official language was unanimous, a myth of a majority of one has been sedulously propagated by a section of the scholarly community as depicted in Box 3.4.

Box 3.4

The Myth of the Majority of One for Hindi as Federal Official Language

Several scholars till this date (2010), believe that the decision on Hindi as official language was taken by the Constituent Assembly by a single vote (78 vs. 77). This is a myth. To quote Granville Austin: "The closeness of the votes on language in the party meetings has given rise to the legend that Hindi became official language of India by a majority of only one vote. This seems very doubtful. The 'one-vote' legend is based on the events at the party meeting of 26th August 1949, when there may have existed briefly one vote majority in favour of Nagari over international numbers. Ambedkar's 'Thoughts on Linguistic States' (Delhi 1955) and Govind Das' autobiography have tended to uphold this legend but both have confused the facts" (pp. 299–300).

Note: The scholars who deserve the strictures of Granville Austin include Asha Sarangi, vide her 'Introduction' in Asha Sarangi (Ed.), *Language and Politics in India* (New Delhi, Oxford University Press, 2009), Footnote 73 on p. 23 and Neerja Gopal Jayal, vide her 'Negotiating Linguistic Diversity' in Bajpai K. Shankar (Ed.), *Democracy & Diversity* (New Delhi, Oxford University Press, 2007), p. 115.

The Unraveling of the Constitutional Settlement

The official language is the language of power in the federal nation and is also taught compulsorily at school stage. As observed by Granville Austin, the constitutional provisions represented a half-hearted or unhappy compromise and are therefore, full of ambiguities. Moreover, they gave an appearance of a centralized elitist model of English being replaced by Hindi, with the role of regional languages being subservient to Hindi, just as earlier they were subservient to English.[31] The path of implementation was not smooth and the resultant outcome was true to the original model, viz., hegemony of English, expanding imperialism of Hindi vis-à-vis regional languages and reduction of regional languages to a subaltern position. This scenario is reviewed below showing how the constitutional settlement as regards official language unraveled including asymmetry of Tamil Nadu. The half-hearted implementation of the three-language formula at the school stage would be reviewed in the chapter on secondary education and the issue of switch over to the regional language as media of instruction at higher education would be dealt with in the relevant chapter.

Hindi as Official Language

There was a perceptible change of sentiment against the time limit of fifteen years. As a result, after the report of the Official Language Commission (1956), also known as Kher Report, which had not envisaged any extension of the time limit of 15 years, carried two strong and symbolic minutes of dissent by Tamil and Bengali-speaking members, i.e., P. Subbarayan and S.K. Chatterji. The Committee of MPs, (presided over by the then Home Minister G.B. Pant), which considered the Kher Report went out of the way and recommended (1958) continuation of English along with Hindi for an indefinite period. In August 1959, while speaking on Frank Anthony's non-official resolution for inclusion of English in the VIII Schedule of the Constitution, Prime Minister Nehru gave an assurance that there would be no imposition (of Hindi) and that English would be an "alternate language as long as people require it and the decision for that I would leave to the non-Hindi knowing people".[32] In April 1960, a Presidential order was issued specifying that after 1965, when Hindi becomes the principal official language of the Union, English should continue as the subsidiary official language.[33]

The transition period from English to Hindi and the role of English in the transition period became a bone of contention between Hindiwallas (who turned into "Remove English" or Angrezi Hatao agitationists belonging to various socialist parties and also the Jan Sangh in the North) and non-Hindi speakers, led particularly by the ruling elite in Tamil Nadu and West Bengal who wanted indefinite continuance of English. The Central Government, however, dragged its feet. The parliamentary legislation in the form of Official Language Act was delayed, being passed only on 10th May 1963. While it went beyond the Presidential order of 1960 and provided that English may continue to be used for all the official purposes (and not only for specified purposes), it failed to incorporate Prime Minister Nehru's assurance of 1959. The intensity of the feeling in the then state of Madras, now Tamil Nadu, on the subject was unfortunately underestimated even by Jawaharlal Nehru who felt that a constitutional amendment restructuring freedom of speech in the interests of sovereignty and integrity of India (effective 1963) would deter DMK in Tamil Nadu. After widespread agitation in Tamil Nadu in January 1965 (when the 15 year period was over), which had the potential of a secessionist threat, the Prime Minister Lal Bahadur Shastri had to announce on 11th February 1965, in an all-India broadcast that Nehru's assurance would be incorporated by amending the 1963 Act. But the projected amendment was delayed apparently because of the Indo-Pakistan war in 1965, the change of Prime Ministership from Shastri to Indira Gandhi, the economic crisis of 1966 and the intervening Third General Elections which give a set back to the congress. In April 1967, the Samyukta Socialist Party (which was a party spearheading 'Remove English' agitation) and the Jan Sangh, also supporting Hindi, made a strong show in the elections in the North but in Tamil Nadu Congress was unsated from power by the DMK led by C.N. Annadurai. The Central Government circulated a Draft Bill providing that English would continue to be an associate official language until resolutions for its discontinuance have been passed separately by the legislatures of non-Hindi-speaking states. This redeemed the Prime Minister Nehru's pledge to Tamil Nadu. However, the Central government (which was under pressure to make concessions to the Hindiwallas), shortly after the passage of amendment Act, passed a parliamentary resolution on 18th January 1968.[34] This was in two parts. The first part reiterated the Central government's commitment to a more intensive and comprehensive programme for the progressive use of Hindi for various official purposes. This appeared to be the main agenda. But this part was coupled with a resolve to take concerted measures for the full development of fourteen major languages of India along with Hindi, and to take effective steps to implement the three language formula in school curriculum, and also an assurance regarding either Hindi or English as a pre-requisite for selection for public services with permissive use of all fourteen major languages as alternative media for all-India and central service examinations. The parliamentary resolution, especially its first part served as a red rag to the Tamil Nadu government which was up in arms and got passed in the state assembly on 23rd January 1968, a resolution repudiating the three-language formula for school education and adopted a two-language formula providing for teaching of Tamil and English only.[35] This stand has been firmly adhered to by the successive Tamil Nadu governments at the meeting of sectoral Inter-State Council, viz., CABE, the Chief Ministers' Conferences and the NDC irrespective of the complexion of the party in power in the state. In effect, the Tamil Nadu government has repudiated Hindi as an educational and official language since January 1968 and this has been officially recognized by the Government of India by providing that Official Language Rules, 1976 would not apply to Tamil Nadu. The repudiation of Hindi as an official language by Tamil Nadu and its official acquiescence by the Central government constitutes an important facet of the asymmetry in the official linguistic and educational discourse of Indian federalism, which may well be listed as the fifth feature in Box 3.3 relating to asymmetrical features of Indian polity.

The Eighth Schedule of Constitution: A Pillar of Linguistic Federalism

So far as the constitutional provisions relating to regional languages are concerned, they are couched in permissive rather than mandatory terms and appear to favour English and Hindi and minority languages and mother tongues. The term 'regional language' is not used in the Constitution except in the title of the group of Art. 345–347. Art. 345 permits legislature of a state to adopt any language in use or Hindi. Art. 347 incorporates special provision relating to recognition by the state of any language spoken by a section of the population of a state. Art. 350A and 350B (added in 1956 after the major linguistic reorganisation) direct states to provide special facilities for instruction in mother tongue at primary stage and for appointment of a Special Officer for Linguistic Minorities to supervise the implementation of the provision. This is apart from the constitutional guarantee of protection of interests of linguistic minorities (vide Articles 29 and 30). The Eighth Schedule of the Constitution, as originally enacted, listed names of all regional languages plus Urdu and Sanskrit. Nehru used to call Eighth Schedule languages as national languages. This was also his reason for opposition to inclusion of English in that schedule (see Box 3.5).

This position was confirmed by the parliamentary resolution of January 1968, which empowered them by calling them 'major languages', thus, reiterating the Nehruvian intent and sending a message that the Eighth Schedule was a pillar of linguistic federalism just as the Eighth Schedule was a pillar of legal federalism. Nehru's policy of restriction on enlargement of the Eighth Schedule was continued till 1992, the only

Box 3.5

Jawaharlal Nehru's Views on Regional Languages of India

Our great provincial languages are no dialects or vernaculars as the ignorant sometimes call them. They are ancient languages with a rich inheritance, each spoken by many millions of persons, each tied up inextricably with the life and culture and ideas of the masses as well as the upper classes. It is axiomatic that the masses can only grow educationally and culturally through the medium of their own language. Therefore, it is inevitable that we lay stress on the provincial languages and carry on most of our work through them.

Source: Jawaharlal Nehru, *The Unity of India* (London, Lindsay Drummond, 1941), p. 243.

exception being addition of Sindhi, a stateless language as a symbolic gesture in 1967, by the Constitution (Twenty-First Amendment) Act, 1967.[36] However, in 1992 when the Congress government was in power, Konkani, Manipuri and Nepali were added and in 2003 when the NDA government was in power, Bodo, Dogri, Santhali and Maithili were super-added, by the Constitution (Ninety-Second Amendment) Act 2003.[37] so that the present number of Eighth Schedule languages is 22. Most of the languages so added had been earlier recognized by the Sahitya Akademi for literary purposes. The inclusion in the Eighth Schedule entitles the language to various facilities in education, employment and administration, competitive examinations, entrance examinations for IITs and IIMS etc. and its expansion under sectional pressures to accommodate languages which are not major regional languages or official languages of newly created states (e.g., Goa, Manipur), does appear to dilute the original intent and devalue the great regional languages of India. Moreover, as pointed out by P.V. Indireshan and N.C. Nigam,[38] the introduction of such of these languages which are not state's official language, has imposed avoidable burden on the conduct of examinations like JEE for admission to IITs. Such concessions to demands of linguistic groups apparently made in response to reports of ad hoc expert committees would need to be accommodated in ways other than the amendment to the Eighth Schedule which should ideally only include official languages of states/UTs enumerated in the First Schedule of the Constitution, which was the intent of the framers of the Constitution, as understood by Nehru, thus preserving the significance of the Eighth Schedule as a pillar of linguistic federalism.

In the light of this constitutional scenario, the role of English, Hindi and other regional languages in the public sphere with special reference to education is considered in the following paragraphs.

Hegemony of English

English though not part of the Eighth Schedule is recognized as an official language in the states of Meghalaya, Mizoram and Nagaland. The National Policy of Education (NPE), 1986, talked of the need specially to strengthen the study of English because "world knowledge is growing at a tremendous pace especially in science and technology" and "India must not only keep up this growth but should also make her own significant contribution". The policy was based on the Kothari Report (1966: 8.38 and 8.47), which did not favour introduction of English as a school subject prior to Class V and which talked of the role of English as a library language in higher education. This was also the view of NCERT's National Curricular Framework (2000), which stated that English language which is considered as a second or third language except in the states of Nagaland, Meghalaya and Mizoram (where it was the first language, being the official language of the state) should be introduced from Standard VI or later. However, in the post-1991 liberalization era, the State Governments, in view of the popularity of English-medium schools and consequent desertion of the state school systems by the general public, began to introduce English from Class I (e.g., Maharashtra in 1999). This has begun a general trend with several other states following suit. Therefore, the NCERT's National Curricular Framework (2005) states that the level of introduction of English is now a matter of political response to people's aspirations rather than an academic feasibility issue and that people's choice about the level of its introduction in the curriculum will have to be respected.[39] This may be called a pragmatic approach but the social forces strengthening this process which is called by some scholars as "anglification of elementary education",[40] and the complicity both of states and the Central government in the same cannot be overlooked. Social forces point to the perpetuation by the middle-class of the public school system with English medium in India in the post-independence period and this system has been strengthened by the Central government through its promotion of a series of centrally financed schools variously called "Central Schools" (for transferable central government employees), "Sainik Schools" and the "Navodaya Vidyalayas-Rural Public Schools" (started by Prime Minister Rajiv Gandhi, even prior to introduction of NPE 1986 and thereafter continued as part of it). It has been observed that far from blurring the urban-rural divide, the Navodaya schools can more accurately be described as the government's capitulation to the pressures from the rural rich who have been fully conscious of the value of English education in consolidating their own hegemony, not unlike Bengali Bhadralok more than a century ago.[41] The Central government's complicity in promoting English is also evidenced by the fact that institutional structures of such a venture were in place as early as 1958 when the Hyderabad-based Central Institute for English was established with assistance from the British Council and the Ford Foundation. This Institute was notified in 1973 as a deemed university and recently the Government of India converted the same into a central university vide the report of the Standing Committee on the subject published by Rajya Sabha Secretariat.[42] One scholar has talked of hegemony of English and this truly describes the current role of English in education and in the centre-state structures. It has been pointed out that even in Tamil Nadu, the State Government had to bow to the pressure of middle classes and resile from its policy of making Tamil the exclusive medium of instruction in junior and senior colleges in 1970–71.[43]

Hindi

The Central Government has followed the parliamentary resolution of January 1968, in letter and spirit so far as promotion of Hindi as official language is concerned. It has established following institutions for promotion of Hindi language: (a) Kendriya Hindi Sansthan, Agra (estd. 1960), devoted to Hindi teacher training from non-Hindi-speaking states and research in the methodology of teaching Hindi as a second/third language, (b) Central Hindi Directorate, New Delhi (1960), which conducts correspondence courses for non-Hindi-speaking people and prepares bilingual, trilingual and multi-lingual dictionaries with Hindi as the base, and (c) more recently (1997) an international Hindi university has been established at Wardha to develop Hindi language and literature in comparative and international perspective with emphasis on translation. According to the report of the Ministry for 2004–05, the University was conducting courses in M.A., M.Phil and Ph.D.

The Central Government established a separate Department of Official Language in June 1975 and issued rules under Official Language Act in July 1976. A Committee of Parliament on Official Languages has been constituted in January 1976 and subsequently it has been reconstituted by every Parliament. A high bureaucracy for implementation of Hindi as official language under this ministry has been created in the form of a new service called Central Secretariat Official Language Service in 1989 with 220 gazetted and 600 translators' posts.[44]

Subalternity of Regional Languages

In terms of the parliamentary resolution of 18th January 1968, which stated that it is necessary in the interest of educational and cultural advancement of the country that concerted measures should be taken for the full development of these languages through centre-state collaboration the Central Government is committed to the development of major Indian languages which are official languages of constituent states of India. It was in terms of this resolution that the Central Institute of Indian Languages (CIIL) came to be set up at Mysore in July 1969 for coordination of the work of State Language Institutes, Tribal Research Institutes and university departments of languages and linguistics. The Institute has not lived up to the expectations of its founders, so far as regional languages are concerned. It runs seven regional centres (five centres at Bhubaneswar, Pune, Mysore, Patiala and Guwahati) and two Urdu teaching and research centres at Solan and Lucknow. Its organizational structure does not provide for representation of the state education departments and its official classification of being a subordinate office of the ministry of education reflects its true status. The Ramamurti Committee had commented on this and on its functional rigidities, comparing its status with CIEFL and Kendriya Hindi Sansthan, the former of which was then a deemed university and the latter enjoyed autonomy. It wanted CIIL to be converted into an autonomous body. It further noted that the capacity of CIIL for teacher training remained considerably underutilized but still, considering the vast training needs, the same may be increased from 360 seats to 1,000 seats.[45] The PoA 1992 does not indicate that these proposals were accepted and the Mysore institute continues as a subordinate office, although CIEFL has been converted into a statutory Central University. The CIIL, however, is being entrusted with additional tasks, viz., work relating to National Testing Service and translation which may dilute its role in the matter of promotion of regional languages. Importantly, it is also likely to undertake a new Linguistic Survey of India.[46]

The Central Government's record in implementing its 1968 resolution in relation to regional languages is not exactly shining. The regional languages find no place at all in the "public" schools and central schools chains, which are focused on English and other foreign languages and on Hindi in their school curricula. Central Government departments also follow no uniform policy regarding the use of regional languages in their state offices about which the Sarkaria Commission commented adversely in its Chapter XX. The Sarkaria Commission writing in 1988 observed that the post for Commissioner for Linguistic Minorities had been lying vacant since March 1978 and the reports of the officer had neither been discussed in Parliament nor had they received adequate attention from Central Government.[47] Since linguistic minorities in one state were linguistic majorities in other states, this only highlights the marginalization of regional languages at the hands of the Central Government. Language planning involves identification, standardization and modernization of major languages. One scholar, deploring the poor state of standardization of modern Indian languages, has advocated establishment of a Lexicographical Survey of India and corresponding state structures, viz., State Lexicographical Institutes, State Institutes of Translation and State Documentation Centres which, in cooperation with the postgraduate modern-language departments of State Universities, can play a role in the development of language infrastructure. There is no indication that the Central Government has any inclination in this direction.[48]

Moreover, all the various language institutions function in isolation. There does not appear to be an effective mechanism to coordinate the work of these institutions and the state language academies or any programme to promote state academies in states, where they do not exist especially when state textbook boards/granth academies are in the doldrums. An Indian Language promotion Council to advise the government on the policy for promotion, development and propagation of all Indian languages to be served by the CIIL had been set up under the NDA dispensation and its first meeting was held in February 2004, chaired by the PM.[49] Apart from the fact that the UPA government which came to power in mid-2004 did not pursue the matter, it needs to be observed that such high level forums cannot deliver results in the crucial tasks of the Central Government relating to implementation of three-language formula, development of major Indian languages as languages of knowledge and media of instruction at higher education stage and redefinition of relationship of regional languages to the twin link languages of Hindi and English. Generally speaking, English is the continuing link language of the university-educated elite and Hindi apart from being the language of the elite in the North has gradually emerged as incipient link language of the masses, thanks to the popular entertainment media like cinema (the so-called Bollywood). The regional languages other than Hindi appear to have become subalterns in the language game.

Asymmetry of Tamil Nadu: Concluding Remarks

Earlier a reference has been made to the asymmetry of Tamil Nadu state within Indian federalism to the extent that the Tamil Nadu has refused to implement the three-language formula. In the same category may be placed Tamil Nadu government's refusal to participate in the Navodaya Vidyalaya scheme of the Central Government started in 1985 because it would amount to Tamil Nadu government accepting three language formula.

Tamil Nadu shares with other states the tendency to change the name of the state and of its capital by way of assertion of identity. Thus, the name of the state was changed from Madras to Tamil Nadu with effect from 14th January 1969, and the name of the capital city was changed from Madras to Chennai in 1996.

In an altogether different category is to be placed the success of the Tamil Nadu government in making Central Government issue a notification about Tamil being a classical language in the year 2004. Subsequently, under pressure from respective State Governments, Kannada and Telugu were similarly notified. This amounts to politicization of the issue of classical status of language.[50] The Central Government has followed up by establishment of a new Central Institute for Classical Tamil in Madurai.[51]

Conclusion

Vesuki Nesiah,[52] after review of the literature on federalism and diversity has proposed the paradigm of evolution of federalism in India from an administrative through contractual to democratic federalism. One has to realize that these are not chronological phases but concurrent ones. Above all, democratic federalism is not a phase but the dominant mode of the evolution of nation-state, that is, India. Indian federalism is work in progress.

Notes

1. Ivo D. Duchacek, *Comparative Federalism: The Territorial Dimension of Politics* (New York: Holt, Rinehart and Winston, 1970). Duchacek has noted that asymmetry is the result of disparity of power ingredients in federal units. These ingredients are: size, population, political power, administrative skills, wealth, economic development etc. (p. 280).
2. Report of Linguistic Provinces Commission vide B. Shiv Rao, *Framing India's Constitution,* Vol. IV, (New Delhi: IIPA, 1966), 448–502.
3. Indian National Congress: Report of the Linguistic Provinces Committee, 2nd Impression (1953) referred to by Y.D. Phadke in his *Politics and Language* (Bombay: Himalaya Publishing, 1979), 128.
4. Joan V. Bondurant, *Regionalism vs. Provincialism: A Study in Problems of Indian National Unity* (Berkeley: University of California Press, 1958).
5. Ramchandra Guha, *India After Gandhi* (New Delhi: Macmillan, 2008).
6. Mohit Bhattacharya, "The Mind of the Founding Fathers", in Nirmal Mukarji and Balveer Arora (Eds.), *Federalism in India: Origins and Development* (New Delhi: Vikas Publishing, 1992), 87–104.
7. Granville Austin, *Indian Constitution: The Corner Stone of a Nation* (New Delhi: Oxford University Press, 1966), 186–216.
8. A.H. Birch, *Federalism, Finance and Social Legislation in Canada, Australia and the US* (Oxford: Clarendon Press, 1955).
9. W.H. Morris Jones, *The Government and Politics of India* (UK: Eothen Press, 1970. Indian Reprint by Universal Book Stall, New Delhi, 1996).

10. Paul R. Brass, *Politics of India since Independence* (New Delhi: Cambridge University Press, 2nd ed., 1994).
11. Vide Footnote 1.
12. Study Group of ARC on UTs (Government of India, Ministry of Home Affairs, 1969).
13. Sarkaria Report, 531–533.
14. Sarkaria Report, 364.
15. Marcus Franda, *West Bengal and the Federalising Process in India* (Princeton: Princeton University Press, 1968).
16. Joan Bondurant, op. cit., pp. 55–70 and 105–109.
17. Sarkaria Report, 240–241.
18. Balveer Arora, "Adapting Federalism to India", in Balveer Arora and Douglas U. Verney (Eds.), *Multiple Identities in a Single State: Indian Federalism in Comparative Perspective* (New Delhi: Konark Publishers, 1995), 83–84.
19. V. Venkat Rao, "North-Eastern Council and Union-State Relations", in N. Sanajaoba (Ed.), *Basic Issues in Union-State Relations* (New Delhi: Omson Publications, 1985), 235–242.
20. Alfred Stepan, "Federalism: Multi-National Societies and Negotiating a Democratic State-Nation", in Bajpai K. Shankar, *Democracy and Diversity* (New Delhi: Oxford University Press, 2007), 225–261.
21. Joan Bondurant, op. cit., 122–127.
22. Sarkaria Commission, 237–243.
23. Rekha Saxena, "Role of Inter-Governmental Agencies in Federal India", in B.D. Dua and M.P. Singh (Eds.), *Indian Federalism in the New Millennium* (New Delhi: Manohar, 2003), 221–227.
24. Rekha Saxena, *Situating Federalism: Mechanisms of Inter-Governmental Relations in India and Canada* (New Delhi: Manohar, 2006), 250–312.
25. Lawrence Saez, *Federalism without Centre* (New Delhi: Sage Publications, 2002).
26. M.P. Singh, "The Impact of Global and Regional Integration on India's Parliamentary Federal System", in B.D. Dua and M.P. Singh (Eds.), *Indian Federalism in the New Millennium* (New Delhi: Manohar, 2003), 379–435.
27. Granville Austin, *Indian Constitution: Corner Stone of Nation* (New Delhi: Oxford University Press, 1966), 265–307.
28. A.K. Majumdar, *The Problems of Hindi: A Study* (Bombay: Bharatiya Vidya Bhavan, 1965).
29. The Article reads: "It shall be the duty of the Union to promote the spread of the Hindi language to develop it so that it may serve as a medium of expression for all the elements of the composite culture of India and to secure its enrichment by assimilating without interfering with its genius, the forms, style and expressions used in Hindustani and in the other

languages of India specified in the Eighth Schedule and by drawing wherever necessary or desirable, for its vocabulary, primarily on Sanskrit and secondarily on other languages".

30. Granville Austin, op. cit., 1966.
31. Hans R. Dua, *Hegemony of English: Future of Developing Languages in the Third World* (Mysore: Yashoda Publications, 1994), 85.
32. K.L. Gandhi, *The Problem of Official Language in India* (New Delhi: Arya Book Depot, 1984), 56–58.
33. K.L. Gandhi, op. cit., 1984, 167–173.
34. *The Official Language Act and Rules Thereunder* (New Delhi: Controller of Publications, 1994).
35. P. Sprott, *DMK in Power* (Bombay: Nachiketa Publications, 1970).
36. According to Paul Brass, who relies on information furnished by E. Annamalai, the inclusion of Sindhi as an ES language was due to the movement by Sindhi speakers in 1950s (and 1960s), and it was facilitated by the perception that it meant recognition by the nation of the Sindhi community, there was no cost involved and it symbolized the rejection in principle of the very idea of partition of India and the separation of the province of Sindh from India. (Paul Brass, "Elite Interests, Popular Passions and Social Power in the Language Politics of India", in Asha Sarangi (Ed.), *Language and Politics in India* (New Delhi: Oxford University Press, 2009), 183–217. Incidentally, inclusion in ES has also enabled Sindhi to have a promotional institution for itself, viz., National Council for Promotion of Sindhi Language, Vadodara.
37. The Sahitya Academy started giving its awards in 1970. The Congress-led government in 1992 did not concede the demand of Dogri Sangharsh Manch for inclusion of Dogri in the ES. The BJP-led government at the Centre accepted the demand and included it in the ES vide 92nd Constitutional Amendment Act 2003. (K. Warikoo, "Language and Politics in J&K: Issues and Perspectives", in Asha Sarangi (Ed.), *Language and Politics in India* (New Delhi: Oxford University Press, 2009), 243–266). So far as Maithili is concerned, Paul Brass interprets its inclusion to BJPs calculations (which was in power at the Centre but not in Bihar at that time) that this step would enable it to establish and consolidate a political base among the upper castes who claimed Maithili as their mother tongue. He notes that 30 years earlier (i.e., in 1973) an elite dominated movement for creation of Maithili state had failed vide Paul Brass in the article mentioned in Footnote 36.
38. P.V. Indireshan and N.C. Nigam, "The Indian Institutes of Technology: Excellence in Peril, in Philip G. Altbach and Suma Chitnis (Eds.), *Higher Education Reforms in India: Experience and Perspectives* (New Delhi: Sage Publications, 1993,), 334–364 (esp. p. 360).
39. NCF 2005 (New Delhi: NCERT, 2006), para 3.1.3.

40. Hans R. Dua, *Science Policy, Education and National Planning* (Mysore: Yashoda Publications, 2001) 312.
41. Gauri Vishwanathan, "English in a Literate Society", in Rajeshwari Sundar Rajan, *The Lie of the Land: English Literary Studies in India* (New Delhi: Oxford University Press, 1992), 29–41.
42. Rajya Sabha Secretariat, 177th Report on CIEFL University Bill 2006 of the department related Parliamentary Standing Committee (New Delhi, 2006).
43. L.S. Saraswathi, "Medium of Instruction in Tamil Nadu", in P.R. Panchamukhi (Ed.), *Studies in Educational Reforms in India*, Vol. IV, (Bombay: Himalaya Publishing Co., 1989), 1–89, esp. 20–22.
44. Government of India: Annual Report of the Department of Official Languages, 2004–05 (2006).
45. Ramamurti Report, 250–273.
46. Sugatha Srinivasaraju, *Keep Faith with the Mother Tongue* (Mysore: Nava Karnataka, 2008), 110–112.
47. Sarkaria Report, 521–530.
48. Pramod Talgeri, "The Fate of Indian Languages: The Need for Standardization and Modernization of Infrastructure", in R.S. Gupta et al., *Language and the State: Perspectives on Eighth Schedule* (New Delhi: Creative Books, 1995), 201–205.
49. Annual Report of Ministry of HRD (2003–2004), 236.
50. A.R. Venkatachalapathy, "The Classical Language Issue" (*EPW,* 10th January 2009), 13–15. See also Idem (Ed.), *Chennai, Not Madras: Perspectives on the City* (Mumbai, Marg Publications, 2006).
51. Ministry of Education, Annual Report (2008–2009).
52. Vesuki Nessiah, "Federalism and Diversity in India", in Yash Ghai (Ed.), *Autonomy and Ethnicity: Negotiating Competing Claims in Multi-Ethnic States* (Cambridge: Cambridge University Press, 2000).

4 The Constitutional Context of Education and Federalism

Education under Dyarchy and Provincial Autonomy

K.C. Wheare has stated his conclusion about the role of education in federal constitutions very guardedly and with many qualifications: "Education is generally, for the most part, under regional control-some supervision and assistance by the general government is advisable and is justified."[1] This is because education is always regarded as important, either as a nation-building activity as in pre-independence India or as a provider of trained manpower for India's drive towards industrialization in the hey-day of central planning or more recently, as an integral part of the strategy of human development. The constitutional role of education was crystallized in India in the course of the reforms of 1919 in an episode fraught with controversy. On the eve of Dyarchy (1917–20) a battle raged in India on the issue as to whether the whole or only a part of education should be a "transferred" provincial subject. The imperial bureaucracy wanted to divide the subject of education and in particular was keen to retain control of higher education institutions. The hero of the battle on the Indian side was undoubtedly Sir Shankaran Nair, Member-in-Charge of Education, as can be seen presently. It was thanks to him that the issue was settled in favour of education as a "transferred" subject in 1920, and this settlement was accepted by the Indian ruling elite in 1950 at the time of the adoption of the Constitution of India and education continued to be a state subject right up to 1977.

The Battle for Provincialization of Education (1919)

The colonial government's decision to make education a provincial subject was framed by three important reports, viz., the Industries Commission Report (1916), the Sadler Report, (1919) and the Montford Report (1919). The Industries Commission (1916) suggested that technical education should be dealt with by the Department of Industries and accordingly, technical education became a transferred subject under the general head "Development of Industries". The recommendations of Sadler Commission, though strictly concerned with the reorganization of

Calcutta University, carried weight because of its composition (a British Vice-Chancellor, Sir Michael Sadler as Chairman and Ashutosh Mukerjee, who was to make name as the Vice-Chancellor of Calcutta University as a member). According to the Sadler Commission, universities should be made much more independent of local governments but should come under the purview of Government of India in respect of legislation, visitation, coordination, research and recruitment. This suggested the idea that the provincial legislation for new universities should be subject to Indian, i.e., central legislation. But, the lead given by the Montford Report was decisive. It viewed education both as a problem and an opportunity. It was a problem because it had made little impact on the masses (only 6 per cent of population was then literate), its distribution was uneven (it was confined to the writing classes like Brahmins and Kayasthas), it failed to form character and train Indians for practical work in manufacture, commerce and application of science to industrial life. But education also offered an opportunity. The Committee talked of the political importance of education,[2] which was two-fold. Firstly, responsibility would mean appreciation of the financial difficulties and willingness to raise taxes for the spread of education. But secondly, to quote the Committee: "Progress must depend on the growth of electorates and intelligent exercise of their powers, and men will be immensely helped to become competent electors by acquiring such education as will enable them to judge candidates for their votes and of the business done in the Council." It was of the opinion that transfer of education to a responsible minister was necessary in the context of a realistic appreciation of financial dimension of the problem as well as in the interest of democracy. In its illustrative list of provincial subjects, it showed education (item 11) covering "primary, secondary, colleges, technical and universities", the exception being 'universities serving more than one province' and some chiefs' colleges, with special consideration for the Indian Universities Act. In its illustrative list of transferred subjects, it showed primary, secondary and technical education.[3] The Committee on the Division of Functions (1919), which was a follow-up of the Montford Report, took its stand on the unity of education and recommended transfer of education as a whole, subject to: (1) the special provisions regarding university legislation in accordance with the recommendations of the Sadler Commission, and (2) exclusion of European and Anglo-Indian education. The justification for its recommendation was that the problem of education should be treated as a whole and any division of education would be unsound in theory and unworkable in practice.[4] It referred to the Montford Report's significant observation that the main defect of the system is "want of coordination between primary and higher education which in turn reacts upon the efficiency of secondary institutions".[5] The Governor-General's Despatch, however, based on the majority recommendation of Governor-General's Council opposed transfer of secondary and higher education including medical education to the inexperienced provincial legislatures.[6]

There was a vigorous minute of dissent by Sir Sankaran Nair, the then member-in-charge of education. He deplored the dual system in the middle stage where vernacular section was controlled by district boards and Anglo-vernacular by the department and also the policy of the department to encourage private enterprise in secondary and college education with a grant-in-aid policy, which discriminated against indigenous societies. He observed: "Primary English education for the masses and higher education for the middle classes are discouraged for political reasons. Higher professional, industrial and technical education is discouraged to favour English industries and recruitment in England of English officials." He strongly supported transfer of Education as a whole.[7] The British Parliament, in effect, supported Sir Sankaran Nair (whose stand was aligned with that of the Montford Report and the Committee on Division of Functions) and rejected the majority recommendation of the Governor-General's Council. The Government of India Act, 1919 read with the Devolution Rules thus made education including agricultural and medical education a transferred subject. Legal and medical profession, however, continued to be a central subject. Thus, education as a whole became a provincial subject.

Between January 1920, when the 1919 Act came into force and April 1937, when the 1935 Act came into effect, there were no developments which necessitated any change in the policy of provincialization of education. If at all, there was expansion. Consequent upon the Muddiman Report (1924), forestry, which was a reserved subject in all provinces except Bombay, was made a transferred subject and thus forestry education became a transferred subject. Also, the subjects of university legislation and the transitional provision about Calcutta University in the context of Sadler Report were also reviewed and became a transferred subject.[8] No doubt, the need for greater central involvement in educational matters came to be emphasized by the Hartog Report (1929), which observed that education is a national service and this can only be realized by the Government of India serving as a centre of educational information, as a means of coordination of the educational experience of different provinces and as a financial provider to some provinces to attain universal primary education. The Committee, however, did not advocate any reduction in the responsibility of the ministries in the provinces,[9] but rather the expansion of the same by de-reservation of European education. The Simon Report recommended abolition of Dyarchy and legislative control over the whole field.[10] Linlithgow Report (1930) on agriculture recommended setting up of an Imperial Council of Agricultural Research but it was clear that agricultural education would remain a provincial subject.[11] The Commission stated that they conceive it as their duty to accept the position with all its implications and frame their recommendations in the light of it. So, the 1935 Act retained education, agriculture, forestry and public health as provincial subjects. No doubt, the Sargent Plan (1944) recommended greater central involvement in higher and technical education and also in the attainment of the goals of universal primary education and eradication of illiteracy but all this was justified primarily as part of the post-war reconstruction plan designed to put in place a national system of education.[12]

Education as a State Subject under the Constitution (1950–1977)

At the stage of the framing of the Constitution, education along with Agriculture and Health Ministries, all dealing with state subjects, were active in suggesting that there should be some element of central supervision by necessary amplification of the Union List. Thus, in April 1948, Maulana Azad, the Education Minister emphasized the imperative need of "central guidance, if not central control, in the sphere of education to combat fissiparous tendencies in the country". The actual entry, sought to be inserted, read: "Supervisory control of post-Secondary education, scientific and technical institutions for the purpose of coordination and maintenance of standards." This appears to be the origin of the phraseology of entry 66 of the Union List. G.B. Pant, the Chief Minister (then called the Premier) of United Provinces opposed the suggested entry on education on the ground that it was not a sound proposition to empower the centre to prescribe the standards of higher education and to place on the units (i.e., states) the responsibility of meeting the necessary expenditure. The general opinion, supported in particular by Jawaharlal Nehru, was in favour of letting the Centre have a say in the matter of standards of higher education.[13]

While the Constituent Assembly was in session, the Radhakrishnan Commission was busy in finalizing its report on university education (it worked for nine months from December 1948 to August 1949). It recommended that university education be placed on the Concurrent List. Significantly, this recommendation was based on the opinion of witnesses including a majority of the provinces. The Commission justified its recommendation on the weighty ground that there is a felt need for a coordinating power to be retained by the Centre to (a) ensure that all provinces act within certain limits or observe certain minimum standards, (b) ensure that where different units wish to develop different special activities, a coherent over-all national policy emerges (which avoids) unnecessary duplication or unfilled gaps, and (c) enable joint planning by provinces where this is necessary.[14]

Radhakrishnan was himself a member of the Constituent Assembly. However, the recommendations of the Radhakrishnan Commission do not appear to have been brought to the notice of the drafting committee – a classic case of absence of effective coordination within the government.[15] The subsequent Sapru Report (1964) speculated as below: "It (Constituent Assembly) appears to have felt that the purposes that the Radhakrishnan Commission (RC) had in mind would be met by vesting the Union Government with powers such as are to be found in entry 66 of List I of the Seventh Schedule. They also seem to have been of the view that the further points made by the RC would be met by authorizing Parliament to declare certain institutions of higher education to be institutions of national importance."[16]

Ultimately, under the Constitution, education in all its ramifications remained a state subject but with important qualifications. The entries are as follows:

State List

6. Public health and sanitation; hospitals and dispensaries.
11. Education including universities subject to the provisions of entries 63, 64 and 66 of List I and entry 20 of List III.
14. Agriculture, including agricultural education and research.
19. Forests.
20. Protection of wild animals and birds.
21. Fisheries.

The Union and Concurrent entries which qualified the State List entries were as below:

Union List

63. The institutions known at the commencement of the Constitution as BHU, AMU and the Delhi University; any other institute declared by Parliament by law to be an institution of national importance.
64. Institutions for scientific or technical education financed by the Government of India wholly or in part and declared by Parliament by law to be institutions of national importance.
66. Coordination and determination of standards in institutions for higher education or research and scientific and technical institutions.

Concurrent List

20. Economic and social planning.
25. Vocational and technical training of labour.
27. Legal, medical and other professions.

These entries are required to be read along with other provisions of the Constitution, viz., those relating to the Fundamental Rights especially of minorities (Art 29 and 30), Directive Principles (Art 45: free and compulsory education and Art. 46: equalization of educational opportunities), where the term 'State' is used as implying both the centre and states (as well as other local bodies) taken together.

There was, however, uneasiness about the constitutional acquiescence in education remaining a state subject. This uneasiness made itself felt as a result of practical experience with the working of the constitutional provisions. For one thing, the establishment of Planning Commission and adoption of central planning resulted in the Central Government playing a leading role in the financing of various development schemes at all stages of education. The establishment of University Grants Commission (UGC) by a resolution in 1953 and statutorily in 1956 led to a situation where UGC found that its policies for regulation of the growth of State Universities as well as affiliated colleges under them required a stronger sanction than merely amendment of the UGC Act. The judiciary also played its part in interpreting Article 66 of the Constitution which vested the Central Government with powers to co-ordinate development and determine standards of higher education. One solution was to follow Radhakrishnan and make higher education alone as a concurrent subject, but such a solution came up against the old chestnut of education being a unified whole or a seamless web whose division may not make for an optimum resolution of the problem. As would be seen, the pendulum swung to the other extreme and in 1976–77, during the course of the Emergency, the whole of education became a Concurrent List subject. The zig-zag course of the adoption of the policy is traced below.

The Battle for Concurrency (1964–77)

J.P. Naik, a veteran educationist and administrator, after an exhaustive examination, concluded in 1961: "There is an element of basic contradiction in the role which the Constitution attempts to assign to the Government of India and in practice, the Government of India has emerged as a Big Brother in what is, in effect, a centre-state partnership".[17] UGC's gentle advice to the states to go slow in the matter of opening of new colleges and universities did not influence the State Governments. Unfortunately, the UGC leadership at this stage lacked initiative which passed to other agencies, vide the Supreme Court decision in Shri Krishna case. In the context of the Gujarat University's powers, the Supreme Court said in effect that no State Governments could prescribe a particular regional language as the sole medium of instruction because that was a matter covered by entry 66 of the Union List.[18] The battle for concurrency was joined with the appointment of the Sapru Committee by the Parliament, which came out with the recommendation that higher education be made a concurrent subject, which was the only way to ensure that State Governments consulted UGC before opening new universities.[19] Other considerations which weighed with the Committee were: common policy in regard to admissions, especially to take care of the interests of SCs/STs, expansion through correspondence courses etc.

The Kothari Commission (1966) had before it the clear-cut recommendation of the Sapru Committee but still chose to recommend status quo, after noting that two of its members (P.N. Kirpal and V.S. Jha) wanted education as a whole to be made a concurrent subject (on the ground that owing to lack of adequate authority at the Centre, national policies even if supported by High Power Commissions or by participative fora like Conferences of Education Ministers/CABE, could not be implemented satisfactorily). The reasons for Kothari Commission's status quo recommendation are worth quoting in full:

> We are not in favour of fragmenting education, which should be treated as a whole. In a vast country like ours, the position given to education in the Constitution is probably the best because it provides for a Central leadership of a stimulating but not a coercive character. Concurrency will lead to undesirable centralization and greater rigidity in a situation where the greatest need is for elasticity and freedom to experiment. There is plenty of scope to evolve a workable Centre-State partnership in education and this has not yet been exploited in the full.
>
> Significantly, as if to placate the opposite view point, the Kothari Commission recommended a review of the problem after ten years.[20]

The Jha Committee (1976), which was reviewing the functioning of the UGC, noted that it was meeting about ten years after the Kothari Commission. It recommended concurrency of higher education alone on the grounds of weight of evidence, to enable UGC to prescribe uniform policies in the important matters regarding (a) minimum age of entry, (b) admissions (merit and extent of reservations), (c) governance structures (university acts and statutes), (d) enrolment policy, and (e) teacher recruitment policy and to make UGC's prescriptions in the matter of co-ordination of development (new universities and colleges) effective.[21] The Committee felt that the power of the Centre to enact necessary legislation in terms of the central entry 66 must be unequivocal and beyond doubt and debate. It hastened to make an interim report incorporating this recommendation in May 1976, because at that time, it was a matter of common knowledge that the Swaran Singh Committee had been appointed by the President of the Congress on 21st February 1976 to consider amendments to the Constitution of India.

The Swaran Singh Committee submitted its report on 14th August 1976.[22] Under the heading 'Centre-State Relations' it made the following observations: "Agriculture and education are subjects of prime importance to the country's rapid progress towards achieving desired socio-economic changes. The need to evolve all-India policies in these two subjects cannot be over-emphasized. It is, therefore, suggested that education and agriculture should be placed on the Concurrent List. It may be clarified that the administration of this subject will remain with the State Governments."[23] The 42nd amendment to the Constitution (based *inter alia* on the Swaran Singh Committee Report) omitted entry 11 from the State List and revised original entry 25 in the Concurrent List to read: "Education, including technical education, medical education and universities, subject to the provisions of entries 63, 64, 65 and 66 of List I; vocational and technical training of labour." The concurrency of education came into force from 3rd January 1977.

The Swaran Singh Committee's recommendation to shift agriculture to Concurrent List, however, was not acted upon under pressure from the CMs except that allied entries 19 and 20 on the State List ("Forests" and "Protection of Wild Animals and Birds") were shifted to the Concurrent List (vide new entries 17–A and 17–B). Thus, during the Emergency, vital subjects like general education, technical education, medical education and forestry education were shifted to the joint control of states/centre. Only agriculture, including agricultural education, remained a state subject.

The Janata government (1977–79) wanted to undo the 42nd amendment and the relevant amendment as passed by the Lok Sabha restored the status quo ante in regard to education. However, in the Rajya Sabha, the Congress party was in a majority. It insisted on retention of some provisions including concurrency of education and the bill as passed by the Rajya Sabha on 31st August 1978 was re-passed by the Lok Sabha on 7th December 1978.[24] Thus, the position of education in the Concurrent List survived the Janata government.

Practical Motives behind Concurrency

It has been seen that in spite of weighty recommendations of expert commissions/committees that higher education alone may be made a concurrent subject (Radhakrishna Commission, Sapru Committee and Jha Committee) and in spite of the Kothari Commission's view that status quo be maintained (i.e., education be retained as a state subject) the Central Government in 1977 made education a Concurrent List subject. Merely because this was done during the Emergency, it may not be assumed that it was a so-called Emergency excess. The practical motives behind this action can easily be surmised from the federal experience in education till then.

Firstly, although the Shri Krishna judgment invoking in terms of entry 66 of the Central List the *doctrine of central legislative supremacy* to interpret entry 11 of the State List effectively made higher education a Central List subject, from a practical point of view, the Shri Krishna judgment did not help the Central Government when it came to the setting up of new universities. Thus, immediately after independence (1951), when Vishva Bharati of Rabindranath Tagore was made a Central University, the Central Government had to adopt the device of declaring it as an institution of national importance under Union List entry 63, because it was located in the state of West Bengal. Similar was the case when, the North-Eastern Hill University (NEHU) was set up as a Central University in 1973 at Shillong in the state of Meghalaya by resorting to the device under Article 252 of getting resolutions of Meghalaya and Nagaland Legislatures and a Central University at Hyderabad was required to be set up to implement the Telengana Award by inserting a new Article 371E in the Constitution. The prospect of resort to various constitutional devices including the need to amend the Constitution each time the Central Government wanted to set up a Central University on a state territory, must have appeared to be frustrating to an impatient executive sworn to the tenets of national integration. Secondly, the Attorney General had also taken the view that prescribing the procedure for appointment of Vice-Chancellor of a State University did not fall within the power of co-ordination and determination of standards in Article 66 of the Constitution.[25] In other words, the Central Government could not lay down a model Act for universities in the country except through concurrency. Thirdly, the view that education is a seamless web, that you cannot separate primary from secondary and secondary from higher and technical education has always appealed to rulers from the time of the Montford Reforms. The Kothari Commission had also taken the same view. Once the ruling elite made up its mind that there should be no legal hindrance to the Central Government operating in the whole field of education, there was no viable alternative to concurrency of the whole of education. Fourthly, the theory of seamless web appealed to Central Government because it very much wanted to do something in the important matters of school education like framing of curriculum, preparation of model textbooks, and affiliation of schools in states. It resented the tyranny of the state boards of Secondary Education. It wanted (a) to indoctrinate the younger generation in the values of national integration and counter the pernicious values of communism in states like Kerala, West Bengal and Tripura, and (b) to counter the undesirable communal ideology in BJP-dominated states like Rajasthan, MP etc. In other words, the Central Government valued its integrative role in school education much more than its role in higher education which by dint of Srikrishna judgment was virtually a central list subject. This came in handy to the Narasimha Rao government while appointing a Steering Committee directly under the Ministry to review textbooks in subjects like history and languages in the various states and to the UPA-I government while framing a National Curricular Framework (2005) to replace NDA government's Curriculum for School Education framed in 2000.

Concurrency in Forestry and Wildlife

The concurrency in forestry education came about through a different route. Indira Gandhi as Prime Minister addressed a major international conservation conference in Delhi in 1969 and in the next four years, the old 'Shikar' ethos in relation to wild animals was replaced by an ethos of conservation. A new Wild Life (Protection) Act with strong punitive powers and a long list of protected species was passed in 1972. Project Tiger was launched in 1973 and Project Crocodile in 1974. Central funding was provided to run reserves in different states. Eventually, the subjects of forest and wildlife were shifted from the State List to the Concurrent List in 1977.

Three examples of the post-1980 period may be cited to underline the federal interest in environmental issues. Firstly, a new central department called Environment Department was set up in 1980 and in 1985, it was converted into a Ministry of Environment and Forests by merging with it forest department, which was traditionally clubbed with agriculture. This had the effect of bringing environmental and conservation activities under the control of the Indian Forest Service, the only all-India service created (in 1966) in the post-independence period and controlled by the Central Government along with the IAS and the IPS. Secondly, the Indian Board for Wild Life, set up in 1952 and chaired by the Prime Minister initially to dignify it, became an activist and an almost aggressive forum under Indira Gandhi. The policy of "no-grazing" was to be implemented so strictly by the Indian Board for Wild Life that it led to the killing of nine persons in October 1982 at the Bharatpur National Park in Rajasthan in 1981.[26] Thirdly, the Forest Conservation Act 1980 made prior approval of Central Government a pre-requisite for diversion of even a smallest parcel of forest land for non-forest purposes in the context of the need for increasing the forest cover in terms of the Forest Policy.[27] Further legislation has followed not only in terms of India's adherence to international conventions on subjects like biodiversity, in terms of entry 14 of the Union List, but also to protect forest dwellers vide Protection of Forests (Tribal and Forest Dwellers) Rights Act, 2005 and thus tightening Central Government's grip over a variety of development projects of the states.

Box 4.1

Concurrency of Education: The Central Role

The substantive financial and administrative implications of the constitutional amendment require a new sharing of responsibility between the Union Government and the states. The Union Government would accept a larger responsibility to reinforce the national and integrative character of education, to maintain quality and standards (including those of the teaching profession at all levels), to study and monitor educational requirements of the country as a whole in regard to manpower for development, to cater to the needs of research and advanced study; to look after the international aspects of education, culture and human resource development and to promote excellence at all levels of the educational pyramid throughout the country.

Source: Para 3.13 of NPE 1986.

In the Box 4.1 is given a slightly adapted quotation from the NPE 1986, which was framed ten years after concurrency, by Indira Gandhi's son and successor Rajiv Gandhi, which begins by noting that the role and responsibilities of the states in regard to education will remain essentially unchanged and ends by asserting that it signifies a meaningful and challenging partnership between the Centre and the states.

The emphasis of the policy on Centre's responsibility for reinforcement of national and integrative character of education and standards in school, and teacher education are significant.

The Sarkaria Commission considered the suggestion of certain State Governments that entry 25 in the Concurrent List should be transferred back to the State List. It was of the view that concurrency in education was essential to achieve desired socio-economic goals including minimizing of inter-state disparities in the level of educational development, helping the states to implement the constitutional directives of universalization of elementary education, enabling Parliament to secure uniformity in standards and syllabi of education and, in the legal sphere, obviating the problems arising out of the Union legislation encroaching on the states' sphere. It, therefore, rejected the suggestion of the states like Tamil Nadu to revert to pre-amendment position. At the same time, it quoted with approval the reference by the NPE 1986 to partnership and talked of the need for "a process of dialogue, discussion and persuasion on the basis of consensus" and "close concert, collaboration and cooperation" between the Union and the states. Finally, it noted that there has been no follow-up legislation by the Union under the concurrent head of education.[28] This raises the question of concurrency in practice.

Concurrency: A Pyrrhic Victory?

The battle for concurrency was won but it has partly, because of the coalition governments at the Centre, not accomplished the lofty objectives of NPE to impart integrative and national character to education. The Janata regime (1977–79) was set against concurrency and as noted above, tried unsuccessfully to restore the status quo ante. The governments under the various avataras of the Janata Party like the UF (1989–91) and the NF (1996–98) as also the NDA (1999–2004) have not hesitated to avail of the practical benefits from the concurrency. After Indira Gandhi came back to power in January 1980, a delegation of the AIU waited on her on 21st August 1980 and invited her attention to the absence of any follow-up legislation to concurrency even four years after the constitutional amendment, and offered to present a joint AIU-UGC draft legislation for consideration of the PM within two months. The PM reportedly welcomed the suggestion.[29] The Ministers of State for Education in their intervention in the debate on successive UGC Amendment Acts 1984 and 1985 had hinted at government's intention to bring forward a comprehensive Bill on the subject of university governance.[30] No such legislation was brought forward during 1980–84. Then came the NPE/PoA 1986 which suggested statutory status for the National Council for Teacher Education, then working as an advisory body of the NCERT as well as AICTE about which a decision was taken even prior to 1986. The legislations were duly passed in 1987 for the AICTE and in 1994 for the NCTE. The Gnanam Committee appointed by the UGC as a follow-up of the NPE 1986, recommended that the Central Government should enact a law setting out the basic structure of the university governance and providing that all legislations by State Government should be around these core provisions. These included defining the powers and designation of the Governor, as the ex-officio Visitor of State Universities. It also suggested model legislation for State Councils for Higher Education.[31] As would be noted in the chapter on Higher Education, these recommendations came to naught. Evidently, the new realities of Indian federalism with coalition governments at the Centre depending on the support of regional parties have halted realization of concurrency to its originally envisaged extent. The period since 1977 has seen legislation to set up new Central Universities outside the UTs, e.g., in Assam (Assam, Tezpur), Maharashtra (Hindi University at Wardha), Andhra Pradesh (Urdu University at Hyderabad) and UP (Ambedkar University at Lucknow). Thus, concurrency has facilitated Central Government's movement in state territory without going through constitutional amendment. There is also considerable activity on the school front. The Central Government is less hesitant in opening new school organizations (e.g., Navodaya Vidyalaya Samiti, not related to any central subject, National Institute of Open Schooling, a new School Board separate from CBSE) and in taking initiatives in school curricula and textbooks vide the hectic activity on the National Curriculum Framework front between 1999 and 2005. More recently, the Central Government has focused on issues bearing on diversities of federalism. It has amended the Constitution (93rd Amendment Act) to facilitate reservation of seats for SCs/STs and OBCs in private institutions leaving detailed legislation to the states. The legislation for setting up a National Commission for Minority Educational Institutions (7th January 2005) enabling minority institutions to seek affiliation to scheduled Central Universities is another piece of legislation which gives evidence of use of concurrency powers to meet challenges of diversity in a federal polity.

The Judiciary vis-à-vis Federalism

The term 'judiciary' comprises the Supreme Court of India and the twenty-one High Courts (as in 2006) in the country. Historically, the High Courts chartered in different provinces from 1862 onwards are at least 75 years older than the Supreme Court which traces its ancestry to the Federal Court which started functioning only from 1937 under the Government of India Act, 1935. The jurisdiction of the Federal Court was limited to that of interpretation of the Government of India Act, 1935 and as a corollary to that power, the protection of civil liberties of the citizens. M.V. Pylee has opined that both in the field of civil liberties and that of federalism, the Federal Court had shown the pioneer's way, except that it was subject to the control of the Privy Council.[32] The Supreme Court of India which started functioning from January 1950, has evolved into one of the most powerful federal courts in the world[33] by dint of its wide jurisdiction including exclusive jurisdiction under Article 131 to determine disputes between the Union and the states which is important in the federal context. Its power as the final interpreter of the Constitution of India has been enhanced by the judgment in Keshavanand Bharati case read with subsequent judgments in Minerva Mills and Waman Rao,[34] in terms of which it can pronounce those constitutional amendments invalid which seek to alter the basic structure of the Constitution. What the basic structure is has not been definitively described but it would appear that the fundamental rights, judicial review, secularism and, after the Bommai judgment (1994),[35] *federalism* are part thereof. In spite of the intention of the framers of the Constitution of India not to introduce into the Indian jurisprudence the American doctrine of due process of law, the Supreme Court introduced via Maneka Gandhi case[36] due process of law in the interpretation of Article 21 so that the procedure for deprivation of life and personal liberty had to be one that was non-arbitrary, fair and reasonable. It has also enhanced its reach by encouraging the Public Interest Litigation (PIL).[37] The growth of the PIL is generally traced to the Supreme Court's attempt to reclaim its reputation in the post-Emergency period.

There is now a scholarly consensus that the Supreme Court is an institution of governance with capacity to influence the agenda of political action. But since it is a non-elective branch of government, it is vulnerable and has to tread cautiously.[38] Its judgments on federalism are required to be read in this background.

Evolution of Supreme Court's Perception of Indian Federalism: From West Bengal Case to Bommai Case

It has generally been observed that judicial interpretation of provisions of federal constitutions has a centralizing tendency. This is especially the case in times of war, when the courts are prone to interpret 'defence' or 'war power' very widely or during a crisis like the Great Depression when the Supreme Court in the US reconciled itself to the New Deal Legislation of President Franklin D. Roosevelt. Even in the absence of such extraordinary circumstances, however, the Supreme Court of India has *ab initio* shown a centralizing tendency. In the first instance, it doubted whether India was a true federation. The landmark case in this regard is *State of West Bengal vs. Union of India*[39], which is among the first cases to be decided by the Supreme Court in exercise of its original jurisdiction under Article 131 of the Constitution. The seven-judge Constitution Bench by a majority held that India was not a true federation and states in India were not sovereign. According to the Supreme Court, there are four characteristics of a true federation: (a) a contract or agreement between sovereign units, (b) supremacy of the Constitution, (c) distribution of powers, and (d) supreme authority of the court to interpret the constitution. The Apex Court held that in our Constitution the characteristic (d) is to be found in full force, (a) and (b) are absent and regarding (c), powers of the states are not co-ordinate with those of the Union, being hedged by numerous restrictions. Pertinently, the Court failed to notice that even in the western countries, federations like Canada and Australia had come into existence not through an agreement but by devolution which was also the case in India. The Court observed (Subbarao J. dissenting) that it would be difficult to hold that Parliament which is competent to destroy a state, is incompetent to acquire the property owned by the state for government purposes.[40]

Justice Subbarao, in his dissenting judgment, observed that the real test to ascertain whether a particular constitution has accepted the federal principle or not is whether the said constitution provides for division of powers in such a way that the general and the regional governments are substantially independent of each other. Applying the test he had no doubt that the Indian Constitution is a federation as the units in normal times exercise sovereign power within the fields allotted to them. Therefore, the correct procedure for the Centre was to obtain possession of state property by a mutual agreement. As for the argument that the power under Article 3 was a power to destroy a state, he countered that it only enabled the Parliament to make a law for formation of a new state (para 92). H.M. Seervai has commented that the discussion on federalism and sovereignty in the majority judgment is very unsatisfactory.[41]

The centralizing force of the Supreme Court's decisions is evident in the economic sphere as well. K.C. Wheare, in his discussion of the federal government and the control of economic affairs, had observed that economic life is one but in federal countries, in the matter of allocation of governmental functions, the legal and political pluralism is imposed upon the alleged unity of economic affairs.[42] However, the Supreme Court of India, while interpreting Articles 301–304 of the Constitution, has tended to interpret freedom of trade and commerce so as to adversely affect states' powers relating to taxation.[43] These two cases (relating to powers of acquisition of mining area and freedom of trade) illustrate the then prevailing majority view of the higher judiciary in India that for various reasons, India was not a true federation. This view had the unfortunate effect that it coloured the Supreme Court's appreciation of the scope of judicial review under Article 356 as well as its interpretation involving powers of states vis-à-vis the Centre under the Commission of Enquiry Act.

Article 355 (duty of the Union to protect states against external aggression and internal disturbances), Article 356 (provisions in case of failure of constitutional machinery) and Article 365 (effect of failure to comply with, or give effect to, directions given by the Union) are required to be read together. As pointed out by H.M. Seervai, these Articles should have formed part of the chapter on Distribution of Legislative Powers, because they are integral to centre-state relations. They are an echo of sections 45 and 93 of 1935 Act.[44] Dr B.R. Ambedkar had hoped that Article 356 would be a dead letter. However, as documented by the Sarkaria Commission, Article 356 has been misused. Out of 75 cases that occurred between 20th June 1951 and 11th May 1987 (a period of 36 years), only in 26 cases could the President's rule be said to be inevitable. The Sarkaria Commission noted that the dissolution of state assemblies by the Janata government in 1977, following its parliamentary victory and the repetition of the same exercise by the Congress government in 1980, amounted to the wholesale use of Article 356 for political purposes.[45] It amounted to subversion of the federal structure of the

Constitution. Its decision in dissolution case carved out the area of judicial review very narrowly holding that the satisfaction of the President is a subjective matter and cannot be put to objective tests.[46] The facts of the dissolution case need to be noted particularly because the action of the Supreme Court in that case is sometimes rationalized as a crucial step in helping the transition from the authoritarian regime (Emergency of 1975–77) to the democratic regime of the Janata government. Within three weeks of the formation of the Janata government, the Home Minister requested nine states ruled by Congress Chief Ministers, to advise the Governors to dissolve the state assemblies in view of the defeat of the Congress party at the central level creating a climate of uncertainty, diffidence and disrespect, thus giving rise to serious threats of law and order. Although the grounds articulated in the Home Minister's letter were wholly extraneous or irrelevant to the exercise of the power under Article 356, still the Supreme Court unanimously went along the same.[47] Supreme Court's tendency to toe the line of the Centre vis-à-vis the states is blatantly evident in another post-Emergency case, viz., Karnataka case.[48] The issue in this case was whether the Central Government could appoint a Commission of Enquiry against the Chief Minister of Karnataka (then Devraj Urs) when the latter had already appointed a Commission to enquire into the allegations of corruption. Since the Act in question barred the Central Commission from investigating the same matter as the State Commission (which was appointed earlier in point of time), the Supreme Court was called on to decide whether matters were the same. Unfortunately, the Supreme Court skirted this issue as being too technical, and upheld the central action, with Kailasam J. dissenting. Upendra Baxi has commented that the majority decision illustrates the trend not to question the political decisions of the Union Government and that Kailasam's judgment showed respect for the values of federalism.[49]

It was in the S.R. Bommai case, a constitutional bench judgment whose main ratio is that the exercise of powers by the Centre under Article 356 can be judicially reviewed that the Supreme Court came to terms with the factum of federalism. In the political literature it has been hailed as upholding democratic norms[50] but for students of federalism, its interest lies in the fact that the minority view of Sikri C.J. in Keshavanand Bharati that federal character of the Constitution is part of the basic structure of the Constitution,[51] became a majority view. Five of the nine judges accepted federalism as an essential feature of the Constitution. Justice B.P. Jeevan Reddi, supported by Justice S.C. Agarwal states: "The fact that under the scheme of our Constitution, greater power is conferred upon the Centre vis-à-vis the states does not mean that the states are mere appendages of the Centre. Within the sphere allotted to them, States are supreme. The Centre cannot tamper with their powers. More particularly, the Courts should not adopt an interpretation which has the effect of whittling down the powers reserved to the States ... the trend the world over is towards strengthening of the Central Government ... all this must put the Centre on guard against any conscious whittling down of the power of the States .... Federalism in the Indian Constitution is not a matter of administrative convenience but one of principle – the outcome of our own historical process and recognition of the ground realities."

After the Bommai case, the incidence of the cases of imposition of the President's Rule under Article 356 might have been marginally reduced, partly because of the political check exercised by one President (K.R. Narayanan as President returning in October 1997, the Prime Minister I.K. Gujaral's recommendation to impose President's Rule in Uttar Pradesh) or by an adverse Upper House (BJP-led NDA government's action of dismissal of Rabri Devi government in Bihar in 1999 being defeated by the Congress-controlled Rajya Sabha) and partly because of the guidance prescribed by the Bommai case (when Uttar Pradesh saw a hung assembly after February 2002 elections, BJP-BSP alliance being able to form a government after a short period of suspended animation of the assembly)[52] but the temptation of the political class to misuse the office of Governor for unwarranted imposition of President's Rule has not diminished as seen by UPA-I government's accepting Governor Buta Singh's recommendation to dissolve the Bihar Assembly on 23rd May 2005. The Supreme Court, in *Rameshwar Prasad vs. Union of India*, decided on 24th January 2006,[53] held that even in the case of installation of new government after fresh elections, the act of the Governor in recommending dissolution of assembly should be only with the sole object of preservation of the Constitution and not promotion of political interest of one or the other party. It held the Governor responsible for filing an irrelevant report and the Central Cabinet for hastily accepting the Governor's report without verifying the facts stated. The judgment was only of academic interest since elections had already been held.

While acknowledging its significance, the impact of Bommai judgment should not however, be exaggerated. Judicial review has its limitations so long as the Article 356 retains its present form or the Governor has the potential of being used as an agent of the Central Government. Incidentally, the logic of the Bommai judgment in upholding the President's rule in Madhya Pradesh, Rajasthan and Himachal Pradesh on grounds of anti-secular postures has been criticized by Raju Ramchandran, who has pointed out that on the same analogy, if a government of a state, driven by compulsion or the ideology of the market, pursues capitalist policies, it would, by the Bommai logic, lend itself to dismissal for failure to follow socialism which is absurd.[54]

Conclusion

This chapter has shown that the provincialization of education ushered in during Dyarchy survived the framing of the Constitution in 1950 but that the political compulsions of national integration have made education, except agricultural education, a Concurrent List subject since 1977; it is noted that the judicial interpretation had already made higher education an effectively central subject. The judiciary initially tended to doubt the factum of federalism but since the Bommai judgment of 1993, federalism has been recognized as a part of the basic structure of the constitution and as a result, the incidence of cases of Governor's rule in states has come down.

Notes

1. K.C. Wheare, *Federal Government* (London: Oxford University Press, 1963, Fourth Edition), 156.
2. Montford Report, 187.
3. Montford Report, 291–297.
4. Committee on the Division of Functions, 45.
5. Montford Report, 196.
6. Committee on Division of Functions, Para 104, 105 and 106.
7. Committee on Division of Functions, 309–331.
8. Sir Gwyer Maurice and A. Appadorai (Eds.), *Speeches and Documents of the Indian Constitution*, Vol.I, (Bombay: Oxford University Press, 1957), 62–63.
9. Hartog Report, 346.
10. Simon Report, Vol. II, 33–35.
11. Linlithgow Report, 44–45.
12. Sargent Plan, Chapters, I, III, V and VI.
13. B. Shiv Rao, *The Framing of India's Constitution* (New Delhi: IIPA, 1968), Vol. IV, 310–317 and Vol. V, 623–646. Granville Austin, *Indian Constitution: Cornerstone of a Nation* (New Delhi: Oxford University Press, 1966), 201.
14. Radhakrishnan Report, 279–281.
15. This contrasts sharply with the Colonial precedent – Montford Report was shown in advance to the members of the Sadler Commission which tailored its recommendations suitably.
16. Sapru Report, 24.

17. J.P. Naik, *Role of Central Government in Education* (New Delhi: Government of India, Ministry of Education, 1961).
18. *State of Gujarat vs. Shri Krishna Ranganath Mudholkar,* AIR 1963 SC 703, decided on 21st September 1962.
19. Sapru Report, 44.
20. Kothari Report, 829–830.
21. Jha Committee Report, 73–93.
22. Granville Austin, *Working of a Democratic Constitution* (New Delhi: Oxford University Press, 1999), 162.
23. Rajeev Dhavan, *The Amendment: Conspiracy or Revolution?* (Allahabad: Wheeler, 1978), 162.
24. Granville Austin (1999) op. cit., 426–427.
25. Sapru Report, 63–65.
26. Michael Lewis, *Inventing Global Ecology: Tracking the Biodiversity Ideas in India* (New Delhi: Orient Longman, 2003).
27. Subhash Kashyap (Ed.), *National Policy Studies* (New Delhi: Tata McGraw Hill Publishing for Lok Sabha Secretariat, 1990), 316.
28. Sarkaria Report, 2.17.08 to 2.17.17.
29. AIU: Proceedings of the 57th Annual Meeting of AIU, 31st January-1st February, 1981 (New Delhi: AIU).
30. Lok Sabha Debates, 21st August, 1984 and 17th December, 1985 and Rajya Sabha Debates, 7th December, 1985.
31. Gnanam Committee Recommendation Nos. 144 and 145.
32. M.V. Pylee, *The Federal Court of India* (Bombay: Manaktala, 1966), 317. According to Rajeev Dhavan, Pylee's account of judicial powers of the Federal Court is exaggerated vide his *Supreme Court of India* (Bombay: N.M. Tripathi, 1977), 15.
33. *The Supreme Court of India: Sentinel of Freedom* (New Delhi: Supreme Court of India, 2000).
34. (a) *Keshavanand Bharati vs. State of Kerala* (1973) 4 SCC 225, (b) *Minerva Mills vs. Union of India* (1980) 2 SCC 362 and (c) *Waman Rao vs. Union of India* (1981) 2 SCC 362.
35. *S.R. Bommai vs. Union of India* (1994) 3 SCC 1919.
36. *Maneka Gandhi vs. Union of India* (1978) 2 SCR 621.
37. (a) S.P. Sathe, *Judicial Activism* (New Delhi: Oxford University Press, 2000), (b) Sangeeta Ahuja, *People, Law and Justice: Case Book of Public Interest Litigation,* Vols. I and II (New Delhi: Orient Longman, 1997).
38. Upendra Baxi, *Supreme Court and Politics* (Lucknow: Eastern Book Co., 1980), passim but especially 10–12.
39. AIR 1963 SC 1241.

40. The same vide para 36.
41. H.M. Seervai, *Constitutional Law of India*, Vol. I, (Bombay: N.M. Tripathi, 9th Ed., 1991), 317.
42. K.C. Wheare, *The Federal Government* (New Delhi: Oxford University Press, 1963), 127.
43. *Atibari Tea Co. vs. Assam* (1961) I SCR 869 which was reconsidered in the subsequent judgment in *Automobile Transport (Rajasthan) Ltd. vs. Rajasthan* (1963) I SCR 491.
44. H.M. Seervai, op. cit., 3rd Ed., Vol. II, 2622. Article 355 incorporates what is called the protection clause (right of every State Government to carry on its government according to the provisions of the Constitution) and Article 356 incorporates the power of the federal government to intervene in case of failure of constitutional machinery. Article 356 gives one example of the failure of the constitutional machinery and is to be read in the background of Article 257(1), (2) and (3) which empowers the Central Government to give directions to a State as provided therein.
45. Sarkaria Report, Vol.1, 166–67.
46. *State of Rajasthan vs. Union of India* (1977) 3 SCC 572.
47. Upendra Baxi (1980) op. cit., 127–133.
48. *State of Karnataka vs. Union of India* (1973) 4 SCC 304.
49. Upendra Baxi (1980) op. cit.
50. J. Dasgupta, "India's Federal Design and Multi-cultural National Constitution", in Atul Kohli (Ed.), *Success of India's Democracy* (Cambridge: Cambridge University Press, 1959), 65.
51. *Keshavanand Case* Supra, 366.
52. The data relating to Post-Bommai Developments are drawn from Ravi P. Bhatia, "Federalism in India and the Supreme Court Rulings", in B.D. Dua and M.P. Singh (Eds.), *Indian Federalism in the New Millennium* (New Delhi: Manohar, 2003), 229–244.
53. 2006 AIR SCW 494.
54. Raju Ramchandran, "The Supreme Court and the Basic Structure Doctrine", in B.N. Kirpal et al. (Eds.), *Supreme but not Infallible* (New Delhi: Oxford University Press, 2000), 107–133.

Part III

Indian Federalism in Action in Education Sector

government which was [illegible] passed in the State [illegible] on 23rd January 1968, a resolution repudiating the three-language [illegible] for school education and adopted a two-language formula providing for teaching of Tamil and English only. This stand has been firmly [illegible] to by the successive Tamil Nadu governments at the meeting of [illegible] Inter-State Council, viz., CABE, the Chief Ministers' Conferences and the NDC irrespective of the complexion of the party in power in the State. In effect, the Tamil Nadu government has repudiated Hindi as [illegible] and official language [illegible] January 1968 and this has been [illegible] by the Government of India by providing that [illegible] 1976 [illegible] Tamil Nadu. The [illegible] official language [illegible] government [illegible]

[illegible] Eighth Schedule of the Constitution: A Pillar of Linguistic Federalism

So far as the Constitutional provisions relating to regional languages are concerned, [illegible] rather than [illegible] and [illegible] Hindi and minority languages [illegible] Art. 347 [illegible] 1908 (added by [illegible] linguistic reorganisation) direct states to provide [illegible] instruction in mother tongue at primary [illegible] provision [illegible] apart from the [illegible] linguistic [illegible] Sanskrit, English [illegible] Schedule languages [illegible] opposition to inclusion [illegible] in that Schedule (see [illegible]).

This position was [illegible] by the parliamentary resolution [illegible] January 1968 which [illegible] all the major languages [illegible] Eighth Schedule was a pillar of linguistic federalism just as the Seventh Schedule was a pillar of legal federalism. Nehru's policy of restriction on enlargement of the Eighth Schedule was continued till 1990 [illegible]

5 Colonial Legacy in Education

In this chapter we would be considering the colonial legacy in education as defined in the 'Introduction'. The encounter, on the one hand, between the West embodied in the British Raj (the rule of a rising West European power) and on the other hand, India (an ancient Eastern civilization) known for its contributions to studies both in physical sciences (astronomy and mathematics) and metaphysical sciences (philosophy), but undergoing a decline at the end of 18th century, marked a paradigmatic shift in the whole approach to knowledge in India. This was partly because of the great importance attached by the colonial power to language. Macaulay's minute of February 1835 on the teaching of European knowledge through the medium of English language, therefore, can be said to have reverberated through the nineteenth and twentieth centuries and has its echoes even in the 21st century.

Locke's Theory of Language and Its Role in the Rise of the British Power

In the West European canon, there was a linkage of attitudes toward language, literacy and development.[1] A view of the uses of language emerged from the English Renaissance of the 17th century, a view attributed to the philosopher Locke, that helped to determine the success of the Industrial Revolution and to establish England for a time as the world's leading power.

The philosophy of Locke embodies an attitude toward language that is fitted for this-worldly success. It reinforces a society that stresses individual initiative, and its demand for clarity and precision of thought facilitates practical communication of all kinds, whether scientific or commercial. The rise of scientific thought (via Bacon) made Locke's views possible and to some extent, the advent of printing was the vehicle for the rise of scientific thought at that time in as much as it gave rise to Protestant Reforms in Germany as argued by Elizabeth Eisenstein.[2] Locke's theory of language connects skill in the manipulation of language with rational knowledge of the truths of life. This equation has had immense importance in shaping the West's psychological and economic devotion to the cause of mass literacy. The literacy percentage in England rose steeply after 1800 and by the end of 19th century, Britain had committed itself to the universal male franchise and had instituted a system of universal education (literacy percentage in 1914 being estimated at 90%). The ideological linkage between literacy and English liberty is provided by Robert Owen and John Stuart Mill. Owen declared in 1849 that in the ideal state all children would be educated and through an accurate investigation of the facts on which the knowledge is based, their minds would be made rational. John Stuart Mill, following the same logic, wrote in 1861 that "universal teaching must precede universal enfranchisement". This, in essence, is the theory that the mastery of the three R's is the royal road to reasonable thought and beyond that, to democratic liberty.[3]

The Anglicist-Orientalist Controversy

It is this belief in literacy in English as an instrument of propagation of European knowledge that led to the enunciation of the famous minute of Macaulay which is framed in India by the Anglicist-Orientalist Controversy (AOC). As is well known, the controversy had to do with provision of funds for advancement of knowledge in terms of Section 43 of the Charter Act 1813.[4] The policy followed by the General Committee of Public Instruction till 1834 was to give financial support and encouragement to traditional Indian studies in Sanskrit, Arabic and Persian with English knowledge engrafted onto it. This Orientalist policy was challenged by the Anglicists like C.E. Trevelyan and Thomas Macaulay, who considered that the great object of the British government is to promote European science and literature among the natives of India through the medium of English language alone. The latter's minute in the matter of 2nd February 1835 was approved by the Governor-General William Bentinck.

Medical Education Avatar

This controversy first manifested itself in India in medical education in the form of C.E. Trevelyan's minute which anticipates Macaulay and its significance needs to be noted. The need for medical education arose because it was felt necessary to train 'native doctors' (who were attached to each regiment as helpers and assistants of the British Medical Officers in the armed forces) in a more systematic and scientific manner. The Medical Board, impressed with the Orientalist discovery of Sanskrit and Arabic treatises devoted to medicine, proposed to government in 1823 to establish a medical institution where western and Indian medicines would be taught side by side. Accordingly, the Native Medical Institution (NMI), Calcutta was established in June 1823, with a student intake of twenty which was increased in 1826 to fifty. The students were taught in Urdu or Sanskrit. European texts were translated into these languages and were also used at the Sanskrit College, Calcutta (estd. 1823) where treatises in Ayurveda were taught and the Madrasa at Calcutta (estd. 1781) where Unani treatises were taught. Only one European doctor worked at the Institute, assisted by a Bengali pundit and other assistants and dissection was carried out only on animal bodies. John Tytler, a noted Orientalist who succeeded Surgeon Bretton as Superintendent, NMI in 1830, set up a 30–bed hospital attached to the Sanskrit College. However, a review of October 1834 by a medical commission was critical of the working of the NMI and the Governor-General approved a proposal for the abolition of the NMI and its replacement by a medical college with effect from 1st February 1835, where English would be compulsory and also European medical Science would be taught. It is interesting to note that the order was issued on 28th January 1835, i.e., precisely five days prior to the minute of Macaulay.[5]

In retrospect, the abolition of NMI was a silent coup staged by English Utilitarians,[6] which prepared the ground for Macaulay's minute and Bentinck's order approving the same. The literature relating to modern medical education generally celebrates the starting of the medical college at Calcutta in 1835 as a landmark but omits to mention that it was established on the ruins of a fine experiment in teaching of a technical subject like modern medicine in Indian languages like Sanskrit and Urdu. The medical commission recommending abolition of NMI included C.E. Trevelyn, Deputy Secretary of the Political Department. It was divided on the issue of the medium of instruction and the balance appears to have been tilted by the following reason for insistence on the knowledge of English as a *sine qua non:* "That knowledge combines with itself the circle of all the sciences and the incalculable wealth of printed works and illustrations, circumstances which give it obvious advantages over oriental languages, in which are only to be found the crudest elements of science or the most irrational substitution for it."[7]

This wording is evidently that of Trevelyan, at that time Macaulay's junior colleague and later on, to be his brother-in-law. To historians of Indian education, he is known for his essay on the education of the people of India.[8]

AOC in General Education

As has been pointed out in the very detailed discussion by Zastoupil et al., Macaulay's minute was not the last word on the subject. There was further correspondence and the matter ended with a compromise by way of a minute by the Governor-General Lord Auckland on 24th November 1839 which was endorsed by the East India Company in its despatch on 20th January 1841. In other words, the general principle that the great object of the British government is to promote European science and literature amongst the natives of India was upheld but endowments of native institutions and financial assistance to native scholars were also continued with some modifications. Since this controversy (AOC) is a staple of the literature of the educational history of the British period and whole books are devoted to it[9] and since it is one of the foundation documents of orientalist discourse,[10] it would be useful to give its basic facts in a tabular form in Box 5.1 below:

Box 5.1

The Contours of the AOC

Anglicists	*Orientalists*
Personnel: Macaulay, C.E. Trevelyan, Bentinck (Predecessors: Charles Grant (1797); James Mill (1812) Indian Supporters/Sympathizers – Raja Ram Mohan Roy	Personnel: H.T. Prinsep, H.H. Wilson (Predecessors: Warren Hastings, William Jones, Elphinstone) Indian Supporters/Sympathizer – Bankim Chandra Chatterji
What did they advocate?	**What did they advocate?**
1. European knowledge should be taught solely in English language. Oriental knowledge in any form should be discarded.	1. Oriental literature had its own utility and should continue to be taught as at present. Stipends should be paid to students pursuing these studies.
2. Oriental Institutions like Calcutta Madrasa, Sanskrit College Banaras and Calcutta Sanskrit College should not be continued and supported.	2. European knowledge should be initially taught through the medium of classical languages (Arabic, Sanskrit) in oriental institutions.
3. Translations of Persian/Arabic and Sanskrit works into English should not be published.	3. An option should be given to students as between instruction through English or instruction through classical languages. Believed in the method of translations.
4. No stipends should be paid to students learning Oriental literature.	4. After vernaculars develop, European knowledge should be taught through vernaculars.
Ideological Orientation: Three Schools	**Ideological Orientation**
1. Evangelicals wanted to give instruction in theology or ethics which would build character. 2. Utilitarians wanted useful knowledge to be taught which was equated with European knowledge. 3. Liberals (Macaulay) wanted English to be taught with a view to prepare Indians to adopt European institutions like responsible and representative self-government.	Attached importance to Indian languages and literature for their instrumental value (knowing about the customs, mores and institutions of oriental people) as much as for its intrinsic value.

Source: Partly based on data in Kalyan K. Chatterjee (1976): *English Education in India* (Delhi, Macmillan).

The Role of English: The Sequel and Significance of Macaulay's Minute

Since Macaulay's minute came to be penned in the process of interpretation of the objectives of Charter Act's financial provision, it was part of routines of transaction of official business and even contemporaneously was not considered an earth-shaking event. If the natural course of events had been allowed free play instead of policy interventions by utilitarians/liberals in the personalities of Bentinck and Macaulay, there might have been a syncretic policy of combined use of local languages (originally interpreted to mean classical languages like Sanskrit and Persian, but later on covering vernaculars also), and English as per requirements of the situation. Unfortunately, there was vertical polarization in the ranks of both the rulers and the natives and the matter fell for decision. Moreover, Macaulay had only recently joined as Law Member. He knew James Mill but did not care to know about exertions of Oriental scholars like Sir William Jones.[11] Macaulay arrogantly ran down native accomplishments and plumped for English, both as a medium of instruction and as a source of knowledge. His minute of 1835 therefore greatly influenced the whole course of evolution of knowledge in India. Indian middle class mastered English but also lost the power of original thinking. Some scholars wonder as to why India could not do what the Japanese of the same period could do, viz., master Western knowledge through their mother tongue. It is not necessary to go into the Japanese side of the history which is recounted by R.P. Dore.[12] The brief answer is not only that India was a colony and was not free to choose but also the diversity of the Indian polity which made a consensus difficult, and the nature of Indian elite which lacked a sense of strategic thinking.

Macaulay's minute did not end the AOC. Moreover, it is more significant in the developing discourse about English as the crucial medium for purveyance of knowledge. As noted by Gauri Vishwanathan,[13] education needed to provide a moral grounding and development of a canon of English literature was the British counterpoint to the Anglicist discourse. So far as the Orientalist discourse was concerned, it was equally complicit with the project of dominance because development of vernaculars had the instrumental role of spreading European knowledge. It is, however, necessary to maintain some perspective in the matter not only in the context of Foucault inspired orientalist discourse á la Edward Said of dominance through a colonial language but also to guard against the tendency of authors like Robert Philipson,[14] who talk of linguistic imperialism of English. As pointed out by Bernard Spolsky, unlike in the case of France, there is no evidence of either England or the USA of having followed a systematic policy of spread of English in the 20th century so that in the 21st century, it became a global language. Rather it reflects local and individual language acquisition decisions responding to change in the complex ecology of world language system.[15]

Macaulay's Minute was followed, of course, by Auckland's Minute of 21st November 1839, but significantly by Wood's despatch in 1854 and review of implementation of Wood's despatch in 1882 by the Education Commission, presided over by Lord Hunter. Their significance is noted in Box 5.2.

Box 5.2

Significance of Auckland Minute, Wood's Despatch and Hunter Report

Auckland Minute 1839

1. Put an end to AOC: existing oriental institutions to continue.
2. Teaching of science through English only.
3. At primary stage, vernacular to be the medium of instruction; at secondary stage, English to be the medium of instruction.
4. Higher education to be restricted to upper classes.

Wood's Despatch, 1854

1. At primary stage, encouragement of indigenous schools side by side with government schools.
2. At secondary stage, vernacular could be the medium of instruction.
3. Establishment of Education Department in provinces, and establishment of universities in presidency towns.
4. Emphasis on teacher training.
5. Importance attached to women's education.
6. Grants-in-aid to private institutions.

Hunter Report, 1882–83

1. Control of primary education be made over to district and municipal boards.
2. Local funds to be used mainly for primary education and government should assist the local funds by a suitable system of grant-in-aid.

Source: Naik and Nurulla (1974), *A Students' History of Education in India* (as interpreted by the author).

The financial provision for education was limited and such controversies did not have great practical outcomes. At this point, it may be useful to refer to another interpretation of Macaulay's system proposed in 2009 by James Tooley in his book *The Beautiful Tree*.[16] As is well-known, this was originally the title of a book by Dharampal[17] on indigenous Indian education and its background is the well-known controversy between Gandhiji and the British educational bureaucrat Philip Hartog, in connection with Gandhiji's visit to London for Round Table Conference in October 1931, when Gandhiji had termed the pre-British indigenous system of education as a beautiful tree which the British had uprooted. Dharampal had collected the reports on indigenous system of education in Bombay (1820), Madras (1823) and Bengal (1835) of which Bengal Reports officially commissioned by the East India Company and written by the missionary John Adam are the most well-known. According to traditional historians, e.g., Nurulla and Naik,[18] the indigenous system was widespread and cost effective but Tooley has reinterpreted the data to suggest that it was, in effect, a privately funded system (because parents paid the teachers) which was sought to be supplemented by Munro, the Governor of Madras by a publicly funded state system in 1828, which remained in operation upto 1835 but was abolished because of its inadequacies. But while Wood's despatch and Hunter Commission paid lip service to indigenous schools, the British bureaucracy, i.e., Provincial Directorates of Public Instruction, promoted secondary education and left mass education to local bodies. As a result, the mass education suffered.

Mass Education on the Ground

Having considered the matter of high theory and policy relating to language and education, when we come to the terra firma of implementation, we find that the British record in the matter of expansion of mass education was very poor. Till 1882, individual provinces were allowed to have their own way. The North-Western Provinces – the modern-day UP – did the most substantial work. James Thomason, Lt. Governor of the province from 1843–1853, devised what is known as Halkabandi (circle) school system which involved (a) encouragement of indigenous schools, (b) levy of voluntary cess of one per cent on land revenue, and (c) a system of visitor at each level – village, pergana, zilla and a Visitor General at provincial level. In 1854, the scheme was in operation in eight districts. Another little known scheme is that of Alan Octovian Hume, District Magistrate of Etawah who ran Elementary Free Schools in the district between 1847 to 1867 with a break between 1857–59. Neither Thomason nor Hume advocated compulsion. This was done by Wingate, Revenue Survey Commissioner in Bombay presidency involving a cess of 5 per cent. His proposal was, however, turned down by the government.

The major reliance however, was placed on the downward filtration theory implicit in Macaulay's minute, i.e., give good education to a few and expect them to spread it more widely. In accordance with Hunter-enunciated policy of the state withdrawal from education,[19] primary education was made the responsibility of the local bodies created under Ripon's Resolution on Local Self-Government (1882). Local bodies had neither the requisite resources nor the leadership. They had to depend on local fund cess, of which only one-third could be used for education. Lord Curzon did assign large recurring grants for primary education as a result of which the number and enrolment in mass education in the period from 1901–02 to 1911–12 increased substantially. What is saddening, as pointed out by Poromesh Acharya,[20] is that the elite (e.g., Bhadralok in Bengal – a collective term for educated classes comprising Brahmins, Kayasthas and Vaids), gave priority to higher education and secondary education rather than to primary education. There were a few exceptions, e.g., Keshub Chandra Sen, the well-known leader of Brahmo Samaj who on return from England, established Indian Reform Association in November 1870 to promote, *inter alia*, mass education in the sense of education of peasants and workers for which he started a paper "Sulabh Samachar" and wrote nine letters to the Queen of England.[21] Naik and Nurulla,[22] in their survey of this area, have concluded that the lag of India during British times in the area of primary education was due not only to the neglect of indigenous schools, but also the failure of introducing compulsion.

What were the efforts made in the direction of compulsory education? The Imperial government was loath to introduce it. The demand for introduction of compulsory education was voiced by G.K. Gokhale in the Central Legislative Assembly in the period 1910–1913. In common with most nationalist leaders, Gokhale linked the failure to introduce legislation for compulsory education to India's being a colony. In England, and in fact, in most European countries, universalization of elementary education was achieved by the third quarter of the 19th century.[23] Gokhale first introduced a resolution on making elementary education free and compulsory and, later on, a bill which was based on the Compulsory Education Acts of 1870 and 1876 of the UK. The bill was rather modest in scope. It was permissive in character and its provisions were to apply only to the areas notified by the municipalities or district boards. The notification required previous provincial government approval and had to fulfil certain tests regarding percentage of children already in school within the limit of the local bodies. Significantly, it was to apply in the first instance only to boys and in this respect, the then prevailing notions of patriarchy appeared to have weighed with Gokhale. Gokhale's bill did not clear the Central Legislative Assembly. However, it had the salutary effect that the 1913 Government Resolution on Education incorporated the following concessions: "The proposition that illiteracy must be broken and that primary education has, in the present circumstances of India, a predominant claim upon the public funds, represent accepted policy no longer open to discussion."[24]

Incidentally, traditional histories while lauding the efforts of G.K. Gokhale in the cause of elementary education omit to mention the role of Jyotiba Phule, who in his petition before the Education Commission (1882) was perhaps the first Indian to underline the need for making primary education free and compulsory up to the age of 12. For his time, Phule was indeed far-sighted, almost prophetic. He advocated priority in funding being accorded to primary education in preference to higher education. He suggested primary schools to be established in all villages with teachers being drawn from the farming communities. His further suggestions were: (a) there should be incentives for spread of primary education by way of scholarships, (b) Urdu schools should be opened for spread of education among the Muslims, and (c) separate schools should be established for the lower castes like Mahars, Mangs etc. He opposed the prevalent system of payment by results which would hamper the spread of education among the lower castes. He wanted the school curriculum to be diversified, vocationalized and ruralized. Jyotiba Phule has been quoted at length because many of his ideas have now become part of conventional wisdom in the measures for access, enrolment and retention of children at the elementary stage of education.[25]

Emulative Federalism

The inter-war period (1918–1947) is notable for considerable progress in the area of mass education, which period, as noted earlier, coincided with the nascent trends of incipient federalism ushered in by the dual reforms of Dyarchy (1919–36) and provincial autonomy (1937–47). One of the most important achievements of Dyarchy was the passing of provincial Acts for compulsory primary education. The spate of legislations took as its model, Vithalbhai Patel's non-official bill passed by the Bombay Legislative Council in December 1917, which applied the principle of compulsion both to the boys and the girls in municipal areas. About 12 provincial Acts were passed even in the absence of any central initiative. The example of spontaneous inter-provincial cooperation can be considered as a striking example of *emulative federalism* in which the successful example of one province inspires other provinces to follow suit. The pity of it, however, was that local bodies/district boards actually notified were small in number, compulsion being in force in 1940–41 in 194 urban areas and 3,297 rural areas, comprising 14,501 villages.[26] This might be because, the discretion to notify was that of local bodies and there was no provision for government advice. In other words, legislation was defective.[27] In terms of the number of schools and enrolment, there was substantial expansion as indicated in the table below:

Table 5.1

Expansion of Schools and Enrolment

Items	*Year 1921–1922*	*Year 1931–1932*	*Year 1936–1937*
Number of Primary Schools	1,55,017	1,96,708	1,92,244
Number of Pupils in Primary Schools	61,09,752	91,62,450	1,02,24,288
Expenditure on Primary Education (Direct) (in Rs)	4,94,69,080	7,87,95,236	8,13,38,015

Source: Naik and Nurulla (1974), pp. 344, 349.

Thus, in the year 1936–37, the enrolment exceeded 1 crore mark, and the expenditure was in excess of Rs 8 crore, which was a little less than double that of 1921–22.

Mass Education in British Times: An Overview

These statistics of expansion however conceal more than they reveal. In 1947, the GER at the elementary stage (6–14 years of age) is estimated to have been very low in urban areas, and it would have been much less in rural areas, among girls and the SCs/STs. Moreover, whatever was achieved was not sustainable because there was a very high level of drop-outs. Hartog Committee which reported in 1929, i.e., barely 18 years prior to independence, presented the following picture regarding mass education in its Chapter IV:

- For British India as a whole, out of every hundred pupils who were in Class I in 1922–23, only 18 were reading in Class IV in 1925–26. In other words, the drop-out rate was as high as 82 per cent. (The Hartog Committee distinguished between wastage (= dropout) and stagnation (= repetition of the class) as the causes).
- It was common for children to remain in one class for more than two years, especially in Class I and some children had remained continuously for as many as seven or eight years in the same class.
- In Bihar and Bengal, owing to preponderance of lower primary schools, with only three classes, a vast number of boys had no chance of reaching Class IV.

The Committee quotes Linlithgow Commission to the following effect:

1. Under present conditions, expenditure on primary education was largely wasted, as the environment of the great majority of Indian pupils who left school at the primary stage was not conducive to retention of literacy and therefore, they tended to relapse into illiteracy,
2. There was a large number of single teacher schools. Their number was in the vicinity of 70 per cent in Bengal, Bihar, Orissa and Assam and about 50 per cent in UP and Bombay,
3. The primary school curriculum was unrelated to the conditions of the village life.

- Distribution of schools across villages was uneven because of competition among teachers. In Bengal, there were large areas without a school while in others, there were many little schools indulging in cut-throat competition.
- Madras led the provinces in providing separate schools for the deprived classes (over 10,000 as against 1,600 in the rest of India).

- Punjab and Bombay led other provinces in the policy of consolidation of primary and upper primary classes.
- A majority of teachers had neither initial qualification nor provision for post-employment training. They were also poorly paid (except in the provinces of Bombay and Punjab).
- The inspecting staff was highly inadequate. During the period 1917 to 1927 when the number of schools had increased, the strength of inspecting staff actually registered a marginal decrease (from 2,209 to 2,147).

The Hartog Committee cautioned that unless a conscious effort was made to follow a policy of consolidation and improvement, there was a grate danger that the continuance of almost valueless schooling such as the children receive in the majority of single-teacher schools, would convert the parents into active opponents of education, especially if any form of compulsion is adopted, and that apathy would become opposition.

Naik and Nurulla[28] criticized the Hartog Committee for this negative approach. They perhaps understood Hartog Committee's criticism to have been aimed at popular provincial governments of inter-war years. However, one has to realize that educational system is slow to change and the popular governments built on what they inherited in 1921 and they worked under the close supervision of their Colonial masters (The Governors of Provinces and the Governor-General at Delhi) and Hartog Committee's indictment is finally that of the British Raj which by its policies implicitly allowed such pathetic conditions in primary schools, which resulted in a very low rate of literacy of 16 per cent in 1951.

Mass Education in Princely States

It is interesting to note that remarkable progress was made by princely states like Travancore, Baroda and Mysore in mass education. The progress in Travancore due to socio-political factors including both state and missionary activity was very impressive even without introduction of compulsory education. According to the 1941 census, the literacy percentage was as high as 47.7 per cent. In Baroda, Compulsory Education Act was introduced and vigorously implemented in the period 1906–1915 and was backed by a network of village, town and state libraries. The Baroda policy owed its success to the farsighted policy of the then ruler Maharaja Sayajirao Gaekwad. Mysore was known as a progressive state and followed various progressive educational policies of British India, thanks to the enlightened Diwans like M. Vishvesvarayya and Mirza Ismail. It introduced compulsion in 1913 and by 1916, 27 centres and by 1920, 250 centres were opened but in 1936 decided not to extend the scheme further.[29]

Pre-primary Education[30]

The definition of education includes pre-primary education. However, it was neglected in India and was not regarded as state responsibility till the Sargent Plan emphasized its significance and recommended that an adequate provision of pre-primary education should be an essential adjunct of a national system of education.

The Sargent Plan

In the background of the pathetic picture of mass education and pre-primary education in the colonial period, the Sargent Plan for post-war educational development made for hopeful reading. It envisaged universal compulsory and free primary or basic education for all children between age 6 and 14 by the year 1984. The report was based on careful calculations and planning and it is unfortunate that Naik and Nurulla criticize it for setting a low aim before the nation. On the other hand, the report of the National Planning Committee (appointed by the Congress party) is not very specific. It suggested that the entire child population of the country should be brought in to the school.[31]

At this stage it is useful to look at the efforts made for eradication of illiteracy.

Adult Education

The idea of teaching adults to read was not accepted till 1921 when a literacy campaign was launched in the Punjab, but after some initial success, it apparently fizzled out. The Hartog Committee reported in 1929 that there were over 11,000 institutions for adult education in British India attended by nearly 3,00,000 people. In the 1930s, India was estimated to contain 325 million illiterates – one-third of the illiterate population of the world. Frank C. Laubach has been held by some scholars to be the father of literacy movement in India. He was financially supported by American missions but his role apparently was that of a social worker. Dr Laubach's Indian tour was around 1936–37. He met Jawaharlal Nehru who reportedly commended the literacy movement. Then, he met Gandhiji who had at one stage expressed doubts about the advisability of teaching (adult) Indians to read because of the pernicious nature of much of the literature that reached the country from the West, but Gandhiji was won over and on Gandhiji's advice, the Congress party on assuming office (under provincial autonomy) in 1938, made teaching of literacy a prime object of policy. Laubach popularized the slogan: *Each One, Teach One* – meaning that those who could read or who had been taught to read should pass on their knowledge to their illiterate brethren.[32]

However, apart from Christian missionaries, the Congress leaders had before them the role model of the Soviet Union also. Thus, it was during the 1937–40 period that adult education movement can be said to have started in India, when the enormity of the problem was realized and the basic techniques of the programme (atmosphere building, campaign mode, involvement of volunteers, linkage with library movement, steps to avoid relapse into illiteracy etc.) were developed and honed. Three states, viz., Mysore, Bombay and Bihar did pioneering work. Mysore State Literacy Council was founded in 1941 and started Vidyapeethas at two places on the lines of Danish Folk Schools, for training of youth leaders. Bombay Adult Education Association was founded in 1934 by the then Vice-Chancellor of Bombay University, Dr John McKenzie.[33]

Syed Mohamud, Education Minister of Bihar who was Chairman of Adult Education Committee of the CABE, played a pioneering role. Some of his remarks are evocative of Latin American radicalism (á la Paul Freire)[34] of future times. He said: "As long as the masses remain steeped in the illiteracy and ignorance, economic and social up-building of the nation will remain a pious dream." He quoted Lenin: "The liquidation of illiteracy is not a political problem. It is a condition without which it is impossible to speak of politics. An illiterate man is outside of politics and before he can be brought in, he must first be taught the alphabet. Without this, there can be no politics – only rumours, gossip tales, superstition." He went on to distinguish between the aim of adult education in India and the western countries. In other countries, adult education aims at extending and expanding the minimum school education received by the labourers and farmers, but in a country like India (with its low literacy and socio-economic backwardness) the objectives of this movement should be: (1) to teach the illiterate adults the three R's, and (2) to impart knowledge closely correlated to his working life and give him a grounding in citizenship.[35]

Various provinces including Bihar and Bombay organized adult education as a "movement" (or as we would now say, campaign mode). Bihar's progress under the inspiring leadership of its Education Minister was spectacular for the time. However, Frank Laubach's assessment was prophetic: "A study of Bihar's statistics reveals the enormous difficulty of making India literate. If Bihar continues, as she is doing, to teach 5 lakh a year, it will take 50 years for her to make those literate who are living today. But meanwhile in 50 years, the population would have increased fifteen millions. Besides this, two-third of the adults now living will be dead and a new batch of illiterates will need to be taught. So we must face a sobering fact. Bihar has far and away the finest record in India but it is not enough even to hold her own."[36]

After the Congress ministers resigned, the adult education programme was continued in a routine administrative manner, but it was not till Independence that it could pick up further momentum. However, the professional association for adult education known as Indian Association for Adult Education was set up in 1939, which played a catalytic role in advancing the cause of adult education in the post-independence India.

Secondary Education

The Hartog Committee[37] called Secondary Education (along with higher education) "education for the directing classes". Its assessment was that by contrast with mass education, the condition of the secondary education was well advanced and with all its defects, it was making a real contribution to its objective, viz., providing education to the directing classes. One reason may be that it was a well regulated system, the academic control being exercised since 1857 by the universities (which admitted students for its matriculation examination) and in some provinces, by the Secondary School Boards since 1920s and the administrative control being exercised by the provincial governments.

There was substantial expansion in the number of secondary schools and pupils which may be seen from the following table:

Table 5.2

Number of Secondary Schools and Pupils (1881–82 – 1946–47)

Year	*No. of Schools*	*No. of Pupils*
1881–82	3,916	2,14,077
1901–02	5,124	5,50,129
1921–22	7,530	11,06,803
1936–37	13,056	22,87,872
1946–47	11,907	26,81,981

Source: Nurulla and Naik, 1974: 197, 335 and 370.

Note: The temporary setback in institutional growth during the period 1936–37 to 1946–47 is attributed to economic situation created by the Second World War.

Most of the schools were private, receiving grants-in-aid from the provincial governments, but some provinces, e.g., Madras and Bombay, maintained one full high school in each district to serve as a model. The devolution of power of the universities in regard to the recognition for matriculation examination and conduct of that examination to school boards in some states (Central Provinces, Bihar, UP, Madras) was in terms of the recommendation of the Sadler Commission. According to the Hartog Committee, the economic level of the provision of new high schools had been reached in Bombay, Bihar and Central Provinces. It also commented adversely on the uniformity in the course in the middle English and high school which was due to influence of matriculation: (a) as an immediate qualification for service, (b) as a gate to university courses, and (c) possession of a higher qualification for service.

Along with lack of diversification of curriculum (which was recommended as far back as 1882 by the Hunter Commission), the domination of the curriculum by the English language as a compulsory subject was characteristic of the secondary system. Most high schools (except 'public' schools) switched over to regional languages as a medium of instruction in other subjects by 1937. However, it was observed that standards of examination in general were low and were deteriorating especially in English. The Hartog Committee also noted the wastage involved because the passing percentage did not generally exceed 50 per cent. Thus, the colonial legacy in secondary education, while not as depressing as in primary education, left a lot to be desired.

Higher Education

Unlike school education, where India had some pre-existing institutional structure in the form of indigenous schools, higher education in India is a foreign plant (Sadler Commission) as quoted by Eric Ashby.[38] Pawan Agarwal's contention that the first college to impart higher western education in India was founded in 1818 at Serampore near Calcutta is not factual.[39] Actually it was initially founded to impart theological training. Hindu College (1817) later renamed Presidency College (1855), was the first institute of higher education in India in whose establishment rich and orthodox Zamindars of Calcutta had taken initiative under leadership of Sir Edward Hyde West (Ram Mohan Roy was in the background).[40] A crop of colleges came up in and around Calcutta and also in other presidencies. By 1855, there were 28 colleges all over India. These colleges came to be affiliated to the three metropolitan universities established in 1857.

Evolution of General Higher Education (1817–1947)

Taking 1882 (the year of appointment of Hunter Commission), 1901 (year of holding of the All-India Education Conference by Lord Curzon), 1921 (start of Dyarchy), 1937 (start of provincial autonomy) and 1947 (year of independence) as representative years, progressive statistics regarding the number of colleges, universities and enrolment are given below:

Table 5.3

No. of Colleges and Universities with their Enrolment (1882–1947)

No. of	*Year 1882*	*Year 1901*	*Year 1921*	*Year 1937*	*Year 1947*
Colleges	59 + 21= 80	191(Arts + Professional)	229(Arts + Professional)	272(Arts Colleges)	420
Universities	03	04	09	16	19
Students enrolled	5,399	23,000 (Approx)	66,258	1,26,228	2,41,369

Note: Data for 1882 are drawn from McCully[41] (1940, p. 161), for 1901 and 1921 from Nurullah and Naik (1974, pp. 444 and 631).

These data show that while the growth of collegiate and university institutions and enrolment was slow in the 19th century, it picked up speed in the first half of 20th century, but especially after 1921. The growth of universities which was slow till 1913, gained momentum thereafter, because of the acknowledged policy of the colonial government (vide Policy Resolution of 1913) to have a university for each province. Thus, while only four universities were set up in the period 1913–1920, viz., Banaras Hindu (1916), Mysore (1916), Patna (1917) and Osmania (1918), the following eleven universities came up in the period (1921–1947) – Lucknow (1921), Aligarh Muslim (1921), Delhi (1922), Nagpur (1923), Andhra (1926), Agra (1927), Annamalai (1929), Kerala (1937), Utkal (1943), Rajputana and Saugar (1946). Many more would have come up if it were not for the critical years of the Great Depression and the World War II. The foundation of such substantial number of universities in close succession can be explained with reference to the linguistic and cultural factors bearing on the future shape of the polity. Thus, Banaras Hindu University was set up on the demand of the Hindu community, which had collected funds for the same and which had given up its demand for having powers of affiliation of colleges all over India. The Central Hindu College of Annie Besant came up only in 1902. Correspondingly, the Aligarh Muslim University, with an older founding college (1877), was set up later because the Muslim community initially was reluctant to give up its demand for all-India affiliation.[42] The Mysore University was set up by the princely state of Kannada-speaking Mysore. The establishment of Patna University was a foregone conclusion after separation of the Hindi-speaking Bihar from Bengal in 1910 at the time of nullification of the partition of Bengal. The Osmania University was set up by a 'firman' of the Nizam of Hyderabad and adopted Urdu, the official language of the princely state, as its medium of instruction. The adoption of Urdu, an Indian language, as a medium of instruction was a novelty, notwithstanding that it was not a regionally rooted language. Nagpur was set up by the province of CP and Berar after long deliberations, going back to 1913. Andhra University, Waltair was set up to cater to the Telugu-speaking population of the Madras Presidency, which had shown early stirrings of linguistic sub-nationalism which logically led to the establishment of the first unilingual state of Andhra, in independent India in 1953. Agra University was set up as a purely affiliating university to take the load of affiliation of colleges off the teaching universities of Lucknow and Allahabad, which were to be made resident teaching universities. Annamalai University was set up in Madras Presidency to avail of a private philanthropic offer. Kerala University started its avatar as Trivandrum University (1937) in the erstwhile princely state of Travancore to cater to the Malayalam-speaking population, relieving the load of Madras University to which the colleges in the princely states of Travancore and Cochin were affiliated. The setting up of the Utkal University even during the war-time indicates the preparedness of the British to meet the aspirations of Oriya-speaking people who were able, a little earlier (1937), to win the first uni-lingual state of (Orissa) in British India during colonial times. As noted, the British had perceived no threat from the Oriya-speaking population. On the other hand, the proposal for establishment of a regional university at Poona was not allowed to make headway prior to independence because of the British prejudice against Poona Brahmins whose leader was B.G. Tilak, the fomenter of disaffection against the British rule and the so-called "Poona School" of thought to which even Dar Commission of the Constituent Assembly of independent India made a sneering reference. Two universities (Rajputana and Saugar) were established shortly after Second World War, but before independence.

Professional Education

The growth of professional colleges was much slower except law colleges whose number increased from 97 in 1886–87 to 116 in 1946–47 and pupils from 1673 to 7098.[43] As noted by Anil Seal, engineering remained the most backward profession and the professions of education and law the most advanced with talk of over-supply of law graduates in Calcutta as early as 1875.[44] In 1900, there were only four engineering colleges in India. By 1947, their number including university departments had increased to 37 of which 11 were established only in 1946–47. The total enrolment was in the region was 2,500.[45] Most institutions taught common civil engineering courses and specialization in areas like electrical, mechanical and mining engineering was limited. In spite of Curzon's initiative (1904) followed by Linlithgow recommendations (1929), agricultural education was neglected with about 29 agricultural colleges, enrolling 5,000 students in 1947. Medical colleges made an early beginning (Calcutta 1835, Bombay 1845) but the progress of medical education was slow with about 30 institutions and 8,850 students in 1942 and medical profession remained essentially urban centred. The Imperial Medical Service was the preserve of English officers.

The main functions of the universities as set up under the 1857 Acts were: (1) examination, and (2) affiliation, and they were not equipped to fulfil the traditional academic functions of teaching and research. Undergraduate teaching was done by colleges and there was very little development of postgraduate teaching and research. The Universities Act of 1904 inspired by Lord Curzon removed the legal difficulty but it was not till after World War I that a few Indian universities began to engage in postgraduate teaching which is a pre-requisite for research. An entrepreneurial Vice-Chancellor like Ashutosh Mukerjee of Calcutta University could make a substantial beginning with the help of donations but the Quinquennial Review for 1922–27[46] shows that the university faced some difficulties after his death. This applied to a university like BHU also which was *ab initio* set up under Pandit Madan Mohan Malaviya's leadership as a teaching university with postgraduate departments.

Research

Naik and Nurulla[47] have made the basic point that the British government curbed the expansion of university education by emphasizing the need to improvement rather than strive to increase the numbers still further. While research saw better days in the period 1920–37, still the output of highly educated manpower as estimated by the Scientific Manpower Committee during the war was far less. Some important developments prior to independence bearing on promotion of research were establishment of (a) Indian Agricultural Research Institute, Pusa (1904), (b) Forest Research Institute, Dehradun (1905), (c) Indian Research Fund Association (1911), (d) Imperial Council of Agricultural Research (1930) (on the basis of recommendation of Linlithgow Commission), and (e) the Council of Scientific and Industrial Research (CSIR in 1944) of which the last mentioned event had a deep influence on the division of academic research in post-independence India as between the government laboratories and the universities.

Academic Profession

As noted by Aparna Basu in her article in the Moonis Raza edited volume,[48] universities in India were instruments for strengthening British cultural, intellectual and political domination and European learning was the staple of the curriculum. The Indian Educational Service (estd. 1864, abolished 1924 as part of Dyarchical Reforms), aspired to organize an academic profession in India by importing talented English teachers. Teaching however, was at best a quasi-profession lacking an established body of technical knowledge and though the IES initially fulfilled the craving of Indian middle classes for learning European knowledge at source, the colonial government ended up by creating a bureaucratic structure which became a source for recruiting raw English graduates to hold high academic positions like Director of Education and similar positions at the imperial government level.[49] However, with the image of the IES before them, graduates of Indian universities began to consider teaching in affiliated colleges as a worthy career. IES officers held positions of professors in government colleges, but their contacts with (Indian) teachers in affiliated colleges were limited to annual meetings of Senate for transacting routine administrative business. Since universities did not support professional chairs till 1920s by which time, recruitment to the IES had ceased, the professors in government colleges and teachers in affiliated colleges led an isolated life. The IES officers continued to rule provincial directorates right till independence and when the Indian teachers took their place, they could not give up their bureaucratic habits. Hence, the absence of a robust academic profession in India is part of the colonial legacy.

Indian universities were modelled on the London University and their basic character as examining and affiliating bodies did not change much with the emphasis on English language as the medium of instruction and with the medium becoming the message à la Marshall MacLuhan, the curriculum was dominated by English/European contents and Indian history, culture and philosophy were neglected. The system of affiliated colleges, the centrality of annual examinations and the control of government over the governance structure of the universities came to characterize Indian higher education. High student: teacher ratio did not encourage the tutorial system. The lecture method with emphasis on cram and memorization did not allow a spirit of enquiry or critical faculty to develop. Although the Sadler Report, known as Calcutta University Commission (1919), made valuable recommendations for reorientation of Indian higher education system, its report came at an inopportune time, when constitutional issues (Dyarchy) tended to monopolize the attention of the Indian elite.

Indian Agency in Higher Education

Indian agency in higher education came to the fore through a variety of channels:

1. Sectarian and communal institutions came to be established from 1875 onwards in the form of Mahomedan Anglo-Oriental College, Aligarh (1877), which became a university in 1920; Central Hindu College, Banaras (1902), became a university much earlier (1916). Dayanand Anglo-Vedic College was founded at Lahore in 1886 and subsequently other DAV colleges came to be established in Punjab (especially in districts which comprise modern Haryana), Delhi Khalsa Diwan which was part of Sangh Sabha Movement (1873) established Khalsa schools and colleges. In all these sectarian and communal institutions, the prescribed official curriculum was followed, with an additionality of sectarian religious teachings.
2. The secular indigenous effort led to the establishment of a variety of institutions:
   (a) Jamshedji Tata offered to donate in 1898 an annual endowment of Rs 1,25,000 (£ 8,000) (which was a substantial amount at that time), fòr establishment of an Indian University of Science in Bombay which envisaged three

faculties: scientific and technical, medical and philosophical/educational. The last faculty was innovative, because it included study of education, ethics, psychology, Indian history and archaeology, statistics, economics and comparative philosophy. But Lord Curzon was skeptical of so ambitious a scheme which was referred to several experts which caused delay. Ultimately, the scheme was reduced to a pure scientific research institute which, thanks to a generous donation of land by the Maharaja of Mysore came to be set up in Bangalore when Lord Hardinge was the Governor-General. Successive Quinquennial Reviews of Education refer to it as the only non-government scientific research institute in India apart from the Bose Institute in Calcutta.

(b) Examples of Indological Research Institutes inspired by NGO efforts were Cama Oriental Institute (for Parsi studies in Bombay), and Bhandarkar Oriental Research Institute (estd. 1917) at Poona.

(c) In the field of social sciences, establishment of Gokhale Institute of Politics and Economics (1928) at Poona is a solitary example.

(d) The nationalist movement inspired:
- establishment of an engineering institute at Jadavpur near Calcutta (1906), which went on to become Jadavpur University, and
- a series of national universities were founded by Gandhiji during the first non-cooperation movement in 1920–22, including Gujarat Vidyapeeth at Ahmedabad, Kashi Vidyapeeth in Banaras, Bihar Vidyapeeth in Patna, Tilak Maharashtra Vidyapeeth at Poona and Jamia Millia Islamia (first set up in Aligarh, but shifted to Delhi). These were national in the sense that they emphasized instruction in Hindi as well as regional languages and the role of character formation. The staff and students were more concerned with building the national movement and fighting the Raj. In fact, recent research shows that they scorned pursuit of learning and held manual labour in high esteem.[50] One alumnus reportedly said that the only education he received was when he was arrested for participation in non-cooperative activities and was sent to a British reform school.
- However, Tagore's Sri Niketan and Shanti Niketan which together made up Vishva Bharati (University) (1921), was

in a different mould. Tagore wanted to synthesize what he called Asian and western values. In practical terms, it did make a name for high quality teaching in art, literature and foreign languages (like Chinese).

Enclavization of Higher Education

It can generally be said that the spread of higher education was limited to port-towns around Bombay, Calcutta, Madras and other administrative centres. This enclavisation of higher education, as observed by Aparna Basu[51] was in conformity with the nature of colonial under-development. It was oriented to meet the needs of elite groups in urban areas (traditional literate groups) with a sprinkling of taluqdars and zamindars. The GER was 0.7 per cent in 1950–51. More than 80 per cent of students were in undergraduate arts and science colleges with only limited postgraduate research or professional education and training. The small intelligentsia imbibed western ideas of liberty and of representative and responsible government but these ideas did not filter down to the masses. Indian universities were transplants no doubt but they were adapted to Indian conditions. Hence, the transition from the British Raj to independent India was comparatively smooth with the Indian elite stepping into the shoes of foreign rulers and continuing the dual and hierarchical system. Recent scholarship has tended to highlight the positive characteristics like openness, modernity and secular values introduced for the first time on the Indian soil by these western plants.[52]

The Incipient Coordinating Bodies

This discussion of higher education may be concluded by referring to the fact that the inter-war period saw the inception of bodies which became coordinating academic authorities in the post-independence India, especially in professional education. Thus, thanks to Munshi Ishwar Sharan moving a resolution in the Legislative Assembly in February 1921, to create an autonomous All-India Bar with powers to regulate legal profession and education, the resultant setting up and recommendations of Chalmers Committee (1923) led to the passing of the Indian Bar Council Act, 1926 under whose auspices provincial Bars in five provinces of Bombay, Bengal, Madras, UP and Bihar came to be set up. The de-recognition of Indian medical degrees by the General Council of Medical Education (GCME) of UK led to the passing by the Central Legislative Assembly of the Medical Council Act, 1933 for maintaining of minimum standards in medical education. The Imperial Council of Agricultural Research (1930), as set up in terms of Linlithgow Report went on to take over the responsibility of agricultural research and education after independence. The Sargent Plan (1944) approved by the CABE led to the setting up of an advisory All-India

Council for Technical Education (1945), and an advisory University Grants Committee for Central Universities (1946). The Bhore Committee Report (1943–46) not only laid out the plan for post-war health development but also led in due course of time to the setting up of All-India Institute of Medical Sciences (AIIMS) at Delhi in 1956. The establishment of IUB (Inter-University Board) in 1925 and its activities meant an informal coordination of higher education till UGC (1953, 1956) was in a position to take over the function.

Thus, the colonial legacy did have the seeds in it of major developments in higher and professional education in the post-independence India.

Notes

1. Robert Pattison, *On Literacy: The Politics of the Word from Homer to the Age of Rock* (New York: Oxford University Press, 1982), 104–109, 138–155. (The discussion relating to language in this chapter is in the context of philosophy of Locke whereas the earlier discussion in chapters 2 and 3 is from the point of view of language as promoting sub-national consciousness).
2. Elizabeth Eisenstein, *The Printing Press as an Agent of Change,* two Volumes, (Cambridge: Cambridge University Press, 1988). (As noted in an earlier chapter, the dissemination of printing in the colonies gave rise to linguistic regional consciousness in the 19th century but this occurred with a considerable time lag.)
3. Robert Pattison, op. cit., 147–148.
4. Lynn Zastoupil and Martin Moir (Eds.), *The Great Education Debate* (London, Curzon Press, 1999).

   (s. 43 provided that "each year, the Company was to set apart at least one lakh rupees of its revenues and apply these funds to the revival and improvement of literature and the encouragement of learned natives of India and the introduction and promotion of knowledge of the sciences among the inhabitants of the British territories in India." In 1833, this section was amended to increase the amount to Rs 10 lakh).
5. Poonam Bala, *Imperialism and Medicine in Bengal: A Socio-historical Perspective* (New Delhi: Sage, 1979). Anil Kumar, *Medicine and the Raj* (New Delhi: Sage, 1978).
6. Eric Stokes, *The English Utilitarians and India* (London: Oxford University Press, 1959; Indian Reprint 1982).
7. Quoted in D.G. Crawford, *A History of Indian Medical Service,* Vols. I and II, (Calcutta: Thacker & Spink, 1914).

8. C.E. Trevelyan, *On the Education of the People of India* (London: Longman, Orme, Green Longman, 1838).
9. B.K. Boman Behram, *Educational Controversies: The Cultural Conquest of India under British Imperialism* (Bombay: Taraporawala & Sons, 1944). Kalyan K. Chatterjee, *English Education in India* (New Delhi: Macmillan, 1976).
10. Edward Said, *Orientalism* (London: Penguin Books, 1978).
11. I have, in chapter 2, underlined the significance of Sir William Jones' Indo-European Hypothesis.
12. R.P. Dore, *The Education in Tokugawa Japan* (London: Routledge, 1965)
13. Gauri Vishwanathan, *The Masks of Conquest* (New York: The Columbia University Press, 1989).
14. Robert Philipson, *Linguistic Imperialism* (Oxford: Oxford University Press, 1972).
15. Bernard Spolsky, *Language Policy* (Cambridge: Cambridge University Press, 2004), 76–91.
16. James Tooley, *The Beautiful Tree: A Personal Journey into How the World's Poorest People are Educating Themselves* (New Delhi: Penguin-Viking, 2009).
17. Dharampal, *The Beautiful Tree: Indigenous Indian Education in the Eighteenth Century* (Coimbature: Keerthi Publishing House, 1983).
18. Regarding Thomason's scheme, see J.P. Naik and Syed Nurulla, *A Student's History of Education in India* (Bombay: Macmillan, 4th ed., 1974), 108–110 and Sudhindra Nath Qanungo, *Historical Background of Compulsory Free Education in India (1830–1893)* (Lucknow: Bharat Press, 1969).
19. Hunter Commission Report, 1882.
20. Poromesh Acharya, "Bengali Bhadralok and the Educational Development in the 19th Century Bengal", in Suresh Chandra Shukla and Rekha Kaul (Eds.), *Educational Development and Under-development* (New Delhi: Sage, 1995).
21. For Keshab Chandra Sen's work in the field of mass education, see David Kopf, *The Brahmo Samaj and the Shaping of the Modern Indian Mind* (Princeton: Princeton University Press, 1979).
22. J.P. Naik and Syed Nurulla, op. cit.
23. Ernest Barker, *The Development of Public Services in W. Europe (1760–1880)* (London: Oxford University Press, 1944).
24. Naik and Nurulla, op. cit., 290.
25. Report of Education Commission: The Bombay Presidency Report, 1882.

    (NB: Jyotiba Phule's recommendations are usefully summarized in Ram Khandge, *Maha-Mahatma Jotirao Phule: Vyakti ani Karya* (Chakan, Pune, Rajashree Prakashan, 2004) (Marathi).
26. Sargent Plan, 1944.

27. Hartog Report, 1929.
28. Naik and Nurulla (1974), 347–349.
29. For princely states, see Nurulla and Naik, *A History of Education in India during the British Period.* (Bombay, Macmillan & Co., first edition 1943, 2nd edition 1951: 875–880; 881–892; 898–908.

    For Mysore see, Government of Mysore, *Report of the Committee for Educational Reforms in Mysore* (Mysore, 1953).
30. For pre-primary education see Kothari Report, 7.03–7.05.
31. K.T. Shah, *The Reports of the National Planning Committee* (Bombay, 1948). Sargent Plan (1944).
32. Charles Jeffries, *Illiteracy: A World Problem* (London: Pall-Mall Press, 1967).
33. W.E. Styler, *Adult Education in India* (Oxford: Oxford University Press, 1966).
34. Paul Freire, *The Pedagogy of the Oppressed* (London: Penguin, 1972).
35. Naik and Nurulla, op. cit., 390–391, 814–824.
36. Frank Laubach (1945), *India shall be Literate* (Nagpur: National Christian Council of India, 1940).
37. Hartog Report, Chapters V and VI.
38. Eric Ashby, *Universities: British, Indian, African: A Study in the Ecology of Higher Education* (Cambridge, MS: Harvard University Press, 1966).
39. Pawan Agarwal, *Indian Higher Education* (New Delhi: Sage, 2009), 19. The background to the establishment of Serampore College is given in E. Daniel Potts, *British Baptist Missionaries in India 1793–1837* (Cambridge: Cambridge University Press, 1967).
40. Although most authorities including Radhakrishnan Report credit Ram Mohan Roy for this achievement, the latest research shows that it was orthodox Zamindars who took a lead in the establishment of Hindu College, vide A.F.S. Ahmed, *Social Ideas and Social Change: Bengal 1819–1835* (Calcutta: Riddhi, 2nd edn.), 201–213.
41. Bruce T. McCully, *English Education and the Origin of Indian Nationalism* (New York: Columbia University Press, 1940).
42. Leah Renold, *A Hindu Education: Early Years of Banaras Hindu University* (New Delhi: Oxford University Press, 2005).
43. Aparna Basu, "Higher Education", in Moonis Raza (Ed.), *Higher Education in India: Retrospect and Prospect* (New Delhi: Association of Indian Universities, 1991), 25.
44. Anil Seal, *The Emergence of Indian Nationalism: The Competition and Collaboration in the late 19th Century* (Cambridge: Cambridge University Press, 1968), 114–130.
45. Radhakrishnan Report, 153–155.

46. Quinquennial Review of Progress of Education in India, 1922–27 (Calcutta, 1928), 60.
47. Naik and Narulla (1974), op. cit., 327.
48. Aparna Basu (1991), op. cit.
49. A. Gilbert Irene, "The Organization of Academic Profession in India: The IES (1864–1974)", in Susanne H. Rudolph and Lloyd I. Rudolph (Eds.), *Education and Politics in India: Studies in Organization, Society and Polity* (Bombay: Oxford University Press, 1972), 319–342.
50. Leah Renold, op. cit., 80–114.
51. Aparna Basu (1991), op. cit., 30.
52. Ramchandra Guha, "Crucibles of Modernity", in Ira Pande (Ed.), *Beyond Degrees: Finding Success in Higher Education* (New Delhi: Harper Collins, 2008), 2–11.

    Guha says that the three presidency universities established in 1857 were in a sense crucibles of modernity. He quotes Andre Beteille as having said: These universities opened new horizons, both intellectually and institutionally that had stood in a conservative hierarchical mode for centuries. These were among the first open and secular institutions in a society that was governed by rules of kinship, caste and religion.

6 Educational Planning

The Federal Framework for Educational Policy Making and Financing

Under the Indian Constitution, economic and social planning is a concurrent subject.[1] Naturally, both the states and the Centre can engage in educational planning which presupposes educational programmes formulated in terms of a policy whose implementation requires adequate financing. When both the states and the Centre are involved, there is need for inter-state coordination. This chapter would therefore deal with the subject of educational planning, policy making, financing and inter-state coordination in the area.

Educational Planning and Financing

Planning and financing as noted presuppose policy making and these functions in the area of education have traditionally been performed by the Central Ministry of Education dating back to 1910.[2] The Planning Commission was established by the Prime Minister Jawaharlal Nehru in 1950, his first act after new Constitution came into force because central socio-economic planning was an integral part of his idea of India.[3] Its role has been to provide a medium-term financial framework as well as annual allocations with reference to the schematic proposals of the Education Ministry and the states have generally followed central guidelines especially since they were accompanied by the financial carrot of the plan grants.

Planning Commission: The Background

Planning Commission, though set up in March 1950, had a long pedigree. Even in the 19th century, Indian thinkers like M.G. Ranade had opposed the British policy of *laissez faire* and had advocated protection of indigenous industry à la Friedrich List in Germany. The Indian National Congress (INC) advocated adoption of planning as an essential part of its political programme as early as 1931. Subhash Chandra Bose, as the President of the INC, shortly after the Congress assumed power under provincial autonomy in 1937, called a Conference of Provincial Industries Ministers, which appointed a National Planning Committee with Jawaharlal Nehru as its chairman. Jawaharlal in his autobiography pointedly but lovingly refers to his work as chairman of the NPC in the following terms: "My other activity was the chairmanship of a National Planning Committee which was formed under Congress auspices with the cooperation of the provincial governments. As we proceeded with this work, *it grew and grew till it embraced almost every phase of national activity*. We appointed twenty-nine sub-committees for common groups of subjects – agricultural, industrial, social, economic, financial – and tried to coordinate their activities so as to *produce a scheme of planned economy of India ... For me this has been a fascinating work, and I have learnt much from it. It is clear that any scheme that we may produce can only be given effect to in a free India*. It is also clear that any effective planning must involve a socialization of the economic structure."[4] The Committee enlisted the help of several experts which produced sectoral plans which infused a planning consciousness among the people and subsequently inspired a Bombay Plan (1944) drawn up by industrialists and a People's Plan drawn up by M.N. Roy. Planning had become a national priority. The colonial government was not far behind. It set up a separate Department of Planning and Development in 1944. The interim government under Nehru had appointed an Advisory Planning Bureau. The terms of reference of the Planning Commission when set up in 1950 were very comprehensive covering assessment of resources, formulation of a plan for their utilization, allocation of resources, determination of the conditions for successful execution of the plan etc.

Role of the Planning Commission

The Planning Commission has continued without any substantial change in its formal constitution. The Prime Minister is the ex-officio Chairman and the Minister for Finance and some other important ministers as designated by the Prime Minister are part-time members and other members are full-time subject experts. Although advisory in character, its advising capacity, as observed by A.H. Hanson may be considered to be almost unlimited.[5] It mainly formulates medium-term (five-year) and short-term (annual) plans within a perspective of 15–20 years in consultation with the states. It conducts a mid-term appraisal of every Five-Year Plan. It has many divisions, but its key divisions are: (1) Perspective Planning Division, (2) Sectoral Divisions (including one for *Education*), (3) State Plan Division, (4) Plan Coordination Division, (5) Programme Evaluation Organization, and (6) Labour and Manpower Division. For its data, it depends on the Registrar-General, Census and the Statistics Department, the latter having been brought under its purview from February 1973.[6] The Department of Programme Implementation was set up in the 1980s to perform the function of monitoring of important plan projects.[7] The Sectoral Divisions of the Planning Commission are concerned both with State Plans and Central Plans of their respective sectors and, in conjunction with the State Plan Division and the Plan Coordination Division (dealing with the NDC) give the Planning Commission its unique character as a federal organization, a lynchpin between the Centre and the states.[8]

The Planning Commission which was a powerful organization in the 1950s began to decline in its importance in the 1960s, the main reason being the crisis of planning associated with the financial difficulties of successive plans including the Fourth Plan, which was required to be deferred.[9] Organizationally, the Planning Commission was downsized following the recommendations of the report of the ARC on Machinery for Planning,[10] which recommended the strengthening of the planning cells of the sectoral ministries and the building up of planning capacity at State Government level. The process of strengthening the Finance Ministry vis-à-vis the Planning Commission was initiated during Prime Minister Lal Bahadur Shastri's time. Another disruption in the plan occurred with the assumption of power by the Janata government in March 1977 (with the Fifth Plan being cut short) but since the Janata government fell in 1979, another Annual Plan intervened (1979–80) before the Sixth Plan started. Thus we have the phenomenon of a four-year Fifth Plan being followed by two Annual Plans. There was a third plan holiday (1990–92) during the regime of the National Front government before the Eighth Plan (1992–97) started. The Ninth Plan (1997–2002) similarly saw several drafts because of political changes. Thus, for a period of 62 years (1950–2012) we have only eleven Five-Year Plans.

In the post-1991 scenario, however, the role of the Planning Commission has become ambivalent. A reference may be made to Arun Shourie's account of the functioning of the Planning Commission in the 1990s. He somewhat unfairly calls the Planning Commission a parking lot,[11] describes how the Annual Plan discussions with the Chief Ministers have become a charade, how the State Plan Advisers have lost touch with their allotted states and how technical divisions like Irrigation feel marginalized, being kept out of policy making of River Valley Projects. However, he also observes that the Commission is the natural body to discharge some vital tasks, which are:

1. The Planning Commission can take a coordinated and a longer view as ministries are splintered and are focused on urgent problems.
2. It can act as the watchdog of interests of backward regions and deprived sections in the Indian polity.
3. Its evaluation (PEO) and manpower (IAMR) organizations can be revitalized to make it a powerful course correction agency.
4. With different political parties being in power in different states and at the Centre, the Planning Commission can work as an impartial arbiter.

5. With governments and political class as a whole finding it impossible to adopt "un-popular" measures, it can prepare the ground for hard decisions.

The Role of the Education Ministry

The tasks of planning at the national level as listed by J.P. Naik,[12] as well as policy making have traditionally been performed by the Education Ministry in conjunction with the Planning Commission. In the context of the Sargent Plan for post-war 'reconstruction', the separate Department of Education originally created in 1910 was revived in 1945. Since then, the Ministry has been renamed as Ministry of HRD at the time of National Policy on Education in 1986. In 2008, education was dealt with by two departments in the ministry, viz., (1) Department of Elementary Education and Literacy, and (2) Department of Higher Education. Of course, the ministry by itself cannot formulate policies. It relies on the three think tanks of NIEPA, now renamed as NUEPA, NCERT and UGC and also several other agencies to frame the policies.

Educational planning is characterized by centralization and the roots of centralization lay in the three-fold imbalance in the following fields: organizational, fiscal and planning procedural.

(a) Organizational imbalance has two aspects: System level and departmental level. At the system level, while there is an organization for overall national planning in the form of the Planning Commission at the Centre, in the State Governments, planning was looked after departmentally till at least 1969. The Planning Commission did not make any move to have counterpart state planning structures, though in the context of rural development, there was talk of district planning from the Second Five-Year Plan onwards.[13] The ARC recommended in 1968 the constitution of State Planning Boards in the states for formulating plans and for evaluating plan performance with three sectoral units including one for social services and functionally an evaluation unit and they were to be manned by personnel with expertise and experience.[14] The Planning Commission introduced a scheme for central support towards the additional cost of strengthening and reorganizing planning departments into planning boards having units for (1) Perspective Planning, (2) Monitoring Plan Information and Evaluation, (3) Project Appraisal, (4) Area/District Planning, and (5) Manpower Planning.[15] The Sarkaria Commission reviewed the progress of implementation of the scheme and found that while some states availed of the scheme and strengthened their planning machinery, several states did not set up Planning Boards and in states where Planning Boards were set up, proper relationship between Planning Departments and Planning Boards had not been established.[16]

(b) The second aspect of organizational imbalance is with regard to the departmental machinery and resources for planning. Whereas the Central Education Ministry had a rudimentary planning staff since the inception of the era of central planning (1950), this was considerably strengthened when in 1968, the ARC took the view that sectoral planning is the function of the sectoral ministries which should have a planning cell entrusted with formulation of plan (preparatory work, necessary studies and research), scrutiny and coordination of schemes and projects and review of progress and evaluation of achievements. The Planning Cell was to be headed by a Joint Secretary and supervised by a Standing Committee for Planning.[17] In the meanwhile, the Central Ministry of Education had also, as part of the implementation of Five-Year Plans and in some cases, with international assistance, created specialized institutions which, in course of time, became national resource bodies or think tanks, named earlier UGC/NCERT/NUEPA.

In the case of State Governments, the ARC had recommended setting up of Planning Cells in sectoral departments of State Governments. However, the planning machinery at the state secretariat departments remained weak. Traditionally, planning and statistical work of the Education Department was looked after by the Directorate of Education. However, the directorates were slow to professionalize.

(c) Fiscal imbalance: In India, the major tax sources assigned to the Centre consist of taxes on non-agricultural income and wealth, customs and manufacturing excises, the bases of which have nation wide mobility. The main items assigned to the states are: sales tax, sumptuary excises on alcoholic beverages, stamp duties and registration fees, taxes on road transport and electricity and tax on agricultural income which remains untapped for political reasons. On the other hand, the major responsibility for providing social and economic services has been assigned to the states. In 1990–91, about 85 per cent of the total expenditure on social and economic services was incurred at the state level. This assignment of tax-powers and expenditure functions has created a high degree of vertical fiscal imbalance. States financed about 43 per cent of their expenditures from their own sources of revenue, meaning that they depended for 57 per cent of their expenditure on the Centre.[18]

(d) Procedures of plan finance: The procedures of plan finance have reduced the leeway available to states. They include: matching grants, requirement of a prior sanction of a central ministry for large sectoral projects of a capital nature, earmarking of funds for Minimum Needs Programme (MNP), fulfilling seven basic needs, which included universalization of elementary education introduced since the Fifth Plan,[19] the requirement of environmental impact assessment and the

requirement of prior clearance under the Forest Conservation Act, 1980 when there is diversion of forestlands for non-forest purposes.

J.P. Naik has pointed out that planning in India is top-heavy, leading to its peripherality and orientation to expenditure.[20] Given this reality, the question arises, what is the record of the ministry in educational planning, in the context of ten completed Five-Year Plans, assorted annual plans and an ongoing Eleventh Plan? The approach is one of comprehensiveness with an attempt to do something for almost all sectors with the preferred planning technique of social demand, which is in consonance with the democratic reality, other planning techniques of "manpower planning" and "rates of return" being combined eclectically.

The role of the Central Government in planning higher and technical education is laid down in the Constitution itself, viz., standard setting and coordination of development for which UGC and AICTE have been set up. A scholar has suggested that the role of the Central Government in school education and adult education was that of providing ideational leadership.[21] His account ends at 1980 but an up-to-date account can easily be gathered from perusal of the successive plan documents. The Ministry was helped in its leadership role not only by the think-tanks referred to earlier but also by its exposure to international organizations like Asian Bank, UNESCO, UNICEF, UNDP, World Bank etc. which pointed to foreign educational models and also provided funds for implementation of schemes in priority areas.

Educational Financing

Financial resources are fungible (of a uniform kind, easily transferable from one head to another), and the tenets of optimum public finance do not approve of earmarking of proceeds of a particular tax for a particular scheme or budget head (save exceptional cases like the education cess introduced in the Central Budget from 2004–05 whose proceeds are earmarked for the programme of universalization of elementary education). Hence, what applies to financing of plan applies to financing of education sector also, except for the fact that there is a target ratio of public expenditure to be allotted to education. The Kher Committee suggested as a matter of rule of thumb 10 per cent of central budget and 20 per cent of state budgets to be allotted to education. The state budgetary ratio has been exceeded by most states. However, both the NPE 1968 and the NPE 1986 following Kothari Commission, talked of a target ratio of 6 per cent of GDP being invested in education as against which the current estimated achievement is 3.8 per cent. Since the centre-state relations are characterized by vertical fiscal imbalance, the way the plan and the non-plan part of education are financed also manifests the centralizing trend of educational financing.

Plan Financing

The State Governments hardly contribute to the financing of central sector education schemes except indirectly as when the Central Government makes grant of free land a pre-condition for location of central institutions (e.g., IITs and Navodaya Vidyalayas). This expenditure hardly figures in the central budget as a source of funding though the State Governments' contribution in terms of market price of land may be very substantial. This aspect needs quantification and further investigation.

However, the central contribution to a states' education plan can be very substantial and takes two forms: centrally assisted schemes and centrally sponsored schemes.

Centrally Assisted Schemes

Centrally assisted schemes in the field of education are part of the State Plan. They may take the form of educational schemes with pattern of assistance attached or block grants. The evolution has been from what in the US are called specific purpose grants to block grants. In the First Plan, all schemes had a pattern of assistance depending on whether the grant was of a revenue or capital nature. In the Second Plan, the pattern of assistance was fixed for the plan period without differentiation as between revenue and capital heads. In the Third Plan, a proforma pattern was prescribed but re-appropriation was permitted. Thus, the system approximated a block grant system.[22] From the Fourth Plan onwards, the Planning Commission introduced the well-known Gadgil formula for determining the quantum of block grant on rational principles. The weightages under Gadgil formula were: (1) population of 1971 Census–60

Table 6.1
Gadgil-Mukherji Formula

Criteria	*Weightage*
Population (1971)	60%
Per capita income	25% This is divided as below: (a) 20% for states having per capita comparable income below the national average based on "deviation" method, (b) for all other States, based on "distance" method–50%
Performance criteria (include tax effort, fiscal management, population control, elimination of illiteracy, on time completion of externally aided projects)	7.5%
Special problems	7.5%

Source: Compilation of Ninth Five-Year Plan, Vol.I (New Delhi: Nabhi Publications, 2000), pp. 291–292.

per cent, (2) per capita income–20 per cent, (3) tax effort 10 per cent, and (4) special projects/problems–10 per cent. The Gadgil formula has been modified from time to time, but substantially in 1991–92 during Deputy Chairmanship of Pranab Kumar Mukherji. According to the current formula, after setting apart the funds required for externally aided projects and reasonable amounts for special area programmes, 30 per cent of the balance is earmarked for ten special category states, and the balance amount is distributed among non-special category states on the basis of listed criteria and weightage. The formula is now known as Gadgil-Mukherji formula. Thus funding for centrally assisted schemes is as much formula based as Central Finance Commission's grants and cannot be faulted on that count.

Centrally Sponsored Schemes

It is through centrally sponsored schemes (CSSs) that the Central Government has tended to distort the priorities of the State Plan. These were introduced in the Second Plan, under the guise of assisting states outside the State Plans for programmes, which were of high priority.[23] Theoretically, a State Government could reject a CSS but the financial bait was too strong. The Setalvad Study Group of ARC went into the matter in great detail. It criticized such schemes on the ground that: (1) in effect they relegate to the Centre the responsibility of settling priorities in the state sphere; (2) they curtail state's sector under the plan; (3) they distort the priorities of the State Plan to a greater extent than centrally assisted schemes; and (4) in principle, it is incorrect to entrust the settlement of such priorities arbitrarily to the Centre when the subject falls within the State List. The Study Group buttressed its case by detailed case studies.[24] The Setalvad Study Group's recommendations were, however, ignored both by the Centre and by the states.[25]

The NDC reviewed the matter at the time of the approval of the Fourth Plan and while supporting the continuance of a system of scheme-wise assistance for a limited number of schemes which require coordination at the national level or where the schemes are of an inter-state nature prescribed the following criteria:

1. They should relate to demonstrations, pilot projects, surveys and research, or
2. they should have a regional or inter-state character, or
3. they should be such as to require lump sum provision to be broken down territorially at a later stage, or
4. they should have an overall significance from the all-India angle.

It further suggested limiting the total monetary value of centrally sponsored schemes to one-seventh or one-sixth of the quantum of central assistance.

The matter was reviewed during the Janata regime at the time of the finalization of the draft Sixth Plan (1978–83). The State Chief Ministers were of the view that the CSSs were drawn too rigidly leaving little flexibility at the operational level and that new schemes introduced during the course of implementation of a plan had resulted in financial hardships to the states, as they had to provide a matching contribution in many of the schemes. In view of this criticism, a Working Group was constituted which recommended 15 schemes to be financed fully by the Union Government, 60 schemes whose cost was to be shared equally between the Centre and the states and the rest 72 CSSs accounting for Rs 2,000 crore of were transferred to the states. However, a subsequent Group under the chairmanship of Ramamurthi, ex-chief Secretary of Orissa, could not verify the implementation of these decisions.[26] On the other hand, it found that the share of CSSs had progressively increased from 47.36 per cent of normal central assistance in 1980–81 to 73.74 per cent in 1984–85 (this was against the norm of 14 per cent to 16 per cent). The Group found that central ministries floated new CSSs for apparently cogent reasons like achievement of national goals, especially in sectors other than irrigation and power, which take a larger proportion of state's resources, to protect social services which are under-funded, to promote innovative schemes for which the State Governments have neither the expertise nor the compulsion, and to provide a degree of uniformity of development in priority areas in different states. The Committee found that no state except Punjab opposed the concept of the CSSs. After careful consideration, the Committee recommended a change in the third and fourth criteria laid down by the NDC at the time of approval of the Fourth Plan and also a ceiling of one-third of block assistance in respect of CSSs and emphasized the need to limit the number of CSSs. However, it did not identify the schemes to be retained as CSS, which work was done by two NDC groups in 1987.[27]

The Seventh Plan outlay of these schemes was Rs 462.50 crore. The implementation of new CSSs like Operation Blackboard, DIETs etc. as part of the NPE 1986, if any thing, increased the pressure of CSSs further. With the adoption of DPEP (District Primary Education Projects) in the 1990s and subsequently Sarva Shiksha Abhiyan (2000) and the establishment of National Literacy Mission, the CSSs in the area of elementary education and literacy have got merged with the respective programmes so that CSSs in secondary education and language schemes alone survive as CSSs. As noted in the footnote 25 the persistence of the CSSs illustrates the phenomenon of picket fence federalism.

Non-Plan Financing: The Role of Central Finance Commission

The Indian Constitution provides for sharing of proceeds of central taxes with the states and making grants to the states from the Consolidated

Fund of India and for this purpose provides for five-yearly appointment of a Finance Commission. The role of the Central Finance Commission in non-plan financing of education is rather limited because its assistance is not earmarked for any particular expenditure head. It is true that the Finance Commission recommends devolution of revenues and also grants in aid for improvement of various public services, which would include education. The successive Finance Commissions have, however, not followed any systematic policy in this regard. Thus, the First Finance Commission recommended grants-in-aid to some of the less developed states to expand primary education. The Second Finance Commission took the view that it was for the Development Plan to ensure an equitable development in the field of social services and saw no room for any grants to education. The Sixth Finance Commission felt that it had a role in bringing up the level of per capita expenditure on education in backward states (it noted that in 1971–72 it was Rs 8.86 in Bihar and Rs 31.03 in Kerala) and made educational grants accordingly. The Eighth Finance Commission recommended upgradation assistance to all those states in which percentage of primary schools without *pucca* buildings exceeded all-India average of 48 per cent and also recommended assistance to those 11 states where the proportion of single-teacher schools exceeded all-India average of 35 per cent. The total assistance recommended was Rs 286.04 crore. Similarly, the Twelfth Finance Commission recommended upgradation grants for education sector and the latest, i.e., the Thirteenth Finance Commission recommended in 2010 a substantial grant of Rs 25,000 crore for five years, in connection with Right to Education Act.

Education expenditure comprises expenditure under both Plan and non-plan headings and with the over-hang of non-plan expenditure of successive plans, non-plan expenditure tends to go up. According to an official committee,[28] the position of plan and non-plan educational expenditures between Centre and states in 1996–97 was as below:

Table 6.2

Plan and Non-Plan Educational Expenditures between Centre and States (1996–97)

(Rs in crore)

	Plan	*Non-Plan*	*Total*
States	5,947.51 (54.26)	30,206.88 (93.01)	36,154.39 (83.28)
Centre-UTs	5,014.26 (45.74)	2,243.77 (06.91)	7,258.03 (16.72)
Total	10,961.77 (100%)	32,450.65 (100%)	43,412.42 (100%)

Note: Figures in brackets indicate percentage of the total.

It is clear that while cumulative non-plan expenditure of the states is as high as almost 94 per cent, the Central/UT share in plan expenditure though less than 50 per cent, is substantially high at almost 46 per cent. Such statements need to be qualified by following considerations: Firstly, 30 per cent of Plan resources go to 10 Backward or 'Special Category' states (8 north-eastern states including Sikkim, Jammu & Kashmir and Himachal Pradesh). Secondly, expenditure of UTs needs to be classified as central expenditure and not as state expenditure. Table 6.2 does this correctly but not all data heed this caution. Thirdly, the Central Government directly or through its autonomous bodies (like UGC) subsidizes education and health-care expenditure in states like UP as seen elsewhere. Fourthly, external financial assistance is controlled by the Central Government through the Ministry of Finance.

It is often suggested that the creation of the Planning Commission has distorted centre-state financial relations. However, apart from the fact that the Planning Commission has come to stay and has proved its usefulness in the Indian federation, an academic study found that allocations made both by the Planning Commission and the Finance Commission did not fit any rational model like pursuit of educational development or educational equity. They could be explained only in terms of a political model.[29]

Education Policy

Policy is defined by NIEPA[30] in very general terms as "a statement of aims, purposes, principles and intentions which serve as continuing guidelines for management in accomplishing objectives". But, in concrete terms, what do the stakeholders understand by the term 'policy'? Firstly, it is a shorthand for a field of activity (e.g., Education Policy). Secondly, it may stand for a specific proposal or a piece of legislation (like a law for free and compulsory education) and thirdly, it may be used for a whole menu of interrelated programmes. In the case of education, the variety of programmes may be correlated with various stages of education (e.g., primary, secondary and tertiary stages), various subjects (e.g., languages, vocational subjects) or various strategies (e.g., priority for universalization of elementary education, decision to allocate 6 per cent of national income for education etc.). The focus in this chapter is on the last sense which is generally called "educational policy statements" (EPS).

A Synopsis of EPS

The period when India was a British colony, i.e., roughly from the middle of 18th century till 1947, was characterized by the dominance of British agency in the formulation and implementation of EPS's at least till 1935. After 1947, the Indian agency becomes dominant though there is also a tendency in the initial years to imitate foreign models, viz., British,

Russian and American. A synoptic statement of EPS's in India is presented below in a tabular form for post-independence period:

Table 6.3

Education Policies

Year	*Nature of Policy Post-Independence*	*Impetus for the Policy*
1953	For coordination of development and maintaining standards in higher education there is need for a University Grants Commission. UGC was set up in 1953.	Radhakrishnan Commission on University Education 1950
1953	Central Government should play a prominent role in planning of secondary education. NCERT was set up in 1961.	Mudaliar Commission on Secondary Education
1966	A revolution of education is needed beginning with a national system of education which can set in motion the much desired social, economic and cultural revolution (para 1.14 to 1.17)	Kothari Commission Report, 1966
1968	National Policy on Education (NPE) 1968	Embodies decisions of MPs' Committee on the Report of Kothari Commission
1977	Education made a concurrent subject in the Constitution	42nd Amendment to the Constitution which was part of the Centralization Agenda of Indira Gandhi during internal Emergency
1986	National Policy on Education (NPE) 1986. Programme of Action 1986 (of NPE 1986)	Rajiv Gandhi as the PM decided to launch long pending revision of 1968 policy preceded by a consultative document called: "Challenge of Education" (1985) to prepare India to face challenges of 21st century
1992	(1) NPE 1986 slightly modified. (2) Revised Programme of Action, 1992	(1) NPE Review Committee (Ramamurti Committee) appointed by NF Government (1990) and CABE Committee on Policy (1992)
2003	86th Constitutional Amendment passed by Parliament in December 2002 making elementary education a fundamental right	Supreme Court judgment in Mohini Jain Case (1992) and Unnikrishnan Case (1993)
2010	Right to Free and Compulsory Education Bill passed by Parliament in 2009 and enforced from 1st April 2010	Report of the CABE Committee on Bill for Free and Compulsory Education, June 2005.

Planning and Policy Making in Education: An Assessment

J.P. Naik, after devoting his life to educational policy making, concluded that no political party in the country is committed to a radical reconstruction of education or for the creation of a national system of education.[31] According to some scholars, education is not high on the agenda of political parties and they have not focused on educational problems as technical problems. They are, however, concerned with the political consequences of educational issues. Hence, there is the paradox of intense political activity accompanied by low educational performance.[32]

This situation, however, is not peculiar to India but it appears to characterize many federal polities. American scholars have, for example, noted the phenomenon of sudden appearance in 1982–83, of about a dozen major reports on the nation's schools, of which the major report was entitled *Nation at Risk* issued by the Federal Government (1983). An analysis of the reports showed that the reports served to take the discussion about education policy making out of the arena of courts and to re-open a debate about the role of government in schooling that had been dormant since the 1960s. To quote: "Educational goals were defined in terms of social justice (equality of educational opportunity for minorities, women and the handicapped) and the courts by virtue of numerous law suits, were charged with a responsibility for the nation's schools in that direction. The reports have directed educational policy making to questions of national defence and economy and re-opened the discussion regarding the proper role of government in education in relation to that of teachers, parents and of school administrators."[33]

Consultative Inter-State Fora in the Field of Education

The consultative fora in the educational field have to some extent moderated the rigour of centralization and are required to be considered in detail. The need for such fora has been underlined in the Sarkaria Report in terms of broad promotion of federal deliberative democracy, both at the political and administrative levels.[34] The effectiveness of the fora depends on their composition, the regularity of their meetings and the impact of their deliberations on the actual outcome by way of policy decisions and their implementation. The cases of two fora are considered, i.e., NDC attached to the PC and CABE attached to the Education Ministry.

National Development Council

The NDC was set up in August 1952 by a government resolution with the prescribed functions of reviewing the working of the National Plan, considering important questions of social and economic policy and recommending measures for the achievement of the aims and targets of the National Plan. It comprised the Prime Minister as chairman, all the chief ministers and all the members of the Planning Commission. Its reorganization in October 1967 in terms of the ARC report on machinery for planning, increased the weight of the Central Government vis-à-vis the

State Governments in the body. The Sarkaria Commission felt that the frequency and duration of the meetings of the NDC were very inadequate and its work was marked by formalism.[35]

Education is an important development sector. While there is no indication of the NPE 1968, having been approved by the NDC, by the 1980s the crucial significance of education in the perspective of human resource development had come to be recognized. Hence, it was considered necessary to place the draft of the NPE 1986 before the NDC for approval in April 1986 after its earlier approval by the CABE.[36] This indicated that the NPE which had implications for the National Plan for all the states and for various departments of the Centre had, so to say, federal approval. Secondly, as a sequel to the World Conference on Education for All (1990), NDC appointed a committee on literacy, whose report was considered by the Chief Ministers' Conference held under the chairmanship of the Prime Minister in February 1994. It is beyond the purview of this work to assess the effectiveness of the performance of NDC as a general Inter-State Council which work has been ably performed by Rekha Saxena,[37] though she has not noted the fact of approval of NPE by the NDC.

Central Advisory Board of Education (CABE)

The role of CABE – a Sectoral Inter-State Council – which serves as a sounding board for educational policies in the Indian federal polity is reviewed in the rest of the chapter. The idea for such a body was first put forward by the Sadler Commission. It was set up in August 1920, abolished in 1923, as a measure of retrenchment and was reconstituted in 1935, with a strong advisory and communicative (clearing house of information) role. The CABE with the central education minister as chairman has state education ministers as members with several nominees of the Government of India, some of them ex-officio. The broad definition of the functions with heavy involvement of states and the composition comprising all education ministers underlines the inter-state character of the CABE.[38] Although Kothari Commission[39] is rather dismissive of CABE, treating it as a mere departmental advisory committee in the limited sense of S.R. Maheshwari,[40] NPE 1986[41] is more appreciative stating that the CABE would play a pivotal role in reviewing educational developments, determining the changes required to improve the system and monitoring implementation. The functions of the CABE, when it was revived and reconstituted after a gap of 10 years (1994–2004) in July 2004 under the UPA-I government included review of the progress of education from time to time, appraisal of implementation of the education policy, and advice regarding coordination between the Centre/states/UTs and NGOs. A copy of the order is enclosed as Appendix-I. Unfortunately, an opportunity of notifying it as an Inter-State Council under Article 263 of the Constitution was not taken.

The POA 1992 had underscored the role of the CABE as a very effective instrument of meaningful partnership between the Centre and the states, particularly at evolving a consensus on the major policy issues in the field of human resource development. Thus, CABE is not only a pivotal body with limited functions in the areas of implementation (reviewing, revision and monitoring), but embodies the ideal of promoting centre-state partnership or, in other words, cooperative federalism in education. It is, thus, clear that CABE is not merely a consultative body attached to the Ministry of Education, as supposed by S.R. Maheshwari, but rather a sectoral inter-governmental body, in the language of Sarkaria Commission, comparable to the Central Council of Health, Central Council of Local Self-government and inter-state bodies in the area of sales tax. Unfortunately, the study of Rekha Saxena, referred to earlier, dealing with a variety of inter-governmental organizations in India refers to Election Commission and some other bodies, but fails to notice the role of the CABE.

In Supreme Court case *Aruna Roy vs. Union of India,* in which judgment was pronounced on 12th September 2002, the National Curricular Framework for School Education (NCFSE) 2000 as drafted and finalized by the NCERT during the NDA regime was challenged, *inter alia* on the ground that the CABE was not consulted by the NCERT in advance. The majority judgment held that CABE was merely an advisory body, that it was not a statutory body and that its functions did not specifically include the approval of the NCFSE. Evidently, the majority judgment took a narrow view of the matter. The minority judgment of Sema J. realistically appreciates the role of the CABE as an inter-state forum. The Judge stated: "The importance of the role played by the CABE cannot be side-tracked on the plea that the body is non-statutory, particularly when it has been playing an important role in the past for evolving a consensus in the major policy decisions involving NPE". The court also directed the government to reconstitute the CABE and seek its opinion on NCFSE. As events unfolded, there was a change of regime in 2004 and CABE came to be reconstituted in July 2004. It was apparently re-constituted in 2007. Unfortunately, on both the occasions, the government did not notify it as an Inter-State Council under Article 263 of the Constitution.

The effectiveness of the CABE, has been affected by three factors relating to (a) its composition, (b) delay in its reconstitution, and (c) its conferencing procedures. Firstly, the CABE as constituted since the 1980s consists of a very large number of central ministers, ex-officio Central

Government officers (heads of academic bodies) and Central Government nominees including MPs, so that state education ministers as a group constitute only one-third of the total membership of about a hundred vide Appendix-I. Secondly, the long gaps in reconstitution of the CABE have occurred twice in the recent past, viz., from 1975 to 1983 and from 1995 to 2003, though the resolution of July 2004 conveniently omits to refer to the gap in the period 1975 to 1983. During Indira Gandhi's time, the tendency developed of omitting any reference to the speeches of state education ministers while drawing up the proceedings of the CABE. After Rajiv Gandhi became the PM and in the context of the NPE 1986/92, CABE was activated and there was talk of Centre-state cooperation and the say of State Governments began to be recorded, even if it was in contradiction to the central policy. Thus, in the meeting of the CABE held in April 1986 (when P.V. Narasimha Rao was the Union HRD Minister), specifically to discuss the draft of NPE, Tamil Nadu government's dissent on three language formula and a few opposition governments' proposals (Punjab, Andhra Pradesh, Karnataka, Tamil Nadu, Tripura and West Bengal) to revert education to the State List were recorded in the proceedings.

The effectiveness of the CABE as an inter-governmental organization in terms of its policy and programme outputs is partly a function of the political and administrative leadership provided by the then education minister/education secretary and partly of the federal political environment. Thus, the period 1935 to August 1967 may be said to be the golden period of the CABE when it played a pivotal role in the educational development especially in the period of what can be termed as 'planning without policy' (1947–67). The period from 1967 to 1983 is one of decline, CABE not having met for 7–8 years between 1975 and 1983 and the authoritarian tendency to ignore opposite viewpoints. The period 1983 to 1994 was a period of revival of the CABE as a platform for inter-state consultation. Between April 1994 and July 2004, the major portion of the period falling partly under UF government under Deve Gowda as PM and under NDA regime with Atal Bihari Vajpayee as the PM (and Murli Manohar Joshi as Education Minister), the CABE was in a limbo till its reconstitution by the UPA-I government in mid-2004, it has been meeting annually since then till at least 2010.

During the UPA-I (2004–2009), when Arjun Singh was Union Education Minister, CABE's activity was evidenced by its committees producing the following important reports in the first two years:

1. Girls' Education and the Common School System (Chairman: Tarun Gogoi, CM, Assam).
2. Universalization of secondary Education (Chairman: Ghanashyam Tiwari, Education Minister, Rajasthan).

3. Integration of Culture Education in the School Curriculum (Chairman: Prof. U.R. Ananthamurthy).
4. Regulatory Mechanisms for Textbooks and Parallel Textbooks Taught in Schools outside the Government System (Chairpersons: Prof. Zoya Hasan and Prof. Gopal Guru).
5. Autonomy in Higher Education Institutions (Chairman: Kanti Biswas, Education Minister, Government of West Bengal).
6. Financing of Higher and Technical Education [Chairman: Prof. Bhalchandra Mungekar, the then Member (Education), Planning Commission].
7. Free and Compulsory Education Bill and other issues related to Elementary Education. (Chairman: Kapil Sibbal, then Union Minister of State for Science and Technology).

NB: The first six reports have been published by the National Book Trust, New Delhi in two printed volumes in 2009.

Most of these reports, particularly those at 2, 3, 5, 6 and 7, appear to have fed into the policy making process and have been quoted in learned literature. Press reports indicate that during its meeting held in the first quarter of 2009, the CABE under Union Minister Arjun Singh considered the report of the National Knowledge Commission relating to higher education. In its most recent meeting held in the first week of September 2009, CABE is reported to have considered the Ministry's new initiatives in the fields of secondary and higher education relating to CBSE, National Council for Higher Education and Research etc.

In Table 6.4 the data relating to the CABE meetings held since 1935 have been presented according to the government in power (colonial, Congress and non-Congress).

It may be noted that in the past, CABE meetings were clubbed with Education Ministers' Conferences. Unfortunately, Education Ministers' Conferences do not have a fixed periodicity and their proceedings are not readily available but there is evidence to show that the UF and NDA governments did hold them, underlining the fact that centre-state consultation has taken place through other channels when the CABE was in the limbo.

Despite the weaknesses of the CABE noted above, it has emerged as one of the most durable inter-governmental sectoral fora and incidentally the oldest. The state education ministers have gradually found a voice and although their speeches follow the party line, and are along expected tracks, the utility of a dialogue at the federal forum and the valuable work of the CABE committees which have turned out weighty reports, has been appreciated.

Table 6.4

CABE Meetings from 1935 to April 2009

Period	*Party in Power*	*Name of Education Minister*	*No. of Years*	*No. of Meetings*	*Average per year*
December 1935 to August 1947	Colonial Government	There were several E.C. Members-in-Charge of Education, the last one being N.R. Sarkar	12 years	13	1.08
August 1947 to March 1977	Congress (PM – J.L. Nehru, L.B. Shastri and Indira Gandhi)	Abul Kalam Azad (Aug. 47 to Feb. 58) Dr K.G. Shrimali (Mar. 58 to Aug. 63) Humayun Kabir (Sept. 63 to Nov. 63) M.C. Chagla (Nov. 63 to Oct. 66) Fakruddin Ali Ahmed (Nov. 66 to Feb. 67) Dr Trigun-Sen (Mar. 67 to Feb. 69) Dr V.K.R.V. Rao (Feb. 69 to Mar. 71) S.S. Ray (Mar. 71 to Mar. 72) Nurul Hasan (Mar. 72 to Mar.77)	29 years and 7 months	25 meetings (Note: No meting held from 1975 to March 1977)	0.8
March 1977 to June 1980	Janata (PM – Morarji Desai and Charan Singh)	Prof. P.C. Chunder (Mar. 77 to July 79) Dr Karan Singh (Aug. 79 to Jan. 80)	2 years and 10 months	Nil	Nil
January 1980 to November 1989	Congress (PM – Indira Gandhi and Rajiv Gandhi)	B. Shankaranand (Jan. 80 to Oct. 80) S.B. Chavan (Oct. 80 to Aug. 81) Smt Sheila Kaul (Aug.81 to Dec. 84) K.C. Pant (Jan.85 to Sept. 85) P.V. Narasimha Rao (Sept. 85 to June 88) P. Shiv Shankar (June 88 to Dec. 89)	9 Years and 11 months	7 meetings	0.7
December 89 to June 1991	NF Government (PM – V.P. Singh and Chandrashekhar)	V.P. Singh (as PM) (Dec. 89 to Nov. 89) Shri Rajmangal Pandey (Nov. 89 to June 91)	1 year and 6 months	1 meeting	0.67

Cont'd...

...Cont'd

June 1991 to May 1996	Congress Government (PM – P.V. Narasimha Rao)	Arjun Singh (June 91 to Dec. 94) P.V. Narasimha Rao (Dec. 94 to Feb. 95) Madhavrao Scindia (Feb. 95 to Jan. 96) P.V.N. Rao (Jan.96 to May 96)	5 years	4 meetings	0.8
June 1996 to March 1998	UF Government (PM – Deve Gowda and I.K. Gujaral)	S.R. Bommai (June 96 to Mar. 98)	1 year and 10 months	Nil	Nil
March 1998 to May 2004	NDA Government (led by BJP) (PM – Atal Bihari Vajpayee)	Murli Manohar Joshi (Mar. 98 to May 2004)	6 years and 3 months	Nil	Nil
May 2004 to April 2009	UPA Government (led by Congress) PM – Manmohan Singh)	Arjun Singh (May 2004 to Apr. 2009)	5 years	6 meetings	1.2

Source: CABE Souvenir for proceedings of 27 meetings and NIEPA Documentation Centre and press reports for proceedings of subsequent meetings.

The SC judgment in the Aruna Roy case might be interpreted as a set back but it serves to underline the need to reconstitute the CABE either as a non-lapsable committee in which there is a change only of non-official members after change of government at the Centre or better still, of notifying the CABE as an Inter-State Council under Article 263 of the Constitution like the Central Councils of Health and of Local Self-Government.

Appendix–I
Government Resolution on CABE

Government of India
Ministry of Human Resource Development
Department of Secondary & Higher Education
New Delhi, 6th July, 2004

Resolution

1. The Central Advisory Board of Education (CABE), the highest advisory body to advise the Central and State Governments in the field of education, was first established in 1920 and dissolved in 1923 as a measure of economy. It was revived in 1935 and had continued to be in existence till 1994. Despite the fact that in the past, important decisions had been taken on the advice of CABE and it had provided a forum for widespread consultation and examination of issues relating to educational and cultural development, it was unfortunately not reconstituted after the expiry of its extended tenure in March, 1994. CABE has a particularly important role to play at the present juncture in view of the significant socio-economic and socio-cultural developments taking place in the country and for the review of the National Policy on Education which is also due. It is a matter of importance therefore, that the Central and State Governments, and educationists and people representing all interests, should increase their interaction and evolve a participative process of decision making in education, which enhances the federal structure of our polity.
2. The Government of India has accordingly decided to reconstitute CABE as per the annexure.
3. The functions of CABE would be:
   (a) to review the progress of education from time to time;
   (b) to appraise the extent and manner in which the education policy has been implemented by the Central and State Governments, and other concerned agencies, and to give appropriate advice in the matter;
   (c) to advise regarding coordination between the Central and State Governments/UT Administrations, State Governments and non-governmental agencies for educational development in accordance with the educational policy; and
   (d) to advise, suo moto, or on a reference made to it by the Central Government or any State Government or a Union Territory administration on any educational question.

4. For the discharge of these functions, the Board may (i) call for information and comments from any Government institution, any other organization or an individual; (ii) appoint committees or groups comprising members of CABE and/or others as may be necessary; and (iii) commission, through Government or any other agency, studies, research or reports on any specific issue requiring the attention of the Board or its committees or groups.
5. (a) Tenure: The tenure of CABE shall be of three years, with effect from the date of this notification.
   (b) Casual Vacancies: (i) All casual vacancies among the members, other than ex-officio members shall be filled by the authority or body which nominated or elected the member whose place falls vacant. (ii) The person nominated or elected to a casual vacancy shall be a member of the Board for the residue of the term for which the member whose place he fills would have been a member.
   (c) Meeting: The Board will meet at least once every year and there shall not be a gap of more than two years between two consecutive meetings of the Board.
   (d) Agenda: (i) The Agenda, the explanatory memorandum and the record of proceedings/minutes will be prepared and circulated by the Ministry of Human Resource Development (Department of Secondary and Higher Education), Government of India. (ii) The Agenda and the explanatory memorandum will ordinarily be circulated to all the members at least 15 days before the date of the meeting of the Board.
   (e) Quorum: The quorum of the meeting of the Board will be 2/3rd of the total membership of the Board.
   (f) Procedure: The Board will adopt its own procedures in respect of matters not provided for above.
   (g) General: No proceedings of the Board shall be invalid merely on the ground of procedural defect or vacancy under any category of membership.

C. Balakrishnan
Joint Secretary to the Government of India

Order

Ordered that a copy of the Resolution be published in the gazette of India for general information.

Also ordered that a copy of the Resolution be forwarded to all the Ministries/Departments of the Government of India, all State Governments/Union Territories Administration, Universities, Institutions/ Organisations of the Department of Secondary and Higher Education, Ministry of Human Resource Development etc. for information. (F.No.2–24/93–PN.I)

C. Balakrishnan
Joint Secretary to the Government of India

To:
The Manager
Government of India Press
Faridabad

Copy forwarded to:

1. All Members of CABE.
2. All Permanent Invitees.
3. All Ministries/Departments of the Government of India.
4. All Attached/Subordinate Offices and Autonomous Statutory Bodies under the Ministry of Human Resource Development.
5. All State Governments/Union Territories.
6. President's Secretariat.
7. Prime Minister's Office.
8. Cabinet Secretariat.
9. Lok Sabha Secretariat.

C. Balakrishnan
Joint Secretary to the Government of India

Composition of the Central Advisory Board of Education

1. Chairman
   Minister of Human Resource Development.
2. Vice-Chairman
   Minister of State for Human Resource Development.
3. Representatives of the Government of India
   (i) Minister of Information and Broadcasting.
   (ii) Minister of Science and Technology.
   (iii) Minister of Health and Family Welfare.
   (iv) Minister of Labour.
   (v) Minister of Social Justice and Empowerment.
   (vi) Minister of Tribal Affairs.
   (vii) Minister of Youth Affairs and Sports.
   (viii) Member (Education), Planning Commission.
4. Representatives of State Governments and UT Administrations
   (i) One Minister in-charge of Education in each State Government (to be nominated by the Chief Minister).
   (ii) Lt. Governor or Minister in-charge of Education in each UT Administration.
5. Elected Members
   (i) Four Members of Parliament from the Lok Sabha.
   (ii) Two Members of Parliament from the Rajya Sabha.
6. Ex-officio Members
   (i) Secretary, Department of Elementary education and Literacy, Government of India.
   (ii) Chairman, University Grants Commission.
   (iii) Chairman, All India Council for Technical education.
   (iv) Chairman, Medical Council of India.
   (v) Chairman, Central Council of Indian Medicine.
   (vi) Director General, Indian Council of Agricultural Research.
   (vii) Chairman, Central Social Welfare Board.
   (viii) Director, National Institute of Educational Planning and Administration.
   (ix) Director, National Council for Educational Research and Training.
   (x) Chairman, Central Board of Secondary Education.
   (xi) Secretary-General, Association of Indian Universities.
   (xii) Chairman, Indian Council of Historical Research.
   (xiii) Chairman, Indian Council for Social Science Research.
   (xiv) Chairman, Indian Council for Philosophical Research.
   (xv) Director-General, National Literacy Mission.

7. Nominated Members – representing different interests

1.	Shri Javed Akhtar 702, Sagar Samrat, Green Field, Juhu Mumbai 400 009	2.	Prof. S.V. Giri Vice-Chancellor, S S Institute of Higher Learning Prashanti Nilayam Anantapur 515 134
3.	Prof. U.R. Ananthamurthy 498 Suragi, HIG House RMV IInd Stage, 6th A Main, Bangalore 560 094	4.	Prof. J.S. Grewal 29 Sector-11, Chandigarh 160 016
5.	Prof. Andre Beteille Sociologist 69, Jor Bagh (Ground Floor) New Delhi 110 003	6.	Prof. Gopal Guru 90, New Transit Hostel Phase-III JNU Campus, New Delhi
7.	Ms. Ela Bhatt General Secretary, SEWA Opp. Victoria Garden, Bhadra, Ahmedabad 380 001	8.	Prof. Zoya Hasan 139 Uttra Khand, JNU, New Delhi 110 067
9.	Shri Praful Bidwai 2st Floor, Anand Villa 1, Jaipur Estate Nizamuddin East, New Delhi 110 003	10.	Prof. P.V. Indiresan B-57, Hill View Apartments, Vasant Vihar, New Delhi 110 057
11.	Shri Charles Correa Charles Correa Associates 9, Mathew Road, Bombay 400 004	12.	Shri J.J. Irani Bombay House, 24, Homi Modi Street Fort, Mumbai 400 001
13.	Ms G. Nirmala Deshpande A 223, Pandara Road, New Delhi	14.	Shri Kiran Karnik Chairman, NASSCOM International Youth Centre, Teen Murti Marg, Chanakyapuri, New Delhi 110 021
15.	Prof. G.P. Deshpande 10 B, Athashree Pashan – Sus Road, Pashan, Pune	16.	Ms. Kiran Shaw Mazumdar Chairperson, BIOCON India Ltd. 20th K.M. Hosur Road, Electronic City, Bangalore 560 100
17.	Ms. Mahashweta Devi 50–B, Prince Gulam Saha Road, Ground Floor, Calcutta 700 032	18.	Prof. Mrinal Miri Vice-Chancellor, North-Eastern Hill University, NEHU Campus, Shillong, Meghalaya 793 002
19.	Prof. Jean Dréze Centre for Development Economics, Department of Economics, Delhi School of Economics, University of Delhi, New Delhi 110 007	20.	Ms. Shubha Mudgal 39–B, MIG Flats, Matia Khan Paharganj, New Delhi
21.	Dr Jayant Narlikar Inter-University Centre for Astronomy & Astrophysics, Post Bag Number 4, Ganesh Khind, Pune 411 007	22.	Shri Sandeep Pande Coordinator Asha (Hope) Lalpur A-893, Indira Nagar, Lucknow 226 016
23.	Shri Azim Premji Chairman, WIPRO, Doddakannelli Sarjapur Road, Bangalore 560 035	24.	Shri Vinod Raina Chair, Arera Council of Fellows E1/193, ARERA Colony, Bhopal 462 016

25. Prof. Anil Sadagopal
Professor of Education,
University of Delhi, E-13 Kalindi,
New Delhi 110 065

26. Ms. Teesta Seetalvad
Editor, *Communalism Combat,*
Sabrang Communications Pvt. Ltd.,
P.B. No. 28253, Juhu Post Office,
Mumbai 400 049

27. Dr Kiran Seth
Associate Professor, Production &
Industrial Engineering, IIT, New Delhi

28. Ms. Kumud Sharma
F-9–G, Munirka, DDA Flats,
New Delhi

29. Dr P.B. Sharma
Principal, Delhi College of Engineering,
Bawana Road, Delhi 110 042

30. Ms. Shanta Sinha
Secretary, M. Venkatarangaiya
Foundation, 28 West Marredpalli,
Road Number 1,
Secundrabad 500 026

31. Ms. Krishna Sobti
505–B, Purvasha Anand Lok Housing
Society, Mayur Vihar, Phase-I,
New Delhi 110 091

8. Member Secretary
Secretary, Department of Secondary and Higher Education, Ministry of Human Resource Development, Government of India.
9. Permanent Invitees:
    (i) Secretary, Department of Women and Child development.
    (ii) Secretary, Department of Youth Affairs and Sports.
    (iii) Secretary, Department of Culture.
    (iv) Secretary, Department of Science and Technology.
    (v) Secretary, Ministry of Social Justice and Empowerment.
    (vi) Secretary, Tribal Affairs.
    (vii) Secretary, Planning Commission.
    (viii) Secretary, Department of Labour.
    (ix) Secretary, Department of Industrial Policy and Promotion.
    (x) Secretary, Ministry of Information Technology.

Notes

1. Vide entry 20 of the Third List of Seventh Schedule of the Constitution.
2. Although a separate Department of Education was first created at the centre in December 1910, it was abolished in April 1923 as an economy measure. In the context of post-War reconstruction, the separate Department of Education was revived on 1st September 1945. In 1986, the Ministry of Human Resource Development (HRD) was set up covering *inter alia* Department of Education. In 2005, education was dealt with by two departments under the ministry, viz. (1) Elementary Education and Literacy and (2) Secondary and Higher Education. As a short hand, this

study will refer to the Education Ministry as the central authority, dealing with school education and general and technical higher education. The historical account is drawn from Cultural Heritage (Ministry of Culture and Tourism, New Delhi: 2002). Department of Culture was earlier part of the HRD Ministry.

3. Sunil Khilnani, *The Idea of India* (New Delhi: Penguin Books, 1997).
4. Jawaharlal Nehru, *Autobiography* (London: Oxford University Press, first edition 1936, epilogue added in 1940), 607.
5. A.H. Hanson, *The Process of Planning: A Study of India's Five Year Plans 1950–64* (London: Oxford University Press, 1966), 537.
6. Vide Draft Fifth Five-Year Plan (1974–79), Vol.II, 292.
7. Sarkaria Commission Report, 363.
8. A.H. Hanson in his detailed study of the Planning Commission over the 14-year period (1950–1964) has awarded high marks to the Commission in regard to its knowledge, status, organization and procedures. He calls.its procedure sophisticated. He faults it on the ground of neglect of social aspects, of the private sector, its failure to remain well-informed regarding crucial developments on the price front, its surrender to ideology in the matters of rural development and cooperative farming. A.H. Hanson, op. cit., 525–538.
9. Paul Streeten and Michael Lipton (Eds.), *The Crisis of Indian Planning: Economic Planning in the 1960s* (London: Oxford University Press, 1968), passim. The Fourth Plan (1969–74) was preceded by three Annual Plans (1966–69).
10. ARC: Report on Machinery for Planning (New Delhi, March 1968).
11. Arun Shourie, *Governance and the Sclerosis that has set in* (New Delhi: ASA/Rupa & Co., 2004), 95–143. Arun Shourie's book is journalistic and lacks a certain balance vide his tedious description of how some decisions about training programmes in the PEO were delayed.
12. J.P. Naik at p. 26 of his *Education in the Fourth Plan* (Bombay: Nachiketa Publications, 1968), lists them as below: (1) Preparing a Programme of Action for implementation of national policy of education as drawn up, *inter alia*, on the basis of constitutional directive principles, (2) Provision of guidance to State Governments in the preparation, implementation and evaluation of plans, (3) Defining minimum targets of national achievements in various sectors from time to time and assisting the less advanced sectors to reach them and (4) Provision of financial assistance to states by way of centrally assisted schemes and centrally sponsored schemes for implementation of the schemes of national significance selected in consultation with the states.

13. R.K. Koundinya and M.R. Kolhatkar, "District Planning and Role of Panchayati Raj Institutions", in S.S. Gadkari and M.R. Kolhatkar (Eds.), *Innovations in Public Administration* (New Delhi: Allied Publishers, 2000), 23.
14. ARC: *Report on Machinery for Planning*, op. cit., 87–93.
15. Draft Fifth Five-Year Plan 1974–79, Vol. II, (New Delhi: GoI, Planning Commission, 1973), 288.
16. Sarkaria Commission, op. cit., 383.
17. ARC Report, op. cit., 34–39.
18. M. Govind Rao, "Indian Fiscal Federalism from a Comparative Perspective", in Balveer Arora and Douglas Verney (Eds.), *Multiple Identities in a Single State* (New Delhi: Konark Publishers, 1995), 272–316.
19. Draft Fifth Five-Year Plan, op. cit., Vol. I, 87–91.
20. J.P. Naik, *Education in Fourth Plan* (Bombay: Nachiketa Publications, 1968), 19–21.
21. A. Mathew, *Ministry of Education: An Organizational History* (New Delhi: NIEPA, 1990), 23–59.
    Mathew stops at 1980. Five-Year Plan documents from the Sixth Plan onwards would give a picture beyond 1980. The precise contours of Tenth Plan programmes including Sarva Shiksha Abhiyan are given in the Tenth Five-Year Plan, Vol. II, (GoI, Planning Commission, 2002), 23–45. For Adult Education, The Annual Report of the Ministry for 2004–05 has been drawn upon (84–96).
22. J.P. Naik, *Educational Planning in India* (Bombay: Allied Publishers, 1965), 165–169.
23. Ibid., 169–170.
24. *Study Team Report on Centre-State Relations*, Vol. I, (New Delhi: ARC, GoI, 1968), 121–130.
25. Since these schemes were outside the State Plan and, therefore, had the effect of augmenting the effective size of a State Plan, states were tempted and central ministries had an interest in pushing their pet projects. This is an example of *picket fence model of federalism* referred to by David C. Nice which draws attention to solidarity among programme specialists (in this case education bureaucrats) irrespective of levels of government. How the CSSs proliferated has been detailed in the text. David C. Nice, *Federalism: The Politics of Inter-Governmental Relations* (New York: St. Martin's Press, 1987), 10–11.
26. This account is drawn from the *Report of the Expert Committee on Centrally Sponsored Schemes* (New Delhi: GoI, Planning Commission, 1985) (Chaired by Shri Ramamurthi).
27. (i) *Report of the Group of Officials on Centrally Sponsored Schemes* (New Delhi: GoI, Planning Commission, April 1987), (ii) *Report of the Committee of NDC*

on Centrally Sponsored Schemes (New Delhi: GoI, Planning Commission, January 1988).

28. Planning Commission, *Report of the Experts' Committee on Educational Expenditure* (Mimeo) (New Delhi, May 1979), 133.
29. J.B.G. Tilak, Centre-State Relations in the Financing of Education in India, *Comparative Educational Review*, Vol. 33, No.4, November, 1987, 450–480.
30. Y.P. Aggarwal and R.S. Thakur, *Concepts and Terms in Education Planning: A Guidebook* (New Delhi: NIEPA, 2003), 8.
31. J.P. Naik, *Education Commission and After* (New Delhi: Allied, 1983), 52–53.
32. H.W. Bjorkman and Kuldeep Mathur, *Policy, Technocracy and Development of Human Capital Policies in The Netherlands and India* (New Delhi: Manohar, 2002).
33. Gail P. Kelly, "Setting the Boundaries of Debate about Education", in Philip G. Altbach (Ed.), *Excellence in Education* (New York: Prometheus Books, 1985), 35–42.
34. Sarkaria Report, 381.
35. Sarkaria Report, 392.
36. S.C. Kashyap, op. cit., 78.
37. Rekha Saxena, *Situating Federalism* (New Delhi: Manohar, 2006), Chapter 7 (250–312).
38. Abu Baker, *The Union and the States in Education* (Ajmer: Shabda Prakashan, 1976), 109.
39. Kothari Report, 18.35.
40. S.R. Maheshwari, *Government through Consultation: Advisory Committees for Independent Administration* (New Delhi: IIPA, 1972), 366.
41. NPE 1986/92, para 10.2.

7 Elementary Education and Literacy

While considering the impact of federalism in the elementary education sub-sector, covering 6–14 age group, we are required to examine also Early Childhood Care and Education (ECCE)(3–6 years of age), which makes elementary education sustainable. The accumulated consequence of failure to universalize elementary education at an early date has given rise to the burden of high illiteracy. Hence, we also need to consider adult illiteracy in the working age group of 15–35.

Early Childhood Care and Education

This programme has suffered because it is a baby of two departments: Women and Child Development Department, and Education Department. Let us first approach it from the angle of Women and Child Development Department.

Role of Women and Child Development Department

As noted earlier, the new research regarding human development shows that the period of 0–6 years of age is the most critical period in the development of the child when his/her capabilities (health, nutrition, learning abilities etc.) are largely determined. The Eleventh Plan document quotes data to show that India has the largest number of children in the world who are malnourished and India's rate of malnutrition is worse than that in Africa on average.[1] About pre-school education, the Planning Commission points out that ICDS was started in 1975 with a view to deliver a package of six services to the women and children[2] of which pre-school education is the weakest link, although there is incontrovertible research that pre-school education is critical to improve primary school readiness of the child of functionally illiterate parents and thus improving drop-out rates.[3] The Planning Commission advocates universalization of ICDS which would of course benefit pre-school education component also. Unfortunately, there was a financial constraint and ICDS could not be extended to all the development blocks.

The number of blocks has increased from 5,652 at the beginning of the Tenth Plan to 6,291 blocks by March 2007 covering 13.8 lakh

Anganwadi centres. However, the second Anganwadi worker is yet to be appointed. The scheme received a much needed boost when the Supreme Court ordered the ICDS to be universalized under its monitoring strategy for the Right to Food.[4] Apart from the resource constraint, an additional negative factor is that the World Bank, the main funding agency is apparently skeptical about the pre-school education component of ICDS. Moreover, the Social Welfare Departments of the State Governments which have to deal with the cadre of Anganwadi workers of the ICDS are also not much enthusiastic about pre-school education component.

Role of Education Department

The Education Commission (1966) called this stage as pre-school education and defined its objectives carefully.[5] It gave credit to the Sargent Plan (1944) which emphasized its significance and recommended adequate provisions therefor. It noted the slow growth in the number of pre-schools between 1950–51 to 1965–66 (from 303 institutions with enrolment of 28,000 to 3,500 institutions with enrolment of 2,50,000, all of them in urban areas) and also acknowledged the role of the Central Social Welfare Board and Community Development Administration which together ran 20,000 'Balwadis' with a total enrolment of 6,00,000. It suggested expansion of pre-school education facilities to cover 5 per cent of children in the age group 3–5, but this was one of the recommendations, which was totally ignored by the committee of the MPs whose report formed the basis of the NPE 1968.

The NPE 1986 gave due emphasis to ECCE. It noted that the National Policy on Children emphasizes investment in the development of young child particularly children from sections of the population in which first generation learners predominate. Hence, it suggested integration of ECCE with Integrated Child Development Scheme (ICDS) and involvement of the local community. It resolved to bring about a full integration of child care and pre-primary education, both as a feeder and strengthening factor for primary education and for human resource development in general.[6]

On the implementation side, the Education Ministry has not shown the same concern. When Article 45 of the Constitution was amended in 2002, ECCE replaced elementary education as a Directive Principle of State Policy but while the original Article 45 had laid down a time limit of 10 years for elementary education, there is no such time limit for ECCE. The Education Ministry is more focused on Sarva Shiksha Abhiyan for UEE and as would be seen, wishes to extend the goal of universalization upward to Secondary education through Rashtriya Madhyamik Shiksha Abhiyan (RMSA). The Tenth Plan mid-term appraisal document, however, does talk about SSA having a component of one year ECCE which can be universalized to cover 2.4 crore children in a phased manner. It is stated that existing coverage of pre-primary classes in schools is over 1.1 crore.[7] So, there is a lot of leeway to be made.

Elementary Education

The progress of school education and literacy in the post-independence India has been profoundly affected by the way federalism operated in the education field. The basic difference between colonial India and independent India is that the latter has a Constitution which has parts dedicated to Fundamental Rights (Part III) and the Directive Principles of State Policy (Part IV), which Granville Austin, calls the conscience of the Constitution comprising respectively the negative and positive obligations towards the goal of social revolution.[8] The initial approach of the Rights Sub-committee of the Constituent Assembly was to make no distinction between positive obligations and negative liberties, but in the context of the role of the court, the positioning of the "Rights" and "Principles" was liable to change. The right to free elementary education was first included among the justiciable rights but then taken out.[9] Article 45 as originally enacted provided that, the State shall endeavour to provide, within a period of ten years from the commencement of the Constitution, for free and compulsory education for all children until they complete the age of 14 years. This has to be read along with the provision of Article 41 which talks, *inter alia*, of state's making effective provision for right to education and work, within the limit of its economic capacity and development and Article 39 about certain principles of policy to be followed by the state of which principle (f) relates to children. This Article in the original Constitution read: "That childhood and youth are protected against exploitation and against moral and material abandonment", which really was in the nature of prevention of abuse. As amplified by the Constitution (42nd Amendment) Act, 1976, it carries a more positive connotation with the addition of the following prefatory remarks: "That children are given opportunities and facilities to develop in a healthy manner." Article 45 was binding on both Central and State Governments and it was the duty of the Planning Commission to plan for implementation and provide funds for the same.

This directive had in effect compressed the Sargent Plan target of 40 years to attain Universalization of elementary education and it is interesting to note the political process which brought about this modification because it was a precursor of periodical conferences of state education ministers to be called in the future by the union education minister. It was a smaller body than the CABE, the political executive committee so to say of CABE. The All-India Education Conference held in January 1948 and presided over by Union Education Minister comprised all State

Education Ministers peremptorily rejected the 40-year limit of Sargent Plan in following words: "After the realization of our independence, we cannot be content with programmes which were considered adequate for the old regime. Thus, no one will for a moment tolerate policy that forty years must elapse before the full scheme of basic education for all the inhabitants of this land can be implemented. In fact even half that period will seem to many to savour of delay and procrastination. Educational progress can be so accelerated that we reach our objective within a much shorter time … . It is the *birthright* of every individual to receive at least the basic education."[10]

Note the reference to old regime and to education as birthright, a terminology reminiscent of the French Revolution which marked the launch of the project of the French nation. As pointed out by John Laska, an American scholar,[11] the education conference departed from the Sargent Plan by limiting the programme of compulsory basic education to five years in the first instance from the original eight years. It was in terms of the decision of this conference that Article 45 reduced the period for attainment of universalization of elementary education to ten years from the original 40 years. CABE shortly thereafter appointed a Committee on Ways and Means of Financing Education, under the chairmanship of B.G. Kher (1949), then Chief Minister of Bombay Province. The Committee assumed that compulsion for age group 6–11 would be introduced within a period of 10 years and that the compulsion could be extended to the age group 11–14 within a further period of five years. In this, the Kher Committee was following the lead given by the Education Conference in January 1949. The Committee estimated the expenditure on compulsory education for the age group 6–11 at Rs 233.41 crore for five years as against which the total provincial budget estimate for 1948–49 was only Rs 30.96 crore for all education including secondary and higher. The Committee did not unfortunately work out a definite plan for meeting the financial obligations except making following recommendations:

- The provincial government should spend 20 per cent of their budget on education.
- The Central Government should spend 10 per cent of its budget on education.
- In respect of provincial plans, 70 per cent of expenditure should be borne by local bodies/provinces and the remaining 30 per cent by the Centre.
- There should be economy in construction of buildings, with the cost per sq. ft. not exceeding Rs 3.
- A higher teacher-pupil ratio of 1:40 for the first five years should be adopted for the sake of economy as well as to overcome shortage of the teachers.

- Private resource mobilization: Charitable trusts should allocate adequate income for expenditure on education.
- This responsibility must be undertaken without detriment to existing facilities for secondary and higher education.

Laska has noted[12] that the CABE while accepting the Kher Report deleted the word 'existing' in the last mentioned recommendation.[13] The Kher Committee recommendation implied that the budgets of existing secondary and higher education institutions should be protected but that there should be no further budgetary support for the same. By deleting the word 'existing', State Education Ministers in effect wanted to have their cake and eat it too, in as much as they wanted expansion of secondary education and higher education side by side with primary education, thus undermining the priority of primary education.

It is all the same surprising to note that after the Constitution was adopted in 1950, the whole matter was not reviewed because, it was no longer a decision of an All-India Education Conference of 1949 or a decision of CABE, but a constitutional directive principle. Action ought to have been taken to provide annual funding through State Plans supplemented by the Central Plan and other means of resource mobilization in addition to those specified by the Kher Committee to achieve the goal by 1966. But in practice it was not taken. The question arises, Why?

It is evident that the Kher Committee report lacked the necessary vision and the foresight to lay down a roadmap for achieving the constitutionally prescribed target and working out the financial ways and means in sufficient annualized and source-wise break-up also showing the resource shares of the Centre, the states and the local bodies. Maulana Azad, the Union Education Minister, pleaded helplessness in the face of resource constraint thus passing the buck to the Planning Commission. In the final analysis, the buck stops at Jawaharhal Nehru. Judith M. Brown, the British biographer of Nehru, has insightfully observed that Nehru stood firmly in support of two of the weakest sections of Indian society, viz., women (vide his support for the Hindu Code Bill) and ex-untouchables vide the passing of Untouchability (Offences) Act and vide the first constitutional amendment providing for 'reservation' of seats in educational institutions for the SCs/STs and did have some amount of success, but when it came to sources of structural inequality in the Indian society, viz., land and education, there was a gulf between Nehru's vision and the numbers in his party who had ideological and vested interests in protecting inequalities in rural society. In the case of education in particular, Article 45 made free mass education part of the *rhetoric of new India's national identity*. The need was great. At independence, literacy stood at only 14 per cent and this masked much lower figures for girls and generally for states like Madhya Pradesh, Rajasthan and Uttar Pradesh, where it was 11 per cent. In the age group 6–11 the GER (Gross Enrolment Ratio) was 25 per cent and in the age group 11–14, it was a little above 8 per cent. Female-male disparity ratio for primary stage was 36 per cent and upper primary 22 per cent. Judith Brown notes that, at least till the inception of the Second Five-Year Plan, Nehru was keenly aware of the need for action. He personally moved the resolution on basic education at the Avadi session of the Congress in January 1955 and his speech shows that he was also aware of the need for ECCE for making basic education sustainable. The resolution called on State Governments to further this policy (of basic education) within a period of ten years but Nehru significantly added: "What I consider very essential is pre-basic training, i.e., training of the child, almost from the very moment of its birth". Brown noted the sad sequel to the Avadi resolution: "Mid-way through the decade in which radical changes in provision of mass education up to the age of fourteen years was supposed to occur, little progress had taken place. Education clearly had a low priority in the government's planned expenditure and allocations to education actually dropped from 8.7 per cent of the total outlay in the First Plan to 6.7 per cent in the Second Plan. Nehru had so much work on his desk that other matters took up his attention and successive education ministers (Maulana Azad till February 1958 and thereafter K.K. Shrimali and Humayun Kabir) who were primarily responsible did not have the authority that Prime Minister might have wielded to push the States forward. In the states, education was not glamorous or politically significant and in the days of the crisis of planning, a massive injection of cash to transform provision was not forthcoming. Consequently, one path way to a long-term change in attitudes and access to a resource which could change lives was still closed off to millions of Indian citizens despite Nehru's understanding of the significance of such facilities to the larger population for growth of the nation".[14]

So it remained and remains an elusive goal; the Education Commission (1966) reset it to 1986, the NPE 1986 shifted it to 2000 and the latest target date was 2010. There is, however, grave doubt whether India would achieve UEE including access, enrolment, retention and achievement even by 2020, especially as regards the most vulnerable sections – the rural, tribal, female sections of the population. As observed by Myron Weiner,[15] social legislation in India is rarely enforced by bureaucracy. The legislation demonstrates that one is committed to all that is modern and progressive and if the laws are not enforced, the fault lies not with the legislators or bureaucrats but with a society that is not responsive to the law's injunctions. The government officials while speaking in international meetings would ascribe the failure to achieve universal education to the country's poverty.

In the light of what is long known but well articulated by Judith Brown, one has to hold that, prima facie it is the centralized federalism dominated by the Congress party at both the Central and State Government levels which was the main culprit behind the tragic failure to achieve universalization by 1966 as envisaged by the Kher Committee. School education was undoubtedly a state subject, but the State Chief ministers followed the lead of the Planning Commission in allowing normal expansion of secondary and higher education and special expansion of technical education to create manpower for plan schemes. Laska after a very careful analysis of the three Five-Year Plans and the Report of the Working Group on Education for the Third Plan notes that while laying down targets for expansion of primary education so as to achieve the GER of 71.7 per cent by 1966 the Working Group did not recommend restriction on the expansion of secondary, higher and technical education. It referred to the "irresistible claims of expansion" and the well-known and persistent public demand for the opening of high-schools even in rural and sparsely populated areas which cannot be denied for any great length of time. It also referred to private enterprise as one of the reasons for excessive expansion of secondary education.[16]

In its detailed analysis of the issues involved in the UEE including universal provision, universal enrolment and universal retention, Education Commission has in fact pointed out that there was increase in wastage and stagnation in the period 1946–47 to 1965–66 as compared with the period 1911–12 to 1946–47. In other words, not only was there failure on the part of politicians and planners but also slackness on the part of educational bureaucracy.[17] The Education Commission recommended that the goal of UEE should be achieved by 1986.

The progress of UEE from 1968, i.e., the year of NPE 1968 till 2010 may be reviewed from two angles: policy and programmes on the one hand and legislation on the other.

Policy and Programmes

The 1968 policy based on the committee of MPs' report could not be categorical. Its formulation in regard to the UEE was: "strenuous efforts should be made for the early fulfilment of the Directive Principle under Article 45 of the Constitution seeking to provide free and compulsory education for all children up to the age of 14". As J.P. Naik observes, this does not take us an inch beyond Article 45 of the Constitution. In his posthumous publication, Naik appears to consider universalization of elementary education realizable by 1990–91 if resort was to be had to non-formal modes of education also.[18]

As is well known, when Rajiv Gandhi came to power in November 1984 he made revision of NPE 1968 as his top priority and the NPE 1986 set the target of the year 2000 for achieving the goal of UEE[19] for which purpose it formulated the well-known programme of Operation Blackboard to strengthen educational infrastructure (school buildings, two teachers and provision of teaching-learning materials). Unfortunately, the enhanced finances could not be sustained in the face of fiscal difficulties and as part of the structural adjustment programme from 1991 onwards, the country was required to rely on foreign assistance for financing District Primary Education Programme (DPEP). DPEP had ambitious targets of reducing drop-out rate to less than 10 per cent, reducing disparities among gender and social groups in the enrolment to less than 5 per cent and improving the level of learning achievement compared to the baseline surveys, and was accompanied by introduction of Mid-Day Meal Programme from 1995. These official programmes were supplemented by innovative programmes like EGS (Education Guarantee Scheme) first started in the state of Madhya Pradesh in 1993, with employment of para teachers to help spread elementary education in the tribal areas. As official programmes were found to be adversely affected by the phenomenon of teacher absenteeism ranging from 25 per cent to 50 per cent, private schools came into existence all of which may not be recognized ones. As foreign assistance decreased, DPEP was replaced by the umbrella scheme called Sarva Shiksha Abhiyan (SSA) in 2000 which included EGS under the nomenclature of Alternative and Innovative Schemes. The target date for universal enrolment, retention and achievement was 2010 as against the World Millennium Development Goals date of 2015.

Legislation for Free and Compulsory Education

When NPE 1986–92 came to be reviewed by the Ramamurti Committee appointed by the NF government of V.P. Singh in 1990, it suggested enshrining the right to education as a fundamental right.[20] But, the CABE Committee on Policy chaired by a Congress party stalwart Janardan Reddy (former CM and Education Minister of Andhra Pradesh), rejected this recommendation on the ground that a legalistic approach to the UEE would not be desirable unless the country is financially and politically in a position to take all measures necessary for enforcing the guarantee.[21] This was apparently a sensible approach but the introduction of legislative compulsion for UEE being part of the Congress ideology since 1911 (Gokhale legislation) as well as having international (UNESCO) support, there was slow but inexorable progress towards the legislative goal whose milestones are traced below.

The Supreme Court in the Mohini Jain case, decided on 31st July 1992, held that the right to education flows directly from right to life under Article 21 and that the state is under a constitutional mandate to provide educational institutions *at all levels* including higher education for the benefit of citizens.[22] Since this was not good law, in the famous Unnikrishnan case (1993), the Supreme Court itself reviewed its earlier decision in Mohini Jain case and relating the fundamental right to the Directive Principle in Article 45 laid down that the right to free education up to the age of 14 years is a fundamental right.[23] This became binding on the government; however, the Congress-led coalition presided over by P.V. Narasimha Rao, simply sat on the issue. It was only after the UF government led by Deve Gowda came to power that the government appointed a Committee of State Education Ministers to study the implications of the proposal in August 1996. The Committee, reporting in June 1997, recommended amendment of the Constitution to make UEE as a fundamental right.[24] While opining against a central legislation, it also recommended constitution of a group of experts to examine financial requirements of the states, to identify measures for mobilization of additional resources and to determine suitable sharing arrangements between the Centre and the State Governments. Such a group was formed in 1997 which reporting in 1999 estimated the financial requirement at Rs 1,36,822 crore for the next 10 years.[25] This may be contrasted with the estimate of Rs 233.41 crore for five years, i.e., Rs 466.82 crore for 10 years made by Kher Committee in 1949.

Meanwhile, the process of constitutional amendment which was set in motion with the introduction in the Rajya Sabha of the 83rd Constitutional Amendment in July 1997 culminated in the Constitution (86th Amendment) being passed on 13th December, 2002. The amendment had three parts: (1) addition of a new Article 21A empowering the state to pass a law of compulsion for age group 6–14, (2) extension of the Directive Principle in Article 45 to early childhood care and education, and (3) addition of a fundamental duty of parents to provide opportunities for education for children in the age group 6–14 vide Article 51–A(k). The amendment to Article 21, though gazetted could not be enforced unless suitable legislation was enacted.

With the programmatic strengthening for elementary education in the form of SSA, the making of education as a fundamental right receded in to the background especially in the context of projected heavy financial implications. When the UPA-I government led by the Congress, came to power in March 2004, it revived the CABE in July 2004 and appointed a CABE committee under the chairmanship of Kapil Sibal, then Minister of State for Science and Technology for framing of appropriate legislation. The Committee reported in June 2005.[26] Notable recommendations of the Committee related to liability of unaided schools to admit at least 25 per cent of children from amongst those belonging to weaker sections, a schedule giving norms and standards for a school and a National Commission for Elementary Education for monitoring and implementation of the Act. The Committee also asked NIEPA to work out financial implications of the enforcement of legislation. These ranged between Rs 4,36,459 crore to Rs 3,21,196 crore for 2006–2012. The higher estimate was on the basis of pupil-teacher ratio (PTR) of 35 and teacher salary as per Kendriya Vidyalaya Sangathan (KVS) scales and the lower estimate was on the basis of the PTR of 35 and teacher salary as per average state scales.

The legislation could not be taken forward partly because of heavy financial implications, but also partly due to the focus of the then Union Minister, HRD on implementation of the OBC quota for admission to prestigious educational institutions like IITs and IIMs. When UPA-II came to power in May 2009 the pending Right to Education Bill received high priority and the requisite legislation was got passed and has been enforced from April 2010. Press reports indicate that the process of passing the legislation and enforcing it was facilitated by reduction of financial estimates to Rs 1,71,000 crore and the award by the Thirteenth Finance Commission to the tune of Rs 25,000 crore for five years to the states for implementation of the Right to Education.[27] This implies that suitable adjustments in PTR for the next three years and salary scales have been made. Even with this adjustment, it is estimated that 12 lakh more teachers especially in the northern states and West Bengal and Orissa would have to be appointed.

As distinguished from the CABE Committee draft Bill, the Right to Education Act provides that the monitoring of the implementation of the Act would be done by the existing National Commission for Protection of Rights of Children and corresponding State Commissions. Many State Governments do not have such authorities and they would have to set up the same. There are several thorny issues relating to the implementation of the Right to Education Act, including adherence to PTR, curriculum and examination policy, role of elite schools etc., but since my main focus is on reaching the goal of UEE of an "equitable quality" (a term used by Kapil Sibal Committee) in the shortest possible time, within the framework of the federal polity, it would suffice to make some observations on issues relating to funding, educational outcomes and the role of the private sector.

Pattern of Centre-State Sharing of Funding

SSA programme would continue to be the vehicle for the implementation of the Act. The current year's (2010–11) centre-state sharing formula (55:45) is not acceptable to most states which are in financial difficulties and the opposition-ruled states have already raised their voice in favour of

100 per cent central funding because of the element of compulsion entailed. The sharing formula is no doubt required to be liberalized, perhaps upto 75:25. It is also noted that major funding from the Centre is flowing from Prarambhik Shiksha Kosh which is made up of revenues received for education cess for elementary education introduced since the budget of 2004–05. One commentator who believes in dominant public sector funding of the UEE, observed with reference to the budgetary allocation for the programme in the financial year 2010–11 (Rs 25,011 crore) that it puts a serious question mark on the seriousness of the Union Government in the implementation of the Right to Education Act.[28]

Quality Dimension of UEE

The UEE has to be considered in all its aspects of access, enrolment, retention, and academic achievement. According to the latest report of Pratham, an NGO (Fifth Annual "State of Education" Report), the government schools appear to fail on the simple test of ability of children of standard V to read standard II level text which is a very modest ability test. The scores vary from 76 per cent in Madhya Pradesh to 20.2 per cent in Jammu & Kashmir. The country average is 50.3 per cent. The worst performers (40% or less) include Assam, Rajasthan, Tamil Nadu and Uttar Pradesh apart from Jammu & Kashmir. The scores on the ability of children in standard V to solve division problems range from 65 per cent in Madhya Pradesh to about 12 per cent in Tamil Nadu.[29] These scores present a very depressing picture regarding the teaching done by the teachers and learning internalized by the students. What if the tests are calibrated higher as they ought to be and how would the country perform if subjected to international comparison? The evolving scenario is quite depressing as regards the academic achievement dimensions.

The Role of Private Unrecognized Schools

It is well known that public schools in India suffer from disfunctionalities like large scale teacher absenteeism and non-performance by teachers actually attending especially in the public sector. This is the reason for low reading and arithmetical scores referred to earlier. According to the findings of the 1999 PROBE (Public Report on Basic Education) Report, covering the five states of Uttar Pradesh, Bihar, Himachal Pradesh, Rajasthan and Madhya Pradesh (a report incidentally with which Amartya Sen was associated), in a large random sample of government schools, in only half was there any teaching activity during a surprise check and in one-third, the Principal was absent. As a result, poor parents not only in urban areas but in rural areas also, are increasingly resorting to private schools and/or tuitions. By 1994, enrolment in rural primary private schools was 30 per cent and in urban areas, the proportion was estimated to be 80 per cent.[30]

But most of these private schools are unrecognized. As the British educationist James Tooley has emphasized, eminent scholars like Amaryta Sen and international organizations like UNESCO have tended to de-emphasize the role of the private schools in the UEE. Their example is naturally followed by the respective national authorities. *Economic Times* reported that post-Right to Education Scenario, lakh of unrecognized schools across the country are liable to face action unless they get themselves regularized within the next three years.[31]

The prevalent prejudice against private schools and private tuitions may be brought home by further evidence of the Pratichi Trust (India) Report entitled, "Child Report on West Bengal".[32] Incidentally, it is a follow-up of PROBE report for the state of West Bengal. A comparison of two successive reports (2001–02 and 2008–09) shows that there has been significant improvement in the performance and coverage of primary education in West Bengal. According to the report, as summarized by Amartya Sen, average attendance increased from 58 per cent to 75 per cent and it may be partly due to mid-day meal scheme. However, in spite of the reduction of proportion of students in classes 3 and 4 who would not write their names going down from 30 per cent to 5 per cent, the report noted that the proportion of primary students in classes 3 and 4, who cannot read is still 17 per cent, those who cannot write is 19 per cent and those who cannot do simple arithmetic is 26 per cent. Moreover, there was real regression in the matter of dependence of children who need private tuition. This proportion had gone up from 57 per cent to 64 per cent. The conclusion of the author is that this is due to the tendency of teachers to give home tasks, and the recommendation is that home work needs to be banned. Unfortunately, the possibility that teachers are not devoting themselves as diligently as they should to their duties in the class is not at all considered. Evidently, parents of first generation learners are bound to resort to private tuition if they find that their children are not taught adequately during school hours.

The issue of private unrecognized schools and private tuition should not be turned into a polemical one. There is need to squarely face the fact that public primary school system in India is highly politicized, that teachers are unionized, that this has resulted in the large-scale disfunctionality of public schooling and that the authorities have to approach the issue of regularization of private unrecognized schools pragmatically. Such private schools of course would charge modest fees but in the goal of UEE, the emphasis has to be on universalization rather than on the "free" (gratuitous) aspect and "compulsory" aspect of it. We have to realize that the horizon of the goal of UEE in independent India has successively receded from the year 1960 through the years 1986, and

2000, to the year 2010. The Right to Education should help in realizing the goal at least by 2020. It should not be allowed to act as a hindrance to attainment of the goal in a situation where in 2005, the drop-out rate at the primary stage was still 50 per cent.[33]

We now turn to the equally important goal of eradication of adult illiteracy.

Adult Literacy

The literacy percentage in independent India has risen very slowly except during the decade 1981–91 as shown in successive censuses:

Table 7.1

Literacy Percentage (1951–2001)

Year	*Percentage of Literacy (Overall)*
1951	16.60
1961	24.00
1971	29.45
1981	36.23
1991	52.02
2001	64.08

Source: Compiled by author from various sources.

India inherited the problem of mass adult illiteracy as a colonial legacy, but the Central Government did not quite get involved in it till the Janata government started the National Adult Education Programme (NAEP) in October 1978. Earlier, the role of the Central Government in the adult literacy programme was limited at the most to providing training support, the States being left to their own devices. There was a lot of terminological confusion, the programme being renamed "social education", immediately after independence, but following the dictates of UNESCO, a Fundamental Education Centre was formed in 1956 in the ministry and became part of NCERT when it was established in 1961 and remained there till 1971. Later on, it was transferred back to the ministry. The setting up of the Directorate Adult Education under the Ministry in 1974 gave an administrative anchor to the programme.[34]

Unfortunately, the detailed analysis, diagnosis and remediation as set out by the Kothari Commission[35] tended to be neglected. It had noted that owing to the failure effectively to universalize elementary education, India was becoming more and more non-literate after every ten years in the sense that while the percentage of literacy was going up, the number of illiterate people was also going up after every census. It called the situation intolerable and bluntly stated that indifference to the problem will not remain unpunished. It emphasized the need for a variety of approaches with major emphasis on a mass campaign approach (as in the period 1937–39). It commended Maharashtra's scheme of *Gram Shikshan Mohim* which exploited the local village patriotism to eliminate illiteracy from the village and required the teachers and all local educated men and women to work for literacy. There were weaknesses in the preparation for the *Mohim* (campaign) and follow-up which needed to be made good. Thus, pilots needed to be replicated and scaled up to taluka and district levels. Unfortunately, the crisis of planning in the period 1965–72 involving a three-year plan holiday (1966–1969), the Indo-Pak war etc. put an end to the enthusiasm for the Gram Shikshan Mohim which through the channel of *emulative federalism* could have improved the situation substantially. Education Commission set before the country the target of eradication of illiteracy within 20 years with the national percentage of literacy projected to go up to 60 per cent by 1971 and 80 per cent by 1976. As noted, this target had not been attained even by the year 2001.

With the launching of the National Adult Education Programme (NAEP) in October 1978 during the Janata regime, the programme became time-bound with the target of covering the entire illiterate adult population within a period of five years. The approach was essentially centre-based. The successor Congress government (1980–84) continued the programme but half-heartedly. Indira Gandhi was suspicious of voluntary organizations which ran the centres under the Janata government believing that they harboured Jayaprakash Narayan's followers. Her political instincts even led her to appoint a Commission to investigate Gandhian institutions. A policy for the Voluntary Organizations (VOs) was framed in the Sixth Plan (1980–85). The programme itself was renamed RFLP (Rural Functional Literacy Project), but without any sense of a mission. The NPE 1986 led to the setting up of National Literacy Mission Authority (NLMA), to supervise the Centre-based programme. The concept of a social mission conveyed a sense of urgency to complete the programme within a time frame, which however was lacking.[36]

The Ramamurti Committee recommended continuance of the NLMA and its campaign approach, but it could not make up its mind about the best model. It was torn between the concepts of "adult literacy" and "adult education". While it recognized that effective UEE alone was the ultimate solution "to ensure that no child in the early nineties shall grow into an illiterate adult in the next century",[37] it could not suggest what to do with the problem of adult illiterates who were on our hands. It suggested further studies to identify the best model. It was only with the success of the Total Literacy Campaign (TLC) in Kerala (Ernakulam district) and Karnataka in the 1990s, that the Centre-based approach gave way to the campaign approach. The TLC as it has evolved and promoted is described as area specific, time-bound, volunteer-based, cost-effective, participatory and outcome oriented. It is conducted in three phases – TLC phase, post-literacy (PL) phase and the continuing education (CE) phase.

At the end of the Tenth Plan over three-fourths of the male population and over half of the female population is literate and sustainable threshold level of 75 per cent was expected to have been achieved by 2007. The goals of AE programme in the Eleventh Plan are to achieve 80 per cent literacy rate, reduce gender gap in literacy to 10 per cent, reduce regional, social and general disparities and extend coverage of NLM programme to 35 and above age-group – all this with a focus on SCs/STs, minorities and rural women, tribal areas etc. More recently, there is a perceived shift to the campaign of Sakshar Bharat (with focus on women). The HRD Minister has stated that adult illiteracy would be eradicated by 2020, the same target year as for UEE.

The Concept of Proximate Literacy

The Ramamurti Committee noted that Ernakulam experiment in which a district with 90 per cent literacy attained 98 per cent literacy in a matter of a year had no lessons for backward North Indian states where large masses of Indian people are alienated from the benefits of education.[38] However, how functional literacy can be attained when there are adequate incentives, was demonstrated by the spread of the Green Revolution in the Punjab and Haryana. This may be dubbed the Punjab model of proximate literacy based on the theorization of Kaushik Basu and James E. Foster,[39] who distinguished between two types of illiterate persons, a proximate illiterate who lives in a household with at least one literate member and hence has access to the public good in the form of agricultural/health information and an isolated illiterate person whose household has no literate member. According to authors, effective literacy rate which is a combination of *usual* literacy rate and *proximate* literacy rate was found to be quite high in states like Haryana and Punjab which correlates with the high rate of diffusion of new technology for farming.

This idea has resonance with the thesis of well-known historian C.A. Bayly, that the North Indian communication network was thicker and hence more effective than apparent.[40] Bayly thesis briefly is as below: Density and flexibility of indigenous routines of social communication explain why North Indians were able to make such striking use of the printing press, the newspaper and the public meeting once these innovations finally began to spread rapidly amongst them in the 1830s and 1840s. The density of social communication helps to explain why political leaders in a poor country with a relatively low rate of general literacy should have been able to create a widely diffused and popular nationalist movement so easily.

Although the Basu-Foster concept of proximate literacy in the background of Bayly thesis, can explain the success of Punjab model, it by no means condones the collective failure of the Centre and the states to eradicate adult illiteracy in India even till 2011 which would mark the centenary year of Gokhale's Draft Bill for the Compulsory Education in the Central Assembly.[41] We may hope that the latest campaign of Sakshar Bharat with focus on females may enable India to attain 80 per cent female literacy by 2020 which in 2001 was 53.7 per cent.

Conclusion

Our analysis of the tortuous path toward UEE/Eradication of Adult Illiteracy (EAI) shows that under the developmental federalist phase of Nehru's leadership it was indecisiveness of the Planning Commission after Jawaharlal Nehru's strategic attention towards this area was diverted by the successive crises of the Second and the Third Plans and national security (in the form of Indo-China war), that was responsible for slow progress, thus allowing free rein to state education ministers to permit the natural expansion of secondary and higher education while paying lip sympathy to the constitutional directive of time-bound UEE. The policy changes of 1968 and 1986 tended to be bureaucratic exercises but it was the intellectual leadership of the (Gandhian) Ramamurti which prompted an activist judiciary to prod the political leadership to amend the Constitution and pass legislation for compulsory elementary education.

Incidentally, one may also note the difference in approach to the problem adopted by various coalitions in the federal parliamentary polity of India. Where coalitions are stable (Congress-led coalition 1991–96, NDA 1999–2004) they are daunted by financial implications and delay the matter by entering into negotiations with the State Governments regarding relative share on which there is generally no unanimity; where coalitions are not stable, there is a tendency to be more radical (NF/UF coalitions).

Notes

1. Eleventh Five-Year Plan, Vol. II, 137.
2. The package of six services comprise: supplementary nutrition, immunization, health check up, health and nutrition education, referral service and pre-school education.
3. Eleventh Five-Year Plan, Vol. II, 149.
4. *Outlook*, 2nd March, 2009.
5. Kothari Report, para 7.03.

6. NPE 1986/92, paras 5.1 to 5.4.
7. As quoted in Eleventh Five-Year Plan, Vol. II, 10.
8. Granville Austin, *The Indian Constitution: Cornerstone of a Nation* (New Delhi: Oxford University Press, 1972), 50.
9. Ibid., 79.
10. Report of the All-India Education Conference, January, (New Delhi: GoI, Ministry of Education, 1948).
11. John A. Laska, *Planning and Educational Development in India* (New York: Teachers' College Press, 1968), 64.
12. Ibid., 65.
13. CABE, Silver Jubilee Souvenir (New Delhi, 1960), 209.
14. Judith M. Brown, *Nehru: A Political Life* (New Haven & London: Yale University Press, 2003), 235–236.
15. Myron Weiner, *The Child and the State in India* (New Delhi: Oxford University Press, 1991), 205.
16. John A. Laska, op. cit.
17. Kothari Report, para 7.19.
18. J.P. Naik, *Education Commission and After* (New Delhi: Allied Publishers, 1983; 1997 Reprint by APH Publishers vide 50, 222).
19. NPE 1986, para 5.12.
20. Ramamurti Report, 124.
21. CABE Committee on Policy, January 1992, 25.
22. *Mohini Jain vs. State of Karnataka*, 1992 (3) SCC 666.
23. *K.P. Unnikrishnan vs. State of Andhra Pradesh*, 1993 (1) SCC 645.
24. Government of India, Ministry of Education: Report of the Committee of State Education Ministers on Implications of the Proposal to make Elementary Education a Fundamental Right (New Delhi, January 1997).
25. Government of India, Ministry of Education: Expert Group Report on Financial Requirements for making Elementary Education a Fundamental Right (New Delhi, 1998).
26. CABE: Report of the Committee on Free and Compulsory Education Bill and other issues related to Elementary Education (New Delhi, June 2005).
27. *Economic Times*, Mumbai, 2nd April, 2010.
28. J.B.G. Tilak, "Budget 2010: Neither Vision nor Policy for Education", *EPW*, 27th March, 2010, 60–64.
29. Quoted in Sudipto Mandal, "Learning about Learning", *Economic Times*, Mumbai, 4th Feb., 2010.
30. PROBE Report as quoted by James Tooley, *The Beautiful Tree: A Personal Journey into How the World's Poorest People are Educating Themselves* (New Delhi: Penguin Books, 2009), 23–25.

31. *Economic Times*, 5th April, 2010.
32. *The Hindu*, 19th and 20th December, 2009 (Child Report on West Bengal, Parts I and II).
33. As quoted in Karin Hulshof, UNICEF India representative, Follow the Learning Curve, vide *Times of India*, 1st April, 2010.
34. A. Mathew, *Ministry of Education: An Organizational History* (New Delhi: NIEPA, 1990), 43–60.
35. Kothari Report, 778–805.
36. NPE 1986, para 4.10–4.13.
37. Ramamurti Report, 201.
38. Ibid., 199.
39. Kaushik Basu and James E. Foster, *On Measuring Literacy* (Washington DC: The World Bank: Office of Sr. Vice-President, Development Economics).
40. C.A. Bayly, *Empire and Information: Intelligence Gathering and Social Communication in India, 1780–1970* (Cambridge: Cambridge University Press, 1996).
41. B.R. Nanda, *Gokhale: The Indian Moderates and the British Raj* (Delhi: Oxford University Press, 1977), 386–394.

8 Secondary and Higher Secondary Education

The Crucial Middle Stage

Whereas the performance of the Indian federal polity in the matter of universalization of elementary education and the allied sub-sectors can be said to be dismal, especially in the context of the Directive Principles of State Policy, the picture presented by the next stage is a mixed one. This chapter is organized as below: Firstly, the general significance of the sector is set out and its growth is reviewed. Secondly, two policy areas, viz., evolution of common pattern of education and the implementation of the three-language formula are examined. Thirdly, the federal footprint in this area which is normally regarded as predominantly a state or regional field of action[1] is reviewed at some length. The chapter ends with a glance at an ambitious agenda for the future, i.e., universalization of secondary education for which Rashtriya Madhyamik Shiksha Abhiyan (RMSA) has been launched in March 2009 on the analogy of Sarva Shiksha Abhiyan (SSA) for elementary education.

Growth

Secondary education is conventionally called a neglected middle, malleable and residuary stage lying between the elementary stage (which is a priority area for most national governments including India as well as for international aid giving bodies like the World Bank) and the higher education (which is a stage associated with the universities with their European origin in the hoary medieval times have their own prestige associated with the function of production and dissemination of knowledge). In India, higher education regulated since 1857 by the metropolitan universities has been cultivated assiduously by the elite sections as the gateway to the job market and as such has won high financial allocations in successive Five-Year Plans in the post-independence India.

But, secondary education is by no means a neglected middle stage; rather it has benefited from natural growth consequent on the efforts to universalize elementary education. The number of secondary schools increased from 4,000 in 1947 to 52,279 in 1982–83 (14–fold increase) and enrolment increased from 7 lakh to 140 lakh (20–fold increase).[2] It is also a crucial stage because it is at this stage that after the mastery of the three R's, students benefit from a rich and variegated curriculum which imparts them life skills and values and empowers them to enter either life (the job market) or to join higher education stage.

The secondary schools play a major part in what the Kothari Commission called for "common school system of public education", which would cover all parts of the country and all stages of school education and strive to provide equality of access to all children.[3] The NPE 1986 talked of the NSE or National System of Education (NPE 1986 Part III) which builds on the common school system and covers a common educational structure at present, (10+2+3) and a national curricular framework. The crucialness of the secondary stage lies also in its involvement in the NSE through the structural as well as curricular aspects. It is because of this characteristic that the Central Government, although well aware that this stage, unlike the two other stages (where the Central Government can claim some voice, in the primary stage because of the Articles 45 of the Constitution and in the higher education stage because of its constitutional role in coordinating development and determination of standards) falls squarely within the arena of states has tended to establish a significant policy and institutional presence as attested by the appointment of Mudaliar Commission in 1952, shortly after independence and the existence of a large number of central institutions and entities.

Secondary Education: High Growth Area

The comparative high growth recorded at secondary stage on various parameters like institutions, enrolment and teachers in the recent period, is reflected in Table 8.1 below:

Table 8.1

Growth of Secondary Education (1993–2002)

(I) Institutions	*Percentage of Growth*	*(Rural Growth in brackets)*
(1) Primary	14.19	(12.91)
(2) Upper Primary	50.66	(24.52)
(3) Secondary	38.43	(14.19)
(4) Higher Secondary	85.75	(97.14)
(II) Enrolment	*Percentage of Growth*	*(Rural Growth in brackets)*
(1) Primary	36.85	(42.35)
(2) Upper Primary	52.46	(66.23)
(3) Secondary	62.73	(79.63)
(4) Higher Secondary	107.32	(156.70)

(III) Teachers	*Percentage of Growth (Rural Growth in brackets)*	
(1) Primary	17.84	(17.87)
(2) Upper Primary	40.01	(40.95)
(3) Secondary	20.09	(15.36)
(4) Higher Secondary	68.69	(77.23)

Source: NCERT (June, 2005): Seventh All India School Education Survey, pp. 1–3.

Note: In all the three dimensions of institutions, enrolment and teachers, the growth in rural area shown in brackets is even higher at higher secondary stage.

The Uniform Pattern of 10+2+3

Adoption of a common pattern of 10+2+3 all over the country means that after eight years of elementary education (as enjoined by the Constitution of India), there would be two years of general school education (8+2), followed by two years of specialized courses (10+2), when a student is fit to join the portal of the university which was one of the most significant reforms in the post-1947 period. The duration of the college degree programme was for a long time of two years. There was a broad uniformity in the British period by having three public examinations: the matriculation, the intermediate and the degree examinations. The Sadler Commission (1919) examined in depth the content of education at the intermediate and undergraduate stages in the context of the practice in the western countries and concluded that the intermediate stage was really a part of the school course and that students at this stage should be more effectively taught by school methods. (It also concluded that the standard of undergraduate education in India at that time was so poor as not to stand in comparison with the first degree in the advanced countries.) It, therefore, recommended that the dividing line between the university and the secondary courses is more appropriately drawn at the Intermediate examination and, for this purpose, there should be established a Board of Secondary and Intermediate (i.e., Higher Secondary) Education. It further recommended that the duration of the undergraduate course for the first degree should be increased to three years.

Unfortunately, the Sadler Commission recommendations were made at the time of the constitutional reforms and also coincided with a period of financial retrenchment and no action was taken except partly in the then United Provinces. After independence, the uniform pattern should have been adopted in the interest of inter-state mobility of educated manpower, but in spite of favourable recommendations of the Radhakrishnan Report, nothing was done. The Sargent Plan and the Mudaliar Report appear not to have given the correct lead. It is to the credit of Kothari Report that the problem was examined in depth and a clear recommendation about 10+2+3 pattern was made.[4] J.P. Naik has sought to underestimate the achievement of Kothari Commission in this regard on the ground that in the educational process, the structure is not as important as the steps taken for improving the quality of education. In any case, the NPE 1968, which was a minimalist document, based on the Kothari Report had the following formulation: "Education Structure: It will be advantageous to have a broadly uniform educational structure in all parts of the country. The ultimate objective should be to adopt 10+2+3 pattern, the higher secondary stage of 2 years being located in schools, college or both according to local conditions."

It would be seen that the policy had to take account of the federal diversity. J.P. Naik had underlined the laudable role played by Nurul Hasan, then Minister of State for Education, in bringing the State Governments round and, in particular, by implementing the reforms in the UTs and in the Central Boards from the academic year 1975–76.[5] J.P. Shukla, who was then Chairman of CBSE has written extensively in this regard.[6] The Challenge of Education (1985), the document preparatory to NPE 1986, says: "Although 10+2+3 pattern was accepted as a policy objective in 1968, many states have not implemented this recommendation. Even today, the states of Rajasthan, Punjab, Himachal Pradesh and Madhya Pradesh have not introduced the 10+2+3 pattern although they have agreed in principle to do so."[7]

The structural change which can be said to have taken about twenty years (1968–1988) to take hold all over the country, has facilitated migration of students across institutions and states and is one of the most far-reaching reforms, in conception going back to 1919.

The Three-Language Formula at the School Stage: Half-Hearted Implementation

The three-language formula was first proposed by the CABE in 1956, in the context of the need for secondary school students to have minimum instruction in Hindi – the prospective official language of the nation. This proposal immediately raised the issue of inequality of academic burden as between Hindi and non-Hindi-speaking states and became a matter of high policy. The formula was approved by the Chief Ministers' Conference in 1961 and the National Integration Council in 1962. The NPE 1968 spells out its contents as below: "At the secondary stage, the State Governments should adopt and vigorously implement the three-language formula which includes the study of a modern Indian language preferably one of the Southern languages, apart from Hindi and English in the Hindi-speaking states and of Hindi, along with regional language and English in the non-Hindi states."[8]

Although, Kothari Commission suggested a modified three-language formula,[9] it did not cut much ice and the 1968 policy formulation was continued in the 1986 policy.[10] The National Curricular Framework (2005) of the NCERT states that the three-language formula needs to be implemented in its spirit, to promote multi-lingual communicative abilities for a multi-lingual country. In practice, Hindi-speaking states have frustrated the implementation of three-language formula, as noted below, on the other hand, the state of Tamil Nadu stuck to two-language formula covering Tamil and English to the exclusion of Hindi.

The Central Government can perhaps be faulted for its connivance at the failure of Hindi-speaking states to faithfully implement the three-language formula, since the refusal of Tamil Nadu government to adhere to it has a different dimension going to the root of federal symmetry. In Hindi-speaking states, the third language is often a language which is not strictly a modern Indian language (thus in Rajasthan and Madhya Pradesh, Sanskrit which is a classical Indian language, is mostly used as the third language) and in Uttar Pradesh and Bihar, Urdu which, in a sense, is a variation of Hindi with change of script and is, therefore, not a real alternative. Most importantly, serious implementation requires money but that too is not forthcoming from the Central Government through Five-Year Plans. In the Second Plan, the Central Government started a centrally sponsored scheme for appointment of Hindi teachers, in non-Hindi-speaking states, under which central assistance on 100 per cent basis was available till 1978–79 but was reduced in the Sixth Plan as part of reduction in the number of the centrally sponsored schemes. The Programme of Action (1986) suggested that 100 per cent assistance for Hindi Teacher Scheme should be restored, and another scheme for cent per cent assistance for Hindi-speaking states for the appointment of southern Indian language teachers be introduced.[11] All this was done in 1993–94. But under financial crunch, there is apparently no expansion of the scheme. The Report of the Ministry for 2004–05 states that both the schemes are being continued with the allocation/expenditure being in the range of Rs 13 crore which is a paltry amount considering the dimension of the problem.[12] Moreover, these two schemes appear to have been linked with a third scheme for appointment of Urdu teachers in the schools in those districts that have a significant minority population. The Report of the Ministry for 2008–09 clarifies the position. The Second Five-Year Plan scheme for appointment of Hindi teachers and the centrally sponsored scheme (1993–94) of the Eighth Plan for appointment of modern Indian language teachers, preferably South Indian Language in the Hindi-speaking states and the centrally sponsored scheme of the Fifth

Plan (1979) for 100 per cent assistance for salary of Urdu teacher in blocks/districts of concentration of economically backward and minorities (a scheme based on Gujral Committee Report) were combined in the Eleventh Plan with the plan provision of Rs 75 crore.[13] Unfortunately, the break up of the allocation inter se the three schemes is not available. The problem with government's approach to the three-language formula is not only that the schemes in this regard are implemented half-heartedly and adequate financial provision has not been made but basically that schemes are not formulated realistically. Thus, when the identity of Hindi states and of the southern languages are known, there should logically be a bracketing of a particular Hindi state and a particular South Indian language, so that training of teachers could be suitably planned, but the whole matter is left to chance giving an impression that the government is not serious about the implementation of the three-language formula.

The Federal Footprint in School Education

The federal government's crucial role in this area is evident from the fact that it maintains and manages a substantial institutional infrastructure. This takes the form of two research and training organizations, two affiliating School Boards and two organizations managing elite public schools. We have thus the following institutions: (a) National Council for Educational Research and Training (NCERT), (b) National Institute of Educational Planning and Administration (NIEPA) since renamed NUEPA, (c) the National Institute of Open Schooling (NIOS), (d) Central Board of Secondary Education (CBSE) affiliating 9,816 schools (as in 2008–09), (e) a central organization for running 981 schools (as in 2008–09) for transferable Central Government employees, called the Kendriya Vidyalaya Sangathan (KVS), and (f) a central organization called the Navodaya Vidyalaya Sangathan (NVS) for running 576 (as in 2008–09) rural public schools, started as part of the NPE 1986.

National Resource Institutions

NCERT

The role of NCERT can be said to resonate with the federal theme. It came to be established in September 1961 by the merger of various separate organizations under the Ministry of Education set up especially in the light of the Report of the Mudaliar Commission. These were: Central Board of Textbook Research (1954), Central Bureau of Educational and Vocational Guidance (1954), Directorate of Extension Programme (1955), National Institute of Basic Education (1956), National Fundamental Education Centre (1956) and National Institute of Audio-Visual Education.[14] The merger was decided upon to create a critical mass of activities, end isolation and facilitate grant of autonomy, which was denied to individual, isolated subordinate organizations of the Ministry. The Regional Colleges of Education, since renamed Regional Institutes of Education (RIEs), were initially set up by the Ministry of Education on the suggestion of the Planning Commission for training teachers for multi-purpose and secondary schools. The administration of these colleges was subsequently transferred to the NCERT. Since they are treated as the primary points of interaction with the states, NCERT's effectiveness vis-à-vis states has suffered somewhat.

NCERT has about 15 departments covering various stages (e.g., elementary education), groups (e.g., children with special needs, women), subjects (science, mathematics, social sciences and humanities, teacher education), activities (research, measurement, evaluation and survey) and services (library and documentation). These academic departments together are called the National Institute of Education (NIE). In addition, there are seven constituent units, two of which are extensions of the NIE, viz., Central Institute of Educational Technology (CIET) at New Delhi and Central Institute of Vocational Education at Bhopal and five other RIEs. These academic departments/institutions and regional institutes together employed in 2003–04, 2,946 academic staff of whom 693 belonged to the Group 'A', the bulk of them being educationists. This is a formidable brainpower under one umbrella bearing on school education.

The NCERT is mandated by its rules to assist and advise the Ministry of Education in implementing policies and major programmes in the field of education particularly research, teacher training, extension services, improved educational techniques and practices, establishment of institutions and preparation of publications. Its major accomplishments include the framing of successive versions of the school curriculum (1975, 1988, 2000 and 2005), preparation and publication of instructional materials/school textbooks (the latter are used by the CBSE affiliated schools including Kendriya/Navodaya Vidyalayas and regarded as models by State Councils of Education Research and Training and state boards of Secondary and Higher Secondary Education), promotion and standardization of teacher education (through the RIEs and the advisory National Council for Teacher Education (NCTE) set up in 1973 till it was hived off as a Statutory Council in 1995), evaluation/examination reforms, promotion of research through its Education, Research and Innovation Committee (ERIC), conduct of periodical research surveys and of periodical school education surveys. In view of its formidable output in this area, including six surveys of research and seven school education surveys, (action for eighth survey has been initiated), NCERT can indeed be termed at once as a brains trust and a think tank of the Education Ministry and has lived up to the role envisaged by the Radhakrishnan

Commission for the Central Institute of Education (which continues as part of Delhi University).

The State Governments historically had two administrative organizations, viz., Directorate of Education going back to the 1850s and the state boards of Secondary Education started in the early years of the 20th century. In course of implementation of the Five-Year Plans, new formations came up, the most important of which were the State Institutes of Education (SIEs) set up in various states in 1963–64 with American assistance with the objectives of improvement of education in elementary schools, elementary teacher education, supervision and training of inspecting staff and production of literature for elementary schools and teachers. In the early 1980s, in order to make in-service education and field research more appropriately tailored to state specific needs and also to enhance the participation and responsibility of state experts in the process of quality improvement in school education, State Councils of Educational Research and Training (SCERTs) were set up in most states with the SIEs serving as the foundation institutions. These SCERTs were modelled after the NCERT and had SIEs as their core. The principle of building a critical mass by amalgamation of all quality enhancing formations/institutes at the state level in the areas of science education, English education, educational technology etc. was, however, not followed by most State Governments. Moreover, the State Governments were reluctant to concede academic, much less administrative and financial, autonomy to the SCERTs. Therefore, SCERTs at state level are a pale shadow of the academically powerful NCERT at the national level. According to Eleventh Plan document, SIEs continue to function in some states as separate institutions.[15]

States Denied Role in Management of NCERT

The rules of the NCERT build in the requirement for the NCERT to assist the states to act as a clearing house of information and ideas and to advise State Governments in matters relating to school education. All the State education ministers and their counterparts in Delhi and Puducherry are ex-officio members of general body of the Council, but their role is rather formal and marginal since the main function of the Governing Body is to approve the draft annual report. The need for greater involvement of the State Governments has repeatedly been emphasized by high-power commissions/committees. Thus, the Education Commission (1966) emphasized the need for a two-way exchange, i.e., interchange and flow of officers from the NCERT to the state departments and vice versa,[16] this was accepted but not followed up. The Nagchaudhuri Review Committee of the NCERT (1969) comprising past and current Education Secretaries, J.P. Naik, M.S. Gore, V.G. Bhide and N.V. Subbarao was a high profile one and recommended that Education Secretaries should be made members of the Council and six Directors of Education, selected in rotation, should be members of the governing body (i.e., the Executive Committee), but the Central Government did not accept these recommendations.

Denial of Autonomy to the NCERT

Successive review committees and the PAC Report (1980–81) had suggested that NCERT may be made autonomous by various devices like (i) declaring it as an institution of national importance (Nagchaudhuri Committee, 1969) or (ii) notifying it as a deemed university (Madhuri Shah Report, 1984), and (iii) an educationist, being appointed chairman of NCERT (PAC Committee, 1980–81). The government resolution of 3rd August 1969 vis-à-vis Nagachaudhuri Review Report rejected autonomy on the ground that there has to be a close and intimate relationship between the Ministry and the Council. The subsequent government resolution of 21st June 1985 vis-à-vis Madhuri Shah Report put it bluntly: "Government has decided not to accept the recommendation about deemed university status, because the NCERT is not only the adviser to the government on academic matters but also the *academic wing of the Government* to which the government turns for advice from time to time and in many cases it is the *only agency for implementation of priority programmes like the review of textbooks from the point of view of national integration*, preparation of guidelines and materials for History of Freedom Movement and the Computer Literacy Project. Thus, the relationship requires a much more intimate linkage between the Ministry and NCERT than would be possible under statutory and full autonomous arrangements. The Education Minister should remain the President of the NCERT."

In 2008, NIEPA, a sister institution of NCERT, was given the status of a deemed university and is now known as NUEPA, but NCERT continues to be an organization subordinate to the Ministry of Education.

Curricular Controversies

Padma Sarangpani noting the distinction made by the UNESCO[17] between syllabus-based and curriculum-based systems of schooling, notes that NPE 1986 with its call for a national system of education, with flexibility built around a common core could be said to mark the shift of Indian education system from being syllabus based to being curriculum based. She says that the first 'National Curriculum Framework' was developed by the NCERT in 1988. (Actually, NCERT's efforts in this direction go back to 1975 and the 1988 curriculum framework had its limitations because of omissions relating to higher secondary and vocational elements.) In that sense, the National Curricular Framework for School Education (2000) was the first comprehensive curriculum covering higher secondary education stage (standards XI and XII) as well as vocational component and can be said to have broken new ground. It was framed under leadership of an academic, who was earlier the chairman of NCTE.[18] However, since it was framed when the NDA government was in power, it was challenged before Supreme Court by a group of activists mainly because it was perceived to promote the rightist agenda, but on the technical ground that it was not approved by the CABE. The challenge was repealed by the Supreme Court on the simple ground that CABE was not a statutory body and there was no legal requirement for the curricular framework to be approved by the CABE.[19] However, after the NDA-I government came to power, the 2,000 document was held in abeyance and 21 Focus Groups were set up comprising 250 scholars guided by a Steering Committee consisting of 35 persons headed by Prof. Yash Pal. This Steering Committee finalized the new National Curricular Framework (2005) which is the official curriculum in force now. That the school curriculum should become an issue to be adjudicated by the highest court of land underlines the symbolic role of the school curriculum as a site of contestation in the federal polity of India in which the NCERT becomes an instrumentality of the ruling dispensation. Incidentally, the National Curriculum Framework, 2005 is not free from controversies, being criticized by some Leftist groups.[20]

Textbook Controversies

Rudolphs[21] have dealt with the genesis and implications of textbook controversy 1977–79. She has pointed out how the Prime Minister Morarji Desai's attempt to de-recognize a few textbooks of NCERT along with some publications written by leftist scholars for the National Book Trust (NBT) on the ground that they depicted Indian history in an undesirable manner, raised issues of secularism in India so far as depiction of Islamic rulers in Medieval India was concerned. The issues of secularism apart, she has, however, pointed out that in a country like India where private publishing is not fully professionalized and malpractices are rampant, "the practice of commissioning and/or selecting texts by agencies of the Central Government in consultation with professional historians has a better chance of protecting scholarly standards than does risking the debilitating effects of an imperfect market". One of the functions of NCERT is to evaluate textbooks prescribed by state boards in sensitive subjects like history and languages, especially in states ruled by opposition parties. Thus, the Ministry of HRD appointed a National Steering Committee to consider evaluation reports of the NCERT (1993–94). They covered states of Uttar Pradesh, West Bengal, Andhra Pradesh, Assam, Tamil Nadu, Kerala and Madhya Pradesh. Some specific institutions were also targeted, e.g., Saraswati Shishu Mandir Prakashan and Vidya Bharati etc. The change of party in power is an occasion for new controversies especially when Education Ministers are ideologues, as when Murli Manohar Joshi was Education Minister during the NDA regime (1998–2004) and Arjun Singh became Education Minister during UPA-I rule (2004–2009). The alleged attempt by the NDA government to "saffronize" the textbooks was an occasion for the 'desaffronization' agenda of the succeeding UPA-I government which wanted the textbooks to reflect the secular pluralist outlook of Indian civilization. A committee of CABE for this purpose was also appointed.

It is possible to draw following conclusions from the above account of NCERT:

- School education in common with other stages was a state subject till 1977. When the Central Government creates a strong organization in that area it is initially seen to fulfil an important nation-building role in the areas of school curriculum, textbooks etc.
- When however, different parties alternate at the central level (e.g., Congress government followed by Janata government in 1977; NDA government following Congress/UF government in 1998; UPA-I following NDA in 2004) school education and NCERT's actions become a zone of contestation.
- NCERT's actions could also become controversial when different ruling parties in states (e.g., West Bengal under Communists, Madhya Pradesh under BJP) question NCERT's prescriptive role.
- Since the school education dominated by the states is the zone of contestation, Central Government especially under the Congress party has shown unwillingness to allow participation of states in the management of the NCERT.
- For the same reason, NCERT which in a way is a national intellectual resource has tended to become an instrumentality of the ruling power. Because of this potential, Central Government is reluctant to concede autonomy to the NCERT.

National Institute of Educational Planning and Administration (NIEPA)

NIEPA began in 1962 as a UNESCO regional centre for the training of educational planners, administrators and supervisors in 14 Asian countries, as part of implementation of the Asian Plan for universal primary education drawn up at Karachi in 1959. It was one of five such regional institutions. Thus, conceptually, NIEPA is an organization in the school sub-sector although its thematic focus makes it Janus-faced, having some interest in the area of higher education also. In 1972, after the expiry of the 10–year period, it was taken over by the National Staff College for Educational Planning and Administration, which was earlier set up in

1970. In 1979, it was renamed as NIEPA with an amended Memorandum of Association. Since then, it has emerged as a small but reputed establishment in its chosen field with academic linkage with the Paris-based International Institute of Educational Planning (IIEP) maintained by the UNESCO.[22]

Structure and Functions with Special Reference to States

The objectives of the NIEPA included organization of training programmes in the areas of educational planning and administration (EPA) for (a) senior educational officers of the Central and State Governments, (b) teacher-educators and university and college administrators, and (c) legislators; undertaking of research in the EPA area; offering of consultancy services to State Governments and other educational institutions; acting as a clearing-house of ideas and information and collaboration with the UGC, universities and management institutions.[23] Its authorities included the Council, the Executive Committee and the Finance Committee. The Union HRD Minister was the ex-officio President of the Council. Its units were partly thematic, partly related to educational level and partly spatial.

The general body of NIEPA called the 'Council' consisted of Education Secretaries of five states and Education Secretary of one UT by rotation plus six Directors of Education. The Executive Committee of NIEPA consisted of seven persons among whom there is one State Education Secretary nominated by the HRD Minister. The Finance Committee had no representation from any state. As compared with the NCERT, the presence of a state representative on the Executive Committee of NIEPA shows that NIEPA had a more participatory approach but the absence of all states on the Council made it less representative.

The sub-national systems unit of NIEPA deals with state/district policies and programmes. Its functions include getting and sharing information regarding educational developments and innovations in various regions and states of India, helping state, district and block level units in development of monitoring and evaluating systems, providing training and consultation to states in educational planning and administration and carrying out research studies on educational needs and problems of states and districts. However, a perusal of the review report of NIEPA shows that consultancy output of this unit was meagre and that the only major states which consulted NIEPA were Haryana and Rajasthan, the rest being smaller states like J&K and Sikkim or UTs like Dadra and Nagar Haveli, Puducherry etc.

During the Seventh Plan, NIEPA unsuccessfully tried to have a centrally sponsored scheme for the establishment of State Institutes of Educational Planning and Administration (SIEPAs). This would have provided NIEPA with its counterpart institutions comparable to the NCERT having SIEs/SCERTs. Subsequently, the World Bank provided assistance as part of District Primary Education Projects (DPEPs) to set up SIEPAs where DPEP was in operation. However, only two states, viz., Maharashtra and Uttar Pradesh, have established institutions called Maharashtra Institute of Educational Planning and Administration (MIEPA) at Aurangabad and State Institute of Educational Management and Training (SIEMAT) at Allahabad,[24] with Assam making a beginning. Thus, the state level capacity in the area of educational, planning and administration remains severely limited.

The conduct of the training programmes takes up 75 per cent of NIEPA faculty time, the two main training programmes being National Diploma Programme for District Education Officers (DEOs) and International Diploma Programme for countries in West Asia, Africa and South-East Asia, in addition to orientation and training programmes for principals of District Institute of Education and Training (DIETs), principals of colleges, functionaries of District Primary Education Programme (DPEP), senior education administrators, university administrators etc. There was a feeling that NIEPA should concentrate on training of trainers and key functionaries. The research output of NIEPA was considerable but much of it is supported by international organizations or the ministry (e.g., the work of the NIEPA on NPE 1986/POA 1986/POA 1992 and earlier, the National Commission on Teachers II (Higher Education)). More recently, NIEPA concentrated on topics like financing of higher education, internationalization of higher education, GATS (General Agreement on Trade in Services), the role of secondary education in the 21st century etc. Thus, in 2004–05 it served as secretariat for CABE Committee on Financing of Higher and Secondary Education.[25] It has conducted two surveys of state administration. It publishes a quarterly *Journal of Educational Planning and Administration*, which enjoys a high academic reputation. It brings out occasional papers on various themes and Best Practices series. NIEPA appeared to suffer from an absence of a critical mass of academic manpower having only 50 academic and senior administrative staff in 2001–02. It needed to be strengthened organizationally and financially, so that it could actively help state level organizations (SIEPAs) to come up. It also needed to build a capacity in the area of district planning and administration and to have an institutional survey and research strategy.

NIEPA as a Deemed University

The Second Review Committee of NIEPA in 2004 at the behest of the Ministry of Finance recommended the continuance of NIEPA. It noted a suggestion to notify NIEPA as a deemed university but made no categorical recommendation. In November 2007 it was notified as a deemed university and renamed NUEPA. This appears to have been done in the context of administrative exigencies rather than as part of a blue print. However, this step may hopefully strengthen the capacity of NIEPA for research and training. Thus, the allocation of NIEPA which was Rs 4.78 crore in 2002–03 was raised to Rs 10.40 crore in 2007–08.[26] The objectives of NIEPA do not appear to have undergone any substantial changes consequent on the re-designation of NIEPA as NUEPA. NUEPA, however, appears to suffer from the usual problems of a quality institution in India, viz., shortage of good teachers and researchers. Its progress especially its interaction with the States would be watched with interest. Its Department of Educational Management and Information System gives valuable support to Sarva Shiksha Abhiyan and brings out periodically national, state and district level reports.

All-India School Boards under Central Auspices

National Institute of Open Schooling (NIOS)

NIOS, which started as an Open School Project under the CBSE in 1978, became the National Open School in 1989 and was re-named as NIOS in 2002. It has a double role – it is an All-India Board as well as a national resource centre of distance education at the school stage. In October 1990, by a government resolution, it was authorized to examine and certify students registered with it up to the pre-degree level courses.

The objectives of NIOS include providing professional advice to the Government of India and to the states regarding the proper development of open and distance learning (ODL) system at the school level, giving financial assistance to the states for establishment and development of state open schools, identifying and promoting standards of learning in the distance education system through research and evaluation and exercising normative and coordinating functions.

Unfortunately, there is only one representative of State Government/State Open School/State Universities on the general body of the NIOS[27] and none at all on the Executive Committee.

The number of students certified has increased from 22,060 and 13,454 in 1991 at secondary and senior secondary stages respectively to 4,57,932 and 2,67,545 in 2003. The number of certified students in professional stream increased from 1,266 in 1993 to 45,507 in 2003. In 2008–2009, 1.5 million learners were reported to be on the roll.[28] The enrolment of NIOS appears to be concentrated in the north (Delhi, Chandigarh, UP) and to a few states in the south (especially Andhra Pradesh). More recently, it has started A, B and C level courses equivalent to classes III, V and VIII (called Open Basic Education Programme) and reportedly certified about 50,000 students in 2003. Such courses would help non-formal education stream students to be mainstreamed. The activities of the NIOS are conducted through eleven regional centres, 2,400 study centres and accredited institutions. The Goa Conference held in January 2005 had decided to revitalize NIOS, to formulate a centrally sponsored scheme for promotion of open schooling in the states, and to set up a National Council for Open Schooling to accredit/grade organizations.[29]

The National Consortium for Open Schooling (NCOS), the main instrumentality for interaction with the states and State Open Schools (comparable with other inter-state resource agencies like COBSE), was set up in 1997 but its achievements appear to be negligible. At present, there are 13 State Open Schools in Andhra Pradesh, Tamil Nadu, Kerala, Karnataka, Madhya Pradesh, Chhattisgarh, Rajasthan, Punjab, Haryana, Jammu and Kashmir, West Bengal, Assam and Delhi. However, the data regarding progress made by these State Open Schools in the matter of certification through open mode/channel are not available, except in the Annual Report for 2002–03,[30] from which it is seen that there is a competition between the Open Universities and the state boards in the matter of housing open schools. The association with the Open Universities may help in sharing the technical facilities, but the ODL system, if it wants to reach the unreached at the school stage, has to concentrate on print media and the state boards are the natural locus for open school initiatives. A scheme for financial assistance for promotion of open schooling has reportedly been framed under which an assistance of Rs 26 lakh was given to Tamil Nadu, Jammu & Kashmir, West Bengal and Karnataka in the three years (2002–05) which is very marginal.[31] The international orientation of NIOS is strong because of the location of the International Centre for Training in Open Schooling (ICTOS) and Open Schooling Association of the Commonwealth (OSAC) within the NIOS. The Annual Report of the Ministry for 2008–09 shows that NIOS is starting the process of on-line admission on pilot basis. The Ministry appears to have decided to involve NIOS substantially in the promotion of education of minorities.[32]

Central Board of Secondary Education (CBSE): An Emergent All-India Organization

The Central Board which began life in 1929 as Board of High School and Intermediate Education, Rajputana with its headquarters at Ajmer[33] was renamed as CBSE in 1952 to affiliate schools in Part C and D states. At one stage, consequent on the states reorganization, its membership dwindled to three but with the merger of the Delhi Board of Secondary Education with CBSE in July 1964, the number of schools increased to 300.[34] Gradually, not only did all schools in the UTs and newly formed states without their own Board (e.g., Sikkim, Jharkhand, Uttarakhand and Chattisgarh) and all Kendriya Vidyalayas and Navodaya Vidyalayas become its members, but even independent schools including schools in Tamil Nadu joined so that the number of schools affiliated to the CBSE as on 31st December 2008 stood at 9,816 schools.[35] The Board's claim to be a National Board, therefore, rings true.

The objectives of the Board are to affiliate institutions and conduct various examinations. The Union Education Secretary is the titular controlling authority but otherwise, the Board functions autonomously under its chairman, who is generally an experienced educationist, supported by a Controller of Examinations and Director (Academic). The Governing Board presided over by the chairman of CBSE has about 40 members with heavy representation of Delhi NCT officers and schools and Education Ministry, NCERT, AICTE, MCI etc. Unfortunately, there is no representative from any State Government or state board of Secondary and Higher Secondary Education.[36]

The Board conducts examinations not only for Class X and Class XII, for the schools affiliated to it but also entrance tests for Navodaya Vidyalayas and All-India Pre-Medical/Pre-Dental and All-India Engineering Entrance Examinations, in effect serving as a National Testing Service (NTS) in terms of the POA 1986.

The Board is also known for having introduced several curricular and examination reforms. This is facilitated by the location of the Board in Delhi and its close interaction with national resource bodies like the NCERT, NIEPA and NIOS as well as the UGC. A leading example is its Open School Project established by it in 1978, which has metamorphosed into the NIOS.

Inter-face with the States

In 1990, the CBSE decentralized its administration[37] and created six regional offices at Delhi, Chandigarh, Allahabad, Guwahati, Ajmer and Chennai. Earlier in 1979, it took the initiative to establish the COBSE (Council of Boards of Secondary Education) which is the coordinating organization of Secondary and Higher Secondary Boards in India. It was COBSE, which facilitated the changeover to 10+2+3 pattern in various states in the country and which is now helping with the introduction of curricular and examination reform by various Boards. COBSE was delinked from the CBSE in 1989, since when its meetings have become more regular.[38] But although COBSE has a separate office and the presidentship rotates between chairmen of different School Boards, chairman of CBSE continues as the executive vice-president and the academic staff is limited, so that the COBSE remains a semi-central body which has yet to realize its potential. The Task Force Report of the Ministry of Education on Boards of Secondary Education has envisaged a few important tasks to be assigned to the COBSE including standardization of rules of recognition of schools, coordination with the Association of Indian Universities regarding entrance examinations for professional courses, evolution of a solution to the problem of inter-variability of standards, assessment of the suitability and quality of textbooks etc. for which the COBSE would need to be strengthened and professionalized.[39]

To some extent, CBSE has evolved from being merely a central body to being an all-India body comparable to the NCERT, at least in the field of examination reforms. This happened firstly, through its role as a virtual National Testing Service for which it was selected by the Supreme Court at the instance of the Education Ministry. Secondly, the NCERT does have a Department of Examination Reforms, but it is hampered because of its lack of practical exposure. CBSE has affiliated to it the pick of the elite schools in India and is in a position to experiment. Thirdly, unlike the NCERT, CBSE has a more coordinative and open-minded approach to its counterpart state formations, viz., state boards, and has operationalized the cooperation through the formation of COBSE. Fourthly, CBSE and state boards are financially independent of Central/State Governments and are in a position to experiment without being hampered by financial constraints, which are faced to a large extent by the SCERTs and, to some extent, by the NCERT.

The press reports indicate that CBSE proposes to go in for examination reforms in a big way including dispensing with a central examination for the 10th standard, but that state boards have chosen not to follow suit. CBSE has also started a new body to look after its international operations. All these initiatives are welcome in so far as they go but CBSE needs to ensure that it maintains its role as a leader of state boards.

Central Sector in School Education

Kendriya Vidyalaya Sanghatan (KVS)

The nucleus of the organization for Central Schools or the Kendriya Vidyalayas (KVs) appears to have been 20 Regimental Schools which were taken over in 1963–64 by the Ministry of Education to be run as Central Schools. The KVs was registered as a body corporate in December 1965.[40] The Indo-Chinese war in 1962 and the Indo-Pakistan war in 1965 appear to have expedited the process of persuading the Government of India of the need to have a separate set of schools primarily meant for transferable Central Government employees including defence personnel and a separate organization to manage those schools. The present position of the institutional network is as below:

Table 8.2

Present Position of KVS Institutional Network

No. of Schools	*No. of Teachers (including Principals/Vice-Principals)*	*No. of Students*	*Annual Budget 2008–09 (Rs. in Crore)*	
981	30,025 (as in 2002–03)	7,50,000	Non-Plan	1,151.00
			Plan	300.00
			Total	1,451.00

Source: Annual Report of Education Ministry.

Note: Data as on 31st December 2008 except in regard to teachers.

KVs tend to be schools with good examination results and with good equipment especially computer and laboratory facilities. Thirty-one KVs were declared as 'smart' schools, which are provided Rs 25 lakh each to enrich the infrastructure and enhance the quality of education through the optimum use of IT and multi-media. With headquarters in Delhi and being under the umbrella of the CBSE and the NCERT, they are the first to adopt innovations, try out experiments etc.

KVs in the Centre-State Context

1. The organizational structure is centralised with the Minister (Education) as Chairman and Additional Secretary of Ministry as Vice-Chairman with heavy representation of defence forces. There is no representation to the State Governments on the Sangathan although its schools are spread all over the country.
2. There is a regional set-up for a group of 40–50 Central Schools and Management Committees for individual schools on which local officials of the State Governments may be represented.
3. All Central Schools are affiliated to the CBSE with a few exceptions.
4. English, Hindi and Sanskrit are compulsory from Class VI to VIII. In Class IX and X, any two languages out of English, Hindi and Sanskrit can be offered. Sanskrit can also be offered as an elective subject at + 2 stage. KVs have no room for the regional languages and they have contributed to strengthening the position of the twin link languages of India, viz., English and Hindi.
5. The cost of education is highly subsidized, with free education for students up to Class VIII, girl students, SC/ST students and wards of staff of KVs up to Class XII, apart from Armed Forces concessions.

Navodaya Vidyalaya Samiti

The existence of Central Schools can be justified by the welfare needs of transferable Central Government employees, but the Navodaya

Vidyalayas (NVS) or rural public schools started as a new project in 1985–86 are more controversial. In the NPE they were referred to as pace-setting schools that would be residential and free of charge.[41] PoA 1986 clarified that the schools would cater to potentially high achievers with 75 per cent reservation for children from rural areas and reservation for SCs (15%), STs (7.5%) and girls (33%).[42] The plan was to have one school per district of the country, the State Governments being expected to provide 30 acres of land free of cost. At the time when the scheme was mooted, it had faced objections from educationists and non-official experts of elitism, curriculum matters and constitutional propriety as school education was a State subject. Three states – Assam, West Bengal and Tamil Nadu – refused to cooperate. Still, the Central Government went ahead and at the time the Ramamurti Committee reviewed the scheme (1990), steps had been taken to start schools in 261 out of about 400 districts in 29 states/UTs. The Committee suggested a freeze on the new starts and posed three alternatives: (i) no new schools but run the existing schools, (ii) take over of schools by the respective State Governments, and (iii) transformation of the NVs into talent-nurturing school complexes.[43] The Janardhan Reddy Committee, by a majority, recommended the continuance of the scheme, suggesting that it should be kept as cost-effective as possible. The Committee particularly commended a new feature of the scheme, viz., migration of students from one linguistic region to the other as conducive to national integration.[44] The position of NVs as in December 2004 was as below:

Table 8.3

Present Position of NVS (December 2004)

No. of Districts	*No. of Schools*	*No. of Students*	*No. of Teachers*
576	576	2,05,820	6,019

The budgetary allocation in 2008–2009 was Non-Plan Rs 259.87 crore + Plan Rs 1,290.00 crore = Total Rs 1,499.87 crore.

Admission to the NVs is made at the level of class VI through a test conducted by the CBSE in the concerned district and annual new admissions are in excess of 36,000. NVs are affiliated to CBSE and have excellent results at class X and class XII. They promote Parent-Teacher Councils (PTCs) and are encouraged to interact with neighbouring schools and share their facilities.

NVs in the Centre-State Context

1. At present, the state of Tamil Nadu remains the only non-participating state. Assam began to participate from 1992–93 and West Bengal from 2001–02.

2. The Minister of HRD serves as the Chairman of the Navodaya Vidyalaya Samiti and an IAS officer works as the Commissioner, NVs. In a committee comprising 25 members, there are four state representatives, i.e., two Education Secretaries and two Directors of Education, both nominated by the minister. This is a token representation and the fact that it is not by rotation but by nomination underlines the centralised character of the management culture of NVs.
3. The three-language formula is strictly followed. Thus, the instruction in the standards VI to VIII is in the regional language.

In conclusion, it may be observed that although the Central Government is devoting large resources for maintenance of a central sector in education in terms of schools and all-India bodies like NCERT, NIEPA, NIOS and CBSE, there are shortcomings from the federal angle. The all-India bodies have not been geared to network with the states (the exception being CBSE through COBSE), the schools are costly and geared to a limited client base. However, KVs are being projected as prototypes of model schools, a large number of which are projected to be set up in the Eleventh Plan (according to press reports, about 3,500).[45]

Universalization of Secondary Education in India by 2020: A New Agenda

More recently, a CABE Committee (2005) has advocated universalization of secondary and higher secondary education by 2020 *inter alia* in the context of the dual pressure – universalization of elementary education being imminent and the need to raise gross enrolment ratio (GER) in higher education, the transition rate between Grade VIII and Grade IX being 85 per cent in 2001–02.[46] The target date appears to be too ambitious, but otherwise this is a goal which needs to be set firmly before the country in the context of national capacity to meet the emerging challenge of development and demography. A World Bank report (2005) emphasizes the need for converting secondary education from being the weakest link in many countries to the cornerstone of the educational structure. According to the report, the reasons the US forged ahead of the European countries after World War II in terms of economic prowess was largely due to the attention paid by the US in the first half of the 20th century to make secondary education universal. It is argued that a powerful case can be made for the expansion of the secondary education in the developing countries on the grounds of growth, poverty reduction, equity and social cohesion.[47] The Eleventh Plan document emphasizes quality aspects and vocationalization of the secondary education which have long been the policy concerns of the Central Government, but which have not been realized fully for various reasons.[48] No reference is made to the universalization of secondary education. However, the Ministry of

HRD approved Rashtriya Madhyamik Shiksha Abhiyan (RMSA) in March 2009, on the eve of the general elections. After the UPA-II came to power in May 2009, the details have been worked out. According to the 2008–09 Annual Report of the Ministry, the objectives of the Mission are: To achieve a GER of 75 per cent for classes IX to X within five years and universal access to secondary education by 2017, i.e., by the end of Twelfth Five-Year Plan and universal retention by 2020.[49] Corresponding objectives relating to quality improvement and equity have been incorporated. The Central Government might spend 25 per cent of the project expenditure during the Eleventh Five-Year Plan and 75 per cent during the Twelfth Five-Year Plan.

Notes

1. In the total government expenditure on secondary education, the share of the Union Government is very limited (5.70% in 2005–06) and this share has been going down in successive years (it decreased from 6.80% in 1994–95). Correspondingly, the share of states/UTs has increased from 93.20% in 1994–95 to 94.30% in 2004–05). Vide J.B.G. Tilak (Ed.), *Financing of Secondary Education in India* (New Delhi: Shipra Publications, 2008), xvii.
2. Challenge of Education (1985), para 3.20.
3. Kothari Report, para 10.05.
4. Ibid., paras 2.10 and 2.11.
5. J.P. Naik, *Education Commission and After* (Bombay: Allied 1983; reprinted by, New Delhi: APH Publishing, 1997), 100–111.
6. J.P. Shukla, *Toward a New Pattern of Education in India* (New Delhi: Sterling Publishers, 1976), 32–42.
7. Challenge of Education (1985), para 3.23.
8. NPE 1968, para 3.
9. Kothari Report, paras 8.34 to 8.37.
10. NPE 1986, para 8.7.
11. PoA 1986, 162.
12. Report of the Ministry of Education (1) 2004–05, p. 235 and (2) 2008–09, pp. 72–73.
13. Report of the Ministry of Education, 2008–09, 72–73.
14. Nagchaudhuri Report, 1969, 3.
15. Eleventh Five-Year Plan, Vol. II, 20.
16. Kothari Report, para 18.36.
17. According to R. Dottrens *Primary School Curriculum* (Paris: UNESCO, 1976) in the syllabus based systems of schooling, standards are set to which all

teachers must conform. In the curriculum based systems, teachers both trained and autonomous, make decisions. (Quoted in Padma M. Sarangpani, vide Footnote 20 below).

18. Prof. J.S. Rajput. After Prof. Rajput left NCTE it deteriorated rapidly. Prof. Rajput, however, fell out of favour with the Union Education Minister during UPA(I).
19. Vide *Aruna Roy vs. Union of India*, 2003.
20. According to Padma M. Sarangpani, NCF 2005 was criticized by Leftist scholars in a seminar organized under the banner of Safdar Hashmi Memorial Trust (SAHMAT) and some of the criticism was published in the issues of *Social Scientist,* Vol. 388–389 in 2005. According to the Leftist critics, philosophy and perspective of NCF pertaining to learner and knowledge were unsound. Vide her article: "The Open Class Room and its Critics," in Preet Rustagi (Ed.), *Concerns, Conflicts and Cohesion: Universalization of Elementary Education in India* (New Delhi: Oxford University Press, 2009), 191–209. As the issues are mainly philosophical, I do not go into details.
21. Lloyd I Rudolph and Susanne H. Rudolph, "Rethinking Secularism: Genesis and Implications of the Textbook Controversy 1977–79", in *Explaining Indian Democracy,* Vol. II, *The Realm of Institutions* (New Delhi: Oxford University Press, 2008), 211–232 (originally published in 1983).
22. G.D. Sharma: NIEPA "Instrumentality of Change", in Prof. P.R. Panchamukhi (Ed.), *Studies in Educational References in India*, Vol. II (Bombay: Himalaya Publishers, 1989), 506–562.

    G.D. Sharma's account has been overtaken by two review committees in 1989 and 2004 and the Notification of NIEPA as a deemed university in 2007.
23. NIEPA: Report of the Review Committee on NIEPA (New Delhi: GoI, Ministry of HRD, 1989), 68–77.
24. Srilekha Majumdar, "Infrastructure and Education Administration", in Marmar Mukhopadhyay and M. Parikh (Eds.), *Education in India: The Fifty Years* (New Delhi: 2000), 229–243.
25. NIEPA: Report of CABE Committee on Financing of Higher and Technical Education (New Delhi, 2005). [Chairman: Prof. Bhalchandra Mungekar, then Member (Education), Planning Commission. The present author of the book was a member of the Committee].
26. Annual Report of NIEPA, 2007–08.
27. MoA and Rules/Regulation No. 4 of National Open School (New Delhi, 1998).
28. Annual Report of the Ministry of Education, 2008–09, 76.
29. Annual Report of the Ministry of Education, 2004–05, 115–124.
30. NIOS Annual Report (2002–03), 96–102.
31. Annual Report of the Ministry of Education, 2004–05, 115–124.

32. Annual Report of the Ministry of Education (2008–09),96–97.
33. Annual Report of CBSE (2003), 8.
34. Platinum Jubilee Souvenir, New Delhi (CBSE, 2003).
35. Annual Report of the Ministry of Education (2008–09), 80–85.
36. PoA 1986, 150.
37. Platinum Jubilee Souvenir, op. cit.
38. P.D. Shukla, "CBSE", in P.R. Panchamukhi (Ed.), *Studies in Educational Reforms in India*, Vol. II, (Bombay: Himalaya Publishing, 1989), 411–443.
39. Report of the Task Force on Boards of Secondary Education (New Delhi: Ministry of Education, 1997) (Mimeo).
40. KVS Annual Report, 1998–99 (New Delhi: KVS), 96.
41. NPE 1986, para 5.14 and 5.15.
42. PoA 1986, III.5.
43. Ramamurthi Report, pp. 94–111.
44. Janardhan Reddy Report, pp. 17–20.
45. *Indian Express*, 24th April, 2010.
46. CABE: Report of the Committee on Universalization of Secondary Education (New Delhi, 2005).
47. The World Bank: *Expanding Opportunities and Building Competencies for Young People: New Agenda for Secondary Education* (Washington DC, 2005).
48. Eleventh Five-Year Plan, Vol. II, 20–22.
49. Report of the Ministry of Education (2008–09), 64–67.

9 Higher General Education

An Elusive Triangle

Higher education is an important social institution. As observed by Philip Altbach, it serves as an avenue for social mobility, as a means of providing the skills needed for a modernizing society, as a 'parking lot' for people who otherwise would be unemployed, as a source of political power and sometimes, even as a business enterprise.[1]

The elusive triangle of Indian education comprising quantity, quality and equality to which J.P. Naik referred[2] applies to higher education as well. In this chapter, the quantitative expansion and its fall out in terms of quality and equality (the latter two aspects as affected by policy interventions) would be dealt with followed by a look at the variety of Central Universities operating in India which serves as an overture to the theme of the next chapter.

Quantitative Expansion: Dimensions

Table 9.1 below underlines the enormous quantitative expansion of higher education system in the period 1950–51 to 2006–07:

Table 9.1

Quantitative Expansion of Higher Education in India (1950–51 to 2007–08)

Particulars	*1950–51*	*2007–08*	*Remarks*
No. of Universities	28	408	14-fold increase
Number of Colleges*	695	22,064	32-fold increase
Student Enrolment	1,74,000	123.77 lakh	71-fold increase
No. of Teachers	21,264	5.22 lakh	23-fold increase

Source: (1) Moonis Raza (Ed.) (1991) (2) Annual Reports of UGC from 1953–2008.

Table 9.2 depicts the development of higher education in India at 10-year intervals up to 1991–92 and thereafter annually up to 2007–08, the latest year for which data are available, in terms of institutions (universities and colleges), student enrolment and teachers.[3]

The growth of enrolment peaked in 1970–71, i.e., at the beginning of the Fourth Five-Year Plan and a period of stabilization and consolidation ensued. Incidentally, 1971 was also the year in which the UGC Act was amended to regulate establishment of new universities. In 1985–86, the rate of growth of enrolment picked up again. Thus, the enrolment has passed through three phases – a high enrolment phase (1947–1970), a stabilization phase (1970–85), and a new but lower growth phase (1985–2008), in which the annual rate of growth is about half of what was achieved in the first phase of growth. Moonis Raza has observed that the annual compound growth rate in the first three plans was 11.2 per cent, 13.5 per cent and 14 per cent respectively.[4] Correspondingly, the growth in the number of colleges has also been high particularly in the 1960s. The growth of colleges has picked up in recent years, apparently reflecting the phenomenon of self-financing institutions floated by the politically influential rural kulaks and urban commercial classes.

Table 9.2

Quantitative Growth of Higher Education: Number of Universities, Colleges, Students and Teachers (1950–51 to 2007–08)

Year	*No. of Universities*	*No. of Colleges*	*Student Enrolment*	*%age Increase Over Previous Year*	*No. of Teachers*
1950–51	28	695	1,74,000	—	21,264
1960–61	44	1,542	5,57,000	—	55,460
1970–71	84	3,604	19,54,000	09.0	1,28,876
1980–81	112	4,722	27,53,000	03.9	1,93,341
1985–86	132	5,816	36,05,029	05.9	2,26,909
1990–91	176	7,121	49,24,868	07.0	2,63,125
1991–92	180	7,513	52,65,886	06.9	2,70,000
1992–93	187	7,958	55,34,966	05.1	2,78,000
1993–94	197	8,210	58,17,249	05.1	2,86,000
1994–95	204	8,613	61,13,929	05.1	3,01,000
1995–96	207	9,278	65,74,005	07.5	3,10,000
1996–97	214	9,703	68,42,598	04.1	3,21,000
1997–98	228	10,555	72,60,418	06.1	3,31,000
1998–99	228	11,089	77,05,520	06.1	3,42,000
1999–2000	236	11,831	80,50,607	04.5	3,51,000
2000–01	245	12,342	83,99,443	04.3	3,95,000
2001–02	253	13,150	89,64,680	06.7	4,27,000
2002–03	300	15,343	95,16,773	06.2	4,36,000
2003–04	320	16,885	99,53,506	04.6	4,57,000
2004–05	343	17,625	1,04,81,042	05.3	4,72,000
2005–06	355	18,064	1,10,28,020	05.2	4,85,000
2006–07	376	20,677	1,16,12,505	05.3	5,05,000
2007–08	408	22,064	1,23,17,000	06.0 (Approx.)	5,22,000

Sources: (1) Moonis Raza (Ed.) (1991); (2) Annual Reports of UGC from 1953–2008.

With its absolute enrolment at 123.17 lakh, India is internationally the third ranking state in the matter of higher education enrolment next only to the US and China. However, in terms of the gross enrolment ratio (GER), or enrolment as a proportion of age-specific population (17–23), India ranks quite low. Its gross enrolment ratio (GER) is estimated to have increased from 0.7 per cent in 1950–51 to 1.4 per cent in 1960–61 and to about 10 per cent in 2001–02. This compares with the following international data: countries in transition (36.5%), developed countries (54.6%), developing countries (11.3%), and the world (23.2%).[5] Ironically, while in the second half of 20th century, UGC was urging State Governments to exercise restraint in expansion, in the first decade of the 21st century, it is now pushing for expansion of higher education by way of raising the GER at least to 15 per cent by the end of the Eleventh Five-Year Plan.

Institutional Growth

Universities

The number of Central Universities has increased from three in 1947 to 25 in 2007–08, an eight-fold increase – many of them in the north-east of India. The number of State Universities including five institutes has increased from 17 to 242, a fourteen-fold increase. The 'deemed' universities and institutions of national importance (categories unknown in 1947) – numbered 103 and 33 respectively. This number excludes seven Indian Institutes of Management (IIMs) which are run by registered societies

Colleges

But the primordial and the most numerous institutions of Higher Education (HEIs) in India are the ubiquitous colleges, whose number increased from 459 in 1947 to 22,064 in 2007–08 – a 48-fold increase. Most of these colleges are affiliated ones, only a few being constituent colleges of universities (estimated to be about 525) and what are under a Fourth Plan scheme recognized as autonomous colleges (281 in 2007–08). A notable feature of the college growth scene is that their number more than doubled in the period from 1997–98 (10,555 colleges) to 2007–08 (22,064 colleges).

Teachers

There has been a 23 fold increase in the number of teachers from 21,264 in 1950–51 to 5.22 lakh in 2007–08. There is evidently a fall off of faculty-student ratio, a sure indicator of the lowering of standards. A structural analysis of expansion shows that, the picture is not very rosy. The share of postgraduate and research students vis-à-vis undergraduate students had deteriorated in 2007–08 as compared with 1950–51. This is an undesirable secular trend, which reflects the result of the clout enjoyed by the state governments in the matter of institutional growth:

Table 9.3

Institutional Growth

Year	*Undergraduate*	*Postgraduate*	*Research*	*Diploma Certificate*
1950–51 *	83.7%	11.5%	0.83%	N.A.
2007–08 **	89.15%	09.26%	0.66%	0.93%

Sources: *Moonis, Raza (1991), ** UGC Annual Report, 2007–08.

Ph.D. degree holders in science, technology and allied fields and their progressive increase might serve as one of the proxies for a nation's progress as a 'knowledge society'. The data in this regard are as below:

Table 9.4

Ph.D. Degree Holders

Year	*Arts, Commerce and Allied*	*Science, Technology and Allied*	*Total*
1961–62	339	476	815
2004–05	7,993	9,905	17,898
2007–08	Arts Faculty 8257	Science Faculty: 5839 Other Faculties: 5535	19,131

Note: The data for 1961–62 and 2004–05 have been reclassified and displayed. Thus Science Ph.Ds in Arts/Science colleges are shown under S&T and not under Arts; Ph.Ds. in law, education and fine arts are shown under Arts. For 2007–08 data classification is as given in the UGC Report.

Sources: (1) Moonis Raza, 1991; (2) UGC Annual Report 2007–08.

Although the number of Ph.D. degree holders has gone up about 25 times in a span of about 45 years, the number of Ph.D. holders in arts and allied fields (commerce, law, education, fine arts etc.) has gone up by a larger factor (22.2%) than the number of Ph.D. holders in science and allied fields (20 times).This is because the faculty-wise enrolment in science, technology and allied areas has gone down from 38.1 per cent to 31.96 per cent as compared with faculty enrolment in arts and allied fields which has gone up from 61.8 per cent to 68.64 per cent vide data in Table 9.5.

Table 9.5

Faculty-wise Enrolment

Years	*1960–61 (%)*	*2007–2008 (%)*
Arts and Allied		
Arts	44.9	44.51
Commerce/Management	10.2	18.13

Cont'd...

...Cont'd

Education	01.5	01.52
Law	02.3	03.07
Others	03.0	00.81
Total	61.9	68.04
Science and Technology and Allied		
Science	30.0	20.55
Engineering/Technology	03.6	07.39
Medical	02.7	03.27
Agricultural	01.3	00.59
Veterinary Science	00.5	00.16
Total	38.1	31.96
Grand Total	100	100

Sources: Moonis Raza, 1991 and UGC, Annual Report, 2007–08.

Quantitative Expansion: Causation

The root causes of the growth in enrolment are: Firstly, India basically followed an 'open door' policy with a permissive approach towards establishment of new institutions and a non-selective policy in the matter of admissions in the arts, science and commerce courses. Since the constitutional reforms of 1919, education was a state subject and continued to be so not only under the Government of India Act of 1935, but even under the Constitution of independent India adopted in 1950, and this was a necessary condition for the surge in enrolment. Secondly, the states themselves were to some extent overwhelmed by the groundswell of 'social' demand for education, which was held in check by the unstable inter-war period characterized successively by retrenchment policies of the Central Government, the Great Depression, the provincial autonomy and the political agitations. Thus, after independence, new regional universities came up to meet aspirations of linguistic regions in areas of Bombay-Maharashtra, Bombay-Gujarat, Madras-Andhra Pradesh, Mysore-Karnataka, Travancore-Cochin-Kerala, etc. The pent-up demand also included unmet demand from the so-called "depressed" classes, from women and from minorities, who were deprived of higher education for generations. There was generally a vertical push from below exercised by the rapid expansion of secondary school education. Thus, the social demand was made up of a complex web of factors. Thirdly, and this is to be categorized as a distinct factor, the partition involved division of two British provinces, viz., the Punjab and Bengal and this entailed not only the loss of certain educational institutions serving the population of the residuary India (e.g., loss of Lahore and Dacca universities to Pakistan), but the influx of refugees from West Pakistan, viz., Sind, Punjab and North-West Frontier Province and East Pakistan, i.e., East Bengal, to neighbouring Indian provinces like Delhi, Rajasthan, Gujarat, Maharashtra and West Bengal necessitating establishment of new institutions to meet the demand for higher education from the increasing influx of refugees. Colleges in West Bengal and especially Calcutta have seen the phenomenon of overcrowding because of waves of refugees from East Pakistan at periodical intervals. Fourthly, morning and evening college classes were started by way of non-formal higher education from 1947 onwards for urban professionals and these were institutionalized by the UGC since the early 1960s through correspondence courses in conventional universities which have now been re-christened as the Correspondence Course Institutes (CCIs) and the opening of a parallel track State Open Universities (SOUs) as well as the IGNOU (estd. 1985). This open distance learning (ODL) system has gradually expanded and accounted for about 24 per cent enrolment in 2002–03 and was estimated to reach 33 per cent in 2007.[6] (Andhra Pradesh was the first state to set up a State Open University in 1982 and the National Open University (IGNOU) followed in 1985, and other states also opened their own open universities subsequently). Although the UGC was initially slow to promote the expansion of the CCIs and the Government of India delayed the setting up of a national open university for almost 15 years (the proposal to open an open university in India having been mooted shortly after UK-OU came up in 1968). The recent proliferation of franchising centres by conventional universities because of slack supervision by the Distance Education Council (DEC) working under the IGNOU, has also helped in expansion though, at the cost of quality, as observed by educational experts.[7]

The expansion had left in its wake certain disturbing features. On the eve of NPE 1986, an official document underlined the following infirmities of the higher education system:

- The growing mismatch between education and employment – between the world of knowledge and world of work.
- The exclusive emphasis on quantitative expansion leading to declining standards of teaching, examination and research.
- The continuance of dysfunctionalities in the form of factors and pressures, which were acting as major roadblocks on the path of implementation of strategic reforms.[8]

The NPE 1986 was modified in 1992. These modifications were overtaken in 1991 by a phase in India's economic growth, when economic compulsions required India to undertake a structural adjustment programme in the backdrop of integration of India with the world financial system and world trade in compliance with the conditionalities of the IMF and the World Bank. This has meant a new scenario of the so-called LPG (liberalization, privatization and globalization) entailing compression of social sector expenditure. The educational expansion since 1991 is not a centrally planned one – it is driven by a blend of state actions, judicial interventions, private initiatives, international factors and unforeseen consequence of past actions. As a result, private sector in higher education has grown and now accounts for 43 per cent of the number of institutions and 30 per cent of enrolment as seen from the table below:

Table 9.6

Higher Education Institutions and Enrolment (by type of management)

	Higher Education Institutions (Universities + Colleges)		*Enrolment (in thousand)*	
Type	*2000–01*	*2005–06*	*2000–01*	*2005–06*
Government	4,342 (245+4,097)	4,493 (268+4,225)	3,443	3,752
Private aided	5,507 (10+4,997)	5,760 (10+5,750)	3,134	3,510
Private (unaided)	3,223 (21+3,202)	7,720 (70+7,650)	1,822	3,219
Total	13,072 (276+12,296)	17,973 (348+17,625)	8,399	10,481

Source: Pawan Agarwal (2009), *Higher Education in India*, p. 91.

The above table indicates that private share of institutional spread and enrolment is high but the fact that the precise turning point came after 1991 is demonstrated by the following table showing the growth of engineering colleges in India:

Table 9.7

Growth of Engineering Colleges in India

Type	*1947*	*1960*	*1970*	*1980*	*1990*	*2000*	*2006*	*2007*
Government and Aided	42	111	135	142	164	202	212	215
Unaided	2	3	4	15	145	467	1,299	1,402
Total	44	114	139	157	309	669	1,511	1,617

Source: Pawan Agarwal (2009), *Higher Education in India*, p. 89.

It is seen that right till 1990, government and aided institutions together made up 164 institutions, which was much higher than 145.

However, within 10 years, the numbers had turned decisively in favour of the private sector (government and aided 202 as against private 467) and the dominance of private sector in 2007 was overwhelming (215 – government/government aided as against 1,402 private).

That the dominance of private sector has spread to all the areas of technical and professional education is shown by Table 9.8. It is seen that the private share of professional courses varies from above 90 per cent (pharmacy, hotel management, physiotherapy and engineering) to 50 per cent in medicine.

Table 9.8

Professional Higher Education Institutions: Growth and Private Share

Name of the Course	*1999–2000*	*July 2007 & (2006–07)*	*Percentage Increase*	*Private Share (%)*
Engineering	669	1,617	142	91
Pharmacy	204	736	261	95
Hotel Management	41	80	95	94
Architecture	78	116	49	67
Computer Applications (MCA)	780	999	28	62
Management (MBA/PGDM)	682	1,150	69	64
Teacher Education (B.Ed.)	1,050	(5,190)	395	68
Medicine (MBBS)	174	(233)	32	50
Dentistry (BDS)	45	(189)	420	59
Physiotherapy	52	(205)	294	92
Total	3,775	10,515	178	80

Source: Pawan Agarwal (2009), *Higher Education in India*, p. 88.

Equity Aspect of Higher Education Development

J.P. Naik[9] pointed out that equality should be the most significant concern of Indian planners because Indian society has been extremely inegalitarian and this is one value on the basis of which Indian society could be humanized and strengthened. Inequities can manifest themselves, in various dimensions like, regional (backward/advanced), class (rich/poor), rural/urban, and the physical handicap or disability. The colonial government had singled out for emphasis the education of the girls for social reasons and education of the depressed classes (SCs) and the Muslims for political reasons. The Indian Constitution, especially since the first constitutional amendment in 1951, has built-in provisions enabling the state to take special measures for the promotion of socially and educationally backward classes. It was assumed that social backwardness and educational backwardness coexisted and modern planners in India have operated primarily in terms of social welfare measures like hostels, scholarships and concessions of fees for Scheduled

Castes (SCs) and Scheduled Tribes (STs). They also acquiesced in affirmative action policies initiated in the southern states even prior to Independence, by way of reservation of seats in central educational institutions at the stage of admission in the postgraduate courses where an open door policy was not feasible and in professional colleges like engineering and medicine. Both the Radhakrishnan Commission (1950), with the memory of communal quotas in Madras, and the Kothari Commission (1966), concerned with quality aspects, were somewhat slow to recognize the intensity of the feelings in the matter. However, reservations were recommended for backward classes by the First Backward Classes Commission (1955) and as noted, the State Governments primarily in the South, were accustomed to operation of communal quotas. Consequent upon the first amendment to the Constitution [Article 15(4)] in 1951, reservation in admission to the seats in colleges and universities received constitutional sanction and they began to be made systematically by state governments, overall reservations in some states like Tamil Nadu exceeding 50 per cent.[10] Partly in pursuance of the recommendations of the Standing Committee on SCs and STs, the UGC introduced a section on SC/ST education facilities in its report in 1975–76 onwards and invited attention of the universities to instructions about reservation of seats for SC/ST students. Reservation in the faculty recruitment at lecturers' level was agreed to in principle by the UGC in July 1975 and mechanisms were worked out in July 1976, significantly during the Emergency. The UGC also constituted a Standing Committee to monitor progress in the matter. State governments have gone further and extended reservations at the reader and professor levels as well.

Table 9.9

Inequalities in Higher Education in terms of GER

	National Average GER	*10.08%*
(a)	1. Rural	8.09
	2. Urban	21.74
(b)	1. Most developed state/UT (Chandigarh)	26.24
	2. Most backward UT (D&N Haveli)	02.23
(c)	1. Male	12.12
	2. Female	08.00
(d)	1. ST	06.43
	2. SC	05.09
	3. OBC	07.00
	4. General	16.74
(e)	1. Poor	02.47
	2. Non-poor	12.41

The Draft Working Group Report on Higher Education in the Eleventh Plan[11] points out vide Table 9.9 inequalities in different dimensions of higher education, mainly in terms of GER.

Moonis Raza[12] has dealt at length with two select aspects of inequities in higher education, viz., the SCs and the regional dimension. His analysis shows that the share of the SCs in total enrolment has been increasing over time though rather slowly. Their share in general education had increased from 5.5 per cent to 7.9 per cent between the period 1964–65 to 1979–80 (as against their share in population of 15%). With regard to regional disparities, Moonis Raza has analysed the data in terms of 77 NSS regions in 1991, which depict a disturbing picture. As many as 20 NSS regions were without a university, whereas the small UT of Delhi had nine university level institutions. While every region had some facility for college, the regional variations in the quantum of available facilities were quite considerable. Inter-regional variations in enrolment per lakh of population were of a high order, varying from as low as 61 in Arunachal Pradesh to as high as 316 in Chandigarh. In terms of faculty, arts enrolment was ubiquitous, accounting for more than 60 per cent of enrolment in Himachal Pradesh, outer hills of J&K, Meghalaya, Nagaland, Tripura, Arunachal Pradesh, eastern and southern Uttar Pradesh and Andaman & Nicobar Islands. The share of science enrolment varied from 'nil' in Assam Hills or nearly 3 per cent in dry areas of Gujarat to as high as nearly 45 per cent in rural Tamil Nadu.

Gender disparities in higher education appear to be declining. In 1950–51 the number of girls per 100 boys was 14 which increased to 35 in 1979–80 and was 68 in 2007–08. Sachar Report on Muslims, which has used the latest socio-economic data, shows that the SCs/STs and Muslims are the most disadvantaged in the matter of higher education (graduate level education) as their respective shares are much lower than their share in population (6% as against 11% in the case of Muslims).[13]

Quality Aspect of Higher Education

The UGC had appointed[14] Sundarrajan Committee on Standards of University Education. Its report concluded that:

- while the quality of the best students is as good as ever, the average product of an Indian university does not compare favourably with his counterparts in some of the well-known universities in the world;
- many of our scholars and scientists have done outstanding work; and
- the various steps taken by the UGC have made a definite contribution to improvement of facilities in universities and colleges ... (but) the resources at the disposal of the Commission have been far from adequate to deal effectively with this problem.

The Committee recommended the concept of autonomous colleges to be given special assistance because colleges were crucial for quality.

The major recommendations of the Education Commission for improving quality of higher education were:

- establishment of five or six major universities,
- strengthening and expansion of UGC programme of establishment of Centres of Advanced Study.

While the recommendation about major universities did not find favour with the government, the latter scheme was given a fillip especially in the Fifth Plan (1974–79).

The issue of deterioration in quality of Indian higher education is serious and any remedy is not in sight. How serious it is, was described by the Education Commission in its report: "There is a general feeling in India that the situation in higher education is unsatisfactory and even alarming in some ways, that the average standards have been falling and that rapid expansion has resulted in lowering quality. The examination results, the reports of Public Service Commissions, the views of employers and the assessment of teachers themselves – all seem to support this conclusion … . Many of our educationists and public men, however, have not fully realized how serious are the actual conditions – academic and physical, that obtain in the colleges and universities. Even those who are broadly aware of the situation fail to notice its poignancy because they have become used to such conditions."[15]

Veteran experts like Amrik Singh[16] had expressed apprehension about the low quality of ODL systems in terms of well equipped and well staffed study centres. The National Assessment and Accreditation Council (NAAC), set up in 1994 in terms of NPE to assess quality, had initially adopted a proactive role in accrediting institutions, but its progress has flagged-off (only 142 universities and 3,271 colleges accredited at end of 2008).

The remedies suggested by the Education Commission were not implemented and as usual government could be blamed. But the major actors like teachers cannot escape their share of blame. N. Jayaram[17] has talked of the "Fall of the Guru" in modern India in following terms: "The decline (of the academic profession) that was noticed over a quarter century ago is now almost complete. Entering the profession with no prior professional preparations other than a postgraduate degree, assured of tenure, doing unchallenging work without any accountability and with their performance being no more than its own reward, teachers at colleges and universities have been largely reduced to the lowest common denominator. Ironically, the improvements in pay-scales and service conditions have come at a time when the profession has almost sunk to its lowest level". Any further comment is superfluous.

Central Higher Educational Institutions

The creeping centralization of higher general education is depicted in the following paragraph by way of initiation to the theme of federal impact in the next chapter.

Central educational institutions are of the following types:

1. Central Universities established under Acts of Parliament.
2. Centrally funded deemed universities.
3. Centrally funded institutions of national importance (e.g., INIs).
4. Central quasi-universities run by registered societies, e.g., IMIs.

Perhaps in no federation other than India do we have a category of Central Universities. In the US, the universities are either private, mainly non-profit, but more recently profit also, or State Universities. In Canada, all and in Australia all except for the Australian National University in Canberra, the capital city, are State Universities. In India, the phenomenon of Central Universities has emerged due to historical reasons.

After 1950 there were repeated demands for starting new Central Universities other than Banaras Hindu, Aligarh Muslim and Delhi, whose names were in the relevant entry of the Seventh Schedule of the Constitution. The question was considered important enough to be specifically referred to the CABE Committee chaired by Karasanbhai Soneri on Gnanam Committee Report in 1991 when their number was 10 which included Vishwabharati, JNU, Hyderabad, NEHU, Pondicherry and Jamia Milia established in that order. It reportedly recommended that a Central University should be opened only to correct a regional imbalance or to cover large gaps in the educational map of the country, and that a Central University should have an all-India character in terms of admission of students and composition of teaching faculty. However, fifteen new Central Universities were started/proposed after the CABE Committee reported (1991), fourteen of them by the Ministry of Education, eight in the north-east, one each for Hindi and Urdu, two in Uttar Pradesh (Lucknow and Allahabad), the Central Tribal University in Madhya Pradesh and the English and Foreign Language University at Hyderabad by conversion of a deemed university and the fifteenth one was the Central Agricultural University started by the Agriculture Ministry in 1993 at Imphal, Manipur, covering the seven north-eastern states excluding Assam, but including Sikkim.

Universities

At the time of independence, there were only three Central Universities. However, the number of Central Universities has gone up since then and deemed universities and INIs have been added to their number. About fifty deemed universities are supported by the Central Government either directly or through the UGC. IIMs run by the Central Government-controlled registered societies are also included since for practical purposes, they are universities granting postgraduate and doctoral degrees. Treating the year 1977, when education became a Concurrent List subject as the watershed, the growth of various types of central education institutes is indicated in the following table:

Table 9.10

Growth of Central Educational Institutions (1947–2008)

Universities	*1947*	*1977*	*2008*
Central	03	07	25
Deemed	—	10	50
INIs (Institutions of National Importance)	—	09	33
Central Quasi-Universities run by Registered Societies (IIMs)	—	03	07
Total	03	29	115

Sources: 1. UGC Annual Reports for various years including Annual Report 2007–08,
2. Press reports in regard to new Central Universities of Allahabad, in the North-East and in Madhya Pradesh (Tribal University).

If we take into account the deemed universities, INIs and IIMs, the effective number of Central Universities as in 2008 increases from 25 to 115 (25 + deemed universities 50 + INIs 33 + IIMs 07), which is a substantial number in a tally of a total 408 university level institutions in the country. This highlights the double need to pierce the veil of nomenclature and to take into account the source of funding to decide the nature of the university (central or state).

The existence of Central Universities mostly located in the north, the east and the north-eastern parts of the country has implications for centre-state financial relations to the extent that they represent substantial financial saving for the respective State Governments and also open up job opportunities. The student admission and teacher recruitment pattern of the Central Universities shows that in most Central Universities, the large majority of students and teachers are from respective or neighbouring states (Delhi, Uttar Pradesh, Bihar, Orissa, West Bengal). Since the Central Universities of BHU and AMU also happen to have constituent or affiliated colleges and faculties of agriculture, engineering and medicine and large hospitals attached to them as part of respective medical faculties, it is evident that part of the central grants in maintaining Central Universities in the respective States effectively subsidize both general collegiate and professional education and health services in those states, otherwise a liability of respective states. The sums involved are substantial. To take a sample, according to 2003–04 Annual Report of the UGC, the non-plan grants for BHU colleges were of the order of Rs 296 lakh as compared to the non-plan grants for all the universities in Maharashtra in the same year, which stood at Rs 219 lakh. The non-plan grants for AMU and BHU as a whole including expenditure on hospitals were in the region of Rs 149 crore and Rs 159 crore respectively.

Deemed Universities

The deemed universities are a comparatively less transparent area of the activities of the Central Government and the UGC. The relevant Section 3 of the UGC Act gives to the Central Government/UGC unregulated power of delegated legislation: an institution can be notified as a deemed university by the Central Government simply on the advice of the UGC which is guided by its own guidelines, there being no appropriate subordinate legislation (rules and regulations). The initial guidelines in force till the year 2000 were that the institutions should be doing work of a high standard in a specialized academic field with 10 years' standing and located in one campus. The modality was for the UGC to appoint a visiting committee, which if favourably inclined, would also suggest a model constitution. An analysis has revealed that initial notifications related to (1) national educational institutions set up in the agitations of 1906 and 1920; (2) government postgraduate and research institutions with high standards; and (3) institutions run by the private charitable societies – non-profit institutions of high standard. In the 1970s, only three institutions were added, one is a Gandhian institution and two central institutions with good credentials. In the 1980s and 1990s, a slightly liberal approach was adopted. However, this situation changed with the revised guidelines of the year 2000. The number of institutions granted deemed university (DU) status in the first 42 years (1958–2000) is about the same as the number of institutions granted the DU status in the three years 2001–2003. This has been done by waiving the original requirement of 10 years' standing and of the institution being single-campus. The main new requirement for private institutions is to have a corpus of Rs 5 crore for technical institutions and Rs 3 crore for social science institutions and to demonstrate that the institutions are engaged in innovative and application-oriented teaching programmes. In regard to government institutions, the regional engineering colleges were decided to be upgraded as deemed universities by renaming them as National Institutes of Technology and further the newly established information technology institutions at Allahabad and Gwalior were ab initio notified as deemed universities. The new guidelines were apparently designed to implement the spirit of the Private Universities Bill, 1995 (which was introduced in the Rajya Sabha in August 1995 but not proceeded with). The unguided discretion has thus involved a policy of 'picking and choosing' institutions for maintenance grants and backdoor 'privatization' because these new non-government DUs are mostly self-financing. According to UGC Annual Report 2007–08, there were 103 deemed universities in India. It is understood from press reports that the UGC under direction of Central Government has issued revised regulations for deemed universities in the month of May 2010 which imply a reversion to pre-2000 guidelines.

Institutions of National Importance (INIs)

The fluidity of the distinction between the deemed universities maintained by the Central Government and the INIs is underlined by the fact that what are for legal purposes treated as deemed universities are classified by respective ministries as national institutions. Thus, the Department of Agricultural Research and Education classifies Indian Agricultural Research Institute (IARI), New Delhi, Indian Veterinary Research Institute (IVRI), Izatnagar (Uttaranchal), National Dairy Research Institute (NDRI), Karnal (Haryana), and the Central Institute of Fisheries Education (CIFE), Mumbai (Maharashtra) as National Institutions. The respective ministries wanted degree-giving powers, but did not want to resort to legislation. So, they adopted the easier route of notifying them as deemed universities.

Coming to INIs proper, they are educational institutions considered by the central political leadership to be of all-India importance. It is, therefore, expected that these institutions should be treated as institutions of all-India rather than merely central importance and that they should also attain international standards. Their governing bodies should reflect their all-India/international character and in the federal context, should give representation not only to the state where an INI is located but also to other states. In practice, these have tended to be treated as another species of Central Universities especially as they are also empowered to award degrees. Of the 33 INIs in the educational field, seven are IITs, four are in the medical field, one relates to statistics and one to Hindi. The number of INIs swelled when 20 regional engineering colleges were converted into INIs via being notified as deemed universities. The way the RECs became INIs illustrates the tendency of centralization by conversion of joint, i.e., state-centre cooperative institutions into INIs (see the note below). At least two INIs started as state level institutions, viz., PGIMER, Chandigarh and the Thiruvananthapuram Medical Institute.

Transformation of Centre-State Institutions into Central Institutions

Seventeen regional engineering colleges (RECs) were sanctioned by the AICTE in all the major states of India between 1960 and 1987 as jointly managed and financed institutions between the Centre and the states. They were an example of cooperative federalism in technical education. There were problems in joint management as there are bound to be. However, in 1998, the Mashelkar Committee after reviewing the functioning of RECs, expressed dissatisfaction with the governance arrangements, and recommended that the RECs (then affiliated to respective universities) be delinked from State Governments and renamed as Regional Institutions of Engineering and Technology. The Central Government decided to rename RECs as National Institutes of Technology (NITs), thus ending their regional/state linkage and declaring them as deemed universities and still later, giving them statutory status. The constitution of the NITs does not provide any representation to the State Governments. Thus, the RECs have ended up by being central institutions euphemistically called national institutions. At present there are 33 INIs including 20 NITs.

Central Quasi-Universities run by Registered Societies: IIMs

As in the case of IITs, IIMs follow an American model and have developed their own 'brand'. Though, all the IIMs (Ahmedabad, Kolkata, Bangalore, Lucknow, Indore, Kochi and Shillong) are registered societies, they can no doubt, be considered to be institutions of national importance. The composition of the Board of Governors provides for representation of the state of location, though its effectiveness is doubtful. During the controversy about reduction of fees of the IIMs (proposed by the NDA government, which proposal was withdrawn by the UPA Government in May 2004), West Bengal and Gujarat governments, which were represented on the Board of Governors of IIM, Kolkata and IIM, Ahmedabad respectively toed the line of the HRD Ministry.

Institutions under Technical Education Bureau of Education Ministry

In the Higher Education Bureau of the Education Ministry, the majority of institutions are maintained by the UGC, the exceptions being (i) the Indian Institute of Advanced Studies, Simla, (ii) Zakir Husain College, Delhi, and (iii) the Indira Gandhi National Open University (IGNOU), which is the only Central University maintained by the Education Ministry directly. The Technical Education Bureau, however, has chosen not to transfer higher technical education institutions for maintenance to the AICTE. Apart from seven IITs and IIMs each, which are supervised by it, the Bureau directly runs following twenty institutions:

1. National Institute of Industrial Engineering (NITIE), Mumbai.
2. Indian School of Mines (deemed university) Dhanbad.
3. National Institute of Foundry and Forge Technology (NIFFT), Ranchi.
4. School of Planning and Architecture,(SPA), New Delhi (deemed university).

5–8. National Institutes of Technical Teachers' Training and Research (NITTTRs) at Bhopal, Chandigarh, Chennai and Kolkata.

9. Indian Institute of Science, Bangalore (deemed university).

10–14. Institutions of Science Education and Research at Kolkata, Pune, Mohali, Bhopal and Thiruvanathapuram.

15–18. Indian Institutes of Information Technology at Allahabad, Gwalior, Jabalpur and Kancheepuram (The Jabalpur Institute deals with design and manufacture also).

Vertically Integrated Technical Education Institutions (which conduct certificate diploma and degree courses on the same campus).

19. Sant Longowal Institute of Engineering and Technology at Longowal, District Sangrur (Punjab).

20. North-Eastern Regional Institute of Science and Technology, Itanagar (Arunachal Pradesh).

Conclusion

Higher education which developed as an enclave in the colonial times has not been able to erase its colonial imprint. According to Moonis Raza, its post-independence development is in the same (enclave) mould, but most worrisome is the professional decline leading to academic stagnation underlined by N. Jayaram.

Edward A. Shils' observations in 1967 appear to retain their validity even now: "An excessively politicized political culture helps to demoralize intellectual institutions and dooms them to ineffectual mediocrity. India is a case in point ... the deficiencies of the Indian university are deficiencies of teaching and research and of *intellectual morale*. The filament that binds minds together into an intellectual community has gone dead or had been ruptured. The Indian universities are supplying manpower to strengthen and expand its modern sector but are unable to supply ideas and judgment that enliven political life. The major task in the development of the Indian intellectual community is the promotion of its intellectual creativity. A new charter is needed for the intellectual community in India and in that charter the universities must come to occupy a more central position than they do at present."[18]

The central message of this diagnosis is the need to reduce politicization of higher education.

Notes

1. Philip Altbach, "The Dilemma of Change in Indian Higher Education", in Suma Chitnis and Philip Altbach (Eds.), *Higher Education Reforms in India: Experience and Perspective* (New Delhi: Sage Publications, 1993), 32.
2. J.P. Naik, *Equality, Quality and Quantity: The Elusive Triangle in Indian Education* (Bombay: Allied Publishers, 1975).

3. Neither the non-statutory interim UGC established in 1953 nor the statutory UGC from 1956 onwards included in the initial years any enrolment statistics in their Reports. The enrolment statistics were presented for the first time in the Annual Report of UGC for 1961–62 and that too in the form of charts rather than statistical tables. UGC started giving statistical tables regarding enrolment for the first time in the Annual Report 1971–72, in which at p. 49, the Growth of Student Enrolment is presented for the ten year period 1961–62 to 1971–72. It is stated that enrolment data includes enrolment in intermediate classes under the Board of High School and Intermediate Education, UP. It is only in NIEPA publications, that we get authentic enrolment data, net of enrolment of the intermediate students. The data given by Moonis Raza are from NIEPA sources.
4. Moonis Raza, *Higher Education in India: Retrospect and Prospect* (New Delhi: Association of Indian Universities, 1991).
5. UGC: Eleventh Plan Proposals, 2007.
6. V.C. Kulandaiswamy, "National Educational Policies vis-à-vis Distance Education", in Suresh Garg et al. (Eds.), *Four Decades of Distance Education in India: Reflections on Policy and Practice* (New Delhi: Viva Books, 2004), 24–38.
7. Amrik Singh, *The Challenge of Education* (Hyderabad: ICFAI Press, 2004), 24–38.
8. Ministry of Education: The Challenge of Education (New Delhi, 1985).
9. Vide Footnote No. 2.
10. Constitutionally protected by inclusion in the Ninth Schedule of the Constitution vide entry 357 A, about the Tamil Nadu Backward Classes, SCs and STs (Reservation of Seats in Educational Institutions and Appointments to posts in the services under the State) Act 1993.
11. Ministry of HRD: Draft Working Group Report on Higher Education in the Eleventh Plan (New Delhi, 2007).
12. Vide Footnote No. 4.
13. Sachar Report, 65–67.
14. University Grants Commission: Report of the Committee on Standards (New Delhi, 1965).
15. Kothari Report, para 1.121.
16. Vide Footnote No. 7.
17. N. Jayaram, "The Fall of the Guru: The Decline of the Academic Profession in India", in Philip Altbach (Ed.), *The Academic Profession in the Developing and the Middle Eastern Countries* (New York: Boston College Press, 2000).
18. Edward A. Shils, "Toward a Modern Intellectual Community in New States", in James S. Coleman (Ed.), *Education and Political Development* (Princeton, N.J.: Princeton University Press, 1967), 498–518.

10 Federal Impact on Higher General Education

Three Case Studies

In this chapter, the general theme of the federal impact on higher education would be illustrated by three case studies relating respectively to the regulatory role of the UGC, the regionalization of medium of instruction and the asymmetry in the role of the President of India and the Governors of states vis-à-vis the universities.

Case Study I
The Regulatory Role of the University Grants Commission

The statutory UGC was set up by the Central Government in 1956, as recommended by Radhakrishnan Commission[1] in terms of the powers under entry 66 of the Central List of the Seventh Schedule of the Indian Constitution. It promotes and coordinates development of higher education in India comprising the variety of institutions referred to in the preceding chapter and works for determination and maintenance of standards of teaching, examinations, research and extension in institutions of higher education.[2] It is not intended in this chapter to make a general review of the functioning of the UGC which has been done masterfully by Amrik Singh.[3] The functioning of the UGC in the federal context up to 1980 has been studied by Marina Pinto[4], a political scientist. Her general conclusion is that the friction points in the federal tie-up between the UGC, the State Governments and the State Universities cannot be taken care of without some coordinating body at the state level (which brings together the UGC, State Government officers, VCs, academicians and experts) in the form of either (a) state UGCs or (b) regional offices of the Central UGC.[5] As would be shown below, State UGCs renamed State Councils of Higher Education (SCHE) have been set up only in a few states and the UGC has not pushed for their further adoption because of the fear of politicization. As for regional offices of UGC, they were set up in 1994–95 but have not made much of a difference in the absence of proper delegation. Two other suggestions by the influential MPs' committee called Sapru Committee – about empowering the UGC to curb the unplanned expansion and having a Model Act for universities have not made any impact, the former because of the wording of the amendment to the UGC Act and the latter because of the opposition of the CABE Committee. The purpose of the present case study is to point out how a coordinating body in higher education sector like the UGC has fared in the Indian federal set-up.

Origin of the UGC

The Central Government initially (i.e., in 1953) wanted to create a powerful body called the Central Council of University Education which would have enjoyed the power to grant initial recognition to a university and to de-recognize, for purposes of government employment, the degree of any university which fails to comply with any direction of the Central Council. The draft bill was opposed by the Inter-University Board (IUB)[6], in the name of the autonomy of the universities,[7] but if we probe a little deeper, we realize that the opposition really came from the academics who belonged to powerful socio-educationally non-forward but upwardly mobile castes in important states and sub-served the purpose of the states as a group. They included A.L. Mudaliar, C. Shanmugan Chetty and others. Of course, the IUB itself coveted the role of the coordinator, but it knew that the colonial state (in Sargent Plan 1944) had rejected that possibility and the Radhakrishnan Commission had done the same. Even the joint committee of Parliament revised the UGC bill in such a way that it made UGC virtually powerless. The only power the UGC has is to withhold grants[8] and while we can blame successive chairmen of the UGC for being soft (and Prof. D.S. Kothari, Chairman for long years 1961–73, was against the option)[9] the fact remains, as pointed out by Rudolphs,[10] that India had a tradition going back to pre-independence days of not enforcing such powers too strictly.

UGC's Inability to Regulate Institutional Expansion

After 1947, the states went on an expansion spree in regard to the opening of new colleges and universities. The UGC, after it was set up in 1953 as an advisory body and in 1956 as a statutory body in its successive Annual Reports deplored the unplanned expansion, but could not do much about it. Its initial focus was on strengthening of college/university plant and buildings, laboratories and libraries and also advocate periodical pay revision of teachers. So far as affiliation of colleges is concerned, the final voice, since the British days, and especially under the university legislation of Lord Curzon, belonged to the State Governments. Even, the Education Commission was compelled to clarify that the State Governments have a role to the extent the opening of new colleges meant financial implications in the terms of financial grants-in-aid.[11] Social forces behind the expansion were the dominant castes in various states, illustratively Lingayats/Vokkaligas in Karnataka, Khammas/Reddis in Andhra Pradesh, Marathas and Malis in Maharashtra, Kayasthas and Bhumihars in Bihar and Zamindars in Uttar Pradesh.

After the report of the Sapru Committee of 1964, there was a two-fold move: (1) to bring higher education on the concurrent list to enable UGC to frame a Model Act for universities, and (2) to amend the UGC Act to give it powers to deny financial assistance to new universities (established without its prior approval). The concurrency of education as a whole was brought about during the Emergency (1977), but no follow-up legislation was passed. As for the amendment of the UGC Act, the bill was delayed (it remained pending between 1966 to 1971 and its proposed provisions underwent substantial changes) and the final shape of the Amendment Act was such that it had the effect of merely delaying the grant of financial assistance to the State Universities. The new universities are required to comply with the so-called 'Fitness for Grants Rules' which envisage allocation of minimum land and investment of minimum capital expenditure by the State Governments and provisions in the University legislation to comply with the norms of the Gajendragadkar Committee on Governance.[12] So, it came about that the State Governments went about establishing new universities and affiliating new colleges according to their agenda, generally driven by regional forces. Jha Committee had occasion to observe that in spite of the amendment of UGC Act in 1971 the number of newly created State Universities had not shown a decline.[13] The UGC promulgated guidelines on affiliation of colleges as late as 1987 but they did not lead to any changes in the University Acts of the states.

As for various development schemes of UGC, State Governments have availed of them for creation of posts but have omitted to incorporate "committed" expenditure in their budgets through grants by the successive Finance Commissions. The State Governments have tended to take a more jaundiced view of the UGC as being a somnolent and ineffective body, whose main priority was pay revision of teachers (hence the well-known phrase: UGC pay scales), and which is demonstrably amenable to pressures of trade unions of teachers based in Delhi. The State Governments have, therefore, shown a healthy skepticism of the UGC's tendency to equate college lecturers (recruited through ad hoc selection committees and lacking even a voluntary code of conduct), with Class I government officers who are recruited through Public Service Commissions, who are promoted on the basis of assessment of CRs and who are governed by strict conduct rules. They have resisted what are considered to be inflated pay scales of college teachers imposing heavy financial burdens on state budgets as could be seen from the deliberations of the Mehrotra Committee and from the writings of scholars like Amrik Singh.[14] So far as trade unions are concerned, the above picture needs to be modified only to the extent that teachers' unions in states like Maharashtra and West Bengal were dominated by the Leftist parties and so was the All-India Federation of Teachers' Union (AIFUCTO).

Regional Offices of UGC

Although advisory All-India Council of Technical Education (AICTE) since its establishment in 1945 has its regional offices (which were continued as part of statutory AICTE after 1987), the UGC had resisted establishment of regional offices for a long time. As a combined effect of the Ramamurti Report[15] and the internal report of Administrative Staff College of India (ASCI) on reorganization of UGC did regional offices of the UGC come up in the year 1993–94. They deal with selected programmes and schemes pertaining to colleges. They are located at Pune, Hyderabad, Bangalore, Calcutta, Guwahati and Bhopal.[16] However, regional offices of UGC are merely exercises in financial decentralization of UGC and in particular, do not interact meaningfully with the State Governments and the local academic community as was envisaged by Marina Pinto.[17]

The Case of State Level UGCs (known as State Councils of Higher Education) (SCHEs)

The UGC during the long reign of D.S. Kothari (1961–73), was opposed in principle to state level UGCs on the ground that such a body would undermine the autonomy and initiative of the universities, create confusion as to the role of the Central UGC and would hinder the direct relationship between the Central UGC and State Universities. This was reflected earlier in the report of the Model Act Committee (1964) and reiterated in the Education Commission Report.[18] However, as a result of efforts of the Gajendragadkar Committee (1969) and the Jha Committee (1977), the idea of having some state level body for coordination became respectable. The UGC itself launched in the Sixth Five-Year Plan a bureaucratic scheme called College Development Council, which was headed by an officer of the level of Pro-Vice-Chancellor.[19] Thanks to the convergence of these ideas, NPE 1986 suggested setting up State Councils of Higher Education for state level planning and coordination of higher education.[20] The idea, however, was apparently jinxed. Just when the UGC brought out a report to operationalize the concept, the Osmania University Teachers' Association challenged a similar body set up by Andhra Pradesh government in 1986, which the Supreme Court struck down as being unconstitutional.[21] Though the UGC revised its guidelines so as to steer clear of any legal challenge, the damage had been done. The idea refused to take off. A final blow was struck when the Gnanam Committee (1990) appointed by the UGC recommended a Model Bill on SCHE and the whole report was referred to CABE Committee. It is understood that CABE Committee refused to accept the idea of a Model Bill. As a result, by 1995–96 there were only four regular Councils (Andhra Pradesh, Tamil Nadu, Uttar Pradesh and West Bengal) and three Advisory Councils (Himachal Pradesh, Tripura and Arunachal Pradesh). There has been no further take up of the idea. Amrik Singh believes that state bureaucrats and State Ministers do not want SCHEs because they feel that such Councils would undermine their position.[22] However, the opposition of the State Governors may also be a factor in the idea of SCHEs not taking off because at present Inter-University Boards in states like Maharashtra are presided over by Governors, whereas SCHEs are to be presided over by an eminent educationist. Incidentally, ICAR, has been able to promote the idea of State Councils for Agricultural Education and Research (SCAER) in states having multiple agricultural universities.[23] But they have not been able to completely depoliticize the office of the chairman of SCAER. When a person like Annasaheb Shinde held the office in Maharashtra, SCAER reportedly did well.[24]

The Case of a Model Act for General Universities

The idea of a Model Act for State Universities is not as new fangled as some might imagine. It has been tried with moderate success by the agricultural universities in India, no doubt under American influence, as reflected in the two reports of the Joint Indo-American Teams respectively in 1954 and in 1959. ICAR developed a Model Act for the Agricultural Universities in 1966[25] which was further revised in 1984 and 1994. State Governments of course, are required to be persuaded to adopt the provisions of the Model Act which is a continuous process.[26]

In the case of general education, however, the idea of a Model Act has not made a success in spite of the fact that UGC has been consistently supportive of the idea. Unlike in the case of ICAR, UGC has, however, been slow to do its homework. Various ideas about the governance of universities have been thrown up by successive committees (Model Act Committee 1964, Gajendragadkar Committee, 1969) and the requirement of following Gajendragadkar norms was made legally binding through 'fitness rules' (1972). In the period 1980–85, the idea of having a model Central Act was very much in the air as is seen by Ministers' replies while piloting UGC Amendment Bills in 1984 and 1985. However, UGC had not prepared a draft Model Act even by 1990 with the Gnanam Committee (1990) which was a follow-up of the NPE 1986 recommending categorically that States should agree to adopt the Model Act for governance of universities. However, as in the case of the Model Bill for SCHEs, the idea of Model Act for governance of universities was reportedly not accepted by the CABE committee. In October

2003, a concept paper for a Model Act for universities of the twenty first century in India was floated by the then Vice-Chairman of UGC but it withered away under barrage of leftist criticism.

Case Study II
Regionalization of Medium of Instruction

The issue of the medium of instruction (which comprises both the medium of instruction and examination) arises in India in a salient manner because of its multi-lingual character and because modern higher education in India began through the alien medium of English. The nationalist movement affected education in two waves: 1905 and 1920. In 1905, it emphasized the use of Indian languages at the school stage and in 1920 the national colleges inspired by Gandhiji emphasized the use of Indian languages at higher education stage. Earlier, in 1918, Osmania University in the princely state of Hyderabad had introduced Urdu, an Indian language as a medium of education. Though, the Constitution in 1950 envisaged replacement of English by Hindi as the official language by 1965, the issue became triangulated and Independent India had three choices before it: (1) continue status quo, i.e., continuance of English, which was supported by some genuine advocates of "national integration", who were also joined by vested interests who raised the bogey of quality, besides emphasizing the role of English as an international link, (2) switchover to regional languages as the medium of education, which was regarded as a natural progression since regional languages were media of instruction at school stage, well prior to Independence (i.e., by about 1937), and (3) switchover to Hindi which had a dual capacity – it was a regional language in some states as well as a constitutionally recognized federal language. It was considered as a natural successor to English as the lingua franca of India and this stance appeared to derive support from Radhakrishnan Report.[27]

For regions other than Hindi-speaking states, the second alternative was a rational one which was also favoured by educationists whereas for Hindi-speaking states, the third choice was suitable. For both regional languages and Hindi, preparation of subject-wise textbooks and the training of teachers to develop competence to teach in respective language was a pre-requisite. The matter was discussed endlessly in the UGC, the IUB, and the Education Ministry, but remained without any final decision. The matter was clinched by the resolution of the National Integration Council (NIC) (1962) in favour of regional languages.[28] The NIC at the same time talked of the importance of development of Hindi as the internal link language. Unfortunately, the fierce opposition from the then Madras State to Hindi as an internal link language which eventuated in the capture of the state by the DMK defeating Congress in the elections held in February 1967, left the Government of India no alternative but to opt for a continuance of the status quo till switch over to the regional languages when textbooks were available. The case for regional languages was ably summarized by the Education Commission both in its introductory chapter as well as in the chapter on Higher Education.[29] The justification was four-fold:

1. The medium at the university stage should enable students to acquire knowledge with facility, express themselves with clarity and to think with precision and vigour. From this point of view, the claims of the mother tongue are pre-eminent.
2. The medium of education at higher and school education stages should generally be the same.
3. The switchover was a matter of profound importance for national integration as observed by the Sampurnanand Committee, 1961.[30]
4. The switchover was also important for development of latent talent in the country and establishing a rapport between the elite and the masses vide the resolution of the National Integration Council.

The Kothari Commission also set out a practical agenda, which comprised UGC and universities to work out a feasible programme within a time horizon of 10 years, comprising production of the needed literature in the Indian languages and making adequate arrangements for the training and retraining of teachers. The Commission deplored the tendency of some universities, attributable to apathy of teachers to conduct teaching in English and allow students the option of taking the examination in a regional language. It dwelt at length on the use of English as a library language and steps to be taken for the same. The NPE 1968 based on the Kothari Report summarized the national consensus on a contentious subject so neatly, that the subsequent NPE 1986 merely reiterated the same,[31] stating that its essential provisions could hardly be improved upon. The 1968 formulation was: "The regional languages are already in use as media of education at the primary and secondary stage; urgent steps should now be taken to adopt them as media of education at the university stage."

The Central Government under Jawaharlal Nehru did have an appreciation of the strategic importance of a language policy and a vision about what needed to be done. In regard to Indian languages, it was realized that there was a need for capacity building and therefore, in terms of the Presidential order of April 1960, the Commission for Scientific and Technical Terminology (CSTT) was constituted in October 1961 with the function, *inter alia*, of coordination and evolution of scientific and technical terminology in Hindi and other languages and preparation of standard scientific textbooks using the new terminology evolved or approved by it. By 1986, the Commission had published 22 glossaries of technical terms. The latest report of the ministry does not unfortunately give clear-cut quantitative information about the achievements of the CSTT.[32]

To implement the NPE 1968, read with the parliamentary resolution of January 1968, the Government of India started a plan scheme in 1968–69 – formally called Scheme for Production of Books at the University Level in Hindi and Regional Languages, sometimes known as *One Crore Scheme for Granth Akademies* – under which Central assistance on 100 per cent basis (revised from 75% under pressure of State Governments) of up to the ceiling of Rs one crore was to be provided by the Central Government, to each of the participating states, subject to the states making a matching contribution. The participating State Governments were to set up University Textbook Boards (called Grantha Academies in Hindi-speaking states), managed by the universities in the state. The Boards were to organize production of original titles as well as translations of renowned textbooks. The textbooks were to be produced strictly according to the syllabus of the university and with some assurance that the Boards of Studies of respective universities would recommend the same in the reading list for the courses. The State Governments were to bear the expenditure on infrastructure and maintenance of the Boards by way of their contribution. The Boards were expected to build a revolving fund out of the sale proceeds of the books produced/translated. Thus, Rs one crore contribution was in a way seed money. In all, 13 states (viz., Maharashtra, Andhra Pradesh, Tamil Nadu, Orissa, Bihar, West Bengal, Kerala, Punjab, Haryana, Uttar Pradesh, Rajasthan, Assam and Karnataka) availed of the scheme. Assam and Karnataka distributed the grants among their universities and the rest had set up the Granth Academies. Till 1977–78, grants totaling a little over Rs 9 crore were released, and 4,800 books in Indian languages were produced and another 3,500 books were under production. Most of them related to undergraduate – arts and science courses. There was little work at postgraduate level or for professional courses. The government considered the scheme to be successful and continued it for another five years.

In March 1987, i.e., shortly after the NPE 1986 had been announced and had reiterated the earlier policy's resolve regarding regional languages as media of education, the Government of India appointed a Review Committee under the chairmanship of Dr Suresh Dalal of SNDT University with the Director of CSTT as its member-secretary. The Committee found that the total number of titles produced were 1,584 of which only 638 were prescribed by the universities and books worth about Rs 10 crore were lying unsold in godowns. The picture was a disappointing one. The Committee's findings were:

1. Less than 50 per cent of universities were providing facilities for education through their regional languages in different subjects at different levels.
2. The main hurdle was not the paucity of textbooks, but unwillingness of the teacher community to switchover to the Indian languages and the absence of a resolution on the part of the university authorities and State Governments.

The Committee's recommendation was to supplement production of textbooks by review journals and books of readings. It also suggested involvement of private publishers in view of the large quantum of unsold stock of books produced. The Committee, however, recommended continuance of the scheme by providing further assistance of Rs 3 crore to each state till end of Eighth Plan.[33]

The Ramamurti Committee,[34] recommended the transfer of the implementation of the scheme to the respective universities. PoA 1992[35] laid the blame for failure of the scheme at the door of the universities and also mentioned lack of employment opportunities as a factor. Government, however, made ad hoc releases to a few Academies. Major releases were made to Haryana, Rajasthan and Uttar Pradesh which had drawn less assistance under the original sanction.

The Government of India appointed in April 1994 a committee under the chairmanship of M.R. Kolhatkar, former Adviser (Education), Planning Commission and Prof. A.N.P. Ummenkutty, Vice-Chancellor, Calicut University as member and Director CSTT as member-secretary, which reported in 1995. The Committee went into the basic question of whether the production of textbooks was a problem of linguistic terminology or an educational problem and having concluded that it was an educational problem, went on to recommend involvement of the UGC and other coordinating bodies (viz., AICTE, ICAR and ICMR) in the basic policy of change over of the medium of education. It noted that the MCI had passed a resolution about continuance of English for an indefinite period, and that the AICTE and ICAR did not have any policy about switchover to regional languages at all. The ICAR did have a book production scheme for university level textbooks, but they were to be in English. The Committee quoted Randhawa Committee as below: "In the case of professional subjects like agriculture, it would be safer to follow the *pragmatic policy of combining both English and regional language*."[36] The same Committee had noted that in Gujarat, Gujarati was the medium of instruction for B.Sc. (Agriculture) and that Pantnagar Agricultural University had a stream of B.Sc. (Agriculture) (Hindi) which was running successfully. The Kolhatkar Committee felt that any scheme for regional language textbooks should be implemented by a consortium of UGC and

AICTE/ICAR/MCI called the National Consortium for Higher Education Textbooks (NC–HET), with specified seed capital to be contributed by each body. The Committee left the details to be worked out by the ministry.[37] Unfortunately, there is no indication regarding implementation of the report of the Committee. The Annual Report of the Ministry for 2004–2005 shows that so far 14,100 books have been published by CSTT of which about 3,100 books are in Hindi, and about 10,500 books in other modern Indian languages.[38] Book production in agriculture, engineering and medicine is undertaken by CSTT itself and about 500 books have been published on these subjects. Considering the number of languages, which are media of instruction and the variety of subjects required to be taught, the work done is evidently far too inadequate. As already, noted, subsequent annual reports are cryptic and the present status of various state level Granth Academies is not known except that press reports indicate that the Government of Maharashtra had decided to close down Maharashtra Textbook Production Board, Nagpur.

N. Jayaram reviewed this whole issue in the overall perspective of language question in higher education, and his conclusions based on considerable research are as below:

1. English is still the predominant medium of instruction in all courses of higher education and the only medium in professional courses. Hindi comes a distant second, being available in 50 per cent of universities in arts and commerce courses, 41 per cent in law and 25 per cent in library science courses.
2. Regional languages are available as a medium of instruction at the undergraduate level, in over 40 per cent of the universities in arts and commerce courses, in over 30 per cent of the universities in education and in nearly 28 per cent in science courses. This compares well with the development of Hindi as a medium of instruction at undergraduate level. But while Hindi has made some headway at the postgraduate level, regional languages have not made any noticeable headway.
3. A complete switchover to regional language as media of instruction is not a possibility in the foreseeable future. The only option that seems to be open is selective bilingualism.
4. As a result, in India at present, there are three categories of the elite educated respectively in English, Hindi and the regional language media contributing to the reproduction of inequality and repudiation of any semblance of a unified academic community.[39]

So far as the textbook scene is concerned, Jayaram's conclusion which was arrived at in 1993 may hold true, mutatis mutandis, in 2010 as well. The reason was underlined by the Dalal Committee which needs reiteration: the main hurdle in the regionalization of medium of instruction is the unwillingness of the teacher community and irresolution of university authorities and State Governments.

Case Study III
Asymmetrical Role of the President and the Governor vis-à-vis Universities

In this case study is highlighted the institution of the Governor in his capacity as the Chancellor of State Universities – a colonial vestige, which has great significance for how Indian federalism functions in practice to promote unintended centralization and to cause asymmetry in the functioning of the Central Universities on the one hand and State Universities on the other.

Role of the President in Governance of Central Universities

So far as the governance of Central Universities is concerned, the first President of India, Dr Rajendra Prasad had the sagacity to consult the Attorney General of India as to the role of the President as the Visitor of these universities and as advised, the successive Presidents have acted on the advice of Union Cabinet without any pretension to discretionary powers in relation to Central Universities. In the states, however, the situation is different.

The Triple Role of the State Governor

In relation to the UTs, the Governor, in terms of Article 239 of the Constitution is the agent of the Central Government but in relation to the states he has a triple role:[40]

1. He is the constitutional head of the state and it is well settled that in India the states as well as the centre operate under a system of parliamentary as distinguished from presidential form of government as held by the Supreme Court in the case of *Shamsher Singh vs. State of Punjab AIR (1974) SC 2192.*
2. He is the representative of the Central Executive as articulated in the Constitution which envisages issue of directions by the President vide Articles 256, 257, 258, 339, 347, 350A and particularly Article 356 dealing with the failure of the constitutional machinery. It is well known that retired politicians of the ruling party at the Centre have come to be appointed as Governors. According to the Sarkaria Commission survey of the appointment of Governors made from independence till October 1984, over 60 per cent of the Governors had taken active part in politics. The Central Government has also shown a marked inclination to use Article 356 to dislodge opposition party governments holding power at the state level. Hence, the image of the Governor is that of an agent of the Central Government rather than a responsible representative of the Central Cabinet. In

this connection, reference may be made to the White Paper issued by the Government of Karnataka on the role of the Governor.[41]

3. The discretionary role, which is specifically provided for in Art. 163 and implicitly in Article 200 and which also allegedly applies to his role as the Chancellor of the State Universities. Hence, its relevance for education. The asymmetry with the President of the Republic vis-à-vis Central Universities is vividly illustrated here. The Governor's power under Article 200 needs some clarification.

Governor's Power in Regard to Various Bills including Educational Bills

The Governor's powers under Article 200 of the Constitution especially when he does not give assent is three-fold: (i) withholding assent, (ii) reserving the bill for consideration of the President, and (iii) returning the Bill (if not a money bill) for reconsideration with his message. If the legislature re-passes the bill, the Governor is required to assent to it.

In relation to Article 200(2) supra, it is provided in Article 201 that the President may, in the case of a reserved bill, assent to it or withhold his assent. He may also send the bill for reconsideration to the State Legislature, but unlike in the case of the Governor, it is not obligatory for the President to give his assent to a reconsidered bill. In other words, the President enjoys a virtual veto over State Legislation reserved for his consideration. And since the President and the Governor in giving or withholding assent to a bill are supposed to be exercising their legislative function, it is stated to be non-justiciable. Thus, the power is indeed absolute.

On this point, the Rajamannar Committee had observed: "In reserving Bills for the President's consideration, the Governor has to act on the advice of the Cabinet because Article 200 does not vest any discretion in the Governor."[42] The view of the Rajamannar Committee is expectedly radical but the ARC study team report also stated that the Article must be interpreted as enabling Presidential intervention only in special circumstances, such as those in which there is a clear violation of Fundamental Rights or a patent unconstitutionality or where legitimate interests of another state or its people are affected.[43] The Sarkaria Commission's statistics relating to reserved bills for 1977–1985 showed that 75 per cent bills related to the Concurrent List though 90 per cent were assented.[44] These 10 per cent bills may well belong to the States ruled by the opposition. *The educational bills including the university bills have become particularly susceptible to reservation since 1977 when education became a concurrent subject*. The Sarkaria Commission observed that repugnancy under Article 254(1) arose only when (i) there is a direct conflict between the provisions of two laws, or (ii) the Union law is intended to be an exhaustive code on the Concurrent List subject. What appears to have happened is that, the *Governors have resorted to the practice of reserving all educational bills for consideration of the President since 1977*, which really means the Central Cabinet, which can use the power to kill the bills. The West Bengal government in its reply to the questionnaire of Sarkaria Commission, gave the examples of the State's Educational Bills to which the President did not give assent. One bill related to amendment of the Primary Education Act and nine bills related to the take over of management or acquisition of colleges. It is evident from the subject matter of the West Bengal bills that they did not require to be reserved for the President's assent in terms of the rule of repugnancy. The West Bengal government suggested the deletion of these Articles or alternatively laying down of time limit (one month for the Governor, six months for the President) for the Governor/President to make up his mind.[45]

The final recommendation of the Sarkaria Commission was that the Governor acting on the advice of the cabinet should be the rule and withholding of assent or reserving of a bill should be an exception to be invoked in rare and exceptional cases. These rare and exceptional cases were: (1) The provisions of the bill are patently unconstitutional (the subject matter is outside State List), (2) provisions of the bill manifestly derogate from the scheme and the framework of the Constitution so as to endanger the sovereignty, unity and integrity of the nation, (3) provisions of the bill clearly violate the Fundamental Rights, or (4) provisions of the bill transgress other constitutional limitations and provisions. In particular, the commission observed that the President should not withhold assent only on the consideration of policy differences or on the ground that the Union is contemplating a comprehensive law in future on the same subject.

According to the report of the Ministry of Home Affairs for 1999–2000, these recommendations of the Sarkaria Commission were considered by the Inter-State Council and it was decided that there should be time-bound clearance of the state bills reserved for President's consideration. The bills should not be reserved for President's consideration in a routine manner and should be reserved only when there is a requirement to do so constitutionally.[46] However, there is no evidence that the NDA government issued any instructions in this regard and the probability of UPA governments, dominated by the Congress party with a record of dignification of the role of the Governor being expected to act in the matter is minimal.

Visitorial Powers of the Governor-Chancellor and University Autonomy

Visitorial powers include all powers regarding inspection/inquiry approval of statutes, annulment of proceedings of the university, inconsistent with the University Act etc., making appointments and nominations, seeking information and issuing directives. These powers are incorporated in most

Acts of the Central/State Universities. The exercise of Visitorial powers by the Indian President on the advice of Central Cabinet/Central Education Minister is considered as part of the supervisory role of the state vis-à-vis universities,[47] following the medieval European fictions, having corporate autonomy. The corporate autonomy of the universities denotes freedom of the universities to lay down admission norms for students, reservation norms for teachers and prescribing course of studies.[48]

However, the Indian discourse of violation of academic autonomy, somehow appears to assume that the State Governments as against Central Government are particularly prone to violate the autonomy of State Universities and that the Governors of the states have a special role to play in protecting the autonomy of the State Universities and insulating them from the State Ministers of Education. The Sarkaria Commission has relied on the Kiran Babu judgment,[49] so as to highlight the discretionary role of the Governor in this area and the Central Government therefore, appears to be unwilling to countenance any amendment of the University Acts which purports to reduce the role of the Governor-Chancellor and for this purpose, the device of the Governor reserving such bills under Article 200 of the Constitution for the assent of the President is freely resorted to. The ARC in its report on state administration perpetuated the fiction of Governor's discretionary powers. This trend therefore, gives rise to a legitimate suspicion that the Governor's discretionary power really operates in the direction of centralization as it does in relation to Article 356 of the Constitution. Various opposition governments, notably Government of Tamil Nadu have protested. The latter in its reply to the questionnaire of Sarkaria Commission stated: "The Governor, in the exercise of his functions, either under the Constitution or under any Act, passed by the State Legislature or by the Parliament has to act on and accept the advice tendered by the Council of Ministers. In the matter of appointment of Vice-Chancellors, the Governor has to act only in accordance with the advice tendered by the Council of Ministers."[50]

But it is forgotten that these discretionary powers are required to be those "by or under the Constitution" and therefore the statutory powers under the University Acts cannot be treated as discretionary. This is confirmed by the well-known jurist D.D. Basu, who pointed out that the appointment of the Governor under a statute relating to university is not made in his personal capacity but ex-officio. Hence, the Governor is appointed to such a statutory office by the legislature only because he is the head of the State Government and therefore, the statutory functions of the Governor must be regarded as included within the 'Business of the Government of the State' under Article 166(3) and within the meaning of 'functions' to be exercised in Article 163 (1). The Rajamannar Committee (1971), therefore rightly held that even in respect of statutory functions ex-officio, the Governor has necessarily to act on the advice of the cabinet but Sarkaria Commission held otherwise. It is true that the Governor's obstructive role comes into play only in the case of State Governments (and therefore State Universities) ruled by opposition parties. Such a random intervention by the Central Government through the Governor in the affairs of State Universities brings this case on all fours with the abuse of Article 356 by the Central Government but has not attracted academic or journalistic attention. The purpose of the case study is precisely to highlight this abuse.

Dysfunctionality of the Role of the Governor as Chancellor

Although there may be anecdotal evidence of some Governors having cleaned up the university administrations, the Governor cannot be cast in the role of a heroic reformer, because he is the appointee of and holds office during the pleasure of the President, i.e., the Central Cabinet. Given the fact that generally the Governor is a retired politician of the ruling party at the Central Government level who may not necessarily be interested in educational matters, the general tendency has been to try to do the bidding of the Central Government. Though, authentically documented accounts of the tussle between the Governor-Chancellors and State Governments belonging to the opposition on matters of university administration are not available, one does know of many such cases as quoted below: (i) Government of Uttar Pradesh (headed by Kalyan Singh, Chief Minister) vs. Governor (Ramesh Bhandari) 1998: The posts of Vice-Chancellor of several universities in UP were falling vacant. The State Government proposed amendment of UP State Universities Act 1973, providing that Chancellor would consult State Government before appointing regular VC, officiating VC and making nomination on the Search Committee/Executive Committee. The bill was pending the assent of the Governor but in the meanwhile, there was change of government at the Centre, which replaced Ramesh Bhandari by Suraj Bhan as Governor. (ii) Government of Madhya Pradesh (headed by Digvijay Singh, CM) vs. Governor (Bhai Mahavir) 1998: Here, the CM was a Congressman and the Governor an appointee of BJP, the ruling party at the Centre. The Chancellor removed and replaced VCs' of two universities (Rewa and Jabalpur) without the Cabinet's advice. The CM got passed MP Universities (Amendment) Bill 1999 replacing the word 'chancellor' by that of 'State Government'. However, the bill could not become Act for want of assent of the Governor.[51]

Thus, the discussion regarding the role of the Governor in the educational sector (as Chancellor of universities and in the matter of withholding assent or reserving educational bills for the consideration of the President) indicates that there is a falsely perceived asymmetry in the role of the President as Visitor of the Central Universities and the role of the Governor as Chancellor of State Universities which may be listed as the sixth feature in Box 3.3 (vide Chapter 3, p. 54). The latest decisions of the Inter-State Council on Sarkaria Report, if followed in letter and spirit, may be expected to act as a check on the Governor's power to reserve educational bills for the President's assent but firstly, there is no evidence of any instructions in specific terms nor do they detract from the need for a formal amendment of University Acts to delete any reference to the Governor as an officer of the State University as also recommended by the Gnanam Committee, and to provide for Governor-Chancellor to consult state government in matters of university governance so as to minimize the potential for the Governor either to act as an agent of the Central Government or for pursuing a personal self-serving agenda.

Conclusion

What is the federal significance of these three case studies? The first case study about UGC shows that the central role in regulation of standards is considerably diluted in practice. The UGC may be a centralized body with late and weak regionalization, but it has to make a lot of adjustments with the states in order to fulfil its standard setting role. It has not been able to curb the institutional expansionist tendency of State Governments or to put on ground inter-face bodies like SCHEs, except in seven states and it has drawn a blank so far as a Model Act for university governance is concerned. The agricultural universities may be considered to be a little more successful, but that was because the ICAR was able to put a Model Bill on the Board in the 1960s, when it was comparatively easy to talk of national models. The case study of failure of regionalization drive in the area of medium of instruction shows that the Central Government may provide funds but the vested interests ensure that states are not able to make much progress. The asymmetrical role of the Governor, in the third case study, however, shows that when the Central Government is so minded, it can exploit the allegedly discretionary role of Governor as Chancellor of State Universities so as to sub-serve the ruling party's agenda of control of States. In other words, the role of the Governor as Chancellor is mixed up with role of the Governor as an agent of Central Government. All the considerations that come into play in the pros and cons of abrogation of Article 356 of Constitution are found at play here. The politics of higher education is indeed complex and is complicit with the functioning of federalism in Indian polity.

Notes

1. Radhakrishnan Commission's recommendations may be seen in Chapter XIII, para 10 of its Report.
   Unfortunately, the Report does not give sufficient credit to the recommendations of Sadler Report which was made even prior to the setting of the University Grants Committee in UK (1919), nor to the Sargent Plan (1944), whose significance was that it recommended combination of power of purse (as in the case of UK-UGC) with powers of coordination. For an account of initial years of UK-UGC, see Robert O. Berdahl, *British Universities and the State* (Berkeley and Los Angeles: University of California Press, 1959).
2. See s. 12 of the UGC Act 1956. The function of extension was added as the third dimension (the first two being Teaching and Research) by the UGC Policy Frame 1978 though the UGC Act was not specifically amended.
3. Amrik Singh, *Fifty Years of Higher Education in India* (New Delhi: Sage Publications, 2004).
4. Marina Pinto, *Federalism and Higher Education: The Indian Experience* (Bombay: Orient Longman, 1982).
5. Pinto, op. cit., 184.
6. IUB was established in 1925 on the analogy of CVCP (Committee of Vice-Chancellors and Principals) in UK. It enjoyed consultative status with CABE in higher education matters till the UGC came into existence. Both Sargent Plan and Radhakrishnan Commission did not think much of it as a coordinating body of universities which it claimed to be. In effect, it was a dignified club of Vice-Chancellors and since 1973 has been renamed as Association of Indian Universities (AIU).
7. Amrik Singh (2004), op. cit.
8. Vide s.14 of the UGC Act.
9. Kothari Report observed that UGC can become an effective instrument of upgradation of standards only if it follows the method of persuasion rather than coercion, vide para 13.74.
10. Susanne H. Rudolph and Lloyd I. Rudolph (Eds.), *Education and Politics in India* (New Delhi: Oxford University Press, 1972), 74–75 and Footnotes 32, 35 and 39 on pp. 402–03.
11. Kothari Report, para 13.53.
12. Vide s. 12 B of the UGC Act. For UGC Rules and Regulations, see UGC Compilation (New Delhi, 2000).
13. Jha Report (1977), 31.
14. Amrik Singh and G.D. Sharma (Eds.), *Higher Education in India: The Institutional Context* (New Delhi: Konark, 1989), 91–131. See also Report of the Committee on Revision of Pay Scales of Universities and Colleges (New Delhi: UGC, 1986), known as Mehrotra Committee after its Chairman.

15. Ramamurti Report, 222.
16. UGC Annual Report, 1994–95, 7–9.
17. Vide Footnote 4 Supra.
18. Kothari Report, para 13.76.
19. The work of CDCs is reviewed by Jayalaxmi Indireson whose assessment is that it was not a successful scheme. See her "Quest for Quality: Intervention vs. Impact", in Suma Chitnis and Philip Altbach (Eds.), *Higher Education Reforms in India* (New Delhi: Sage, 1993).
20. NPE 1986, para 5.30.
21. *Osmania University Teachers' Association vs. State of AP*, AIR 1987 SC 2034.
22. Amrik Singh (2004), op. cit.
23. ICAR Review Committee, 1988.
24. Vide Savita Bhave, *Krishik Krantiche Senani: Annasaheb Shinde* (Pune: Kalpana, June 1994), 126–129 (Marathi).
25. This was done on the basis of Agricultural Universities Committee chaired by Dr Ralph W. Cummings (1962).
26. ICAR Review Committee, op. cit.
27. Radhakrishnan Report, 207–222.
28. S.S. Bhandarkar, *Association of Indian Universities, 1925–85* (New Delhi: AIU, 1985).
29. Kothari Report, para Nos. 1.51, 1.52, 11.58.
30. Report of the Emotional Integration Committee (New Delhi, 1961) (Chairman: Sampurnananda).
31. NPE 1986/92, para 8.7.
32. Report of the Ministry of Education, 2008–09 (New Delhi, 2009), 235–237.
33. Report of the Committee on the Scheme of University level Book Production in Indian Languages (New Delhi, 1989) (Mimeo) (Chairman: Suresh Dalal).
34. Ramamurti Report, 265–266.
35. NPE/PoA 1992, 94.
36. Report of the Review Committee on Agricultural Universities (New Delhi, 1978), paras 4.20 and 4.21 (Chairman: M.S. Randhawa).
37. Based on personal knowledge of the author. (It is not clear if the Report is in public domain.)
38. Annual Report of the Ministry of Education (2004–05), 236–237.
39. N. Jayaram, "Language Question in Higher Education: Trends and Issues", in Suma Chitnis and Philip Altbach (Eds.), *Higher Education Reforms in India* (New Delhi: Sage Publications, 1993), 74–114.

40. M.C. Setalvad, *Union and State Relations under the Indian Constitution* (Calcutta: Eastern Law House, 1974). Sarkaria Report, 131–132.
41. Sarkaria Report, Vol. II, 260–272.
42. Report of the Committee on Centre-State Relations (Madras, 1971) (Chairman: Justice Rajamannar).
43. ARC Report on State Administration (New Delhi, 1969).
44. Sarkaria Report, Vol. II, 139–159.
45. Ibid., Vol. II, 600–601.
46. P. 53 of the Annual Report of Ministry of Home Affairs, 1999–2000.
47. Report of Gajendragadkar Committee, 1969.
48. Kothari Report, para nos. 13.03–13.15.
49. *Kiran Babu vs. State of Andhra Pradesh* (AIR 1986 AP 275).
50. Sarkaria Report, Vol. II, 487.
51. Anirudh Prasad, *University Education: Administration and the Law* (New Delhi: Deep & Deep Publishers, 2000), 108–110.

11 Technical and Professional Education

Since 1977 technical and professional education has been a concurrent subject except for agricultural education and research, which continues to be a state subject.[1] However, historically, the Central Government has played a prominent role in the expansion of technical institutions. Thus, entry 64 in the Central List of the Seventh Schedule deals with institutions for scientific or technical education financed by the Government of India and declared by Parliament to be institutions of national importance (INIs). It is under this entry that IITs as well as All India Institute of Medical Sciences, New Delhi and Postgraduate Institute of Medical Education and Research, Chandigarh were set up in the 1950s. This is apart from powers of coordination and determination of standard under entry 66 in the Central List in relation to scientific and technical institutions. By entry 26 in the Concurrent List of the Seventh Schedule, legal, medical and other professions are concurrent subjects. Naturally, it is the Central Government which has passed the Indian Medical Council Act, 1956 under which Medical Council of India has been set up and the Advocates' Act, 1961, under which the Bar Council of India has been set up. These Acts provide for the setting up of professional bodies which regulate not only the respective professions (medical and legal) but also medical and legal education with the qualification that the postgraduate legal education is the responsibility of the UGC and the Health Ministry has a decisive voice in the postgraduate medical education. Moreover, the Supreme Court of India has transformed legal education into a central subject by its judgment in the Mahendru case,[2] which held that Advocates' Act, 1961 has been passed by the Parliament by virtue of entries 77 and 78 of List I of Seventh Schedule (entries relating to persons entitled to practise in the Supreme Court and the High Courts).

Since Indian medical education is a dualist system comprising both modern and traditional education, it is dealt with separately. However, the modern medicine has allied/ancillary branches and there are other areas of technical and professional education which have their own regulatory/professional bodies. These are listed below in a chronological order:

1. Indian Council for Agricultural Research (ICAR) set up in 1929 under the Societies Act and dealing also with agricultural education since Sargent Plan (1944).
2. All India Council of Technical Education set up by an executive order in 1945 and given statutory status under the All India Council for Technical Education Act, 1987.
3. Nursing Council of India set up under the Nursing Council Act, 1947.
4. Dental Council of India set up under the Dentists' Act, 1948.
5. Pharmacy Council of India set up under the Pharmacy Act, 1948.
6. Council of Architects (CoA) set up under the Architects Act, 1972.
7. National Council for Teacher Education – advisory under the NCERT since 1973 and given statutory status since 1994 by the National Council for Teacher Education Act.
8. Veterinary Council of India set up under the Veterinary Council Act, 1984.
9. Rehabilitation Council of India set up by an executive order in 1986 and given statutory status under the Rehabilitation Council of India Act, 1992.
10. Indian Council for Forestry Research and Education (ICFRE) set up in 1987 in the same way as ICAR.

Of the above ten bodies, three each deal with technical education (AICTE, Pharmacy Council of India and the Council of Architects), modern medicine (Dental Council, Nursing Council and Rehabilitation Council), and agriculture, animal husbandry and forestry (ICAR, VCI and ICFRE) and one is a regulatory body for teacher education. These bodies, to the extent they deal with co-ordination of development and maintenance of standards, are supposed to have been constituted in terms of the Central Government's powers under entry 66 of Central List/Seventh Schedule of the Constitution, the same entry under which the UGC has been set up.

From the federal point of view, it is to be noted that the Dental Council/Pharmacy Council and Bar Council of India have statutory State Councils built into the respective Acts. The State Medical Councils have been formed under the respective State Acts, rather than under the Indian Medical Council Act, 1956 which had its origin in a 1933 Act.

In the technical and professional education field, except in agricultural education, the following processes appear to be at work:

1. Expansion and diversification of educational courses and institutions.
2. Tendency toward regional imbalance in the distribution of professional education facilities.
3. Commercialization and privatization of educational institutions which processes do not appear to be unrelated.
4. A dualist system of medical education comprising 'scientific' medicine concentrated in urban areas and the indigenous systems of medicine comprising Ayurveda Siddha, Naturapathy, Yunani and Homeopathy, which are reduced to the position of sub-alternity.

5. Creation of a few central institutions as centres of excellence, some of which even have an international brand but which tend to be dominated by the elite of the society.

Expansion and Diversification

The process of expansion and diversification may be illustrated by referring to the technical education institutions. Not only are the courses diversified (thus, the original civil, mechanical and electrical engineering courses at diploma and degree level have been diversified into new courses like architecture, computer applications and information technology, applied arts and crafts, industrial designing, pharmacy, hotel management and business management), but postgraduate courses in a variety of disciplines and Ph.D. courses have been introduced. At the time of independence, India simply had 39 degree level and 53 diploma level institutions with an intake capacity of 2,940 and 3,670 engineers. In 2008, the number of degree institutions had increased to 6,244 and diploma institutions had increased to 2,324; correspondingly annual intake had increased to 11.47 lakh (degree) and 5.08 lakh (diploma) respectively. The relevant data are given in Table 11.1 by way of illustration. Comparable expansion has taken place in other professional fields.

Table 11.1

Number of AICTE Approved Technical Education Institutions and their Annual Intake (as on 31st August, 2008)

Programme	*Degree Institutions*	*Annual Intake*	*Diploma Institutions*	*Annual Intake*
Engineering	2,388	8.41 lakh	1659	4.71 lakh
Architecture	106	0.04 lakh	—	—
MCA	1,137	0.82 lakh	—	—
Pharmacy	1,001	0.62 lakh	575	0.32 lakh
Applied Arts & Crafts	10	0.008 lakh	4	480 (absolute no.)
Management				
(a) MBA	1,231	1.15 lakh	—	—
(b) PGDM	285	0.36 lakh	—	—
Hotel Management	86	0.06 lakh	86	4,490 (absolute no.)
Total	6,244	11.47 lakh	2,324	5.08 lakh
Institutions (Grand Total)		8,568		
Intake (Grand Total)		16.55 lakh		

Note: There are 13 IITs in 2008–09 with intake capacity of about 2950.
There are seven IIMs with intake capacity of about 1,400.
Totals may not tally because of rounding off the figures.

Source: Annual Report of the Department of SE&L and Higher Education (2008–09), Ministry of HRD, New Delhi, p. 144.

Tendency toward Regional Imbalance

The data collected by the Review Committee of the AICTE[3] clearly bring out the regional imbalance in the distribution of technical education facilities in regard to both the number of institutions and the intake capacity. Thus:

- More than 52 per cent of degree engineering colleges are located in the south and south-west whereas east and north account for just around 7 per cent and 10 per cent respectively. While the five states in the south-west, viz., Tamil Nadu, Andhra Pradesh, Karnataka, Kerala and Maharashtra account for 250, 215, 211, 73 and 151 of degree engineering institutions respectively, states like Bihar, Assam, Himachal Pradesh, north-eastern states, J&K and Jharkhand have less than seven institutions each.
- 43 per cent of MBA institutions and 59 per cent of MCA (Master of Computer Application) institutions with an intake of 35 per cent and 57 per cent of students in the above disciplines are in the south and south-west.
- Similar is the case with pharmacy and architecture.
- In hotel management, the regional inequity is so great that almost 50 per cent of institutions and intake is in south-west alone, and that too in Karnataka.

Commercialization and Privatization of Technical Education Institutions

These processes are not of recent, i.e., post-liberalization (1991), origin. They go back to the initial years of independence and in fact were a response to the fact of imbalance between demand and supply for technical education. A technical/professional qualification is a passport to job and in an economy characterized by 'scarcity'[4] at least part of which was attributable to government supported reservations for socially and educationally backward class students, guardians of young meritorious students from non-backward classes were prepared to pay higher level of fees. The Pai's of Manipal in Karnataka started private professional (medical and technical) institutions from late 1940s, accepting higher fees upfront (that is against receipt) initially from students outside the state, but the CABE appears to have taken high moral ground and desired the chief ministers of states to stop the practice.[5] There was, as usual, no follow up. What Pai's of Manipal had started was really non-profit privatization as in the case of the USA in the previous centuries (17th, 18th and 19th) as distinguished from corporate privatization which made its appearance in the USA only in the second half of 20th century. Commercialization in the sense of treating education as a commodity for sale coupled with the practice of accepting higher fees under the table by way of establishment of capitation fee colleges first made its appearance again in Karnataka under the chief ministership of Devraj Urs in late 1980s. Such predatory commercialization was backed especially by the State Governments of Karnataka and Andhra Pradesh as seen from the various court judgments like Mohini Jain (Karnataka), Unnikrishnan (Andhra Pradesh) etc. Rekha Kaul[6] has studied the phenomenon in Karnataka and identified it with the rise of and competition among the dominant castes like Lingayats and Vokkaligas, whose leaders started their own institutions with the support of State Governments. It would appear from the data for Mysore collected by some scholars in 1965–66[7] that Vokkaligas were not as active as Lingayats in the 1960s, but by late 1980s, they had apparently followed the lead of the Lingayats. These scholars noted that the powerful Karnataka Lingayat Education Society of Belgaum cleverly changed its name from 'Lingayat' to 'Liberal' thus, camouflaging the caste identity of the society. Apparently, the Muslims and Christians also (the latter with national and international funding) had taken the benefit of the constitutional protection for linguistic and religious minorities to start a large number of professional colleges in Karnataka. Madan and Habar also found that in the institutions run by the respective communities, the teaching staff is dominated by the managing community.

The so-called Acts for prohibition of capitation fees were really Acts to regularize the collection, at the admission stage, of capitation fees which were permitted to be collected at a higher rate in the case of non-local, i.e., non-domiciled students. A perusal of the Supreme Court judgments in Mohini Jain (1992) and Unnikrishnan (1993) helps us to piece together following facts:[8] In 1983, Andhra Pradesh State Government enacted Andhra Pradesh Educational Institutions (Regulation of Admission and Prohibition of Capitation Fees) Act 1983. The Act was brief and the actual task of the fixing of level of fees was left to the rules. The state of Karnataka appears to have taken a leaf out of the book of Andhra Pradesh and enacted in 1984 the Karnataka Educational Institutions (Prohibition of Capitation Fees) Act. A notification issued in June 1987, enabled private educational institutions from the academic year 1989–90 to charge differential capitation fees in respect of "government seats" and "non-government seats" for Karnataka and non-Karnataka students. In effect, higher fees were charged for non-government (management) seats and non-Karnataka students. Evidently, fees for outside students allotted management quota seats would be the highest among the four categories. It was this notification that Mohini Jain, a non-Karnataka student had challenged in the Supreme Court. The Supreme Court took note of the testimony of experts like Dr

K.S. Chugh of PGIMER, Chandigarh that there has been a mushroom growth of medical colleges (increase in the number from 25 in 1947 to 172 in 1991) turning out 20,000 medical graduates per year which was far more than the norms laid down by the Mudliar Committee on Health Survey and Planning (1961). The Supreme Court held the charging of capitation fees by private educational institutions to be illegal. This judgment adversely affected the managements of unaided private professional colleges in the four states of Karnataka, Andhra Pradesh, Tamil Nadu and Maharashtra, which challenged the same. The matter was referred to a seven–judge Constitution Bench, which delivered its judgment in the Unnikrishnan case of 1993. The eponymous party in that judgment had challenged the Andhra Pradesh legislation in 1992, but the judgment applied to the parties from Maharashtra and Tamil Nadu also which had followed Andhra Pradesh and Karnataka in passing their legislation in 1987 and 1992 respectively. The Unnikrishnan judgment was overruled in the Pai judgment in 2002,[9] which permitted managements of unaided institutions to set the fees though subject to regulation by the government committees dealing respectively with admission and fees. The basic point regarding the trend toward commercialization, however, remains substantiated.

The NPE 1986 had this grand formulation about commercialization: "In the interests of maintaining standards and for several other valid reasons, the commercialization of teaching and professional education will be curbed. An alternative system will be devised to involve private and voluntary efforts in this sector of education, in conformity with accepted norms and goals."[10] Requisite provisions were made in the AICTE Act, 1987, Medical Council Act (by ordinance in 1990) and NCTE (1994), but these were not complied with. Both the NCTE and AICTE, although autonomous, followed the dictates of the government of the day leading to mindless expansion. The Medical Council of India (MCI) was required to obtain approval of the government in health ministry for new institutions and the ministry permitted expansion, apparently without raising any question. The malpractices indulged in by the new medical colleges which at the time of inspection temporarily borrowed faculty from other colleges and pretended that it was a regularly appointed faculty were known but a blind eye was turned to them. In a few cases when the disgruntled parties approached court, a few malpractices were exposed, but the culprits were not punished.

Something needs to be said about the record of the MCI which came in the news in April 2010 because of the arrest of Ketan Desai, its second-time President by the CBI, for allegedly taking a bribe of Rs two crore, to grant recognition to a medical college in Punjab.[11] The case makes a startling reading because the same Ketan Desai was earlier indicted by Delhi High Court in December 2001 for corrupt practices and abuse of power. The facts of that case were narrated by Sunil Pandya, Editor Emeritus of the *Journal of Indian Medical Ethics* in its July–September 2009 issue. Neither Desai nor the MCI challenged these statements published in the journal but Ketan Desai had not only escaped any action but had got himself re-elected as the President of the MCI. There can be no escape from the conclusion that persons like Ketan Desai enjoy the support of the political establishment and that the medical academic community is apathetic. In Maharashtra, press reports indicate that the Governor of the state had ordered an inquiry and had received a report, enumerating various malpractices, of the newly set up medical colleges, but the ministers who were the final authority ensured that the reports were not made public and there was no action.

The NPE 1986/1992 talked of an alternative system for participation by private sector. This was sought to be provided in a straight forward manner by Madhavrao Scindia, the Union Education Minister, under the Private Universities (Establishment and Regulation) Bill 1995, which was introduced in the Rajya Sabha on 25th August 1995. The bill provided for a legal framework for private universities and the basic financial safeguard was to have a permanent endowment of Rs 10 crore, which amount could be directed to be raised by the Central Government. UGC was to send its recommendations to the Central Government on the project report of the sponsors of a private university. This would have ensured an orderly framework for the establishment of non-profit private universities, but the outcry by leftist sympathizers of the ruling establishment against even any talk of "privatization" ensured that the Bill made no further progress.

The bill having stalled, the Central Government, appears to have adopted an ingenious device. Apparently, under directions of the Central Government, UGC framed revised guidelines for deemed universities in 2000 which provided for entertaining applications of societies/trusts interested in starting *de novo* institutions with proof of specific corpus of Rs 5 crore (for technical institutions) and Rs 3 crore (for social scientific institutions). A large number of self-financed institutions[12] apparently floated either by the politically influential rural rich or the commercially powerful corporate or family groups came to be notified as deemed universities. This was privatization by the backdoor.

More recently, press reports[13] indicated that the Central Government had on the basis of report of a committee to investigate deemed universities had decided to close down 44 deemed universities, but several of them obtained a stay from the High Courts. The latest position is that the matter has landed in the Supreme Court which has stayed action.

Dualist System of Medical Education: Scientific Medicine vs. Indigenous Systems

At present, the indigenous systems of medicine are known by the evocative term of AYUSH (Ayurveda, Unani, Siddha and Homeopathy), Siddha, being a branch of Ayurveda prevalent in Tamil Nadu. There were hopes that after independence, the problem of dualism between the "scientific" western medicine and the indigenous systems would be resolved, but it was not, the reason apparently being firstly, the internal divisions within the Ayurveda lobby as between the supporters of 'Shuddha Ayurvedic' education and 'integrated' Ayurvedic education and secondly, the opposition of the modern system of medicine. There is a separate regulatory system for traditional medical education as below:

1. Indian Medicine Central Council Act, 1970
2. The Homeopathy Central Council Act, 1973

The former Act covers Ayurveda, Siddha and Unani. The Homeopathic system is not indigenous. It was a European system, specifically German, which was popular in Europe till mid-1850s. It was naturalized in India, especially in Bengal and has enjoyed popular and state patronage even after its virtual disappearance from the western countries. In the UK, it is part of the National Health System as an alternative therapy but in early 2010 its scientific validity and any continued official subsidization has been questioned in an official report. The Health Ministry perhaps needs to take note of the same and re-examine the issue of Government of India's support to such a non-indigenous therapy.

T.N. Madan[14] has noted: "A strong plea for a rational approach to the evolution of an integrated system of Ayurvedic education was made by no less a person than the General President of the Indian Science Congress who drew attention to the fact that the practice of modern medicine also had its unscientific aspects, but modern doctors in India have opposed integration. Traditional practitioners have their own debates regarding a 'pure' vs. modernizing approach". On the basis of analysis by Paul Brass[15] who has studied and characterized the efforts for modernization of Ayurvedic education as part of a revivalist agenda, a tabular statement (Table 11.2) is presented below, which underlines the nature of socio-political backing enjoyed by respective groups. These debates, says Madan, are ultimately concerned with the nature of the new society that is in the process of being made in India since independence. The hopeful developments are: establishment of a separate department under the Health Ministry in 1995 which has announced a separate policy for AYUSH medicine which contains two important features: (1) need for improving the quality of training and research in Indian systems, and (2) the need to check the quality of indigenous medicines by enforcing hygienic production and batch manufacturing.

Table 11.2

Support for Integrated Medicine and Shuddha Ayurveda

Support for Integrated Medicine	*Support for Shuddha Ayurveda*
• Chopra Committee (1952)	• Mudaliar Committee (1959)
• Udupa Committee (1959)	• Vyas Committee (1962)
• Health Ministry	• Morarji Desai (PM)
• Honorary Adviser for Ayurveda	• Gulzarilal Nanda (Home Minister)
• Central Council of Ayurvedic Research	• Planning Commission (Panel on Ayurveda)
• Council of state boards and Faculties of Indian Medicine	• Hon. Adviser: Pt. Shiv Sharma
• National Medical Association	• Central Council of Health
• States of Uttar Pradesh and Maharashtra	• Central Board of Shuddha Ayurvedic Education

The Eleventh Plan[16] notes that the past investment in AYUSH education institutions has never exceeded three per cent of the Union health budget and the picture of the state budgets was no better. The plan indicates the intention of gradually increasing public investment in AYUSH sector. Specifically, the strategy is stated to be upgrading the undergraduate and postgraduate educational institutions under AYUSH by better regulations and establishing a system of NET type testing of AYUSH teachers and NAAC type assessment and accreditation of AYUSH undergraduate and postgraduate colleges. AYUSH system is proposed to be mainstreamed in the National Health Care Delivery System. All these steps are commendable but they also underline the fact that it will take a long time for the AYUSH system to end its sub-alternity within the national medical education system.

Centres of Excellence in Different Fields

IITs

IITs in technical education sub-field have by now emerged as Indian brands with its alumni holding responsible corporate positions internationally. In the first instance, four IITs were set up between 1951 and 1963 on the recommendation of the Sarkar Committee (1946) with a common vision to set up a chain of MIT type institutions in the four corners of India – Kharagpur (east), Bombay (west), Kanpur (north) and Madras (south). The Delhi College of Engineering was added in 1963 (perhaps as a concession to Delhi being the capital of India) and was named IIT, Delhi. The intention was to set up de novo institutions – it is therefore clearly against the original intent to 'convert' a State University like Roorkee University into an IIT in 2001. The IIT, Shillong established in 1995 was the last one of what may be called the first generation IITs. The Eleventh Plan envisages setting up of eight new IITs.[17]

All the IITs are regulated by a common Act (The Indian Institutes of Technology Act, 1961) under which the President of India is the Visitor of IITs (which means, in the prevalent cabinet system of government, that the Union Cabinet is the final decision-making authority). There is a broad-based IIT Council chaired by the Union Minister in charge of Technical Education, which lays down general policy guidelines for the IIT system. The administrative and academic autonomy are vested respectively in the Board chaired by an independent eminent person and the Senate chaired by the Director of the Institute. No bureaucrat or politician finds a place on these bodies. Its undergraduate curriculum has a strong core programme consisting of courses in sciences, humanities, technical arts and engineering sciences. Its postgraduate programme places emphasis on research. The admission to undergraduate courses is through the Joint Entrance Examination (JEE) and to postgraduate programmes through Graduate Aptitude Test Examination (GATE). The undergraduate programme is, by far, more prestigious. It is observed that postgraduate facilities are mostly availed of by the non-IIT graduates. Students are subjected to continuous evaluation and are not required to take annual examinations. The lecture method is supplemented by seminars, tutorials and guided studies. The faculty-student ratio is generally 1:10 and the faculty is excellent. Four countries extended technical assistance to specified IITs – USA (Kanpur), Germany (Madras), UK (Delhi) and Soviet Union (Bombay) – and the academic traditions of these countries have to some extent affected the nature of equipment but all the IITs follow a common approach to curriculum. Because of the higher investment and low faculty-student ratio, expenditure per student is much higher in the IITs than in comparable central institutions like regional engineering colleges (RECs) (now renamed NITs) or state engineering colleges. Indiresan estimates the difference in the range of 4:1. The quality of an IIT graduate is much higher than that of graduates in those latter institutions.[18]

In the IITs the reservation policy was implemented for the first time in 1973 perhaps in the context of the government's declared commitment (1971) to "Garibi Hatao" (Eradicate Poverty).[19] The unique aspect of the reservations in the IITs (15% for SCs, 7.5% for STs) is the total absence of compromised standards (such as grace marks). The concessions offered are: reduced cut-off point at entry (two-thirds of marks obtained by the last general category (GC) students), reduced course load during semester (22 credits vs 28 credits for GC students) and extension of one year to complete the B.Tech programme. Since 1983, a preparatory course has also been started for students who score less than two-third marks. A careful study of the impact of reservations in the five IITs based on the data for 1989–92 concludes that the apprehensions of excellence in peril because of reservations[20] are somewhat exaggerated and that given a number of pre-and post-entry strategies, implementation of reservation can be taken beyond tokenism, SC/ST students can be socio-culturally integrated and contribute to development.[21]

There were proposals since the 1980s for reservation of seats for the OBCs and this demand was finally conceded by the Government of India for which central legislation was passed in 2007. Its validity has since been upheld by the Supreme Court.[22] The government has also increased the number of seats in the IITs specifically to compensate for the reduction of non-reserved seats. Since in the southern states like Tamil Nadu and Karnataka, OBC students are even otherwise able to get admission on their own steam, the reservation for OBCs in IITs is not problematic for quality, though logically speaking, such statistical finding could put a question mark over the very need for OBC reservations. The OBC reservation policy is apparently designed to make a point about the OBCs having arrived.

Earlier, IITs were admired for their quality of education but were also blamed for the brain-drain going up to 30 per cent[23] and not contributing to industrial development in India. After 1991, as alumni of the IITs were seen to occupy key positions in the developed countries, especially in the USA, IITs came to be regarded as institutions with an Indian brand with international recognition. Shortly after India had created a niche for itself in the software industry, mainly owing to the Indian computer software professionals' skills in working out solutions for Y2K (Year 2000) switchover, the consultancy firm McKinsey submitted its report "Shaping the Knowledge Economy in India: The Need to set up a National Mission for Technology Education in India" in December 2000. It was pointed out in the report that though the IITs may be centres of excellence within India, they were in danger of falling behind in the international race. Thus, they were short of faculty in some cases to the extent of 50 per cent, research output and patents were very low in comparison with MIT and Stanford and governance was sub-optimal. It was pointed out that the Council for IITs had not met for several years. In February 2009, the press reported that the IIT Council had met after a gap of four years. (The HRD Minister is the Chairman). The McKinsey Report recommended that the IITs must triple their scale, expand doctoral programmes and improve quality of research, the IIT Directors must be given more autonomy and held accountable, the salaries of teachers must be raised and that the IIT budgets must be increased.[24] In this connection, it may be noted that till 2003, IITs were wholly funded by the Central Government, but thereafter they have been allowed to raise fees. It was always possible to raise funds from alumni or otherwise. Anecdotal evidence indicates that some steps toward implementation of the McKinsey Report might have been under way but the Government of India appears to be focused during the Eleventh Plan on opening more IITs.

IIMs

IIMs are another Indian brand with international recognition, though on a smaller scale. The first two IIMs were set up in 1961 – at Ahmedabad and Calcutta respectively – also with international collaboration (Harvard Business School in the case of Ahmedabad and Sloan School of Management of MIT at Calcutta). Their two-year postgraduate programmes (PGPs) established a reputation for excellence and later on, both started Fellowship Programme equivalent to Ph.D. New IIMs came up at Bangalore (1972), Lucknow (1984) and Kochi. IIMs are not statutory bodies, but are run by registered societies, with management vested in a Board of Governors constituted by the Government of India. Unlike IITs, the Board has representation from the Central Government. Recently, IIT graduates have started joining IIM programmes and IIMs have thus partly assumed the shape of finishing schools. This has also raised their brand value. IIMs have come into conflict with the Central Government and the issue of autonomy of IIMs has emerged prominently. While IITs are statutory bodies and outside the purview of AICTE, IIMs fall within the purview of Board of Management Studies of the AICTE. More recently (2008), the Review Committee on the IIMs chaired by R.C. Bhargava, submitted its recommendations, but they have not been well received, being perceived as suggesting larger Government control over IIMs. Some time back, *EPW* editorially commented on IIMs as below: "The transplantation of US style management education through a continuous, systematic and indiscriminate adoption of concepts, theoretical frameworks, contents and pedagogy and the underlying ideological orientation, albeit reshaped on Indian soil has been more thorough-going in the IIMs than in other emerging economies. At the end of their two year stay on campus, the services of the top-20 students of the IIMs at Ahmedabad, Kolkata and Bangalore are increasingly demanded by and supplied to transnational finance and management consultant firms ... The IIMs are thus seen to have a distinct competitive advantage in the international realm."[25]

These observations convey some of the grudging admiration evoked by IIMs even from left-academic quarters. No wonder, IIMs are perceived as the elite among 450 or so institutions of management co-existing with them.

As in the case of the IITs, the Eleventh Plan envisages setting up of seven new IIMs, thus expanding opportunities for quality management education.

In the federal context, elite institutions like IITs and IIMs appear to promote a tendency toward homogenization. They cater, as pointed out in the *EPW* critique of IIMs, to the modern corporation. But India's requirements of management personnel are diverse, covering the government sector, NGO sector, agriculture and rural areas. The question is: how to make the IITs and IIMs subserve the needs of diversity of the modern Indian federal polity? In a situation where financial incentives play by far the largest role in recruiting technical and management talent, the question poses a serious challenge to policymakers. It needs to be noted however, that the prevalence of a dualist system of education, the co-existence of centres of excellence and the run-of-the-mill institutions meant for the common man, is not a phenomenon peculiar to technical education field. It occurs in other areas too as noted below.

Medical Education

In medical education, the aspiration to set up all-India institutions with the best equipment, with a variety of faculties and with excellent facilities of education at all levels – graduate and postgraduate – as also research, goes back to pre-independence days. The Bhore Committee observed: "At least a few institutions which will concentrate on quality, should be established at suitable centres in different parts of the country."[26] In the first instance, an All India Medical Institute was recommended to be established in Delhi with the following objectives:

- to bring together in one place educational facilities of the very highest order for the training of all the more important types of health personnel,
- to promote research of the highest type in all the branches of study,
- to coordinate training and research,
- to provide postgraduate training of an advanced character,
- to inspire all trainers with high ideals of the profession, and
- to promote in them a community outlook and a higher degree of culture.[27]

The All India Institute of Medical Sciences, New Delhi was established in 1956 and the Medical Institute established at Chandigarh by the Punjab Government was taken over and renamed Postgraduate Institute of Medical Education and Research. Both were declared by law to be institutions of national importance. These two institutions, along with the Tiruvanantpuram Institute of Medical Science and Technology under the CSIR and the National Institute for Pharmaceutical Education and Research (1987) under the Department of Pharmaceuticals, are centres of excellence in medical education. They receive applications for admission far in excess of their intake capacity. The Mid-Term Appraisal of the Tenth Plan indicated the intention of setting up such tertiary level institutions in the six backward states of Bihar, Madhya Pradesh, Orissa, Rajasthan, Chattisgarh and Uttarakhand and of upgrading one prominent medical institute in Uttar Pradesh, Tamil Nadu, Jammu & Kashmir, Jharkhand, West Bengal and Andhra Pradesh. to the level of AIIMs. However, the relevant paras of the Eleventh Plan do not give any indication about the setting up of such new institutions. They do indicate however, that thanks to the establishment of Public Health Foundation of India (which is apparently an initiative in the Public Private Partnership – PPP mode). New Public Health Schools would be set up independently as well as part of AIIMs, PGIMER etc.[28]

Legal Education

In legal education, the movement for creating "centres of excellence" was a late starter (the National Law School University at Bangalore under state legislation, but managed by the Bar Council of India Trust having been set up only in 1986). The movement for setting up more such law universities uniformly implementing 5–year integrated course of LL.B. gathered momentum with the Supreme Court Judges' Committee on Reforms in law education (1994) and the Resolution of Law Ministers' Conference at Bhubaneshwar.[29] As a result, such universities have come up at Bhopal, Madhya Pradesh (1997), Hyderabad, Andhra Pradesh (1998), Jodhpur, Rajasthan (1999), Kolkata, West Bengal (1999) and some more in the following years. Not all of these institutions match the standards of National Law School University, Bangalore, which has been hailed as the best in India and comparable to the best any where abroad, but they replicate what may be called IIT/IIM model of being "centres of excellence" in the field of legal education. The placement record of these institutions is also good but not surprisingly, the alumni of these institutions have tended to veer toward corporate law practice. Thus, the "centres of excellence" in legal education have not been of much help to the common man who wants help in garden-variety criminal and civil cases.

Agricultural Education

It is necessary to take note of evolution of this stream of education which, in most accounts of higher education, tends to be neglected. Significantly, it has been inspired by American precedents. Radhakrishnan Commission had talked of setting up rural universities (RUs), which were to be an extension in higher education of the basic education pattern of Mahatma Gandhi (which was originally restricted to elementary education). However, thanks to the reports of the first (1954–55) and second (1959–60) Joint Indo-American Teams, the American agricultural experts were able to sell the idea of setting up land grant colleges in India now called State Agricultural Universities' (SAUs). They were to combine agricultural education, research and extension and they came up in collaboration with five land grant universities of Illinois, Ohio, Kansas, Missouri and Tennessee. It must be conceded that the Radhakrishnan RUs were not well-defined and the equation of SAUs and RUs may not be borne out by record. The difference between the American system and the Indian system is brought home by noting that one state one university idea could not be maintained in regionally diverse and bigger states in India like Maharashtra, Uttar Pradesh etc. At present, India has about 34 state agricultural universities. Many states have multiple universities for reasons indicated earlier. While not all agricultural universities can be called elite institutions, those at Pant Nagar in Uttarakhand, Ludhiana in Punjab, Hyderabad in Andhra Pradesh, Bangalore in Karnataka and Coimbatore in Tamil Nadu are regarded as a cut above the rest. These four-five universities along with four National Institutes under ICAR, which all are deemed universities (IARI, New Delhi; IVRI, Izat Nagar; NDRI, Karnal and Fisheries Education Institute, Mumbai) are coveted agricultural institutes for purposes of admission and can be said to replicate the IIT/IIM syndrome in the area of agricultural education.

But, the irony of the situation of agricultural universities and in particular, the disillusionment of the political leadership with the way agricultural universities came to evolve as centres of education research and extension became evident when during the Emergency, i.e., in January 1977, the Union Agricultural Ministry set up a Committee for Review of Agricultural Universities with the following terms of reference: "To assess how far agricultural universities are meeting the needs of trained manpower at different levels and producing non-elite graduates with motivation for self-employment in agriculture, with competence to identify and resolve practical problems and with an attitude to demonstrate to the farmers even by working on farms. In this context, the committee would assess the quality of educational programmes, adequacy of opportunities for work experience, internal efficiency and relevance of research programmes of the university, particular attention being given to orientation of home science education to suit Indian conditions, more particularly rural India." The then Union Agriculture Minister (Jagjivan Ram), brought out his concern in his inaugural address of 25th January 1977. He stated that the number of agricultural universities and also national institutes had multiplied with an annual intake of 7,000 and outturn of 5,000. The number was far less than the requirement of rural agriculture. For example, only 10 agricultural graduates per district, one veterinary graduate and one home science graduate per district are available, statistically speaking. But many of the graduates were unemployed because they did not want to practise their skills, but only wanted a government job. They were urban based students, who were not prepared to go to the villages. Home science graduates could have engaged in imparting training in post-harvest technology (including e.g., avoidance of spoilage of fruits and vegetables by applying the technique of processing and preservation). The committee,[30] chaired by the veteran Dr M.S. Randhawa, made appropriate recommendations, but it cannot be said that the situation has improved to any considerable extent even after a lapse of 20 years.

Socio-political Forces at Work in Professional Education

The above analysis of professional education in post-independence India with the evidence of certain trends is a preliminary one. We have to see as to what are the socio-political processes at work which have given rise to these trends. The trend toward regional imbalance evidently is the result of north-south divide which developed in colonial times due to the systems of land administration (Zamindari and permanent settlement of land revenue system in the north and the east as against the Ryatwari land revenue system in the south and the west, which the latter is associated with greater political awareness, spread of education etc.). The north-south divide is manifested in the various measures of social development (literacy, male and female and infant and maternal mortality). In all these measures, the south scores over the north. This north-south divide is also reflected in the population growth with high fertility rates prevalent in the north which harbours the so-called BIMARU states (Bihar along with Jharkhand, Madhya Pradesh along with Chattisgarh, Uttar Pradesh, Orissa and Rajasthan).

The sub-alternity of indigenous systems of medicine is rooted in the deliberate colonial neglect of these systems (compare the approach to Ayurveda of the renowned Bhore Committee which was otherwise quite advanced in its views about the need to develop preventive and social medicine) which has been perpetuated by post-colonial practitioners of modern medicine combined with the rural-urban divide in India with the modern medical practitioners concentrated in urban areas and vaids and hakims mostly practising in rural areas but above all, being the main source of health care provision in the villages of India. India's failure to achieve universalization of elementary education and eradication of adult illiteracy is matched by India's poor record in reaching the goal of Health for All.

The commercialization and privatization of medical and technical education is partly rooted in the linguistic and religious diversity in India with safeguards for linguistic and religious minorities. These safeguards serve as an incentive for various communities like Muslims, Christians and resourceful linguistic minorities in various states to start professional institutions. The role of dominant castes in the south and south-west also cannot be neglected. Those self-financed institutions are expected to be supervised and regulated by the administrators of a secular State but such regulation tends to be politicized in India. As pointed out by Rudolphs,[31] politicization involves appropriation of educational structures and resources and displacement of educational goals by organized political and community (religious, castes, locality) interests. The effect of politicization is to subsume the educational goals and processes of particular educational institutions to those of organized extra-educational interests. Rudolphs have also pointed out that there are three separate processes at work, viz., politicization of educational structures, political influence exercised by educational structures and assertion by the state of public interest in education. These three relationships are not easy to distinguish in concrete empirical situations. Since politicization of educational institutions is part of a larger process of politicization in India, the results may not always be in the best interest of education. For example, a politician may set up a college through political influence, and the college may exercise its influence by sending its nominees to decision-making bodies of the university but since the university works in close relation with the state, the university may come to affect state policy. This has happened in practice in the states and at the Centre in India so that the state may be slow or slack in regulation. The phenomenon of capitation fee colleges and the inability of UGC or AICTE or MCI to regulate these has to be understood in these terms. Since the central level is remote, it tends to be regarded as a saviour when politicization assumes pathological proportion.

Judicial activism is sometimes interpreted in terms of judicial response to the vacuum created by the failure of the executive power to act and the democratic demand for redressal of people's grievances. But, the judicial activism is not an un-mixed blessing. Thus, the Supreme Court through a series of judgments beginning with Pradeep Jain[32] took away the control of 15 per cent of undergraduate medical seats and of 25 per cent of postgraduate medical seats from the states and municipal bodies and placed them under the control of a Central Government agency. T.R. Andhyarujina[33] termed the result as nationalization. It is also pointed out that a byproduct of this nationalization of medical education was part – centralization of school curricula in various states to approximate to the CBSE curriculum to respond to the requirements of JEE.

Moreover, it has been noted that the concept of NRI quota in medical education is of judicial origin and not part of the public, i.e., legislative or NGO discourse. This only underlines the moral hazard involved when one Arm of the government apparently encroaches on the territory of another Arm.

These processes/tendencies do not exhaust the list of forces at work but they indicate how the social role of education in the direction of reproducing social inequalities has operated in practice. Unfortunately, the political elite has played a role which gives an impression of the state being transformed into a hand maiden of commercial forces. There is a certain brazenness about the resultant system which is in need of urgent reform. Some analysts rely on the activist judiciary to do the trick but the judicial process has its limitations and the activist judiciary has itself contributed to the unbearable burden of arrears of litigation. There has to be a movement for reform from within the system.

In this connection, one notes the accomplishments of an administrator statesman like Abraham Flexner in the USA, who, with his strategic location in the Rockfeller Foundation was able to initiate a process of reform in the medical education in the USA in 1910 and onwards.[34] Some modern scholars[35] have claimed that the malpractices by way of the proliferation of commercial medical colleges in the USA were identified by the American Medical Association itself which engineered the Flexner Report. If so, the case and need for internally initiated reform in India's professional education sector would appear to be stronger. Unfortunately, the professionalization of the medical guild in India is itself weak. The same needs to be aided by the government agencies like Election Commission (to conduct elections to Medical Councils, Bar Councils etc.), C&AG (to conduct proprietary audit of the accounts of various professional, educational and research bodies), and the Central Vigilance Commission (to expose, *inter alia,* the malpractices like capitation fees in medical and engineering colleges). This amounts to bringing the state back in, in a matter rooted in social factors but for the present, there appears to be no other alternative.

Notes

1. Vide entry 14 of State List of Schedule VII of the Constitution of India.
2. *O.N. Mahendru vs. Bar Council,* AIR 1968 SC 888.
3. Government of India: Ministry of Education: Report of the Review Committee of AICTE (New Delhi, 2003) (Mimeo).
4. Weiner Myron, *The Politics of Scarcity* (Bombay: Asia Publishing, 1963).
5. The question of capitation fees was discussed by the CABE in its 16th meeting held in January 1950 and in its 18th meeting held in January 1951. In the 16th meeting the agenda item was: To consider the proposal to abolish the system of capitation fees charged by some educational institutions from students coming from other provinces or States. Although the agenda item is

cryptic, the reference is presumed to be to the practice of private engineering colleges in some States especially the then Mysore state. The Board's decision was that the system of capitation fees was not in keeping with the spirit of national unity and the provincial governments may be requested to re-examine the question. In its 18th meeting, the decision recorded is as below: "The Board regrets to note the position in regard to levy of capitation fees. The states concerned may once again be urged in the interest of the national unity and harmony and justice to students in less flourishing states to abolish capitation fees in respect of states not sponsored by State Governments" (vide Ministry of Education, CABE Silver Jubilee Souvenir (1936–1960), pp. 240, 263). Any comment is superfluous!

6. Rekha Kaul, *Caste, Class and Education* (New Delhi: Sage, 1993).
7. T.N. Madan and B.G. Halbar, "Caste and Communities in the Private and Public Education of Mysore State", in Susanne H. Rudolph and Lloyd I. Rudolph (Eds.), *Education and Politics in India* (Delhi: Oxford University Press, 1972), 121–147.
8. *Mohini Jain vs. State of Karnataka*, 1992 (2) SCC 645 and *J.P. Unnikrishnan vs. State of Andhra Pradesh*, 1993 (1) SCC 645.
9. *TMA Pai Foundation vs. State of Karnataka* (2002) 6 SCC 481.
10. NPE 1986/92 para 6.20.
11. *Indian Express* (Mumbai), 26th April, 2010.
12. K.B. Powar, "Deemed to be Universities: Their Genesis and History, Present Status and Future Prospects", *University News*, Vol. 43, No. 13, 29th March, 2004.
13. Press Reports in March, 2010.
14. T.N. Madan, *Doctors and Society: Three Asian Case Studies: India, Malaysia and Sri Lanka* (New Delhi: Vikas, 1980), 25–26.
15. Paul R. Brass, "The Politics of Ayurvedic Education: A Case Study of Revivalism and Modernism in India", in Susanne H. Rudolph and Lloyd I. Rudolph (Eds.), *Education and Politics in India* (Delhi: Oxford University Press, 1972), 342–371.
16. Eleventh Five-Year Plan, Vol. II, 125–129.
17. Eleventh Five-Year Plan, Vol. II, para 1.3.41.
18. P.V. Indiresan et al., "The IITs: Excellence in Peril", in Suma Chitnis and Philip Altbach (Eds.), *Higher Education Reforms in India: Experience and Perspectives* (New Delhi: Sage Publications, 1993), 334–364.
19. Viney Kripal and Meenakshi Gupta (Eds.), *Equality through Reservations* (Jaipur and New Delhi: Rawat Publications, 1999).
20. See Footnote 18.
21. See Footnote 19.

22. In the well-known case of *Ashok Kumar Thakur vs. Union of India* decided in 2008.
23. See Footnote 18.
24. Sandipan Deb, *IITians: Story of a Remarkable Indian Institute and how its Alumni have Reshaped Indian Society* (New Delhi: Penguin, 2004).
25. *EPW*, 25th February 2006, 669.
26. Health Development and Planning Committee, (New Delhi, GoI, 1946), Vol. IV, 60.
27. As quoted in T.N. Madan (F.N. 14).
28. Eleventh Five-Year Plan, Vol. II, 94–96.
29. *Indian Bar Review*, Vol. XXII(4), 1995: 7–34.
30. Report on Review of Agricultural Universities (Chairman: M.S. Randhwa) (New Delhi, 1983).
31. Rudolph and Rudolph, op. cit. (1972), 6–10.
32. *Pradeep Jain vs. Union of India* (AIR 1984 SC 1420).
33. T.R. Andhyarujina, *Judicial Activism and Constitutional Democracy* (Bombay: N.M. Tripathi, 1992).
34. Abraham Flexner, *Medical Education in the US and Canada: A Report to the Carnegie Foundation for the Advancement of Teaching* (New York: Bulletin No. 4, 1910. Idem: *Medical Education in Europe: A Report to the Carnegie Foundation for the Advancement of Teaching* (New York: Bulletin No. 6), 1912.
35. Paul Starr, *The Social Transformation of American Medicine* (New York: Basic Books, 1982).

12 The Research Dimension

Sunil Khilnani refers to the Temples of the Future[1] and implies that Nehru's *idea of India* zeroed in on the Planning Commission (with P.C. Mahalanobis as its influential member), which was set the task of bringing about all-round economic development. Unfortunately, he fails to take adequate notice of Nehru's vision of the role of science and by extension, technology in the project of economic development. As early as 1937, while addressing the Indian Science Congress (Calcutta, December 1937), Nehru recalled his days at Cambridge, that house of science, and observed: "Science was not only an abstraction but was the very texture of life, without which our modern world would vanish away. It was science alone that could solve these problems of hunger and poverty, of insanitation and illiteracy, of superstitions and deadening customs and traditions, of vast resources running to waste, of a rich country inhabited by starving people."[2] Very briefly, Nehru believed that science is the solvent of most problems of India and, therefore, after Independence, he set up a chain of scientific laboratories under the CSIR of which he as the PM was the President. But he also knew the close relationship between science and technology, the latter of which contributed to solving the problems of the real life. Hence, irrigation projects which were, in a sense, technological application of the engineering science, to solve the water problems of India and which, therefore, he called "temples of the future".

This chapter is organized as below: First of all, the federal context of the proliferation of central science and technology (S&T) organizations is noted, being rooted in the two-fold policy decision taken by the first Prime Minister Jawaharlal Nehru, regarding research and industrial policy. As a result, firstly, research is predominantly conducted in independent central laboratories rather than in the universities. Secondly, the research is mainly conducted by the Centre rather than the states. Thereafter, general issues regarding S&T policy making, funding and measures of research performance are examined. Lastly, functioning of research councils in social sciences and allied fields is examined.

Federal Context of Central S&T Organizations

At the time of independence, India had only a few scientific research laboratories and organizations in the areas of survey, agriculture and medicine. In the post-independence India, the dominant role in conducting research in natural, biological and social sciences has been played by specialized Central Government agencies. As for research, thanks to the influence of scientific advisers like Homi Bhabha and S.C. Bhatnagar, it was decided to carry out basic research in the Central Government funded laboratories rather than in the universities or in regional research organizations under the control of one or more State Governments. As observed by the document 'Challenge of Education': "Research in the university system is widespread and is known to be cost effective but major national inputs have gone to laboratories outside the universities."[3] The number of research institutions funded by the Central Government through its various ministries has increased from about a dozen in 1947 to about 457 in 2002. Apart from institutions under the Defence Research and Development Organization (DRDO), space, atomic energy and ocean development numbering 78, which operate in the exclusive domain of the Central Government, about 379 institutions are in areas which are related to agriculture, health, industry etc. in the state domain, thus underlining the fact that the research in central scientific research institutions is at the cost of research in state level organizations including universities. This has affected the balance in centre-state relations.

As for industrial policy, with the passing of the Industries (Development and Regulation) Act, 1948, the Industrial Policy Resolutions of 1948 and 1956 and the creation of Directorate-General of Technical Development in the Central Industries Ministry, coupled with the creation of CSIR and other laboratories, the industrial research establishments of State Governments which had grown up in the inter-war period due to industry being a provincial subject under Dyarchy/provincial autonomy declined or became moribund. The main research currently conducted by the State Governments is in the area of agriculture, with agricultural universities accounting for 88 per cent of the research activity of State Governments. As against over 450 central S&T research institutions, State Governments do not have any research institutions worth the name.

Proliferation of Central S&T Research Organizations

The phenomenon of proliferation is due to the process of cloning. As observed by Aquiel Ahmed, every time the government wanted to promote a new field, it did so by 'cloning' a separate organization from the primordial structures,[4] so that at present the Government of India has about a dozen departments with heavy S&T content. These departments[5] are:

1. Department of Health and Family Welfare
2. Department of Agriculture and Research (DARE)

3. Ministry of Science and Technology which comprises three separate departments:
   (i) Department of Science and Technology
   (ii) Department of Scientific and Industrial Research (DSIR), an umbrella for CSIR
   (iii) Department Biotechnology
4. Department of Atomic Energy
5. Defence Research and Development Organization
6. Department of Space
7. Department of Ocean Development
8. Department of Information Technology
9. Ministry of Non-Conventional Energy Sciences
10. Ministry of Environment and Forests
11. Ministry of Earth and Geo Sciences

Two points regarding the organization need to be noted, viz., the Commission form and the Mission mode of implementation which the S&T departments have adopted. The Commission form is interesting because its autonomy is backed by high level leadership (PM as chairman), freedom from the Central Finance Ministry in crucial matters (with Finance Secretary being a member), freedom from UPSC control in recruitment and freedom from the Supply Department in the procurement of equipment. The leading examples of Commission form are: the Atomic Energy Commission and the Space Commission. The Mission mode of performing and completing time-bound tasks has been adopted by the S&T departments from the US (e.g., the American mission of sending the man to the moon) and has been emulated by "soft" departments like education also, e.g., National Literacy Mission.

The Premier Research Council: Council for Scientific and Industrial Research

CSIR established in 1942 has now focused on funding its own laboratories apart from a few fellowships. (It had 38 laboratories and 47 regional centres in 2003–04.) Since it has served as a role model for other research councils, it is worth noting that it has a highly centralised set-up. The original Memorandum of Association provided for some provincial representation but in the rules framed after independence, neither in the society nor in the governing body, are the State Governments represented.[6] It has five Regional Research Laboratories (RRLs) at Hyderabad, Jammu, Jorhat, Bhubaneswar and Thiruvanantapuram but they each focus on a particular scientific discipline. In the Silver Jubilee publication brought out by the CSIR, there are ample references to liaison with industries but absolutely no reference to any states or regions.[7] Since 1996, CSIR has emerged as a model organization for scientific and industrial research and a path-setter in the shifting paradigm of self-financing R&D and global R&D platform, providing competitive R&D and high quality science-based services the world over.[8] Nearer home, it should serve as an exemplar for other Research Councils, e.g., ICAR, ICMR etc.[9]

Policy Making and Funding

The exercises in S&T policy making and funding underline the fact that these activities are highly centralized without much involvement of the states. The Scientific Policy Resolution (SPR) of March 1958 was the result of a backroom exercise done by the PM's advisers. Parliament approved the SPR in 1958 which aimed to:

- Foster, promote and sustain scientific research in all its aspects – pure, applied and educational.
- Ensure adequate supply of research scientists of the highest quality.
- Encourage the programme for the training of scientific and technical personnel to fulfil the country's needs in science, education, agriculture, industry and defence.
- Encourage dissemination and discovery of knowledge in an atmosphere of scientific freedom.[10]

From Nehru's point of view, education policy was incorporated in the Science Policy.

The goal of national investment in R&D at the end of the Fifth Plan being one per cent of GDP was laid down by the National Committee on S&T (NCST)[11] on the eve of the Fifth Plan. The Janata regime (1977–79) coincided with a phase of introspection in the S&T community in India, in which concerns with social, environmental and rural/regional aspects of development came to the fore. In the Technology Policy Statement issued in January 1983, some of these concerns were articulated but it did not spell out the role of the State Governments in the scientific and industrial research.[12] The latest S&T Policy 2003[13] committing the Government of India to raise the level of investment in S&T (including contribution by industry) to two per cent of GDP by the end of tenth Plan (2007) is, however, notable for recognizing the need for coordination with social sciences and for underlining the role of State Governments. Its intention that states would be encouraged and assisted in the use of S&T for developmental purposes and in establishing linkages with national institutions for solving their regional and local scientific problems, is welcome. However, the succeeding UPA governments appear to treat the policy as an NDA exercise and hardly refer to it. Except for Andhra Pradesh, which reportedly issued a biotechnology policy, no State Government boasts of its own S&T policy.[14] The Government of Maharashtra has reportedly set up a Rajiv Gandhi S&T Mission in

2005–06. Corresponding to the ambitious targets, funding for S&T sector has been progressively stepped up. In 2000–01, it was Rs 17,680.21 crore,[15] broken up as below: Central Government 62.5 per cent, public sector industries 5.0 per cent, higher education sector 2.9 per cent, State Governments 8.0 per cent and private sector industries 21.6 per cent. If we consider the government sector alone, as much as 89.4 per cent of the expenditure incurred from government sources came from the Central Government and only 10.6 per cent from the State Governments. The latest data regarding R&D expenditure are as below:

2002–03	Rs 180 billion
2003–04	Rs 197.27 billion
2004–05	Rs 216.4 billion

Against the target of 2 per cent of GDP for research spending, the actual achievement has been 1.03 per cent (2.76% in the USA and 1.61% in China).[16]

Science and Engineering Research Council

The mainstay of research assistance from the S&T sector to higher education institutions is the Science and Engineering Research Council (SERC) set up in 1973, under the DST. In the year 2003–04, SERC approved 214 projects costing Rs 3.73 crore.[17] Moreover, almost every scientific department of the Central Government operates a scheme for research assistance and fellowships in its chosen area, by way of "assistance for extra-mural projects" and in the year 1998–99, the central scientific agencies gave an assistance of Rs 125.32 crore to universities/deemed universities.[18] This may be compared to the miniscule assistance of Rs 4.82 crore given for research by UGC in the same year.

The Mid-Term Appraisal of the Tenth Plan proposed to set up an Indian Science Foundation (ISF) on the lines of the National Science Foundation (NSF) of the USA, tasked with supporting all fields of fundamental research and engineering, identifying relevant new initiatives and the leading Indian scientists in the field and providing necessary guidance and for enabling them to excel. It stated that in addition to funding basic research in the traditional areas, the proposed NSF may identify and support "high risk, high pay off" ideas.[19]

The Eleventh Plan states that for funding internationally, competitive and front ranking major research programmes, the existing SERC would be restructured into National Science and Engineering Research Board (NSERB) and a special programme for rejuvenation of research in universities would be initiated.[20]

The Annual Report of UGC for 2007–08 indicates that there has been some follow up. The Ministry of HRD set up a Task Force for rejuvenation of basic scientific research in Indian universities, under chairmanship of Prof. M.M. Sharma, former Director, UICT, Mumbai. An amount of Rs 205 crore has been allocated for implementation of recommendations of the Committee of which Rs 157 crore Has been sanctioned. An 'Operation Faculty Research' is being launched under which 1,000 faculty positions are being created to be filled at national level through global advertisement. In a significant development a six-member committee has been constituted with Chairman, UGC and Director General, CSIR as co-Chairman, to work out modalities for creating formal linkages between universities and CSIR laboratories under the collaborative programme.[21] One gets an impression that funding is not a constraint so far as research is concerned and that in addition to usual schemes, there is a lot of emphasis on post-doctoral fellowships. However, one has to keep an open mind regarding performance on the ground.

Measures of Research Performance

India's comparative position on various input and output measures, both in basic research (publications and citations) and applied research (patents) is shown in Table 12.1, where data regarding USA, China and Japan are also presented:

Table 12.1

S&T Indicators for India in Comparative Perspective

S&T Indicators	*US*	*China*	*Japan*	*India*
R&D expenditure				
As percentage of GDP, 2007	2.47	1.61	3.40	1.03
Percentage performed by HEIs	16.8	10.1	13.9	4.1
Research manpower				
Researchers (per million population)	4,484	663	5,287	119
Technicians (per million population)	—	—	528	102
Rank in Growth Competitiveness Index	2	49	12	50
Patent – PCT applications, 2007	52,480	5,456	27,731	648
Publications/Citations, 1994–2004				
Number of papers (Rank)	1	9	2	13
Number of citations (Rank)	1	18	4	21
Citations per paper (Rank)	1	121	11	113
High technology exports				
Volume (US$ billion)	216.02	161.60	124.04	2.84
As percentage of manufactured	32	30	24	5
Royalties and licence fees				
Receipts (in US$ billion)	52.64	0.24	15.70	0.03
Payments (in US$ billion)	23.90	4.50	13.64	0.42

Source: Adapted from Pawan Agarwal, *Higher Education in India*, 2009, p. 271.

Research Councils in Social Science and Allied Fields

The successive Annual Reports of the Ministry of Education (2002–05) refer to five research councils functioning outside the university system namely, Indian Council of Social Science Research (ICSSR), Indian Council of Historical Research (NCHR), Indian Council of Philosophical Research (ICPR), Indian Institute of Advanced Studies (IIAS) and National Council of Rural Institutes (NCRI).[22] Of these, the last two mentioned are not research councils at all, the former being an advanced centre of research modelled on the Institute of Advanced Studies, Princeton USA/All Souls' College, Oxford/UK and the latter is an incipient coordinating body for rural higher education.

Indian Council of Social Science Research (ICSSR)

Structure and Functions

The establishment of ICSSR in 1969 was based on the recommendations of the report of a committee chaired by V.K.R.V. Rao appointed by the Planning Commission in August 1965 to survey the current situation in relation to research in social sciences in the country and to make recommendations regarding the future line of development. The Committee harked back to the Science Policy Resolution of 1958, which had emphasized the role of science in the progress of the nation. The Council was expected to supplement UGC's structural role (development of departments) by providing facilities like documentation, data library, promotional facilities for seminars, workshops and conferences. In regard to organizational pattern, the specific model of the CSIR was commended.[23]

The primary objective of the ICSSR is to promote research in social sciences and to facilitate its utilization. For this purpose, it may review progress of research, sponsor research programme and projects, and finance seminars. Special emphasis is placed on promotion of research in universities, especially by young social scientists and on international cooperation. It may also support documentation/data services.

The Neglect of the Role of State Governments

In social science research and allied fields, states/regions can have much more interest academically than in the fields of natural science and technology. The ICSSR adopted a policy statement on its role in October 1971.[24] A paper was placed before the ICSSR (on the basis of which the Policy Statement was adopted) in which reference was made to the report on 'Social Science Research in India' submitted by Mr Shonfield and Prof. Cherns, making some important suggestions in regard to close relations with State Governments. Shonfield-Cherns Report stated: "The relationship of the Council with the State Governments is of especial importance. Not only are some State Governments major sponsors of social science research, all are potential users and many of the results of research invite interest and action more within the ambit of State Governments than of the Central Government. Although ICSSR receives its funds from the Federal Government, it should avoid being seen by State Governments as an exclusive servant of the Centre. It must be recognized, however, that the social science policy is not something which is best determined at state level; every aspect of it transcends state boundaries and State responsibilities. Thus, the ICSSR needs to be seen by the States as a resource, a source of help and advice, as the voice of social science community as a whole, but not as an embodiment of superior power."[25]

Unfortunately, the ICSSR's final decision treated State Governments as 'Other Agencies' and simply stated that the Council would also have to develop relations with State Governments who had begun to take greater interest in social science research and especially in relation to the regional social science documentation centres.[26] Since then the devaluation and derogation of states has continued apace and the ICSSR, as feared by Shonfield and Cherns, is perceived by the States as purely a central agency.

There are voluminous data relating to ICSSR which undertook three self-assessments in 1973, 1978 and 1986.[27] After a break, an assessment was done in 2008, under A.Vaidyanathan which is called the Fourth Review of ICSSR and reported in *EPW*,[28] but it is not clear if ICSSR is taking action on the same. The latest S&T Policy Statement (2003) says that closer interaction of those involved in the natural sciences and technology, social sciences, humanities and other scholarly pursuits will be facilitated to bring about mutual reinforcement, added value and impact. In relation to social science research, in the founding Conference of Association of Social Science Research Councils of Asia (ASREC), held at Simla in May 1973, Malcolm Adisheshaiah enunciated a goal of 5 per cent of total investment in S&T to be invested in social science in any given year. Since investment in S&T was 17,660.21 crore in 2000–01, in the social science field, it should have been Rs 883 crore as per this norm. Actually it was in the region of Rs 40 crore (Rs 31.50 crore by Research Councils and Rs 8 crore under UGC). The Research Council-wise break up was: ICSSR – Rs 25.50 crore, ICHR – Rs 3.86 crore and ICPR –Rs 2.14 crore.

ICSSR has sought to decentralize its operations by setting up regional centres at Mumbai (western), Hyderabad (southern), Kolkata (eastern), JNU New Delhi (northern), Shillong (north-eastern) and Chandigarh (north-western). Among other things, the regional centres are to be responsible for promoting the policies and programmes of the ICSSR in the region, assist in the organization of programmes of the ICSSR within the region, assist the ICSSR in identifying young social scientists in the region, maintain documentation and bibliographical services especially in the modern Indian languages, operate the programmes of study grants and fellowships assigned to them and collect, preserve and make available research materials about the region (and in the regional languages) to all social scientists in the country. In 2001, the Council decided to make the regional centres an integral part of the ICSSR and granted its employees the status of ICSSR employees which really meant deconcentration and not devolution.

Regional Research Institutes

A second aspect of decentralization, originally envisaged by the V.K.R.V. Rao Committee was regional research institutes (RRIs), which do not constitute either affiliated or constituent institutions of statutory universities and that are entitled both to maintenance and development grants from the ICSSR. The Third Review Committee noted that beginning with nine institutes in 1974–75, their number was expected to rise to 25 in the Seventh Plan period (1985–90), and that they accounted for 42 per cent of Sixth Plan expenditure of the Council. The Annual Report of ICSSR for 2002–03 shows that there are 27 such research institutes and that State Governments paid them grants totalling Rs 747 lakh as against Rs 1,152 lakh paid as grants by the ICSSR. Five of the Institutes were located in Delhi, being effectively central institutions and they got Rs 525 lakh as grants.

The Third Review Committee rightly emphasized the regional role of the RRIs, stating: "They have played a significant role in expanding and raising the quality of research and in strengthening the research capability in regions away from Delhi. Their close links with the State Governments, planning bodies and public sector organizations have led to greater consciousness about the use of research to help policy makers." Unfortunately, the Council bureaucracy does not appear to have accepted the recommendation in the spirit in which it was made. The tendency is to keep aloof from State Governments and the Council itself remains preoccupied with financial ceilings. As a result, both the RRIs and the regions/states have suffered.

Role of ICSSR in Empowerment of Women in India

The account of ICSSR may be aptly concluded by referring to the Report of the Committee on the Status of Women in India (R-CSW) entitled "Towards Equality" which was produced by the ICSSR in 1975. The report is the precursor to a variety of research, teaching and activist initiatives in women's movement which were a spin off from that report. These may be listed as:

1. Women's studies initially visualized as an area of action and policy on issues of women.
2. Women's studies as a discipline in the higher education system where teaching became crucial along with research and documentation.
3. Women's studies as a structure established by the UGC from 1983 onward in the form of Women's Studies Centres for promoting research, teaching and action.[29]

Prof. M.N. Srinivas, in his inaugural address to the XI World Congress of Sociology in 1986 underlined the significance of women's studies as the only significant development in Indian social science in the last two decades – a thrust from below. His allusion to a thrust from below refers to the fact that women's studies *ab initio* are associated with activism which leads to change. Knowledge is empowering and gender perspective empowers women to comprehend complexities of subordination and also impels them to change gender relations. It is noted by Menon and Nigam[30] that in the 1980s the "second wave" of women's movement saw the emergence of vocal and visible autonomous women's groups which placed feminist issues firmly in the public agenda. They include dowry, rape and violence against women, but not education, but it was also affected by R-CSW.

R-CSW's Impact on Education Policy

In the context of women's education, NPE 1968 may be compared with NPE 1986, the latter of which underlines the sea-change that came about. NPE 1968 has a single reference to women's education in the para about equalization of educational opportunity across regions, castes, etc. It says: "The education of girls should receive emphasis not only on grounds of social justice but also because it accelerates social transformation" (para 4.10). However, the NPE 1986 devotes two paragraphs to the subject under the heading: "Education for Women's Equality", whose very wording[31] reflects a paradigm shift in the approach which is the direct fall out of RC-SW and the 'second wave' of women's movement generated by it referred to earlier.

ICSSR in Perspective

An international review has deplored perception of the decline of the role of ICSSR as an apex body of the social science research since the latter half of 1980s, the two symptoms of decline being (1) physical expansion of the administrative apparatus that consumed an ever-increasing share of resources, and (2) a perception of delays, hassles and unimaginative routinization of ICSSR's procedures for awards, grants and fellowships.[32]

On the other hand, in the federal context, the plight of ICSSR's RRI's is symptomatic of the centralization ethos of the Central Government. The concept of a region and a service organization for a regional hinterland is abhorred. While regional institutes are thus centralized and euphemistically called national institutes, there is no parallel movement within ICSSR to set up new regional/state centres or re-define the role of existing research institutes. The distance between central organizations and State Governments goes on increasing. The state political class is indifferent and the state level bureaucracy does not care. It is the universities and especially college teachers in the remote areas of individual states, who suffer. There is, therefore, a need to have a fresh look at the role of regional centres and research institutes of the ICSSR.

Other Research Councils

In the matter of projects financed and level of funding, Indian Council of Historical Research (ICHR) and Indian Council of Philosophical Research (ICPR) have always been junior partners of ICSSR. Their funding is about one-fourth or less than that of ICSSR. The comparative financial allocation for a single year for which comparable data are available is as below:

Table 12.2

Comparative Financial Allocation (2002–03)

Name of Council	*Final Outlay (Rs in crore)*
ICSSR	33.61
ICHR	7.31
ICPR	4.37

Indian Council of Historical Research

ICHR was set up because it was felt that "there was a need to promote historical research to strengthen national consciousness and identity, to promote application of historical method to the study of social sciences and to enunciate and implement a national policy of historical research."[33] A Working Group was set up in December 1971 by the Ministry of Education to work out the details of such a body, its objectives, functions and organizational set-up. The Council was inaugurated on 27th March 1972, when Prof. Nurul Hasan, who was himself a historian, was Minister of State for Education. The ICHR's 'objects' contain a specific reference to State Governments, i.e., about the Council entering into arrangements with Government of India, State Governments and other public or private organizations for furtherance of its objectives. There is no indication however that it has acted in terms of this object. Review Committees for ICHR were reportedly appointed in 1982, 1999 and 2004 but their reports have not been disseminated as was done by ICSSR. Unlike the ICSSR, ICHR has no regional institutions, but it has regional centres at Bangalore (now Bengaluru) and in the north-east.

Indian Council of Philosophical Research

There was a time gap between registration of ICPR in March 1977 and its activation in July 1981. It appears that in the mid-seventies a team of scholars made a careful study of the whole question relating to the revitalization of the Indian tradition of philosophizing and suggested that in addition to other efforts, the Government of India should come forward to establish an Indian Council of Philosophical Research (ICPR). Its first chairman was Prof. D.P. Chattopadhyaya. ICPR has an academic centre at Lucknow and hence some linkage with Uttar Pradesh government but otherwise it has no regional/state linkages.

There is one organizational lacuna, namely absence of a council for promotion of arts and humanities. In the UK which has served as a model for India in regard to setting up of Social Science Research Council, there was a Research Board for Arts and Humanities since converted into a regular Council.[34] There is also a post of Director General, Research Councils to coordinate activities of all such councils. One alternative is to allow the ICSSR, which is the senior Council, to assume the role of a coordinator as well as regional facilitator on behalf of the two remaining councils. But, this requires inter-council coordination, which is lacking. A heartening step was taken recently by the UGC which constituted a committee involving the academic heads not only of ICSSR, ICHR and ICPR but also the Sahitya Akademi and the first meeting was held under the chairmanship of Vice-Chairman of UGC in July 2003.[35] But this was an isolated initiative without any continuity.

Conclusion

This account of the research dimension shows the imbalance between research in S&T departments and research under the auspices of universities and the UGC. There is need to correct the imbalance, but on present indication this may not happen soon. The research in social and allied sciences is not substantial in terms of funding but underlines India's distinctiveness as compared with other developing countries. Research in Arts and Humanities is required to be better organized and funded.

Notes

1. Sunil Khilnani, *The Idea of India* (New Delhi: Penguin, 1997), 61–106.
2. S. Gopal (Ed.), *Jawaharlal Nehru: An Anthology* (Delhi: Oxford University Press, 1980), 42.
3. Challenge of Education, 1985, 48.
4. Aqueil Ahmed, "S&T in India: Policy, Management and Institutions", in Michael Gibbons et al. (Eds.), *S&T Policy in the 1980s and Beyond* (London: Longman, 1984).

5. P.M. Bhargava and Chandana Chakraborty, *The Saga of Indian Science* (Hyderabad: Academic Publishers, 2003).
6. CSIR: Memorandum of Association and Rules and Regulations and Byelaws of CSIR, New Delhi.
7. Twenty-five Years of CSIR (CSIR, New Delhi, 1967).
8. CSIR's Vision was based on the report of an internal committee which appears to have been developed further into a case study in management schools. Vide Sumantra Ghosal et al. (Eds.), *World Class in India* (New Delhi: Penguin India, 2001), 293–318.
9. It is significant to note that DARE appointed a Reorganization Committee under chairmanship of R.A. Mashelkar, DG, CSIR in 2004 which reported in July 2005.
10. Science Policy Resolution, 1958.
11. Report of the National Committee on S&T (New Delhi, Government of India, Department of S&T, 1973).
12. Technology Policy Statement, June 1983 (New Delhi, GoI, DST).
13. Science and Technology Policy, 2003 (New Delhi, GoI, Ministry of S&T).
14. Vide P.M. Bhargava and Chandana Chakraborty, op. cit., 145.
15. R&D Statistics, 2001–02 (New Delhi, GoI, Department of S&T).
16. Pawan Agarwal, *Indian Higher Education* (New Delhi: Sage Publication, 2009), 252–253.
17. Annual Report of DST, 2003–04.
18. R&D Statistics, op. cit., 23–28.
19. Tenth Plan MTA (New Delhi, Planning Commission, 2005), 144.
20. Eleventh Plan, Vol. II, 31.
21. UGC Annual Report, 2007–08, 197–212.
22. Report of the Ministry of Education, Annual Report 2002–03, 20. Annual Report 2003–04, 12 and Annual Report, 2004–05, 14.
23. Report of V.K.R.V. Rao Committee (New Delhi, Planning Commission, 1967).
24. Role, Responsibilities, Functions, Programmes and Organization of ICSSR (Occasional Monograph No. 7), New Delhi, ICSSR, 1971, 19.
25. Vide Andrew Shonfield and Albert B. Cherns, *Social Science Research in India: A Report submitted to ICSSR* (ICSSR Pamphlet No. 20, 1971), paras 74 and 75.
26. Vide publication cited at Footnote No. 24.
27. Vide (a) Report of Social Sciences in India: Retrospective and Prospective, Vol. I & II (ICSSR, New Delhi, 1970), (b) Report of the Second Review Committee (ICSSR, New Delhi, 1978), (c) Report of the Third Review Committee (ICSSR, New Delhi, 1986).
28. *EPW*, 2nd February 2008, pp. 21–24.

29. Neera Desai, "Women's Studies: Pursuit at Widening Horizons of Knowledge", in Ranjana Harish and Bharathi Harishankar (Eds.), *Shakti: Multi-Disciplinary Perspectives on Empowerment of Women* (New Delhi and Jaipur: Rawat Publications, 2003), 131–144.
30. Nivedita Menon and Aditya Nigam, *Power and Contestation: India since 1989,* (Hyderabad: Orient Longman, 2008), 28.
31. NPE 1986, 4.2/4.3.
32. Social Science Research Council: *Social Science Research Capacity in South Asia* (New York, 2002), 43–44. It is pointed out in this review that in 1996–97, ICSSR's own administration accounted for 23 per cent of resources, 48 per cent was distributed as grants to ICSSR Research Institutes and just over 4 per cent (about Rs 40 lakh) was given as research grants to scholars.
33. This account draws on the Report of the ICHR Review Committee (ICHR, New Delhi, 1982) (Mimeo) and recent Annual Reports of ICHR for years 2000–04.
34. Vide issues of *Times Higher Education Supplement*, London for 2005.
35. *UGC News*, issues for 2003.

13 Proposals for Reform in Higher Education

NCHE, NKC and Yashpal Committee

In the post-liberalization era, the earlier proposals for reform of higher education, including the Gnanam Report (1990), have become largely outdated. In this chapter, would be considered the major reform proposals of the recent times, viz., report of the National Knowledge Commission on Higher Education (2006) and the report of the Yashpal Committee on Renovation and Rejuvenation of Higher Education (2009). Both these reports, however, are responses to the NPE 1986/1992 proposal for setting up of a National Council of Higher Education (NCHE). Hence, the same would be dealt with first. Lastly, the clutch of legislations proposed by the government including one for regulation of foreign universities would be looked into.

National Council for Higher Education: A Super Co-ordinator

That there is fragmentation in higher education by way of different branches like general, technical, agricultural, legal and medical, that there is a multiplicity of coordinating bodies, and that there is need for coordination among them all and therefore for an organization for bringing about the same has been recognized since the time of Radhakrishnan Commission which had hoped that the UGC, a statutory body, would perform the function.[1] The Sapru Committee categorically recommended that professional education should come within the purview of the UGC.[2] The UGC, however, did not develop in the requisite direction. The Kothari Commission cautiously suggested that the UGC and UGC type organizations to be set up (in technical, agricultural and medical fields) should have overlapping membership and should meet periodically to review and coordinate their programmes.[3] The Jha Committee not only flagged the problem of segmentation of the areas of education but also included legal education and scientific and social science research as additional areas needing coordination and noted that the UGC had been lukewarm to CSIR's proposal regarding coordination between universities and scientific laboratories. It further noted that the Planning Commission had taken initiative in constituting a committee to look into matters of coordination between health and agricultural education as well as other university education, but no concrete results were achieved.[4] All this thinking has been crystallized in NPE 1986 as below:

> In the interest of greater coordination and consistency of policy, sharing of facilities and developing inter-disciplinary research, a national body covering higher education in general, agricultural, medical, technical, legal and other IT professional fields will be set up.[5]

The PoA 1986 contains the most detailed formulation. Firstly, it says that separate bodies would be set up for agriculture, medicine, engineering, distance learning etc. As can be readily seen, the recommendations have been implemented only in respect of engineering (AICTE), distance learning (DEC) and teacher education (NCTE), with action remaining to be taken in respect of agriculture and forestry, medicine and legal education in all of which areas the existing legal provisions are outmoded. Significantly, PoA 1986 identified the major functions to be performed by the apex body as below: (a) to advise the government on policy, (b) to coordinate activities of the other bodies in different fields, (c) to encourage interdisciplinary activities and promotion of interface among different areas, (d) to allocate resources, (e) establishment and management of common infrastructures and institutions, and (f) coordination of policy concerning external academic relations. Of these functions, the one at (b) is the most important and needs detailed spelling out. At the least, it would cover the norms of admission and fee structure in professional education where commercialization is rampant. The other a dozen or so areas would be found spelt out in AICTE Act 1987 section 10 and NCTE Act 1993 section 12, including staff development, ODL methods, accreditation and assessment.

Gnanam Committee's remit was limited and it only dealt with the interface of university/industry/national laboratories.[6] The 66th Report of the Estimates Committee wanted the government to take expeditious action to set up the proposed National Council for Higher Education (NCHE).[7] The Committee also wanted the government to include voluntary agencies in the set up though it did not amplify the point. In its Ninth Report on Action Taken on the Estimates Committee Report, the government told the Committee that (i) the topic has been under discussion with the concerned departments and agencies, (ii) two alternative models were suggested: a National Council to be chaired by the Prime Minister or a statutory body managed by professionals, and (iii) government was, therefore, considering the appointment of an expert committee to work out details.[8] As expected, the Estimates Committee was unhappy about the matter and urged the ministry to take a final decision in the matter.[9] The PoA 1992 states that a proposal was prepared but a consensus on structure and functioning could not be reached.[10]

There is no indication in the published reports since 1992 about the progress in the matter. 'Horizontal coordination' at the central level is a pre-requisite for a smooth movement of the 'vertical' modalities (e.g., SCHE in higher education, SCAER in agricultural education) involved in the centre-state relations. Evidently, inter-ministerial rivalries appear to be standing in the way of such a body taking shape. There is no doubt that what is needed is a professional body divided into two-co-ordinate wings: one for research co-ordination and another for education coordination. For research co-ordination, there is a precedent in the UK of having a Directorate General of Research Councils. As for the locus of the coordinating bodies, which issue might be at the root of inter-ministerial rivalry, the Planning Commission appears to be the obvious choice. The Jha Committee had indicated the interest taken by the Planning Commission in coordination between agricultural, medical and general education. Planning Commission, as compared with the Education Ministry or UGC, would be a neutral body with a long-standing coordinating role in developmental planning which could be acceptable to powerful scientific ministries (for research) and professional education ministries (for agricultural, medical and legal education). Moreover, the Planning Commission has taken interest in the exercises relating to India's emergence as a Knowledge Society.[11] These exercises were done during the NDA rule but the UPA-I government, being aware of the issue, appointed a National Knowledge Commission under the chairmanship of Sam Pitroda in 2005. Perhaps, the member in charge of S&T in the Planning Commission, who is of the rank of a Minister of State, could preside over the forum for research coordination and Deputy Chairman, Planning Commission, who is of the rank of Cabinet Minister could preside over the NCHE. There would have to be appropriate administrative support. Thus, the Planning Commission, which is a federal body, involved with the state plan-making is eminently qualified to function as a super-coordinator in the field of higher education and research.[12] The appendix to the chapter contains a compendium of 28 educational and research coordinating bodies in India with details like whether states participate in its governance, whether it has regional offices and whether it has state-level counterparts.

National Knowledge Commission

Genesis

The National Knowledge Commission (NKC) was constituted by the UPA-I Government on 13th June 2005 as a high-level advisory body to the Prime Minister, who observed at its inauguration, that the time had come to create a second wave of institution building and of excellence in the fields of education, research and capacity building. The Prime Minister's reference to the second wave of institution building has to be construed as meaning that this second wave was a logical but necessary sequel to the first wave of institution building inaugurated by the first Prime Minister of India, Jawaharlal Nehru, in the form of creation of several national laboratories, the IITs and the IIMs in the period 1947–64.

The characterization of modern society as a Knowledge Society owes its origin to the sociologist Daniel Bell[13] who talked of the dominance of services but especially knowledge services in the post-industrial society. In the 1980s, the term 'Information Society' became more common. Thus, William J. Martin[14] distinguished between data, information and knowledge. Data are recorded symbols without any real world reference; information is that property of data which represents and measures effects of processing them. Knowledge means information that has stood the test of time and has, by accretion, and integration, formed a structure. It has a cognitive base and a pragmatic significance. At the inception of the 21st century, the term 'Knowledge Society' has become common currency. During the NDA regime (1998–2003), there was talk of making India as a knowledge super-power.[15] This vision was rather narrow and began with the IT specific goal of maximizing India's software service exports with a target of $ 50 billion in 2008 and elaborated supporting education specific structures like additional Indian Institutes of Information Technology. It is, indeed fitting that Dr Manmohan Singh, without making educational goals as a sub-set of economic goals, has made institution building in higher education as primary goals.

The World Bank, in its World Development Report 1998–99,[16] had also addressed the problem of knowledge societies and had distinguished between knowledge on technical know-how and knowledge about attributes and stressed the need for addressing the problem of knowledge gaps and information problems which were faced by developing countries. It particularly emphasized the need for tertiary (i.e., higher education) institutions for research and the absorption and transmission of research.

The latest composition of NKC was as below: Dr Sam Pitroda, Chairman; Dr Ashok Ganguly, Dr P. Balaram, Dr Joyati Ghosh, Dr Deepak Nayyar, Dr Nandan Nilekani and Dr Sujatha Ramdorai (members). The composition is apparently technocratic, except for two economists (viz., Dr Ghosh and Dr Nayyar). In the context of education ministry's bill for reservation of seats in the IITs/IIMs for OBCs to the extent of 27 per cent of seats, the NKC was called on to give its views. Its formulation was qualified (reservations are essential but are only a part and one form of affirmative action. There is a need to address the multi-dimensionality of differences, e.g., construction of "a deprivation index" to supplement a student's examination score etc.). Two members, namely, Pratap Bhanu Mehta, a political scientist, and Andrè Beteille, a sociologist, dissented and resigned. The Vice-Chairman, P.M. Bhargava, a microbiologist who was a pro-reservationist, also resigned because of differences with the chairman. The NKC, therefore, was reconstituted as indicated above without the benefit of advice of any soft social scientist. The NKC's original tenure was for three years. The press reports[17] indicated that its tenure had been extended for six months to enable it to suggest ways in which the government can expedite the implementation of its recommendations.

The term of reference of the NKC in so far as its related to higher education was: Build excellence in the educational system to meet the knowledge challenges of the 21st century and increase India's competitive advantage in the world of knowledge.

Proposals

The NKC reports on several subjects were initially available on-line. Later on, they were published.[18] The general thrust of the NKC's recommendations on higher education submitted in November 2006 is to have an umbrella body which it calls Independent Regulatory Authority for Higher Education – IRAHE – and to have standing committees on sub-fields of higher education like medical education, legal education, management education and ODE. In regard to professional bodies, it proposed to restrict the role of the Medical Council and the Bar Council of India to enforcement of professional ethics and to the issue of licences to practise. Management education which is under AICTE is to be delinked from the same. Similarly, ODE would be delinked from IGNOU. IRAHE is to be set up by an Act of Parliament. It would be the only agency which would be authorized to accord degree-granting powers to higher education institutions. It would also be responsible for monitoring standards and settling disputes. It should also be thought of as an authority for licensing accreditation agencies. The chairman and members of the IRAHE would be appointed by the Prime Minister based on the recommendation of a Search Committee.

Management Education

The separation of management education from AICTE would be a welcome step. This is because management education is an interdisciplinary subject in the broad field of social sciences rather than a technical one. Its yoking to the AICTE was *ab initio* illogical. However, there may have to be a state-level Council for Management Education to assist the central body.

Legal Education

The NKC proposed to have Standing Committee of IRAHE for legal education separated from the BCI. However, apart from about 8–9 National Law Universities, there are now more than 400 law colleges all over India most of them of indifferent quality, affiliated to respective State Universities. The Standing Committee may find it difficult to deal with all the colleges directly and therefore, there may have to be State Councils for legal education which could deal with the Standing Committee.[19]

Medical Education

Once the medical colleges are de-linked from the MCI as well as the affiliating universities, there would be no alternative but to have State Councils for Medical Education. There is also need to have a separate body for colleges in para-medical disciplines like physiotherapy.[20]

Traditional Health Systems

NKC's recommendations on the topic of traditional health systems are too general. One needs to be clear if there would be a separate Standing Committee on AYUSH disciplines and what to do with 'poor colleges' and sub-critical research institutions. A basic approach of a Flexner type review may have to be adopted with large-scale consolidation of viable but small institutions and closure of sub-standard institutions.[21]

Open and Distance Education

The government has already decided to delink DEC from IGNOU, and to set it up as an independent council. It needs to be followed up.

The NKC has recommended that the number of universities should be expanded from the present about 400 to 1,500 with a view to achieve GER of 15 per cent, and that in addition there should be 50 national universities as multidisciplinary exemplars. The recommendation that UGC should be a purely grant giving body and a body for maintenance of Central Universities appear to underestimate the performance of UGC in the matter of development and standards of higher education in India.

There has been criticism of the NKC recommendations.[22] Firstly, it is stated that NKC has not based its recommendation about expansion on any detailed analysis and that its data about GER are wrong. This is a trivial objection. Thus, the CABE Committee[23] on Financing of Higher and Technical Education had recommended not 15 per cent, but 20 per cent as the GER to be aimed at in the medium term. That type of GER would certainly justify a large number of institutions, though not as many as recommended by the NKC. Secondly, NKC recommendation that minimum 20 per cent increase in fees should be aimed at is criticized, since CABE recommended 20 per cent as the maximum. It is acknowledged that the NKC's recommendation is supported by authorities like Punnayya Committee and Swaminathan Committee. The basic criticism is that the overall approach of the NKC is neo-liberal and even anti-public. Whether NKC is neo-liberal is a matter of argument and Sudhanshu Bhushan[24] has presented a plausible case, but to call the NKC's approach as anti-public appears to be unfair. It is said that the private universities account for 75 per cent of the universities in the US, but only 35 per cent of student enrolment and thus, it is futile to hope that private universities in India would increase educational opportunities for higher education. But not-for-profit private higher education is almost non-existent in India except for a few institutions of Tatas (TISS, TIFR in Mumbai and IISc in Bengaluru) and Birlas (BITS, Pilani and Mesra in Jharkhand). The proportion of endowments in 1984 has gone down to 5.4 per cent from 13.8 per cent in 1947. There is a limit to the raising of resources through enhancement of fees which is also opposed by certain scholars. The issue is that government resources for higher education are limited; and there has to be diversification of revenue sources. Universalization of elementary education, eradication of adult illiteracy and near universalization of secondary education in a time-bound manner, say by 2020, have a prior claim on government resources, and this is the reason for limitation on government resources for higher education. Universalization of elementary education and secondary education is moreover a precondition for raising the GER in higher education and therefore, endowments have to be increased as a source of funds and philanthropy has to be promoted as a secular trend as in the western countries. In this connection, reference may be made to Sanjay Subramanyam's observation in this regard,[25] that foreign (Dutch and English) traders had seen a great tradition of giving among Indian princes and magnates in the 16th and 17th centuries, but it petered out with the onset of the colonial rule, and that since liberalization from 1991 onwards or even earlier, has created a new generation of affluent ("high-net-worth") Indians in recent years, the Indian government can promote philanthropy for higher education through proper tax incentives as the US did in the 19th and 20th centuries.

There are however grave doubts about the viability of the structure envisaged by the NKC in the form of a top heavy IRAHE and Central and state boards for Under Graduate Education. As in the case of Japan and Korea, India may require a large number of Central and State Universities, though not as many as proposed by the NKC. They may need to be supplemented by private universities to cope with the problem of reaching the higher GER but a single apex body like IRAHE for a vast country like India is apparently impracticable. Federal complications arising out of constitutional division of powers is an additional factor. The idea of community colleges suggested by NKC might not be saleable in India and therefore the best course is to have affiliating model universities as set out in the relevant chapter of the Gnanam Report.[26]

In regard to Research Councils, NKC has advocated the setting up of a single National Science and Social Science Foundation (NSSF), which compares with the British mechanism of Advisory Board of Research Councils (ABRCs). This is apparently an optimum arrangement from the point of view of policy and funding coordination.

As NKC Report on Higher Education was subjected to criticism by the leftist circles, the former HRD Minister (Arjun Singh) had reportedly placed the same before the CABE which had turned down the recommendations. Since the CABE is the highest policy making body in education sector, NKC recommendations are defunct for practical purposes, though apparently one may refer to them for scholarly purposes.

Yashpal Committee Report

It was in this vacuum that a Review Committee was constituted under the chairmanship of Prof. Yashpal, ex-Chairman, UGC, by Education Ministry in February 2008 to review the role of (1) UGC, and (2) AICTE, in the context of changes in higher professional and technical education in the country and demands of new knowledge economy. The terms of reference of the Review Committee were very detailed and its composition was weighty (comprising about 25 members) (See Appendix II). The Review Committee submitted its Report to the newly constituted UPA government on 24th June 2009,[27] of which the main recommendation was that there should be a National Commission for Higher Education and Research, which should be a constitutional body comparable to the Election Commission and that it should supersede all other coordinating bodies like UGC, AICTE, NCTE etc. and also bodies in functional areas like medicine, law etc.

This narrative would give a false impression regarding the committee's smooth progress. The press reports indicate that the first few meetings of the Commission did not even have a quorum. This should cause no surprise in view of the following considerations:

1. Firstly, the terms of reference and the composition did not match. The terms of reference expected the Committee to do review of functioning of two bodies, viz., UGC and AICTE, requiring whole-time attention of members who had the requisite aptitude and the time to spare. But such was not the ground reality. The Chairman, a professional space scientist, was known as a man of ideas. He had only recently led a team of eminent academics, who

had formulated the National Curricular Framework (2005) of the NCERT. But there he had presided over a Steering Group of experts and NGOs which had the support of dedicated NCERT and other educationists who had produced massive Task Force Reports. In the present Review Committee, he had with him a team comprising as members, very busy government officers like Finance Secretary, Planning Commission Secretary etc., equally engaged Vice-Chancellors and heads of IITs etc. and other dignitaries with very different ideas, orientation and specialization.

2. Secondly, the Committee did not have a strong back room research support as in the case of NCERT vis-à-vis NCF. UGC, over the years, had failed to develop any think-tank in the area of higher education policies and programmes with a comparative international perspective. The reasons as to why NUEPA was not involved are not clear. The main academic support for the Commission appears to have been a consultant who was drawn from the Hindi Department of the University of Delhi.

Under the circumstances, the chairman on 21st September 2008 approached the ministry with the following request: "Right at the beginning of our work, I had mentioned that I would not want to be involved in a routine administrative exercise but would be prepared to take on the responsibility to go deep into the causes of the malaise of our education system just like the work we did in connection with drafting a curriculum framework at school level – something that led to NCF 1995". Apparently, the Chairman had met the minister on 14th September and had left a note with the Minister suggesting a change in the name of the Committee as "Committee to Advise on Renovation and Rejuvenation of Higher Education". "I was pleased that you were not visibly antagonistic toward my way of thinking ... we would be in position to prepare an interim report in a couple of months" (all quotations are from the report as available).

The results of this remarkable initiative of the Chairman are officially visible in the OM of the ministry dated 14th October 2008. It conveyed the decision to rename the Committee but significantly added that the composition and terms of reference of the Committee remain unchanged. After five-and-a-half months from the renaming of the Committee, an interim Draft Report was submitted by the Committee in March 2009. The press reports indicate that the Chairman of the Committee wanted the government to disseminate the interim report for public discussion, but that the Committee itself was asked to do the needful (this was apparently because the government was election-bound). As noted, the Committee after further debate finalized the report. The UPA-II assumed power in mid-May 2009 and the report was submitted in June 2009.

The Yashpal Committee's report is couched in very abstract terms. Its recommendations may be summarized as below:

1. All universities must have a full range of knowledge areas. Do not create specialized universities. This also applies to IITs and IIMs, which should be diversified and not devoted to single disciplines. Universities should be responsible for deciding the academic content of professional courses.
2. Universities should be autonomous and not subject to inspection by external agencies.
3. Create accreditation bodies within states.
4. Coordination of existing regulatory structure is difficult. Hence, integrate functions of existing regulatory systems into a single National Council for Higher Education and Research (NCHER) as recommended.
5. Deemed universities and private HEIs have become exploitative. No more deemed universities should be notified. Functioning of existing deemed universities should be reviewed.
6. Foreign universities should not be given an open licence; only the best universities should be welcomed and not those which want to make money.

The basic criticism of the Yashpal Committee is that it did not deal with its basic terms of reference and its recommendations were not based on any research or investigation, but based on some theoretical notions about the ideal university. The Committee does not list regulatory bodies like ICAR, VEC and ICFRE, all of which are in the agriculture-related areas, nor does it list coordinating bodies in the Indian systems of medicine. Evidently, the Committee did not get in touch with any of the regulatory bodies all ten of which would be found listed on preceding page 226 or their controlling ministries regarding their latest plans.

The recommendations of the Yashpal Committee's report were accepted by the government and also placed before CABE for approval. The report was included in the educational agenda of the HRD Minister to be implemented within 100 days of the assumption of power by UPA-II government. The draft NCHER bill has been prepared. A recent commentary in *EPW* opined that the provisions of NCHER bill, though supposed to be based on Yashpal Committee, appear to draw inspiration from NKC's centralization agenda. NCHER will concentrate in itself all functions – academic and non-academic, accreditation, advisory, regulatory, monetary and funding. NCHER would maintain a registry of qualified persons for the appointment as Vice-Chancellors and State and

Central Governments would have to select a Vice-Chancellor from among a panel of five persons sent by NCHER. NCHER is likely to end any measure of autonomy with the State Universities. The commentary ended with a forecast that NCHER may possibly end with exactly the same problem (as the UGC).[28]

Moreover, press reports indicate that the scope of NCHER would be narrower than was envisaged by the Yashpal Committee, confining its coordinating role to the educational fields under the Education Ministry proper, viz., the fields covered by the existing UGC, AICTE and NCTE.

Apparently, the proposal to amend the Constitution to give parity to NCHER with Election Commission has not been accepted by the government. In the field of medicine, the Health Ministry's proposal for National Council for Human Resources in Health appears set to be revived especially because it was part of the President's address to Parliament in 2009. Agricultural education has been excluded from the purview of NCHER on the spurious ground that it is a state subject, but there is no indication that ICAR and Veterinary Council of India (VCI), under Union Ministry of Agriculture as well as ICFRE, under Department of Forests, of Ministry of Environment are under threat of abolition. As for legal education, the Law Minister was reportedly against the proposal to cover legal education under the NCHER, and apparently, status quo would continue, i.e., undergraduate education would be regulated by the Bar Council of India and postgraduate education might be under the newly set-up NCHER.

The Yashpal Committee report has thus been only partly implemented so far as can be judged from available information. We are back to a situation where legal, medical and agricultural education and S&T research under the banner of various scientific departments, would be outside the purview of a national coordinating body. This appears to be the result of Yashpal Committee's failure to come to grips with its original terms of reference. Yashpal Committee's report can well be said to be a "lost opportunity".[29]

Other Legislative Initiatives of the Central Government: Regulation of Foreign Universities

Just before the Parliament adjourned its budget session in May 2010, the HRD Minister introduced four bills relating to education. They were:

1. Prohibition of Unfair Practices in Technical, Medical and Educational Institutions and Universities Bill empowering the Centre to initiate criminal proceedings against private institutions that charge capitation fees and cheat students.
2. Educational Tribunal Bill providing for a three-tier system of Tribunals – District, State and National, to deal with disputes between students, teachers and institutions.

3. National Accreditation Authority for Higher Education Institutions Bill proposing to make accreditation mandatory for all educational institutions.
4. Foreign Educational Institutions (Regulation of Entry and Operation) Bill providing for a red-tape free and time-bound transparent form of approval process to grant passage to quality foreign universities in India.

While the first three measures are self-explanatory, the introduction of the Bill relating to the entry of foreign universities in India needs comment.

The bill may, perhaps, be considered as India's response to the nascent process of globalization. As pointed out by the UNDP Human Development Report (1999), globalization involves a three-fold change of landscape: (1) shrinking space, (2) shrinking time, and (3) disappearing borders. The process of globalization that is now under way involves new financial consumer markets, new actors like multi-lateral corporations; WTO, international criminal law system, international network of NGOs, new rules and norms (e.g., conventions and agreements in global environment, human rights etc.) and new and faster tools of communication including internet and cellular phones. The role of WTO as an international regulator is particularly to be noted.

WTO and GATS

WTO is a culminating body from GATT (General Agreement on Tariff and Trade) under which there were eight rounds of negotiations between 1947 and 1993. It is a permanent inter-governmental body governing and regulating international trade in goods and services, with headquarter at Geneva. It administers 28 agreements including GATS (General Agreement for Trade in Services), which envisages four modes of supply as below:

Mode 1

Cross-border supply (from one territory to territory of another – distance education and internet education/virtual university).

Mode 2

Consumption abroad (student mobility across borders).

Mode 3

Commercial presence (setting up facilities abroad by educational producers).

Mode 4

Presence of natural persons (faculty movement).

It is clear that government is not required to do much in regard to Mode 2. This is because Indian students have been going for education abroad since 19th century. The government appears to be keen to promote export of Indian faculty abroad (Mode 4). But the matter for worry is: how to regulate trade in educational services under Mode 1 and Mode 3. Mode 1 does not specifically involve commercialization but Mode 3 does. This is the background to the bill to regulate entry and operation of foreign higher education institutions, but its effectiveness is being doubted.

The renowned international authority on comparative education, Philip G. Altbach, while referring to Indian legislation commented that the Bill had incorporated higher barriers to entry, viz., million dollar deposits and ban on repatriation of profits. Foreign universities are not likely to fulfil Indian expectations that they will solve India's problems of access, quality and shortage of financial and academic resources. Foreign universities are there to make money and India may well find its hopes of riding the branch campus phenomenon belied.[30]

An Assessment of Reform Proposals

This author is inclined to agree with the assessment of Sudhanshu Bhushan[31] that Yashpal Committee Report is based on an idealistic theory of knowledge and is not in synch with modern approach to development of higher education which has to adjust to the trend toward globalization. Whether the NKC is actuated by neo-liberalism or not, it is no doubt inspired by a managerial approach and the recommendation for setting up of IRAHE by overriding the role of Central and State Governments in a federal polity is unsustainable. The number of universities (1,500) proposed by it also errs on the higher side. The existing coordinating bodies like UGC, professional bodies like ICAR and Bar Council of India etc. would need to be retained but streamlined and both research and higher education can be coordinated under the neutral auspices of the Planning Commission as proposed by the present author. The proposed bill for regulating foreign universities needs a major revamp.

Appendix I
The Matrix of Coordinating Bodies in India

	Name of the Organization and whether Statutory or not	*Participation of States in*		*Regional Offices if any, and whether states participate*	*State counterparts, if any*
		General Body	*Executive Body*		
(1)	*(2)*	*(3)*	*(4)*	*(5)*	*(6)*
School Education					
1.	National Council of Educational Research & Training (Registered Government Society)	Yes Universal (all States/UTs)	No (Nagchoudhury Committee Recommendations Rejected)	Yes – Five regional offices at Ajmer, Bhopal, Mysore, Bhubaneswar and Shillong. (However posts of State Field Officers abolished in 1990s.)	Yes – State Councils of Educational Research & Training.
2.	National Institute of Educational Planning & Administration (Registered Government Society)	Yes, but partial. (5 State Education/UT Secretaries, and 6 Directors of Education)	One State Education Secretary out of 7 members nominated by Union HRD Minister	Nil	Two (Maharashtra and UP)
3.	National Institute of Open Schooling (Registered Government Society)	Yes, but partial (Only one representative)	No	Ten Regional Centres at Delhi Zone I, Delhi Zone II, Chandigarh, Jaipur, Patna, Allahabad, Pune, Kochi, Kolkata and Guwahati, but no state participation	Ten State Open Schools (AP, TN, Kerala, Karnataka, MP, Rajasthan, Punjab, Haryana, J& K and West Bengal)
4.	Central Board of Secondary Education (Set up by Government Resolution)	No	No	Six (Delhi, Chandigarh, Allahabad, Guwahati, Ajmer and Chennai) but no state participation	Yes – all States have state boards of Secondary & Higher Secondary Education. There is also a consultative body-COBSE.

Cont'd...

...Cont'd

Higher Education					
5.	University Grants Commission (Statutory under 1956 Act)	No general body	Nil	Six since 1992 – Kolkata, Guwahati, Bhopal, Poona, Hyderabad and Bangalore, but no State representation	Yes – since 1992 four (Andhra Pradesh, Tamil Nadu, West Bengal and Uttar Pradesh)
6.	National Assessment & Accreditation Council (Registered Society under UGC Act)	No	No	Nil	No
7.	Distance Education Council (Statutory under IGNOU Act) 1985	No	No	Nil	Ten states have OUs – Andhra Pradesh, Chattisgarh, Maharashtra, Rajasthan, Madhya Pradesh, Bihar, West Bengal, Jharkhand, Gujarat and Karnataka
8.	All-India Council for Technical Education (Statutory under 1987 Act)	Universal (All States/ UTs)	Four States in a 21 strong body	Seven (Kanpur, Chennai, Mumbai, Kolkata, Bangalore, Bhopal and Chandigarh) with state representation	Yes – state boards of Technical Education dealing with Diploma programmes
9.	Indian Pharmacy Council (Statutory under 1948 Act)	N.A.	N.A.	Nil	There are about 24 State Pharmacy Councils
10.	Council of Architects (Statutory under 1972 Act)	N.A.	N.A.	Nil	Nil – No provision in the Act
11.	National Council for Hotel Management & Catering Technology (By Government Resolution)	N.A.	N.A.	Nil	N.A.

Cont'd...

...*Cont'd*

12.	Indian Council of Agricultural Research (Registered Government Society)	Universal (all States/UTs)	Nil (Hemendra Kumar Committee recommendations rejected)	Nil	34 State Agricultural Universities
13.	Veterinary Council of India (Statutory under 1984 Act)	Nine states in a body of 27	N.A.	Nil	About ten States
14.	Indian Council of Forestry Education & Research (Registered Government Society)	Partial (Six out of 45)	N.A.	Nil	Nil
15.	Bar Council of India (Statutory under 1961 Act)	N.A.	N.A.	Nil	16 State Bar Councils
16.	Medical Council of India (Statutory under 1956 Act)	Universal	N.A.	Nil	Yes; about 24 states have Medical Councils
17.	Dental Council of India (Statutory under 1948 Act)	Universal	N.A.	Nil	Yes; about 24 states have State Dental Councils
18.	Nursing Council of India (Statutory – 1947 Act)	Partial (50% states at a time)	N.A.	Nil	There are Provincial Nursing Councils since Dyarchy
19.	Central Council of Indian Medicine (Statutory under 1970 Act)	Universal	N.A.	Nil	Most states (except North-Eastern States) have state level Councils
20.	Central Council of Homoeopathy (Statutory under 1970 Act)	Universal	N.A.	Nil	Most states (except North-Eastern States) have state level Councils
21.	Rehabilitation Council of India (Statutory under 1992 Act)	No representation for states or professionals from states	Nil	Nil	Nil

Cont'd...

...*Cont'd*

22.	Indian Council for Medical Research (ICMR) (Registered Society)	Nil	Nil	Nil	Six Regional Centres at Bhubaneshwar, Dibrugarh, Port Blair, Jabalpur, Jodhpur and Belgaum
23.	Indian Council for Social Science Research (ICSSR) (Registered Society)	Nil	Nil	Six regional offices – Mumbai, Hyderabad, Kolkata, New Delhi, Shillong and Chandigarh	There are 21 Social Science Research Institutes partly supported by State Governments
24.	Indian Council of Historical Research (ICHR) (Registered Society)	Nil	Nil	Two (Bangalore and Shillong)	Nil
25.	Indian Council of Philosophical Research (ICPR) (Registered Society)	Nil	Nil	One (Lucknow)	Nil
26.	Central Council for Research in Ayurveda and Siddha	Nil	Nil	Nil	Nil
27.	Central Council for Research in Unani Medicine	Nil	Nil	Nil	Nil
28.	Central Council for Research in Homeopathy	Nil	Nil	Nil	Nil

Note: N.A. = Information Not Available.

Appendix II
Government Resolution on Yashpal Committee

No.4–4/2008–U.I(A)
Government of India
Ministry of Human Resource Development
(Department of Higher Education)
New Delhi, dated the 28th February, 2008

Notification

Subject: Constitution of a UGC/AICTE Review Committee to review the functions of UGC/AICTE in the wake of changes in higher, professional and technical education in India and demands of a new knowledge economy.

There is a need to review the role of statutory bodies like the University Grants Commission (UGC) and the All India Council for Technical Education (AICTE) in the context of changes in higher, professional and technical education in the country and demands of a new knowledge economy. Accordingly, the Government constitutes a Review Committee with the following members;

(i)	Prof. Yashpal, former Chairman, University Grants Commission	Chairman
(ii)	Prof. N.R. Madhava Menon, Member, Centre-State Relations and former Vice-Chancellor, National Law School, Bangalore and Director, National Judicial Academy, Bhopal	Member
(iii)	Prof. Pulin B. Nayak, Professor, Department of Economics, Delhi School of Economics, University of Delhi	Member
(iv)	Prof. L.M. Patnaik, Professor of Computer Science, IISc., Bangalore	Member
(v)	Prof. Kaushik Basu, Professor of Economics & Karl Marx, Professor of International Studies, Department of Economics, Uris Hall, Cornell University	Member
(vi)	Shri S.V. Giri, former Secretary, Department of Education, Government of India and former Vice-Chancellor, Sri Satya Sai Institute of Higher Learning, Prasanthi Nilayam, Puttaparthi, Andhra Pradesh	Member
(vii)	Prof. J.K. Chaddha, former Vice-Chancellor, JNU and present Member, Economic Advisory Council to the PM, Vigyan Bhawan Annexe, New Delhi	Member
(viii)	Prof. (Ms.) Malini Bhattacharya, Member, National Commission for Women	Member
(ix)	Prof. Goverdhan Mehta, Chairman, NAAC and former Director, IISc., Bangalore	Member
(x)	Prof. Sukhadeo Thorat, Chairman, UGC	Member
(xi)	Chairman, All India Council for Technical Education	Member

(xii)	One Vice-Chancellor of a State University	Member *
(xiii)	One Secretary to a State Government dealing with Higher/Technical Education	Member *
(xiv)	Dr, Ramdas M. Pail, President, Manipal University	Member
(xv)	Prof. Ananda Krishnan, Chairman, IIT, Kanpur	Member
(xvi)	Prof. M.S. Ananth, Director, IIT, Chennai	Member
(xvii)	Prof. Pankaj Chandra, Director, IIM, Bangalore	Member
(xviii)	Prof. Mushirul Hasan, Vice-Chancellor, Jamia Millia Islamia	Member
(xix)	Secretary, Planning Commission	Member
(xx)	Finance Secretary, Government of India	Member
(xxi)	Secretary, Department of Higher Education, GoI	Member
(xxii)	Joint Secretary (Higher Education) Department of Higher Education, GoI	Member Secretary

* To be nominated by the Ministry of HRD.

2. The following are the terms of reference of the Committee:
   (a) To review the functioning of the UGC/AICTE and to critically assess the role of the UGC/AICTE and their preparedness to provide institutional leadership to the emerging demands of access, equity, relevance and quality of higher education/technical education and the university system.
   (b) To review the provisions of the University Grants Commission Act, 1956 and the All India Council for Technical Education Act, 1987 and various suggestions for amendments to the said Acts by earlier Committees such as the Prof. Amreek Singh Committee.
   (c) The role of the UGC in coordinating standards of higher education vis-à-vis the functional role of other statutory bodies such as AICTE, MCI, DCI, NCI, NCTE, DEC, etc.
   (d) An assessment of the requirements of autonomy of the UGC vis-à-vis the Central Government and that of the university system vis-à-vis the UGC.
   (e) The role of the UGC/AICTE in determining and enforcing standards of higher education/technical education in State Universities and the possibility of introducing a system of incentives and disincentives so that national standards of higher education/technical education are not compromised or diluted.
   (f) Recommendations in regard to an effective and efficient mechanism for flow of resources from the UGC to the universities for their timely utilization including a mechanism of feedback thereto.
   (g) The requirement of transparency and efficiency in the functioning of the UGC/AICTE.

(h) The role of the UGC vis-à-vis declaration of institutions to be deemed universities and recommendations for streamlining the process adopted by the UGC.

(i) Recommendations about the need to change the eligibility criteria for becoming eligible to receive grants under Section 12B of the UGC Act 1956.

(j) Any other issue arising out of or relating to the above terms of reference and, the functioning of the UGC/AICTE which the Government or the Committee on its own, may desire to look into.

3. The Committee shall submit its report within a period of one year from the date on which this notification comes into effect.
4. UGC shall provide all secretarial assistance and logistics support to the Chairman and Members of the Committee. This will include expenditure on travel and accommodation of the Committee on its visits to different parts of the country for interaction with institutions and academics.
5. The Committee may devise its own methodology and processes for its functioning.

Sd/-
(Ravi Mathur)
Joint Secretary (Higher Education)

To: Chairman and all Members

Notes

1. Radhakrishnan Report, 279–281.
2. Sapru Report, 45.
3. Kothari Report, 13–70.
4. Jha Report, 28–31.
5. NPE 1986, para 5.34.
6. Gnanam Committee Report, 44–47.
7. 66th Report of the Estimates Committee, 1988–89.
8. Action Taken Report, 1990–91.
9. Estimates Committee Report, 2–3.
10. PoA 1992, 12.3.
11. Planning Commission, Government of India: (a) India as a Knowledge Super Power: Strategy for Transformation: Task Force Report (New Delhi, June 2001), (b) Report of the Committee on India: Vision 2020 (New Delhi, December 2002).

12. This idea of the author was first put forward in July 2006 being the date of the submission of the Thesis. The Late Prof. Amrik Singh, the well-known educationist, when he was made aware of the same in February 2007 found it attractive.
13. Daniel Bell, *The Coming of Post-Industrial Society* (New York: Basic Books, 1973).
14. William J. Martin, *The Global Information Society* (London, Aslib Gower, 1985).
15. Vide Footnote 11.
16. The World Bank: Knowledge for Development – The World Development Report, 1998–99, (Washington DC, 1999), 1–14.
17. *Times of India* (Mumbai Edition) 14th October, 2008.
18. The Recommendations of NKC (New Delhi: Academic Foundation, 2008).
19. A suggestion similar to NKC's in regard to legal education was made by the present author in July 2006.

    He was inspired by the suggestion made by Dr B.R. Ambedkar vide his "Thoughts on the Reforms of Legal Education in the Bombay Presidency" (*Magazine of the Government Law College*, Vol. VII, No. 1, January 1936, 1–17).
20. This author had advocated in July 2006 establishment of Medical Education Commission in place of Medical Council of India.
21. Abraham Flexner on behalf of the Carnegie Commission for Advancement of Teaching submitted two reports re. Medical Education in the US and Europe in 1910 and 1912 respectively. Vide Bulletin No. 4 and 6.
22. J.B.G. Tilak, Knowledge Commission and Higher Education (*University News,* 26th November to 21st December, 2007, 59–62).
23. CABE Committee on Financing of Higher and Technical Education (New Delhi, 2005).
24. Shudhanshu Bhushan, *Restructuring Higher Education in India* (Jaipur and New Delhi: Rawat Publication, 2009), 103–160.
25. *India Today*, 6th October, 2008, 51–57.
26. Gnanam Report (New Delhi, 1990) (Chapter XVIII).
27. Report of Yashpal Committee as available on the internet.
28. J.B.G. Tilak, The Proposed NCHE: A Solution Worse than the Disease? (*EPW,* 1st May, 2010, 11–13).
29. See the author's article on YPC in *Samaj Prabodhan Patrika*. (Belgaon, July-December, 2009 (Marathi)).
30. Philip Altbach, Open Door in Higher Education: Unsustainable and Probably Ill-advised, (*EPW,* March 27, 2010, 13–15).
31. Vide Note No. 24.

Part IV

Conclusion

14 Conclusion

An Overview and Prospects

Summary of Argument

Indian federal polity's nature and its impact on the 'education sector' and their inter-relationship which is the focus of present study has been traced so far in about thirteen chapters in three parts. In the introductory chapter, the dynamics of education and federalism are broadly examined. The stages of education from the pre-primary to adult education and their objectives and broad curricula are brought under review. Thereafter, educational diversity and institutional differentiation are distinguished and the changing perceptions of education from its role in socialization to the modern view of education as the master determinant of development are described from a sociological viewpoint. Consequent upon world crisis in education in 1965–68 and the following destabilization, there is a consensus that education at all stages is important. The attention is then shifted to federal morphology. The interlocking characteristics of federalism in its "font et origo", that is, the USA are noted (division of powers between levels of government, separation of powers among three organs of government – legislative, executive and judiciary, checks and balances among these organs and especially the triple E senate: elected, equal and effective, limited government, popular sovereignty, judicial review and regional parties). Canada and Australia departed from the American model in combining parliamentary with federal system of government, involving 'executive' federalism and national parties. India has followed suit and resembles Canada in its diversity, K.C. Wheare has called India a quasi-federation because of its centralized features (including power to create new states and imposing central rule in the states). The precedents of the present study, its methodology and its special features are set out, followed by a description of the chapter scheme.

The second part looks at the shaping up of India's federalism. In chapter two, its evolution during the inter-war years (1918–1947) has been traced. S.P. Aiyar's discussion of the federal idea is critically examined. It is pointed out that it was not the provincial autonomy (1935–1947) but Dyarchy (1917–1935), popularly reviled but basically benign, which laid the foundation of federalism in India. Edwin

Montague, the joint author of Montford Report, was a genuinely liberal Secretary of State and advocated Dyarchy involving, at the provincial level, division of powers combined with division of revenue and expenditure heads as between the Centre and the provinces. The report had referred prophetically to the eventual future of India as a sisterhood of states, over which would preside a Central Government. The All-Party Motilal Nehru Report (1929) endorsed the concept though it was in favour of as close a union as possible. The Government of India Act, 1935 merely abolished 'reserved' subjects, shifted the two lists of subjects to regular schedules in the body of the Act and introduced a third list of concurrent subjects, with the three-fold aim of securing uniformity of law, encouraging provincial efforts and dealing with externalities in matters like epidemic diseases. The Montford Report also presciently recognized the need to revise the political geography of India on a linguistic basis. The historical linguistic roots of the language problem in India are traced in the context of colonial role in the discovery of Indo-European languages, the introduction of printing and the phenomenon of Vernacular Renaissance and the consequent rise of linguistic regionalism in India. A separate section is devoted to the official language problem, since official language automatically tends to become the language of education. Hindi-Urdu controversy in the north especially in Uttar Pradesh and Bihar regions, is traced and it is pointed out that in the context of the discovery of Dravidian family of languages in the south, Tamil laid a claim to great antiquity and to the classical status rivaling that of Sanskrit. The result was the foundation of Tamil asymmetry and its politicization.

In the third chapter, the reconstruction of the Indian federalism and the role of language policy in the post-independence period are described. India evolved from a centralized polity into a federal nation-state characterized by multiple asymmetries. The asymmetry may be constitutionally based (as in J&K) or may be due to differences in area and population resulting from the state reorganizations which have gone through the phases of (a) integration of princely states, (b) liberation of foreign enclaves, (c) linguistic reorganization in 1953, 1956, 1960 and 1966, and (d) the reorganization of tribal states in two phases: (i) north-eastern states between 1963 and 1987, and the (ii) central-northern states of Uttarakhand, Jharkhand and Chhattisgarh in 2000. Next, the language policy and planning are dealt with in terms of the repercussions of the adoption of Hindi as the official language. It is pointed out that after the amendment to the Official Language Act, 1963 to implement Jawaharlal Nehru's assurance about indefinite continuance of English as an associate official language was passed in 1967, there were three important developments. Firstly, the parliamentary resolution of 18th January 1968 which followed the amendment was repudiated by the Tamil Nadu so far as its emphasis on the development of Hindi as an office language and language of education was concerned. Secondly, Central Government has committed itself to the development of regional languages as listed in the original Eighth Schedule of the Constitution which thus becomes a pillar of linguistic federalism in India, just as the Seventh Schedule of the Constitution is the pillar of legal federalism. Thirdly, Official Language Rules, 1976 do not apply to Tamil Nadu, thus giving statutory status to Tamil Nadu's stand on repudiation of Hindi as an official language and as a language of education by way of three–language formula. However, the Central Government has not taken adequate action to develop regional languages; thus the Central Institute of Indian Languages has been neglected and there is an impression of hegemony of English (Anglification of school curriculum has been endorsed by the National Curricular Framework of 2005) and of Hindi (OL bureaucracy has been expanded), and the subalternity of regional languages. The three-language formula has not been implemented in its proper spirit either by the Tamil Nadu or by the Hindi-speaking states and the recent haphazard expansion of the Eighth Schedule by addition of non-state official languages betrays a lack of policy coherence in this area.

The fourth chapter sets out the constitutional context of education. The provincialization of education at the time of Dyarchy was due to the efforts of then Education Member, Sir Sankaran Nair. At the time of adoption of the Constitution in 1950, the provincial chief ministers opposed any major change in the status of education as a state subject but thanks to Jawaharlal Nehru, co-ordination and determination of standards in higher and technical education remained a central subject, apart from three Central Universities. Though the experience of UGC which failed to control unplanned expansion of universities and colleges led to a policy consensus about the need for concurrency of higher education, by the 42nd amendment to the Constitution during the Emergency, education as a whole along with forestry and wild life but excluding agricultural education were made concurrent subjects. The impulse behind concurrency was the Central Government's desire to control school curriculum. However, concurrency has not led to any meaningful legislation except new Central Universities, new School Boards and the NCTE. More recently, federal diversity (in the form of existence of religious minorities and socially and educationally backward classes especially the OBCs) has occasioned new legislation. The chapter concludes with a review of judicial approach to Indian federalism. It took the Supreme Court 43 years to recognize federalism as part of the basic structure of the Constitution, thus underlining the centralizing tendency of judicial interpretation.

Now begins the third part containing nine chapters dealing with education sector. The fifth chapter deals with the colonial legacy of education which was built on the foundation of English both as the official language (language of power) and medium of instruction (language of knowledge). The equation "language = knowledge + democracy", combined with the 'downward filtration theory' led to the belief that Macaulay's famous Minute of 1835 was the solvent of the Indian problem of illiteracy. The chapter points out that Charles Trevelyan's Minute of January 1835 putting an end to the Native Medical Institution (NMI) in Calcutta (which was the ground of a fine experiment in the use of Indian languages for imparting instruction in medical education), was a dress rehearsal for Macaulay's Minute of February 1835. After dealing with the Anglicist-Orientalist Controversy (AOC) (of which Macaulay's Minute was the culmination) in terms of its ideologies and leaders, the chapter points out that on the terra firma of policy implementation, pragmatic vernacularism prevailed. However, the neglect of indigenous primary institutions (which Gandhiji had hailed as the Beautiful Tree) and the ideologically oriented transfer of primary education as a subject to financially starved and inadequately supervised local bodies and the failure to introduce compulsion resulted in very low level of mass education and literacy in 1947. All this is clearly brought out by the data of the official Hartog Report. The progress of the compulsory primary education bills of the provincial governments passed during the Dyarchy is illustrative of the phenomenon of emulative federalism which, however, was not enough to make a dent in the problem. As for adult literacy its first Indian advocate was the Bengali reformer Keshab Chandra Sen, whose interest in the matter was, however, short-lived. The Indian leadership in the inter-war years appears to have been impressed by the Soviet success in the area but a short spurt of activity in 1937–39 could not achieve much. Secondary education fared better than primary education, but even here, the colonial legacy is apparent in the dominance of government-grant-receiving private institutions and lack of diversification of curriculum dominated by English as a subject. The first higher education institution was the Hindu College, Calcutta (1817); the establishment of metropolitan universities in 1857 was meant to regulate not only affiliated colleges but, above all, the matriculation examination (a gate way to the job market). In 1947, India had about 425 colleges, 20 universities and 2.5 lakh students. The higher education had a literary bias and the growth of technical and professional education was severely limited. There were a few tentative attempts at co-ordination of medical and legal education and agricultural research. Higher education development in the form of enclaves, the affiliation system of colleges, the examination-led curriculum and the role of English language as the medium of instruction with adverse effects on regional languages – this was the colonial legacy in higher education.

The sixth chapter deals with educational planning as providing the federal framework for educational policy making and financing. The Central Planning Commission set up in 1950 realized Jawaharlal Nehru's pre-independence dream of a scheme of a planned economy for India. With its Perspective, Five-Year and Annual Plans covering all sectors and involving all states, the Planning Commission has emerged as a unique federal organization, a lynchpin between the Centre and the states. The National Development Council (NDC) provides an interface with the states. Planning Commission's influence declined after 1967 but it has the potential of coming into its own. Educational planning, however, is the responsibility of the Education Ministry. It suffers from organizational, fiscal and planning-procedural imbalances. The progress of education policy statements is traced from 1968 policy (based on Kothari Report, but a minimalist version based on the differences among MPs) through 1986 policy (a bureaucratic exercise under Rajiv Gandhi which lost steam when Rajiv Gandhi got embroiled in controversies), to the modifications made in 1992 (which policy was a cross between Acharya Ramamurti's vision of decentralization and an Andhra politician's pragmatism). But, by 1992, the education policy statement had lost its significance because of the change of context (structural adjustment programme of 1991). In the matter of financing, the chapter refers to formula based central assistance to State Plans supplemented by the centrally sponsored schemes (CSSs) which are a manifestation of the phenomenon of picket fence federalism [meaning that there is solidarity among programme specialists (in this case educational planners) irrespective of levels of government, e.g., central and state]. The chapter is concluded by a review of the functioning of CABE as a sectoral Inter-State Council. This is the first detailed study of CABE in literature because neither Sarkaria Commission nor the students of federalism have taken notice of its existence. It notes two disruptions in the working of CABE (1975–1983 and 1995–2003) and also a Supreme Court judgment on CABE (Aruna Roy). A detailed chart of the working of CABE from 1935 to 2010 has been incorporated.

Chapter seven on elementary education and literacy extends its coverage to take in early childhood care and education. In spite of the Directive Principle in Article 45, the failure to achieve universalization of elementary education targeted to be achieved in 1960–1965 may be blamed on the lack of timely action on national leadership's and especially Jawaharlal Nehru's part but ultimately it is due to the ruling elite's lack of interest in the matter, in which the leadership of the State Governments cannot escape the blame. The chapter deals with programmes and policies including Sarva Shiksha Abhiyan as well as the legislative measures. The NPE 1968 and the NPE 1986 (especially the latter, with its Operation Blackboard) could not achieve much. The Gandhian Acharya Ramamurti's recommendation of treating elementary education as a fundamental right (1990) was followed by the Supreme Court's judicially declaring it as a fundamental right in the Unnikrishnan case (1993). In due course, the Constitution was amended (2002) and the legislation for compulsion has been passed (2009) and enforced with effect from 1st April 2010. Programmatically, Sarva Shiksha Abhiyan has been a moderate success, but it needs to be watched if India would manage to achieve UEE and EAI even by 2020. The international community (UNICEF) and efforts of Supreme Court to monitor food security have led to the decision to universalize ICDS blocks, which would give a push to ECCE. The constitutional amendment (ECCE being made a directive principle in the amended Article 45) is at the most a symbolic gesture.

India's progress in adult literacy is dismal, the literacy having increased from 16.6 per cent in 1951 to 66.38 per cent in 2001. Between 1947 and 1978, there was not much activity, 1978 marking the adoption of the national adult education programme by the Janata government. The centre-based approach of the government, however, turned out to be ineffective and it was only with the adoption of TLC (Total Literacy Campaign) approach in the 1990s that substantial progress could be made. The Prime Minister has placed before the nation the target of universal female literacy by 2014. The chapter concludes by referring to the Punjab model of proximate literacy which made Green Revolution a success in spite of low level of literacy. The Punjab model is explained in terms of British scholar, C.A. Bayly's thesis of "density and flexibilities of Indian routines of social communication".

Chapter eight deals with secondary and higher secondary education which is a residuary stage, falling between the priority stage of elementary education and the prestigious stage relating to higher education. After reviewing the overall growth of secondary education, two policy areas, viz., evolution of the common pattern of education (10+2+3) and the implementation of the three language formula are examined. The former is a success which the latter is a failure. The federal footprint in this area which is normally regarded as a state or regional field of action is examined. The federal footprint is manifested in two research-cum-training institutions, viz., NCERT and NUEPA, two examining Boards, viz., CBSE and National Institute of Open Schooling and two organizations conducting elite central schools, viz., Kendriya Vidyalaya Sangathan and the Navodaya Vidyalaya Samiti, the latter of which runs rural public schools all over India except in Tamil Nadu.

NCERT is a secondary school resource complex set up by the Central Government in 1961 with one of the largest expertise in school curriculum, textbooks, teacher education, research and surveys. The states, however, have very little role in its management and the Central Government has also consistently opposed granting of autonomy to NCERT. NUEPA, which is a deemed university since 2007, specializes in the area of educational planning and administration. CBSE has spun off a body called COBSE which co-ordinates the work of all State School Boards. The chapter ends with reference to the new agenda for universalization of secondary education by 2020 for which a Rashtriya Madhyamik Shiksha Abhiyan (RMSA), i.e., a national campaign for secondary education has been launched in March 2009.

Chapter nine deals with higher general education and its elusive triangle of quantity, quality and equality. The expansion in terms of enrolment (1.24 crore), institutions (408 universities, 20,064 colleges) and teachers (5.22 lakh) is considerable but GER is still low (about 11%). The structural trends are adverse: Postgraduate enrolment has gone down from 11.5 per cent to 9.42 per cent between 1950–51 and 2006–07, Ph.D holders from 0.83 per cent to 0.66 per cent between 1950–51 and 2007–08 the science faculty enrolment has gone down from 38.3 per cent to 31.96 per cent between 1960–61 and 2006–07. The socio-economic causative factors are analysed. The inequalities in terms of rural-urban, gender, class, caste and community divides have not shown any substantial decline. A most significant trend since 1990 has been large-scale expansion of private sector, both in institutional growth and enrolment. Most worryingly, there is a perceptible fall in quality and there has not been any improvement in spite of the measures taken by the UGC to implement the recommendations of the Govindarajulu Committee (1965) and the Education Commission. The number of autonomous colleges (a standard remedy) has not substantially increased. One commentator has talked of "fall of the Guru" in India. A distinguished foreign scholar has urged the need for promotion of intellectual creativity. At the end of the chapter is a note on the central higher education institutions, their number and variety partly reflecting effects of federalism.

The challenge of education is implicit in the pressure of numbers at the two stages of secondary/higher secondary and higher education. It is this pressure which has accentuated the trend toward privatization of enrolment and institutions and compelled the government to mount two campaigns – one campaign for universalization of secondary education/higher secondary education and another for mass higher education which involves enrolment of 15 to 20 per cent in the age group 17–23.

Chapter ten considers three case studies in higher education. The first one is about the regulatory effectiveness of the UGC which has not been able to control the unplanned institutional expansion of colleges and universities, nor to promote model bills for university governance nor in setting up State Councils of Higher Education of which only seven have come up. This case study brings out that the problem of the triangular relationship between the UGC, the State Governments and universities/colleges, identified by a scholar as crucial in a Federation, has not been solved. The second case study about regionalization of medium of instruction which has been on the policy agenda since 1960s, shows that in spite of the activities of an expert body like CSTT, substantial funding by the Central Government and institutionalization through Granth Academies/Textbook Production Boards at the state level, English remains the sole medium in professional courses, and at the postgraduate level and the dominant medium at the undergraduate level. The main hurdle reportedly is unwillingness of the teacher community and irresolution of the university authorities and the State Governments. The third case study relates to the issue of whether Governors have any discretion in dealing with the State Universities. Whereas it is an accepted position that the President of India in relation to Central Universities is bound by the advice of Cabinet/Education Minister, the position and role of the State Governors is presumed to be different. It is pointed out that the State Governor, being an appointee of the Central Government and also enjoying the power of refusing assent to any state bill, including the education bills, the Governor's assumed discretionary power really amounts to the creation of a gridlock for State Governments. The Sarkaria Commission held that the power of a Governor to withhold assent is to be used only in specified and rare cases, and the same having been accepted by the ISC, the matter should be beyond doubt but is not so in practice. The false asymmetry between Governor's role and President's role needs to be rectified.

Chapter eleven deals with technical and professional education whose special constitutional status is underlined by entry 64 of the Central List dealing with INIs (Institutions of National Importance), set up and financed by the Central Government (e.g., IITs, AIIMS) and entry 26 of the Concurrent List covering legal, medical and other professions. Professional bodies like the Medical Council of India, Bar Council of India etc. ensure minimum standards of undergraduate education as well as norms of professional conduct, the postgraduate medical education and postgraduate legal education being the concern of the Health Ministry and the UGC respectively. For other streams, viz., technical education, agricultural education and teacher education for which the regulatory bodies are: All-India Council for Technical Education (AICTE), advisory since 1945 and statutory since 1987; Indian Council for Agricultural Research, setup under Societies Registration Act in 1929 and National Council for Teacher Education (NCTE), advisory since 1973 and statutory since 1995). The development of technical and professional education in India has been characterized by trends of (a) expansion and diversification of courses and institutions, (b) regional imbalances in the distribution of technical and professional education facilities, (c) commercialization and privatization of educational institutions (which trends are mutually related), (d) a dualist system of medical education comprising 'scientific' (allopathic) medicine and indigenous system of medicine now called AYUSH (Ayurvedic, Unani, Siddha and Homeopathic) and, lastly (e) co-existence in this sub-sector of the common run of institutions with the INIs like IITs/IIMs/AIIMS etc. enjoying an international 'brand'. The trends toward expansion and diversification and regional imbalances are statistically illustrated by data relating to engineering and management education. Regional imbalance is seen in the concentration of a majority of institutions in the three southern states of Karnataka, Andhra Pradesh and Tamil Nadu and the western state of Maharashtra. It is pointed out that the trend to privatization got under way when the Manipal-based non-profit engineering and medical colleges began to attract higher fee paying students consequent on backward class favouring legally – backed reservations. From 1980s, commercialization by way of "capitation fee" – demanding, dominant-caste/minority managed technical professional education institutions made their appearance. They had tacit political support; hence the regulatory bodies looked the other way. Then the Supreme Court stepped in and through a series of judgments beginning with Mohini Jain (1992), Unnikrishnan (1993) and TMA Pai Foundation (2002) declared "under the table" capitation fees illegal but allowed these self-financed private institutions to charge higher fees subject to regulation by state level committees dealing with admissions and fees respectively. However, malpractices are rampant even at the stage of sanctioning of new professional colleges where teaching faculty from other existing professional colleges is 'borrowed' temporarily. AICTE and NCTE are legally autonomous but have abdicated their responsibility. In medical education, press reports indicate that the Health Ministry was compelled in May 2010 to issue an ordinance to dissolve the MCI and to set up an ad hoc Board of Governors to look after its work. The reason was that the Chairman was arrested by the CBI in April 2010 for allegedly taking a bribe for sanctioning new medical colleges. The malpractices in the professional colleges are well documented in official reports which, however, never see the light of the day. Madhavrao Scindia as Union

Education Minister, under P.V. Narasimha Rao, had introduced in the Rajya Sabha a bill for regulation of private universities in August 1995 but it was never proceeded with because of the ideology inspired political opposition. Another clandestine route of privatization is notification of de novo institutions as deemed universities since 2000 under the revised UGC guidelines in the matter. As for dualist medical education system, it is colonially rooted and after independence, the internal dissensions within the Ayurveda education establishment between "Shuddha" and "integrated" medicine as well as staunch opposition of the allopathic lobby have ensured that the indigenous systems remain subaltern although they have all the paraphernalia of professional regulatory and research councils. The only hopeful sign is that an independent department for AYUSH has been set up in 1995 and a separate policy for AYUSH has been announced which shows that the Central Government is committed not only to improving the quality of training and research in Indian systems but also to enforcing hygienic production and batch manufacturing practices in regard to Ayurvedic medicines based on standardized pharmacopoeia. Finally, centres of excellence established and maintained by the Central Government like IITs/IIMs/AIIMs/National Legal Universities etc. are dealt with. IITs set up on the MIT model were earlier criticized for the brain-drain (to the extent of 30%) but now they have achieved international 'brand'. A recent McKinsey Report (2000) on IITs shows that they require further investment by way of upgradation to maintain their standards internationally. Finally, it is pointed out that the social forces behind the various trends in this area are the underlying north south divide, basic inegalitarian structure of society and politicization of education. The solution may well lie in a 'Flexner' type consolidation and reform as was done in American medical education in 1910s.

Chapter twelve deals with the dimension of research which along with teaching is an important function of higher education. However, a policy decision was taken by the first Prime Minister of India that scientific and industrial research would be conducted in a separate and well financed sector called S&T so that the research conducted in universities is a very small proportion of overall research (less than 3%). Similarly, research is conducted in national laboratories rather than state laboratories. After marshalling the data regarding financial provision and initiatives like science policy, technology policy and the latest S&T policy 2003 it is pointed out that there are about 12 S&T departments which conduct research in about 500 research institutions/laboratories under various councils and commissions. The functioning of S&T councils like CSIR is highly centralized with very little participation by the states. Three research councils function under the Education Ministry, viz., ICSSR

(Social Sciences), ICHR (History) and ICPR (Philosophy). ICSSR is by far the best regarded of the research councils, it has regional centres and regional research institutions. Its report on Status of Women in India had important positive fallouts in the form of women's study centres etc. On the whole, the quantum of research in India in comparative world perspective is meagre, various indicators regarding research effectiveness in terms of publications and patents are low and India suffers in comparison with developed countries as well as its competitors like China.

Chapter thirteen deals with proposals for reforms in higher education. These proposals are four-fold. Firstly, in the context of coexistence of coordinating bodies like UGC, AICTE, NCTE etc. side by side with professional bodies like Medical Council, Bar Council, ICAR etc. a need is felt for a coordinating mechanism. The NPE 1986–92 suggested NCHE (National Council for Higher Education). There was no consensus till recently on the final form of the coordinating mechanism. The National Knowledge Commission in 2006 and Yashpal Committee in 2009 made their own suggestions regarding central mechanisms. These have been examined and are found wanting though Yashpal Committee-proposed National Council for Higher Education and Research (NCHER) appears to enjoy official backing. Other proposals for reform include regulation of foreign universities which has to be considered in the context of WTO negotiations.

Prospects

In the background of the overview, the prospects for education and federalism in the second decade of 21st century may be considered, which, in the ultimate analysis involves considering the capacity of federalism to meet the emerging challenge of education sector in the secondary/higher secondary and higher education stages.

The Evolution of Federalism in India

While the education sector had its moment of disjuncture in 1966–69, the federal system in India had its moment of disjuncture in the post-Emergency Janata regime (1977–79). It was then, that the single party dominance at the central level was ended with a coalition of parties forming government and advocating a new policy of decentralization and rural development. No doubt, 1989 is traditionally regarded as the defining year but in federal terms, it really revived the forces which lay dormant because of the unforeseen rejuvenation of the Congress party in two elections of 1980 and 1984 on the strength of a sympathy 'wave'. The significance of 1989 is that it brought to the fore regional parties as active agents in federal management. The central disarray was evident in the wobbling on policy front both under Indira Gandhi (1980–84) and Rajiv

Gandhi (1984–89). The appointment of Sarkaria Commission (1983–1988) on Centre-State Relations by Indira Gandhi was really under duress, the opposition having united under a few powerful chief ministers led by Andhra Pradesh's N.T. Rama Rao in 1982–83. Sarkaria Commission in a way diagnosed a problem and offered solutions which were no longer relevant to the new political reality in India. The parliamentary system combined with discontinuous one-party dominance till 1989 made Indian federalism even more centralized than the designers of the Constitution had envisaged. The charismatic leadership of Jawaharlal Nehru in the first seventeen years gave the federal polity stable democratic institutions, minimum economic growth and cultural-educational capacity which served the nation-state well and enabled it to weather the times of trouble caused by the Indo-China (1962) and the Indo-Pak (1965, 1971) wars and turbulence of the internal Emergency and the succeeding decade. Thus in 1989, when the era of coalition of regional parties began, India had not only adequate democratic experience but also a sturdy policy framework in the areas of science and technology, school and higher education, languages and social sciences, with institutional infrastructure in the form of national science laboratories, Central Universities, institutions of national importance like the IITs/IIMs and the complex web of think tanks in the form of research councils in school education, social sciences, history and philosophy.

The federalization-localization process which began in 1977–79 was accentuated after 1989, by following developments:

1. The structural innovation of creation of a third tier of federalism in the form of Panchayati Raj and municipalities through constitutional amendments for which Rajiv Gandhi set the ball rolling and which fructified during P.V. Narasimha Rao's time in 1993. Rajiv Gandhi in his turn was following the practice of Karnataka (under Ramakrishna Hegde), Kerala and West Bengal, particularly under Left governments, in the matter of democratic decentralization.
2. Regional parties becoming stronger and becoming part of the central decision-making as a result of which the incidence of President's rule in the states has declined.
3. Greater federal consultation through old mechanisms like (NDC/CABE) as well as new consultative fora (e.g., Inter-State Council set up in 1990).
4. The activist role of the Supreme Court in upholding federalism as a basic feature of the Constitution (Bommai judgment of 1994) and also in upholding and protecting fundamental human rights to environment, education, food etc. as facets of right to life and liberty in Article 21.

There have been some countervailing processes like the transformation of Rajya Sabha into a mere parliamentary second chamber, but it has been pointed out by the author[1] that this set back can be counterbalanced by the revitalization of second chamber at the state level. It is part of the signs of time that states which had abolished Legislative Councils (e.g., Andhra Pradesh and Tamil Nadu) are reviving them and states which never had them are trying to institute them (e.g., Madhya Pradesh).

Do Recommendations of the Punchchi Commission Make a Difference?

At this stage, it may be interesting to take note of the mind of the Punchchi Commission on Centre-State Relations,[2] which reportedly submitted its report in April 2010 and some of whose recommendations have appeared in the press in May 2010.[3] The Commission is reported to have made 200 recommendations. From the available material, the Commission's recommendations are not very radical, broadly following the path laid down by the Sarkaria Commission, the Venkatachaliah Report (NCRWC) and the ARC Report. Some of the recommendations highlighted in the press may be noted:

1. Amend Articles 355 and 356 to enable the Centre to bring 'areas' under its rule for a limited period. (This means that parts of a state may be brought under President's rule.)
2. Set up structures like US Homeland Security.
3. Give more teeth to the National Integration Council (NIC). It has been suggested that it should meet at least once a year. In case of any communal incidents, a team of the NIC should visit the affected area within two days and submit a fact-finding report. However, it has rejected the suggestion of the Liberhan Commission that the NIC be accorded a constitutional status.
4. Need for laying down clear guidelines for the appointment of Chief Ministers.
5. Recommendations as to the Governor's office.

The Punchchi Commission appears to be following the Sarkaria Commission when it suggests that the Governor should not have participated in active politics of the state concerned, that he should be an eminent person and that he should not belong to the state where he is to be posted. It follows the NCRWC in suggesting the composition of a panel which should select the Governor. It differs from Sarkaria in suggesting that Governors be given a fixed five year tenure. It says that Governors should not be arbitrarily dismissed. It suggests provisions for impeachment of Governor by the state legislatures along the same lines as that of the President by Parliament. Significantly, it says that the Governor should not be associated with State Universities which is a matter of convention, that the scope of his discretionary powers under Article 163(2) should be limited, and that the Governors should not sit on a decision and must decide a matter within a four-month period. This tallies with what the author suggested in the chapter on higher education vis-à-vis discretionary powers of Governor to withhold assent to a State Bill.

A Second States Reorganization?

At this stage, a reference may be made to the demand for smaller states which has a bearing on the future shape of Indian federalism. It is well known that in the context of the long pending demand for creation of a separate state of Telangana and particularly the agitation of the Telangana Rashtra Samiti (TRS), (in June 2010) a view has emerged favouring creation of smaller states. The background is as below: During the chief ministership of late Rajashekhar Reddy in the Andhra Pradesh, the demand for Telangana had more or less subsided. After his death, the chief of TRS went on fast unto death. At a crucial juncture, probably based on inadequate information, Union Home Minister announced in Parliament in December 2009 that the Central Government would initiate steps for formation of a separate state of Telangana. Later, the Centre stated that there was need for holding wide-ranging consultations following protests in Rayalseema and coastal Andhra Pradesh. The Central Government also appointed a committee under the chairmanship of a retired Supreme Court Judge, to go into the pros and cons of the formation of a separate state of Telangana and make recommendations and the report is awaited at the time of writing. The Centre's apparent conceding the demand for a separate Telangana has given a fillip to the dormant new state demands like Vidarbha in Maharashtra etc. It has also begun to be argued that newly created states like Uttarakhand and Chattisgarh have been economic success stories. As for Jharkhand, while it could not be called a success, the residuary state of Bihar is said to have recently experienced a high rate of growth. Therefore, it is being suggested that, there should be a second wave of states reorganization and not only Telengana but also Vidarbha (Maharashtra), Bundelkhand (Uttar Pradesh) and Harit Pradesh (Uttar Pradesh), all small states should be created.[4]

The author feels that the creation of new states within the Indian federalism at this juncture, i.e., when the country is poised to enter a crucial growth phase in the background of world recession, goes to the root of federal stability in India and that any such exercise should not be undertaken lightly. In all this, the general recommendations of the SRC (Fazal Ali Commission) in the matter of creation of new states needs to be kept in view. The SRC had propounded the 'balanced budget' standard for creation of a new state (meaning that, over a fairly short period, the revenue budget should be balanced) and held that excessive dependence of any state on the Centre detracted from the federal principle. In the matter of size, it had favoured larger rather than smaller states. It observed that every grievance regarding an alleged unfair and unequal distribution of development expenditure cannot be made into a ground for creation of a new state. Rather, there should be a permanent body attached to the NDC to investigate the complaints and to report thereon so that emerging grievances were nipped in the bud.

Secondly, the case for small states like Jharkhand, Chattisgarh and Uttarakhand is by no means proven. Random and medium term data for 4–5 years can not be pressed to arrive at a judgment. The data need to be long run and robust. Lastly, merely because there may be a general case for smaller state, it should not be assumed that new small states are required to be established in India at the present moment.

If it is accepted that, there needs to be a closure to the creation of new states in India, one needs to think in terms of a consensus in favour of a requisite constitutional amendment. This would enable Indian federation to attain a measure of stability and evolve healthy federal conventions.

Given the suggestion for freezing the federal system, one is required to make a futuristic projection for education and this can best be done by looking at the LPG scenario.

LPG Deciphered

The post-1991 scenario, especially nationally, is said to be characterized by the so-called LPG – the triple trend of liberalization, privatization and globalization – and this is bound to be reflected in the future of education under federalism. As noted by M.P. Singh,[5] the recent economic reforms in India are marked relatively more by regulation and partial privatization than by globalization of trade and investment. To the extent decontrol and privatization reduce the intervention of the federal state in the affairs of industry, business and State Governments, the forces of federalization as contrasted to parliamentary executive centralization and of localization are reinforced.

It needs to be pointed out that both the processes of federalization and localization have deeper historical roots and are a result of a dialectical process. Jawaharlal Nehru (1947–64) was a moderate centralizer but even during his time, federalization was under way. Thus, Marcus Franda talked of the federalizing process being at work in West Bengal because West Bengal has had more independence in centre-state relations than, for example, Madhya Pradesh because Bengalis under the leadership of B.C. Roy had been more effectively mobilized in centre-state disputes.[6] Nehru was succeeded by Indira Gandhi who was a hyper-centralizer. Her rule culminated in the dark period of Emergency (1975–77). The thrust of the Janata interregnum of 1977–79 was towards greater decentralization with an emphasis on rural development.[7] It is to be noted that Mandal Commission on Backward Classes was appointed by the Janata government. Indira Gandhi on her return to power (1980–84) managed to put a lid on the Mandal Report. Her successor Rajiv Gandhi tried to pursue her project centralization but was required to enter into various regional accords in the north-east and Punjab. The National Front regime of V.P. Singh (1989–91) unleashed a process of Mandalization, which was really a phase of regionalization or federalization of politics in India.

So far as the localization in the form of third tier of federalism is concerned, it has a chequered history. The first wave of Panchayati Raj (1959–77), inaugurated by Balwantrai Mehta Committee,[8] lost steam because its motivating factor, of increase in agricultural productivity lost its relevance after the Green Revolution (1966–67). The Panchayati Raj, therefore, was reduced to administrative decentralization. The second wave (1977–1988) was launched by Ashok Mehta Committee Report,[9] and it was mainly marked by the democratic decentralization initiatives of opposition ruled states of West Bengal, Karnataka, Andhra Pradesh and Kerala,[10] with the Sarkaria Report in 1988 making it an official policy.[11] Rajiv Gandhi government tried to fashion Zilla Parishads as centrally guided bodies but this project was frustrated by the defeat of the constitutional amendment piloted by him and it was only during the Prime Ministership of a more conciliatory P.V. Narasimha Rao, that constitutional entrenchment of Panchayati Raj and the municipalities became a reality. Moreover, it is axiomatic in the constitutional law of the first federation, viz., the US that in terms of Dillon's rule, local bodies are creatures of State Governments,[12] and the Indian Supreme Court has adopted the same approach. The more important aspect of the weakness of Panchayati Raj bodies in India is not only that they do not have the heart-felt support of the State Governments, which regard them as the Trojan horse of the Central Government, but also that State Governments are not adequately empowered, not having the requisite technical and expert capacities.[13] In other words, the emerging scenario of federalization and localization of the political system is a variation on the theme of centralization/decentralization, going back to the Montford Report which according to the present study is the leit motif of the federal role in education sector. It hardly needs to be added that, it is not enough to identify and name a new trend. Its modalities are required to be spelt out which in the case of federalization process are stated to be regional party representatives in the federal coalition conveying their views directly to the Prime Minister for action.[14] This modality is purely opportunistic and highly contingent. Different regional parties come to power in different coalitions (e.g., NDA between 1999 to 2004 UPA-I from mid-May 2004 and UPA-II from May 2009 onwards). Serious students of federalism are required to consider organizational devices to make meaningful empowerment of states as a system vis-à-vis Centre.

As for globalization, it is a complex phenomenon going beyond internationalization, and has multiple dimensions, economic, political, social and cultural. It got under way in the 1980s and gathered momentum after the fall of the Berlin Wall (1989). The tendency in the 1990s to equate it predominantly with economic aspects and to assume as if the territorial nation-state has become irrelevant has given way especially after the Terrorist Friday (11th September 2001 in New York), to recognition of the role of political and cultural facets of globalization, including regional and local factors.[15] From this point of view, the process of 'glocalization' which results from the interaction of global and local factors could be held to subsume federalization also. If economic dimension of glocalization is manifested in the State Governments competing among themselves for foreign direct investment, the cultural dimension of glocalization is manifested through the activities of the NRIs/PIOs (Persons of Indian Origin), who have their roots in the linguistic cultures of the respective states. In the present situation, LPG really mean LFPG-L = Localization, Federalization, Privatization and Glocalization.

The question then arises: Why does the Centre mistrust the states, what have the states managed to accomplish especially in educational – cultural fields in spite of this attitude and what are the devices which could be adopted to enable Indian federation to face the emerging challenges of education in the post-2010 period?

States: Perception vs. Deeds

The reasons for the mistrust of the states in India at a general level have been spelt out by the social psychologist Ashis Nandy in graphic terms. "The idea of the modern state especially in the third world has a clear technocratic context to it. Not only does the idea legitimize centralised structures for the purposes of social engineering, it tends to see the diversity and empowering of the lower political order as positively inefficient, diversionary and disruptive. Any decentralization or reconceptualization of the states as a truly federal entity requires a confidence and trust in the citizens and in local communities, which is next to impossible in the post-colonial polities, with their imitative technocratic states and westernized elites, fully convinced of their historical role as a cultural vanguard."[16] At a more particularized level, states are regarded as highly politicized and non-professional in their approach to the urgent problems of a crucial sector like education with its human development potential. In the present study, such a criticism of states has been noted in areas like technical education (e.g., Mashelkar Committee's criticism of

State Governments' interference in the management of the RECs)[17] or in social science research management (e.g., the ICSSR Third Review Committee's criticism of the states', handling of the problems of jointly financed regional social science institutions).[18] The whole approach of the UGC to the states is pervaded by a profound distrust of states as evidenced by the grounding of the SCHER initiative. The recognition of some validity of criticism directed against State Governments should not lead to the conclusion that states in India have been mere greedy recipients of the financial largesse of the centre in the charade of picket-fence federalism or passive spectators of Central aggrandizement in the institutional spheres of higher education and science and technology. As a matter of fact, the Central government has been equally prone to the vice of politicization[19] and the states have been known for major innovations in the field of education. We consider examples under the four headings: institutional innovations, cultural innovations, programmatic innovations and policy innovations.

Institutional Innovations

- Two states, vis., Punjab and Kerala, were founders of institutions, which were so excellent that the Centre took them over as institutions of national importance, namely PGIMER, Chandigarh, originally founded by Pratap Singh Kairon then Chief Minister of Punjab which, was taken over by the Central Health Ministry and Sree Chitra Tirunal Institute of Medical Science and Technology, Thiruvanthapuram which was taken over by CSIR.
- Andhra Pradesh set up the first Open University in the country (1982) (ahead of IGNOU in 1985), the first Health University (1987) and the first State Council for Higher Education (1983).
- Tamil Nadu pushed for and won UGC clearance for its Tamil University in 1981.
- Bihar set up K.S. Darbhanga Sanskrit University, 1961, the first language university in the country, in spite of strong opposition from the Kothari Commission which observed that they cannot support the idea of Sanskrit University.[20] By now, not only Bihar but Uttar Pradesh, Orissa, Maharashtra and Kerala have such Sanskrit universities.
- States have also set up separate women's universities (Maharashtra, Tamil Nadu, Andhra Pradesh) and separate journalism and music universities (Madhya Pradesh).

In general, the states with their concern for promotion of local culture, upgradation of century-old local institutions and traditional learning have experimented with single-faculty universities to which

UGC/Central Government were initially opposed. Agriculture Ministry is opposed to the establishment of separate Animal Sciences universities but West Bengal, Maharashtra, Tamil Nadu and Karnataka have gone ahead and set up such universities partly in response to regional demands and partly with a view to upgrade century-old veterinary colleges. State Agricultural Universities, State Open Universities, State Law Universities and State Health Universities have by now the support of the Central Government.

Cultural Innovations

These encompass what may be called manifestations of 'glocalization' and are directly related to linguistic reorganization. The states with the financial help of Indian diaspora of regional origin, have been organizing what are euphemistically called "World Regional Language Conferences" in the face of initial opposition or in any case lack of sympathy of the Ministry of External Affairs, which with its blindness to the reality of regional cultures, would have nothing to do with promotion of anything which fell short of the cachet of Indian national culture. Tamil was the first regional language which, with its history of Tamilian diaspora in Sri Lanka, Singapore, Malaysia etc. going back to the colonial times, organized such a world conference in 1968 when the language agitation was at its height. Telugu and Kannada have followed suit and there is even a World Marathi Conference, being organized since 1992. The Central Government has since established a separate Ministry for PIOs acknowledging the politico-economic significance of this segment, though it is not yet clear if the Ministry of External Affairs, that bastion of diplomatic orthodoxy, has overcome its myopia and begun to recognize the validity of regional cultures not antagonistic to a national culture.

Programmatic Innovations

Programmatic innovations are as numerous as institutional ones: (1) Maharashtra is known for its pioneering Gram Shikshan Mohim (Social Education Campaign) in the 1960s, popularization of the school complex idea first mooted by the Kothari Commission and a scheme for adoption of girls (Savitribai Dattak Palak Yojana) for spread of girls' education. (2) Kerala is known for its people's campaign for decentralized planning[21] as well as for the campaign for 100 per cent literacy in Kottayam district which led to the Total Literacy Campaign being adopted by the National Literacy Mission. (3) Tamil Nadu pioneered the noon-meal scheme during chief ministership of K. Kamraj (1954 onwards), which was adopted as the Mid-day Meal Programme at the national level in 1995. Even a backward state like Madhya Pradesh became known in the 1990s for its innovative Education Guarantee Scheme (EGS),[22] under which tribal education was effectively promoted by appointment of locally recruited para-teachers.

Policy Innovations

Policy innovations by State Governments are comparatively rare and generally emulative of the Central Government but, all the same, provide important lessons. A White Paper on Education was floated in April 1968 by an idealistic Education Minister in Maharashtra, who was an active participant in the CABE deliberations relating to school and social education leading up to the formulation of NPE 1968. The White Paper aimed to integrate the school systems in the three regions of the state (western Maharashtra, Vidarbha and Marathwada), modernize the curriculum and prepare the state to face the challenge of the Industrial Age. However, the good intentions of the White Paper ran into the sand of debate rooted in urban/rural and forward caste-backward caste divide as a result of which the revised White Paper of February 1970 was a sanitized version of the 1968 version.[23] An American scholar noted that both the sides to the debate shared common assumptions and did not make any move for early universalization of elementary education and the main effect of the debate was to ensure that rural politicians are regularly included among those whose interests must be consulted in education policy making and implementation.[24] More recently, Andhra Pradesh under Chandrababu Naidu as Chief Minister became known for its advanced policies in the field of information technology, bio-technology etc. More significantly, it also devised a strategy of countering left wing extremism popularly known as Naxalism, under chief ministership of late Raj Shekhar Reddy. In the context of the Prime Minister having identified Left Wing Extremism as the greatest internal security threat faced by Indian state today, the details of strategy are of interest. This consisted of police getting additional staff, superior training in arms, vehicles and communications and government building an intensive network of roads in the jungles of the four worst affected northern districts. The new road network helped to set-up the full range of government services. At the end of four years from 2005 to 2009 Left wing extremism was on the retreat.

All such initiatives were neither centrally designed nor centrally assisted at the time of their conception. Thus, states left to themselves are not devoid of educational and strategic innovations. What is necessary is to give voice and operational leeway to the states, setting in motion a process of multiplication of such innovations through the pathway of emulative federalism. This amounts to following Daniel Elazar's dictum of non-centralization, which would bear fruit in the form of optimum functioning of a dynamic Indian federalism in aid of socio-economic services including education.

What is, therefore, suggested is that the states could be encouraged to associate voluntarily as a counterpoise to the centrally designed consultative bodies like the NDC, ISC, CABE etc. and that there are comparative precedents and constitutional backing for such a body and that such a body may be better equipped to meet emerging challenges of education.

Fulfilling the Federal Mission: A "Fraternity"-based Forum

Meaningful educational structures in a federation need a federal forum to underpin them. CABE as a consultative forum has been useful in the past but its locus in the Education Ministry limits its role. The NDC is too focused on issues relating to the Five-Year Plans and the ISC has turned out to be not as effective as expected.[25] Moreover, all these are essentially central fora with an imperial hangover. There is need for an autonomous forum in which the initiative lies with, and the agenda is set by, the states. A quest for constitutional foundation for such a body needs to begin with the original preamble of the Constitution, referring to the four values of justice, liberty, equality and fraternity each of which has found a practical expression in the post-independence India[26] except fraternity about which Dr Ambedkar explained: "Fraternity means a sense of common brotherhood of all Indians. In a country like ours with so many disruptive forces of regionalism, communalism and languages, it is necessary to emphasize and re-emphasize that the unity and integrity of India can be preserved only by a spirit of brotherhood. India has one common citizenship and every citizen should feel that he is Indian first irrespective of other basis. In this view of the matter, any means of bringing about equality should be welcome."[27] This is eloquent but tends to equate fraternity with equality. Seervai, the noted constitutional lawyer, has adopted a literal interpretation of the term, linking it with common citizenship (Article 5), and adding that division of states on linguistic lines and the provisions relating to language militate against fraternity. He appears to overlook that Indian languages are metaphorically called sisters, having a common ancestor. His conclusion that this is a moral and political ideal and that there is no provision of the Constitution, which gives a clear content to it would appear to be defeatist.[28] Pursuing the idea of fraternity as a moral or political ideal, it is possible to suggest that it is a political ideal of a collectivity rather than of individual citizens as both Ambedkar and Seervai appear to have assumed. Ivo Duchacek has quoted an author who calls a federation as "a brotherhood of tempered rivalry." Morton Grodzins spoke of federalism as antagonistic rivalry to indicate that groups can indeed engage in joint ventures on a regular basis even as they react to each other antagonistically.[29] In this theoretical background and with the Supreme Court having recognised federalism as part of the basic structure of the Constitution, it is suggested that, it is federalism as an ideology of the collectivity of states, which is the right vehicle to articulate the value of fraternity. Here, let us again recall the prophetic vision of the Montford Report of future India as a sorority or fraternity[30] of states which bears repetition: "Our conception of the eventual future of India is a *sisterhood of states*, self-governing in all matters of purely local and provincial interest over which would preside a Central Government, representative and responsible to the people of them all."[31]

Foreign Precedents

Precedents in other countries may be noted here. Rekha Saxena's study quoted earlier deals with First Ministers' Conference in Canada, but it is an official agency comparable to, but more effective than, the Indian Inter-State Council.[32] Australia appears to have started a new institutional mechanism called Council of Australian Governments (COAG) in 1990 as a parallel body to Premiers' Conference which latter body was known for its acrimonious bargaining. The agenda of the new body was set by states though it was chaired by the prime minister of the Commonwealth.[33] The US appears to provide more relevant models for innovative mechanisms for inter-governmental cooperation including constitutionally recognized inter-state agreements. The National Governors' Association established in 1908 to enable the nation's governors collectively to influence development and implementation of national policy has reportedly emerged as a strong lobby,[34] but it can have no parallel in India with its parliamentary system. The Council of State Governments established in 1935 with headquarters in Chicago appears to be of great relevance. In 1946, it codified its reform agenda in the post-war era. It has been publishing a "Book of the States", a biennial publication. Given the separation of powers in the US, it is naturally oriented towards the problems of legislatures.[35]

The New Federal Forum in India

In this background, India can have a fraternity-promoting Forum comprising all states, in whose formation the states could take the initiative, as a counterpart body of the Inter-State Council/NDC set up by Central Government. It can be tentatively called Forum of Fraternal States of India for Cooperative Action (FFSI-CA). The headquarters of the proposed body could be at some central location like Bhopal, Nagpur or Hyderabad rather than Delhi. It could have its own Constitution and appropriate deliberative, decision-making and think-tank structures. The Forum should aim to promote, in the words of C.J. Freidrich, federal spirit, loyalty and comity as vital behavioural features of federalism.[36] Three priority items on its reform agenda could be:

(a) to bring about stability in the federal system by suggesting amendment of Article 3 of the Constitution, so that the number and identity of states is no longer an issue within the discretion of the Centre but would require a special amendment as in the case of Seventh Schedule vide proviso of Article 368(2),

(b) to change the mode of appointment of Governors who should no longer be perceived as the agents of Central Government, who should, in the words of Soli S. Sorabjee, be *sages rather than saboteurs*,[37] and

(c) to project the Rajya Sabha as a real upper house, representative of states not so much on the analogy of the German Constitution but in the light of Article 249 of the Indian Constitution which is a pointer to the intention of the framers of the Indian Constitution.[38]

There could be a sectoral council for education under the new body, representing all sub-sectors of education including medical, agricultural and legal, spearheading educational reforms on a broad front. This forum could have its own think-tank which could also serve as a clearing house of information, whose existence is a pre-requisite for promoting emulative federalism. One of the first action agenda for the new body would be to help NDC in fulfilling the National Mission for Skill Development which could help the nation in reaping the demographic dividend in the next 20–25 years (2010–2035) as explained below.

Role of the President of India

Who should preside over the forum? Not the Prime Minister (who presides over the NDC and the Inter-State Council, which, though serving as countervailing forces to the project of Centralization, are not very effective as instruments of non-centralization), but rather the President of India who by constitutional design as well as practice is ideally suited to promote the third dimension of the central role in federalism transcending narrow state and central concerns. He is elected by an electorate on which are represented, not only the Parliament, but also the State Assemblies. Several provisions of Constitution refer to the President as distinguished from the Central Government (e.g., Article 3 relating to formation of states state that a bill for the purpose cannot be introduced except on the recommendation of the President).[39] Since 1989, he is a referee in the game of government formation and since 1994, (after Bommai case) he can return the recommendation of the Prime Minister to impose Presidential rule in a state under Article 356. He is sworn to protect India's Constitution including its federal values.

The third dimension of central role in federalism referred to above is not an idle phrase. According to the Australian author Sawer, we are required to incorporate in our discussion a higher level of Federalism called by the German Jurist Hans Kelsen as *Gesamstaat* which could be translated as "organic federalism" and conveys the same idea as general welfare in the preamble of the US Constitution. In the Indian context, it means the federal authority representing both the Centre and states/UTs.

Meeting the Challenge of Education and Skill Development before the Indian Federation: 2010–2035[40]

The challenge before Indian federalism in 2010 and following few years is to utilize the demographic advantage through education and skill development at secondary and post-secondary/tertiary stages.

The UN Population Division estimates that over the next few years, India's working age population (age-group 15–64) is set to grow by a cumulative 138 million (annual increase of 13.8 million), significantly greater than the expected increase of 33 million in China. Among the large countries in the world, India would continue to have the best demographic trend as measured in terms of low dependency ratio (ratio of non-working population, i.e., the young, the old and non-working women to working population). If India can create productive jobs for the expanding workforce with the requisite skill sets, it can earn demographic dividend in terms of higher savings, investment and economic growth.

The significance of the year 2035 (It is to be noted that these are all estimates) is that at that point, India's working age population may have peaked. So, the next 25–30 years represent a demographic window of opportunity.

As against this, the situation on the ground in terms of universal literacy and universal elementary education leaves much to be desired. NSS data show that only 5 per cent of 11–25 age group in India have some skills compared to 96 per cent in South Korea. There is, therefore, a huge skill gap. The skill gap needs to be filled up by expansion of secondary education followed by skill training (ITI type training). There is also scope for expansion of polytechnic education and vocation oriented higher education. This is a challenge of education and labour sectors in India. The Education/Labour Ministries of the Centre and the states in India need to rise to occasion.

The government is launching a Mission for Skill Development in the Eleventh Plan. The plan document states: "It is envisaged to evolve a comprehensive scheme for creating a diverse and wide-range of skills for our youth that would enable the country to reap the scientific and demographic dividend. The emphases will be on demand-driven vocational education programmes in partnership with employers. Clear strategies for encouraging access to VET (Vocational Education and Training) for marginalized groups including SCs, STs, OBCs, minorities, girls, street children, working children and differently abled children will be adopted."[41]

The implications of the extract from the plan document need to be spelt out:

1. From the start of planning in 1950, India has followed a man-power planning approach – a directorate of manpower was established in 1950s under the Ministry of Home Affairs and now the Indian Institute of Applied Manpower Research functions under Planning Commission. The emphasis from the start has been on the *supply side* of the labour market. The Eleventh Plan document marks a radical shift when it refers to *demand driven vocational education programmes* in partnership with employers.
2. Government programmes even on the supply side of the market are fragmented among seventeen ministries and departments. There needs to be co-ordination among them.
3. As suggested by the economist Bibek Debroy, the existing 50,000 skill development centres are required to be augmented by a factor of five.
4. There is need to address the training needs of the unorganized sector which accounts for over 90 per cent of the workforce.
5. Finally and most importantly, implementation remains a State subject. The National Skill Development Mission should have its counterparts in state level missions. The states need to gear for action on a variety of fronts – literacy and UEE, skills in English, strengthening of secondary and vocational education etc.

According to the author, the NDC together with the new federal forum under the President can guide and supervise the implementation of the missions of RMSE and SD (Skill Development). If Indian federation successfully tackles the educational/skills challenges of the next 25–30 years, it could well be said to have met the federal survival test comparable to the civil war in the US.

Notes

1. M.R. Kolhatkar, Second Chamber in States: Role in the Three Tier Federalism (*Journal of Constitutional and Parliamentary Studies*, January-June, 2007), 89–98.
2. The Commission on Centre-State Relations was constituted in 2006. Its composition was: Justice M.M. Punchchi, ex-CJI (Chairman), Dhirendra Singh, V.K. Duggal, ex-Secretaries to GoI; N.R. Madhav Menon, ex-Director, NLS in Bangalore as Members; the Secretary, Inter-State Council was the Member-Secretary. The vacancy of Dr Amresh Bagchi who expired on 20th February, 2008 was unfortunately not filled. The

Commission issued a questionnaire in April 2008. Evidently, the composition of the Commission left a lot to be desired, especially since then there was no social scientist on the Commission.

3. *Indian Express* (Mumbai), 10th May, 2010.
4. See the following: Bibek Debroy: 'From 28 to 45?' (*Indian Express*, 15th December, 2009), Pratap Bhanu Mehta: 'Sizeable Matters' (*Indian Express,* 15th December, 2009), Swaminathan S.A. Aiyar: 'The Economic Case for Creating Small States' (*Economic Times*, 20th December, 2009) and Karthik Muralidharan: 'Too Small to Fail' (*Indian Express*, 17th December, 2009).
5. M.P. Singh, "The Impact of Global and Regional Integration", in B.D. Dua and M.P. Singh (Eds.), *Indian Federalism in the New Millennium* (New Delhi, Manohar, 2003), 370–435.
6. Marcus Franda, *West Bengal and the Federalizing Process in India* (Princeton: Princeton University Press, 1968).
7. Idem: *Small is Politics: Organizational Alternatives to India's Rural Development* (New Delhi: Wiley Eastern, 1979).
8. Planning Commission: *Report of Study Team for CD and NES* (New Delhi, November 1957).
9. Ministry of Agriculture and Irrigation: *Report of the Committee on Panchayati Raj Institutions* (New Delhi, August 1978).
10. Vide Article by George Mathew, "Federal Principles in Local Government", in B.D. Dua and M.P. Singh (Eds.) *Indian Federalism and the New Millennium* (New Delhi: Manohar, 2005) 218–265.
11. Sarkaria Report, 543–544.
12. Dillon's rule is so-called after Judge John Dillon of Iowa Supreme Court, which was upheld by the US Supreme Court. Vide Nicholas Henry, *Public Administration and Public Affairs* (New Delhi: Prentice Hall of India, 2001), 372.
13. Capacity is defined as government's ability to respond effectively to change, make decisions efficiently and responsibly and manage conflict. Vide Ann O'M Bowman et al., *State and Local Government* (Boston: Houghton Mifflin, 2002), 3.
14. Rekha Saxena, *Situating Federalism: Mechanisms of Inter-Governmental Relations in Canada and India* (New Delhi: Manohar, 2006), 316.
15. Ronald Munck, "Globalization and Democracy" (*Annals of the American Academy of Political and Social Science*, May 2002, 10–12).
16. Ashis Nandy, "Federalism, the Ideology of the State and Cultural Pluralism", in Nirmal Mukarji and Balveer Arora (Eds.), *Federalism in India: Origins and Development* (New Delhi: Vikas), 27–40.
17. See the chapter on Higher General Education – Note on Central Educational Institutions.

18. See the chapter on Research Dimension.
19. Politicization of education has been defined by Rudolphs (in *Education and Politics in India* (New Delhi: Oxford University Press, 1972), 87–88) as the propensity to subordinate educational goals to those of political groups on the one hand and to those of private and community groups on the other. The Central Government which has actively promoted Mandalization of IITs and IIMs on the eve of elections in the major states of Tamil Nadu, West Bengal, Kerala and Assam in 2006 is hardly innocent of politicization of education.
20. Kothari Report, para 8.79.
21. T.M. Thomas Isaac with Richard N. Frank, *Local Democracy and Development: People's Campaign for Decentralized Planning in Kerala* (New Delhi: Left Word, August 2000).
22. R. Gopal Krishnan and A. Sharma, Education Guarantee Scheme in Madhya Pradesh, *EPW*, Vol. 33, No. 29, 26th September, 1998.
23. Donald B. Rosenthal, *The Expansive Elite: District Politics and State Policy-making in India* (Berkeley and Los Angeles: University of California Press, 1977), 152–190.
24. N. Chandrababu Naidu with N. Shevanti, *Plain Speaking* (Bombay: Viking Penguin: 2000).
25. Rekha Saxena, *Situating Federalism*, op. cit., especially Chapter 7.
26. Among appropriate structures to implement them may be mentioned (a) the Supreme Court and High Courts (addressing the value of justice), (b) the National Human Rights Commission (addressing the value of liberty), and (c) a large number of Commissions to promote equality as exemplified by the National Commission for the SCs (Article 338), National Commission for the STs (Article 338 A), National Commission for OBCs, for the Minorities and for the Women (all of the latter by a Statute).
27. As quoted in R.C. Lahoti, *Preamble: The Spirit and the Background of the Constitution of India* (Lucknow: Frontier Book Co., 2004), 106.
28. H.M. Seervai, *Constitutional Law of India,* Vol. I, (Bombay: N.M. Tripathi, 1998), 281–82.
29. Ivo Duchacek, *Comparative Federalism: The Territorial Dimension of Politics* (New York: Holt, Rinehart and Winston, 1970), 192.
30. The word 'sorority' is derived from a Latin word "sor" meaning sister. Although in the US, the term sorority has come to mean "a female students' society in a university or college", the term is used here following Montford Report in the literal sense of sisterhood, which is equivalent to brotherhood or fraternity.
31. Montford Report, para 349.
32. Rekha Saxena, op. cit., 224–249.

33. J.C. Bannor, "From Confrontation to Cooperation: Australian Commonwealth State Relations in the 1980s–1990s", in Ian Copland and John Rickard (Eds.), *Federalism: Studies in Indian and Australian Federalism* (New Delhi: Manohar, 1998), 240–248.
34. Robert D. Behn (Ed.), *Governors on Governing* (Lanham: University Press of America, 1991).
35. John Teaford, *The Rise of the State: The Evolution of American States* (Baltimore, Johns Hopkins University Press, 2002).
36. C.J. Friderich, *Trends in Federalism: Theory and Practice* (London: Pall-Mall Press, 1968), 176.
37. Soli S. Sorabjee (Ed.), *Governor: Sage or Saboteur*? (New Delhi: Roli Books, 1985).
38. Article 249 broadly provides: If the Council of States has declared by resolution that it is necessary/expedient in the national interest that Parliament should make laws with respect to any matter enumerated in the State List, it shall be lawful for Parliament to make laws with respect to that matter.
39. James Manor, 'The Presidency', in Devesh Kapur and Pratap Bhanu Mehta (Eds.), *Public Institutions in India: Performance and Design* (New Delhi: Oxford University Press, 2005), 105–127.
40. The following paragraphs are based on a synthesis of a variety of sources including the following: Bibek Debroy: 'Moving in for the Kill: Getting Serious on the Skills Deficit Would Need Going Beyond the Government's Roadmap', *Indian Express*, 9th December, 2009).

    Chetan Ahya: 'Tracking India's Talent Supply' (*Economic Times*, 21st December, 2009).

    Neeraj Kaushal: 'Where Are the Skilled Indians?' (*Economic Times*, 31st December, 2009).

    Manish Sabbarwal: 'Learning While Earning' (*India Today*, 27th July, 2009).
41. Eleventh Plan Document, Vol. II, 20–21.

Bibliography

The Bibliography is in three parts: (I) Official Documents (divided into pre-independence and post-independence and under post-independence according to ministries/departments and according to nature of governments, i.e., Central/State/Foreign/ International etc.), (II) Books and (III) Articles. Here aka stands for 'also known as'.

I. Official Documents

A. Reports of Central Government and its Organizations

Pre-Independence Reports

Report of the Education Commission 1882–83 (aka Hunter Report).

Report of the Universities Commission 1902 (aka Raleigh Report).

Report of the Indian Industries Commission 1916 (aka Holland Report).

Report on the Indian Constitutional Reforms 1918 (aka Montford Report).

Report of the Calcutta University Commission 1919 (aka Sadler Report).

Report of the Committee on Division of Functions and Related Reports 1919.

Report of the Royal Commission on Agriculture 1928 (aka Linlithgow Report).

Report of the Auxiliary Committee of the Indian Statutory Commission 1929 (aka Hartog Report).

Report of the All-Parties Conference 1929 (AICC, Allahabad) (aka Motilal Nehru Report).

Quinquennial Review of Progress of Education 1922–27, 1927–32.

Report of the Statutory Commission, Vols. I and II, 1930 (aka Simon Report).

Report of the Joint Committee on Indian Constitutional Reforms, 1933–34.

Report of CABE on Post-war Educational Development 1944 (aka Sargent Report).

Reports of the Committees appointed by CABE (1943–46) (1947) (Pamphlet No. 57).

Report of the Committee on Health Survey and Development 1946 (aka Bhore Report).

Interim Report of the CABE Committee on Technological Institutions 1946, reprinted 1950 (aka Sarkar Report).

Post-Independence Reports

Government of India (Hereinafter referred to as GoI) (place of publication New Delhi unless otherwise indicated)

Constituent Assembly

Report of the Linguistic Provinces Commission.

Ministry of Agriculture

Ministry of Agriculture and Irrigation (Now Ministry of Rural Development) Report of the Review Committee on Panchayati Raj (1978).

Department of Agricultural-Education and Research, Annual Reports 1997–1998 to 2004–2005.

Department of Animal Husbandry and Dairying: Annual Reports 2001–2005.

ICAR

Memorandum of Association, Rules and Byelaws of the ICAR Society as corrected upto 12th July 2002 (August 2002).

Reports of the First and Second Joint Indo-American Teams on Agricultural Research and Extension (ICAR, New Delhi, 1954 and 1960)

Report of ICAR Enquiry Committee (1973). (aka Gajendragadkar Committee Report)

Report of the Review Committee on Agricultural Universities (1978). (aka Randhawa Committee Report)

Report of the ICAR Review Committee (1988). (aka G.V.K. Rao Committee Report)

Model Act for Agricultural Universities in India (as revised in 1994) (1994).

Accreditation for Quality Assurance in Agricultural Education (1998).

Report of the Committee set up to Review Administrative Structure of the ICAR at headquarter and its linkages with Institutions and SAUs (2003). (aka Hemendra Kumar Committee)

Accelerating ICAR's Journey towards Excellence: Report of the ICAR Reorganization Committee (July 2005) (Chairman: R.A. Mashelkar).

Ministry of Education

Progress of Education in India 1937–47 (1949).

Report of University Education Commission (1949). (aka Radhakrishnan Report)

Report of Secondary Education Commission (1954). (aka Mudaliar Report)

Report of the Sanskrit Commission (1956–57).

Report of the Committee of Members of Parliament on Higher Education (1964). (aka Sapru Report)

Report of the Committee on Model Act for Universities (1964).

Education and National Development: Report of the Education Commission (1966). (aka Kothari Report)

Report of Committee of MPs on National Policy of Education (1967). National Policy on Education, 1968.

Report of the Review Committee on the University Grants Commission (January 1977). (aka Jha Report)

Report of the Review Committee on the Curriculum for the Ten-Year School (1977). (aka Ishwarbhai Patel Report)

National Review Committee on Higher Secondary Education with special reference to Vocationalization (1978). (aka Adisheshaiah Report)

Draft National Policy on Education 1979.

Challenge of Education: A Policy Perspective 1985.

National Policy on Education, 1986: Programme of Action 1986.

Report of the National Commission on Teachers-I (School Education) 1985. (aka Chattopadhyaya Report)

Report of the National Commission on Teachers-II (Higher Education) 1985. (aka Rais Ahmed Report)

Report of the Review Committee on NIEPA (1989).

Toward an Enlightened and Humane Society: Report of the Committee for Review of NPE 1986 (December 1990). (aka Ramamurti Report)

National Policy on Education 1986 as modified in 1992.

NPE 1986/92: Programme of Action 1992.

Learning without Burden: Report of National Advisory Committee 1993.

Report of the Group to Examine Feasibility of Recommendations supra 1993.

Report of the Committee of State Education Ministers on Implications of the Proposal to make Elementary Education a Fundamental Right (New Delhi, January 1997) (Mimeo).

Report of Expert Group on Financial Requirements for making Elementary Education a Fundamental Right (1997) (Mimeo).

Task Force Report on Boards of Secondary Education (1997) (Mimeo).

Interim Report of the Committee on Operationalization of Suggestions to Teach Fundamental Duties (January 1999).

Annual Reports of the Ministry 2000–2009.

Elementary Education: A Fundamental Right (New Delhi, 1998).

Draft Working Group Report on Higher Education in the Eleventh Plan (New Delhi, Ministry of HRD, 2007).

CABE

Central Advisory Board of Education: Silver Jubilee Souvenir (1960).

Proceedings of the Post-1960 Meetings of CABE (as available in NIEPA Library).

Report of the Committee on Ways and Means of Financing Education (1949). (aka Kher Report)

Report of the CABE Committee on Policy (1992).

Report of the CABE Committee on Decentralized Management of Education (1994).

Report of the CABE Committee on Distance Education (February 1994).

Report of the Committee on Universalization of Secondary Education (New Delhi, 2005).

Report of the Committee on Financing of Higher and Technical Education (NIEPA, New Delhi, June 2005).

Report of the Committee on Free and Compulsory Education Bill and other issues related to Elementary Education (New Delhi, June 2005).

Report of the Committee on Girls Education and Common School System (New Delhi, 2005).

Report of the Committee on Integration of Cultural Education in the School Curriculum (New Delhi, 2005).

Repot of the Committee on Regulatory Mechanism for Textbooks and Parallel Textbooks taught in Schools outside the Government System (New Delhi, 2005).

Report of the Committee on Autonomy in Higher Education Institutions (New Delhi, 2005).

AICTE

Report of the Committee to Review RECs (Chairman: Prof. Jaikrishna) (1974).

Technical Education in Independent India 1947–97 (1997).

Report of the High-level Committee to Review the working of the RECs (Chairman: R.A. Mashelkar) (2002).

Review Committee Report of AICTE (2003) (Mimeo).

Annual Reports 1988–2008.

AIU

Proceedings of the 57th Annual Meeting of AIU, 31st January–1st February, 1981 (New Delhi, AIU).

Central Board of Secondary Education (CBSE)

Annual Reports 2002, 2003 and 2004.

Platinum Jubilee Souvenir (2003).

Kendriya Vidyalaya Sangathan (KVS)

Annual Report 2002–2003.

Navodaya Vidyalaya Samiti (NVS)

Annual Report 2002–2003.

National Institute for Educational Planning and Administration (NIEPA)

Annual Reports 2002–2008.

National Institute of Open Schooling (NIOS) (Earlier National Open School)

Annual Report 2002–2003.

ICHR

Annual Reports 2000–2003.

ICHR Review Committee (Mimeo) (1982).

ICPR

ICPR: A Profile 2002.

Annual Report 2000–2003.

ICSSR

Report of First Review Committee: Social Sciences in India: Retrospective and Prospective, Vols. I & II (1970).

ICSSR: Role, Responsibilities, Functions, Programmes and Organization of ICSSR (Occasional Monograph No. 7, 1971).

ICSSR: Social Science Research in India: A Report submitted to ICSSR by Andrew Shonfield and Albert B. Cherns (ICSSR Pamphlet No. 20) (1971).

Report of Second Review Committee (1978).

Report of Third Review Committee (1986).

ICSSR: Newsletters 2002–2005.

ICSSR: Annual Report 2002–2003.

IGNOU, New Delhi

IGNOU Act 1985 (No. 58 of 1985).

Annual Reports of IGNOU 1999–2003.

IGNOU: A Profile 2005.

DEC: Guidelines for Support to State Open Universities and Correspondence Course Institutes (1999).

Indian National Congress

Report of the Linguistic Provinces Committee, 2nd Impression (1953).

NCERT

Future Development of NCERT: Report of Review Committee (1969). (aka Nagchaudhuri Report)

Memorandum of Association (December 1974).

The Curriculum for Ten-Year School: A Framework (1975).

Framework for Curriculum for Teacher Education (1978).

Report of the Task Force of NCERT (New Delhi, 1985).

The National Curriculum for Elementary and Secondary Education: A Framework (1988).

Framework for Curriculum for Teacher Education (1988).

National Curricular Framework for School Education (2000).

The Curriculum Framework for Teacher Education (February 2004).

National Curriculum Framework (2005).

NCTE

Policy Perspectives in Teacher Education: Critique and Documentation (1998).

Annual Reports for the years 2000–2004.

NCTE: (Form of application for recognition, the time of submission of application, determination of norms and standards for recognition of teacher education programmes and permission to start new courses or training) Regulations, 2002.

UGC

UGC Report (December 1953 to March 1957) (New Delhi, 1958).

Annual Reports 1958–1959 to 2007–2008.

Report of the Committee on Governance of Universities and Colleges, Part I: Governance of Universities (1971) (aka Gajendragadkar Report).

Development of Higher Education in India: The Policy Framework (1978).

Report of the Review Committee on Development Programmes (1981) (aka Satish Chandra Report).

Report of the Committee to Enquire into the Working of the Central Universities (1984). (aka Madhuri Shah Report)

Report of the UGC Committee on State Councils of Higher Education (1986).

Guidelines for Affiliation of Colleges (December 1987).

Report of the UGC Committee: Towards New Educational Management (1990) (Chairman: A. Gnanam).

Report of Committee for Funding of Institutions of Higher Education 1992–93 (1994) (aka Dr Punnayya Report).

Report of the Working Group of Higher Education: Ninth Five Year Plan (June 1996).

UGC News (Issues from 2002 to 2004).

Report of UGC's Reconstituted Panel on Law submitted on 27th December, 1994.

Guidelines for Autonomous Colleges (1995).

Guidelines for Considering Proposals for Declaring an Institution as Deemed to be University under s.3 of UGC Act (2000).

UGC Act 1956 and Rules and Regulations under the Act. (aka UGC Compendium) (October 2000).

Towards Formulation of a Model Act for Universities of the Twenty-First Century in India: A Concept Paper (October 2003).

NAAC (Bangalore)

Annual Report 2002–2003.

Total Quality Management for Tertiary Education, Government of Karnataka Initiative (Bangalore, June 2003).

Guidelines for Establishment of State-level Quality Assurance Committee and Quality Assurance Cell (Bangalore, December 2004).

NAAC: A Profile 2005.

NAAC: Newsletter, July 2005.

Ministry of Environment and Forestry

National Forest Policy, 1952.

National Forest Policy, 1988.

Indian Council for Forestry Research and Education (ICFRE): Draft Annual Report 2000–2001 (Dehradun 2002).

National Forestry Action Programme: India: Executive Summary (1999).

Ministry of Finance

The Report of the Third Central Pay Commission, Vols. I & II (New Delhi, 1973).

Finance Commission

Twelfth Finance Commission: Fifty Years of Indian Federalism (April 2003).

Ministry of Health and Family Welfare

Report of the Committee on Health Survey and Planning (1959).

(Chairman: A.L. Mudaliar).

Group on Medical Education and Support Manpower (1975). (aka J.B. Srivastava Report)

National Health Policy 1982.

Medical Education Review Committee 1983.

Compendium of Recommendations of various Committees on Health Sciences 1943–75 (1985).

Health Manpower Planning, Production and Management: Report of Expert Committee (1987). (aka Bajaj Committee Report)

National Education Policy in Health Sciences (1989).

National Health Policy 2001.

Annual Reports of the Ministry: 2001 to 2004.

Report of the Working Group on Development of Human Resources in Health (10th Plan) (2001).

Department of ISM and Homoeopathy: Indian Systems of Medicine and Homoeopathy in India 1998 (1999).

Central Council of Health

CHS

Proceedings and Resolutions of Seventh Conference, 1998.

Proceedings and Resolutions of Eighth Conference, 2002.

Dental Council of India: Silver Jubilee Volume (1973).

Medical Council of India: Annual Report 2002–2003 (Mimeo).

Ministry of Home Affairs

Report of the States Reorganization Commission (1955).

Report of the Official Language Commission (1956).

Report of the Committee on National Integration (1962). (aka Sampurnanand Report)

Reports of the Administrative Reforms Commission on:

1. Machinery for Planning: Interim Report (1967) and Final Report (1968).
2. Administration of Union Territories and NEFA (1967).
3. The Machinery of the Government of India and its Procedures of Work (1968).
4. Centre-State Relationship (1969).
5. Scientific Departments (1969).

Study Group of ARC on UTS (1969).

Report of the Study Group of ARC on Centre-State Relationship (1967).

Report of the Commission on Centre-State Relations, Vols. I & II (1987).

Others

The Official Language Act and Rules thereunder (New Delhi, Controller of Publications, 1994).

Department of Official Languages: Annual Report 2004–2005 (New Delhi, 2006).

Ministry of Law and Justice

Report of All India Bar Committee (1953).

Law Commission of India: Fourteenth Report (Reform of Judicial Administration) 1958.

—: 160th Report on Amendment of AICTE Act (1998) under Minister of Low Justice.

Bar Council of India

Annual Reports 2000–2002.

Ministry of Science and Technology

DS&T

Scientific Policy Resolution 1958.

Report of the National Committee on S&T (New Delhi, 1973).

Technology Policy Statement, June 1983.

Guidelines and Format for Submission of Project Proposals under the Scheme: Assistance for Development of State S&T Council (No date).

Research and Development Statistics (2000–01) (May 2002).

Science and Technology Policy 2003.

Annual Reports of DST for the years 1996–1997 to 2003–2004.

Department of Scientific and Industrial Research

CSIR

Twenty-Five Years of CSIR (New Delhi, 1967).

Memorandum of Association and Rules and Regulations and Byelaws of CSIR (New Delhi, no date but probably 1987).

Report of Reorganization Committee under the Chairmanship of R.A. Mashelkar (CSIR, 2004).

Planning Commission (PC):

Plan Documents: First Plan to Eleventh Plan.

Committee on Plan Projects: Report of the Study Team on CD/NES (1957). (aka Balwantrai Mehta Report)

The Committee on Social Science Research 1967. (aka VKRV Rao Committee)

Draft Fifth Five Year Plan (1974–79), Vol. II.

Report of the Expert Committee on Centrally Sponsored Schemes (1985). (Chairman: Shri Ramamurthi, Chief Secretary of Orissa Govt.)

Report of the Group of Officials on Centrally Sponsored Schemes (April 1987).

Report of the Committee of NDC on Centrally Sponsored Schemes (January 1988).

Report of the Experts' Committee on Educational Expenditure (May 1999).

Mid-Term Appraisal of the Ninth Five Year Plan (October 2000).

Task Force Report on India as Knowledge Super-Power: Strategy for Transformation (June 2001).

Report of the Committee on India: Vision 2020 (December 2002).

Report of the Task Group on Revamping and Refocusing National Agricultural Research (January 2005).

National Development Council (NDC):

Record of Discussions of Various Meetings of the National Development Council. (as available in Planning Commission Library).

Report of NDC Committee on Micro-Level Planning and Involvement of People at Grass Roots (April 1993).

Report of NDC Committee on Literacy (June 1993).

Ministry of Programme Implementation and Statistics

Report of National Statistical Commission, Vol. I (New Delhi, 2003).

B. Reports of Parliament of India

Parliamentary Debates

Lok Sabha Debates (21st August, 1984) (Seventh Series, Vol. No. 20, Columns 498–520) on UGC Amendment Bill 1984.

Rajya Sabha Debates (9th December, 1985) on UGC Amendment Bill 1985 (Columns 243–286).

Lok Sabha Debates (17th December, 1985), on UGC Amendment Bill (Columns 374–386).

Rajya Sabha Debate (7th December, 1993) on Medical Council of India (Amendment) Bill.

Parliamentary Committee Reports

Eighty-Second Report of the Estimates Committee (1964–65) on the University of Delhi (Lok Sabha Secretariat, April 1965).

One-Hundred and Fourteenth Report of the Public Accounts Committee (1969–70) (Lok Sabha Secretariat, New Delhi, April 1970).

Ninth Report of the Estimates Committee (1977–78) on Higher Technical Education (Lok Sabha Secretariat, New Delhi, January 1977).

Seventy-Third Report of the Public Accounts Committee (1977–78) on UGC (Lok Sabha Secretariat, 1978).

Forty-Eighth Report of the Public Accounts Committee (1980–81) on NCERT (Lok Sabha Secretariat, New Delhi, April 1981).

Eighty-First Report (Action Taken Report on Supra) March 1982.

Sixty-Sixth Report of the Estimates Committee (1988–89) on UGC.

(Lok Sabha Secretariat, New Delhi, March 1989).

Ninth Report of Estimates Committee (1990–91) on UGC, Action Taken Report on Supra (Lok Sabha Secretariat, August 1990).

Fifteenth Report of the Committee on Subordinate Legislation Presented to Lok Sabha on 16th December, 1994 (Law Ministry).

Rajya Sabha Secretariat: 177th Report on CIEFL University Bill 2006 of the Department-related Parliamentary Standing Committee (New Delhi, 2006).

C. Reports of State Governments and their Organizations

Government of Andhra Pradesh

Report of the Committee on Establishment of an Open University (1982).

Report of the Committee for Evaluation of Administration and Programme of the Universities of AP (August 1995).

Government of Maharashtra: (pre 1960 – Government of Bombay)

A Review of Education in Bombay State 1855–1955 (Poona, 1958).

Cooperation and Rural Development: Report of the Committee on Democratic Decentralization (1961).

Maharashtra Medical Council Act 1965.

Text of Prime Minister Rajiv Gandhi's Address to the Nation (DGI & PR, Bombay, 1985).

Government of Karnataka

National Law School of India Act, 1986.

Report of the University Review Commission (1986).

Government of Tamil Nadu

Report of the Centre-State Relations Inquiry Committee (1971). (aka Rajamannar Report)

Government of West Bengal

Report of Universities Commission (1988).

D. Reports of International Organizations

World Bank, Washington DC

Higher Education: The Lessons of Experience (May 1994).

Priorities and Strategies for Education: A World Bank Review (1995).

Report of the Task Force on Higher Education and Society: Higher Education in Developing Countries: Peril and Promise (Washington DC, 2000).

Constructing Knowledge Societies: New Challenges for Tertiary Education (2002).

Lifelong Learning in the Global Knowledge Economy (2003).

Expanding Opportunities and Building Competencies for Young People: A New Agenda for Secondary Education (Washington DC, 2005).

United Nations Organization (UNO)

Our Global Neighbourhood: Report of the Commission on Global Governance (1995).

UNESCO, Paris

1. Learning to Be: The World of Education: Today and Tomorrow (Paris, 1972). (Chairman: Edgar Faure)
2. Learning: The Treasure Within: Report of International Commission on Education for the Twenty-First Century (Paris, 1996). (Chairman: Jacques Delors)

UNDP, New York

Human Development Reports: (for 15 years-> 1990–2005).

All published by Oxford University Press, New Delhi.

UNICEF

Final Report of World Conference on Education for All: Meeting Basic Learning Needs (New York, 1990).

E. Reports of Foreign Governments (and their Organizations)

UK

1. Report of the Committee on Higher Education appointed by the Prime Minister (of UK) 1961–63 (London, HMSO (CMd, No. 2154)). (aka Robbins Report).
2. Report of the Open University Planning Committee (HMSO, 1968).
3. An Enquiry in to the Social Science Research council by Lord Rothshild (May 1982) (London, HMSO (M. No. 8554)).

USA

The Council of State Governments: The Forty-Eight State School Systems (Chicago: Illinois, 1949).

II. Books

Abbi, A. "Vanishing Diversities and Submerging Identities: An Indian Case", in Asha Sarangi (Ed.), *Language and Politics in India* (New Delhi: Oxford University Press, 2009).

Acharya Poromesh. "Bengali Bhadralok and the Educational Development in the 19th Century Bengal", in Suresh Chandra Shukla and Rekha Kaul (Eds.), *Educational Development and Under-development* (New Delhi: Sage, 1995).

Agarwal, Pawan. *Indian Higher Education* (New Delhi: Sage, 2009).

Agarwal, V.P. *Forests: Environmental and Production Frontier* (New Delhi: Oxford and IBH Publishing Co., 1985).

Aggarwal, J.C. *Landmarks in the History of Modern Indian Education* (New Delhi: Vikas Publishing, Third Revised Ed., 1996).

Aggarwal, Santosh. *Three-Language Formula: An Educational Problem* (New Delhi: Gian Publishers, 1991).

Aggarwal, Y.P. and R.S. Thakur. *Concepts and Terms in Educational Planning: A Guidebook* (New Delhi: NIEPA, 2003).

Agrawal, S.K. (Ed.). *Legal Education in India: Problems and Perspectives* (Bombay: N.M. Tripathi, 1973).

Ahmed, Aqueil. "Science and Technology in India: Policy, Management Institutions", in Michael Gibbons et al. (Eds.), *Science and Technology Policy in the 1980s and Beyond* (London: Longman, 1984).

Ahmed, A.F.S. *Social Ideas and Social Change in Bengal 1818–1835* (Calcutta: Riddhi, 2nd Ed., 1976).

Ahuja, Sangeeta. *People, Law and Justice: Case Book of Public Interest Litigation*, Vols. I and II (New Delhi: Orient Longman, 1997).

AIU. Diminishing Autonomy of Indian Universities: Final Report (New Delhi: AIU, 2000).

——. Handbook of Universities, 29th Edition (2002) and 30th Edition (2004) (New Delhi).

——. Report of the National Colloquium on Right to Education as a Fundamental Right (September 1992).

Aiyar, S.P. *Federalism and Social Change* (Bombay: Asia Publishing, 1961).

——. "The Federal Idea in India", in S.P. Aiyar and Usha Mehta (Eds.), *Essays in Indian Federalism* (Bombay: Allied, 1965).

Alexander, P.C. *Through the Corridors of Power: An Inside Story* (New Delhi: Harper Collins, 2004).

Allen, Hollis P. *Federal Government in Education* (New York: McGraw Hill Book Co., 1950).

Altbach, Philip. "The Dilemma of Change in Indian Higher Education", in Suma Chitnis and Philip Altbach (Eds.), *Higher Education Reforms in India: Experience and Perspectives* (New Delhi: Sage Publications, 1993).

Ambedkar, B.R. *The Evolution of Provincial Finances in British India: A Study in the Provincial Decentralization of Fiscal Finance* (London: P.S. King and Sons Ltd., 1925).

——. *Federation vs. Freedom* (Poona: Gokhale Institute of Politics and Economics, 1939).

Amrik, Singh and G.D. Sharma (Eds.). *Higher Education in India: The Social Context* (New Delhi: Konark, 1988).

Amrik, Singh and Philip Altbach (Eds.). *The Higher Learning in India* (New Delhi: Vikas, 1974).

——. *Redeeming Higher Education: Essays in Educational Policy* (New Delhi: Ajanta Publications, 1985).

——. *Fifty Years of Higher Education in India* (New Delhi: Sage Publishers, 2004).

Amrik, Singh. *Challenge of Education* (Hyderabad: ICFAI University Press, 2004).

Anderson, Benedict. *Imagined Communities: Reflections on the Origin and Spread of Nationalism* (London: New York, Verso, 1983, 2nd Ed., 1991).

Andhyarujina, T.R. *Judicial Activism and Constitutional Democracy* (Bombay: N.M. Tripathi, 1992).

Appadorai, A. *Dyarchy in Practice* (London: Longmans, Green & Company, 1937).

Arora, Balveer. "Adapting Federalism to India: Multi-level and Asymmetrical Innovations", in Balveer Arora and Douglas Verney (Eds.), *Multiple Identities in a Single State: Indian Federalism in Comparative Perspective* (New Delhi: Konark, 1995).

——. "Multiple-level Federalism", in V.A. Pai Panandikar (Ed.), *A Survey of Research in Public Administration* (New Delhi: Konark, 1997).

——. "Negotiating Differences in Federal Coalitions and National Cohesion", in Francine R. Frankel et al. (Eds.), *Transforming India: Social and Political Dynamics of Democracy* (New Delhi: Oxford University Press, 2000).

——. "Political Parties and the Party System", in S.C. Kashyap et al. (Eds.), *Reviewing the Constitution* (New Delhi: Shipra, 2000).

——. "The Indian Parliament and Democracy", in Ajay K. Mehra and G.W. Kueck (Eds.), *Indian Parliament: A Comparative Perspective* (New Delhi: Konark Publishers, 2003).

Arora, Balveer and Douglas V. Verney (Eds.), *Multiple Identities in a Single State: Indian Federalism in Comparative Perspective* (New Delhi: Konark, 1995).

Ashby, Eric. *Universities: British, Indian, African: A Study in the Ecology of Higher Education* (Cambridge: Harvard University Press, MS, 1966).

Atal, Yogesh (Ed.). *Social Science in Asia* (New Delhi: Abhinav Publishers, 1974).

Austin, Granville. *Indian Constitution: The Cornerstone of a Nation* (New Delhi: Oxford University Press, 1966).

——. *Working of a Democratic Constitution* (New Delhi: Oxford University Press, 1999).

Baker, Abu. *The Union and the States in Education* (Ajmer: Shabda Prakashan, 1976).

Banerjee, Ashish. "The Ideology and Politics of India's National Identity", in Zoya Hasan et al. (Eds.), *The State, Political Process and Identity* (New Delhi: Sage Publications, 1983).

Bannor, J.C. "From Confrontation to Cooperation: Australian Commonwealth State Relations in the 1980s and 1990s", in Ian Copland and John Rickard (Eds.), *Federalism: Studies in Indian and Australian Federalism* (New Delhi: Manohar, 1998).

Barker, Ernest. *The Development of Public Services in Western Europe (1760–1880)* (London: Oxford University Press, 1944).

Basu, Aparna (Ed.). *Imperialism, Nationalism and Regionalism in Canadian and Modern American History* (New Delhi: Manohar, 1989).

——. "Higher Education", in Moonis Raza (Ed.), *Higher Education in India: Retrospect and Prospect* (New Delhi: Association of Indian Universities, 1991).

Basu, D.D. *Commentary on the Constitution of India*, Vol. 3 (New Delhi: Deep & Deep Publications, 1969).

——. *Shorter Constitution of India* (New Delhi: Prentice Hall of India, 12th Ed., 1996).

Basu, Kaushik and James E. Foster. *On Measuring Literacy* (Washington DC: Office of Sr. Vice-President, Development Economics) The World Bank.

Bayly, C.A. *Empire and Information: Intelligence Gathering and Social Communication in India, 1780–1870* (Cambridge: Cambridge University Press, 1996).

Baxi, Upendra (Ed.). *Socially Relevant Legal Education* (New Delhi: UGC, 1977).

——. *Supreme Court and Politics* (Lucknow: Eastern Book Co., 1980).

Behn, Robert D. (Ed.). *Governors on Governing* (Lanham: University Press of America, 1991).

Berdahl, Robert O. *British Universities and the State* (Berkeley and Los Angeles: University of California Press, 1959).

Bhambri, C.P. "Federal Politics: A Trend Report", in ICSSR: *A Survey of Research in Political Science*, Vol. III: *Political Science* (New Delhi: Allied, 1981).

Bhandarkar, S.S. *Association of Indian Universities 1925–1985* (New Delhi: AIU, 1985).

Bhardwaj, Surendra M. "Homeopathy in India", in Giriraj Gupta (Ed.), *Social and Cultural Context of Education in India* (New Delhi: Vikas, 1980).

Bhargava, P.M. and Chandana Chakraborty. *The Saga of Indian Science* (Hyderabad: Academic Publishers, 2003).

Bhat, P.N. "Veterinary Education in India", in S.L. Mehta and B.N. Mathur (Eds.), *Fifty Years of Agricultural Education in India* (New Delhi: ICAR, 2000).

Bhatia, Ravi P. "Federalism in India and Supreme Court Rulings", in B.D. Dua and M.P. Singh (Eds.), *Indian Federalism in the New Millennium* (New Delhi: Manohar, 2003).

Bhatt, Alok and Sudhir Chandra (Eds.). *Indian Response to Colonialism in the 19th Century* (New Delhi: Sterling Publishers, 1993).

Bhattacharya, Mohit. "The Mind of the Founding Fathers", in Nirmal Mukarji and Balveer Arora (Eds.), *Federalism in India: Origin and Development* (New Delhi: Vikas Publishing, 1992).

Bhave, Savita. *Krishik Krantiche Senani: Annasaheb Shinde* (Pune: Kalpana, June 1994) (Marathi).

Bhushan, Sudhanshu. *Restructuring Higher Education in India* (Jaipur/New Delhi: Rawat Publications, 2009).

Birch, A.H. *Federalism, Finance and Social Legislation in Canada, Australia and the US* (Oxford: Clarendon Press, 1955).

Bjorkman, H.W. and Kuldeep Mathur. *Policy, Technocracy and Development of Human Capital Policies in the Netherlands and India* (New Delhi: Manohar, 2002).

Blackburn, Stuart. *Print, Folklore and Nationalism in Colonial South India* (New Delhi: Permanent Black, 2003).

Bombwall, K.R. *Indian Politics and Government* (New Delhi: Atmaram and Sons, 1951).

——. *Foundations of Indian Federalism* (Bombay: Asia Publishing House, 1967).

Bondurant, Joan V. *Regionalism vs. Provincialism: A Study in Problems of Indian National Unity* (Berkeley: University of California Press, 1958).

Bowman, Ann O'M and R.C. Kearney. *State and Local Government* (Boston: Houghton Mifflin, 2002).

Brass, Paul. "The Politics of Ayurvedic Education: A Case Study of Revivalism and Modernization in India", in Susanne H. Rudolph and Lloyd I. Rudolph (Eds.), *Education and Politics in India* (New Delhi: Oxford University Press, 1972).

——. *Language, Religion and Politics in North India* (Cambridge: Cambridge University Press, 1974, Indian Ed., New Delhi: Vikas, 1975).

——. *Politics of India since Independence* (Cambridge: Cambridge University Press, 2nd Ed., 1994).

——. "Elite Interests, Popular Passions and Social Power in the Language Politics of India", in Asha Sarangi (Ed.), *Language and Politics in India* (New Delhi: Oxford University Press, 2009).

Brint, Steven. *The Future of the City of Intellect: The Changing American University* (Stanford: Stanford University, 2002).

Brown, Judith M. *Nehru: A Political Life* (New Haven and London: Yale University Press, 2003).

Chandra, Naresh. *Federalism and Linguistic States* (Calcutta: Firma K.L. Mukhopadhyaya, 1962).

Chatterjee, Meera. *Reaching Health for All* (New Delhi: Oxford University Press, 1992).

Chintamani, Sir C.Y. and M.R. Masani. *India's Constitution at Work* (Bombay: Allied Publishers, 1940).

Clerk, Burton R. et al. "Education", in David Sills (Ed.), *International Encyclopedia of Social Sciences*, Vol. 4 (London: Macmillan, 1968), pp. 509–16.

Cochran, Clarke E. et al. *American Public Policy: An Introduction* (Belmont, C.A.: Wadsworth Thomson Learning, 7th Ed., 2003).

Coleman, James S. (Ed.). *Education and Political Development* (Princeton, NJ: Princeton University Press, 1965).

Conlan, Timothy. *From New Federalism to Devolution* (Washington DC: The Brookings Institution, 1998).

Coombs, Philip H. *The World Educational Crisis: A System Analysis* (New York: Oxford University Press, 1968).

——. *The World Crisis in Education: The View from the Eighties* (New York: Oxford University Press, 1985).

Copland, Ian and John Rickard. *Federalism: Studies in Indian and Australian Federalism* (New Delhi: Manohar, 1998).

Curtis, Lionel. *Dyarchy* (Oxford: Clarendon Press, 1920).

Dalmia, Vasudha. *The Nationalization of Hindu Tradition* (New Delhi: Oxford University Press, 1996).

Daniel, John. *Mega Universities and Knowledge Media: Technology Strategies for Higher Education* (London: Kegan Paul, 1996).

Dasgupta, Jyotirindra. *Language Conflict and National Development* (Bombay: Oxford University Press, 1970).

——. "Democracy, Development and Federalism: Some Implications of Constructive Constitutionalism in India", in Subrata K. Mitra and Dietmar Rothermund (Eds.), *Legitimacy and Conflict in South Asia* (New Delhi: Manohar, 1997), pp. 82–106.

——. "India's Federal Design and Multi-cultural National Construction", in Atul Kohli (Ed.), *The Success of India's Democracy* (Cambridge: Cambridge University Press, 2001).

Dasgupta, Subrata. *The Bengal Renaissance: Identity and Creativity from Ram Mohan Roy to Rabindranath Tagore* (New Delhi: Permanent Black, 2007).

Denison, E.F. *The Sources of Economic Growth in the United States and the Alternative before Us* (New York: Committee for Economic Development, 1962).

Deolalikar, Anil B. *Attaining the Millennium Development Goals in India* (New Delhi: Oxford University Press, 2005).

Desai, Ashok H. and S. Murlidhar. "Public Interest Litigation: Potential and Problems", in B.N. Kirpal et al. (Eds.), *Supreme but not Infallible* (New Delhi: Oxford University Press, 2000).

Desai, D.M. *Universal, Compulsory and Free Primary Education in India* (Bombay: Indian Institute of Education, 1953).

Desai, Neera. "Women's Studies: Pursuit at Widening Horizons of Knowledge", in Ranjana Harsh and Bharathi Harishankar (Eds.), *Shakti: Multidisciplinary Perspectives on Empowerment of Women* (New Delhi and Jaipur: Rawat Publications, 2003), pp. 131–44.

Deshpande, M.M. *Sanskrit ani Prakrit Bhasha* (Pune: Shubhada Saraswat, 1995) (Marathi).

Dharampal. *The Beautiful Tree: Indigenous Indian Education in the Eighteenth Century* (Coimbatore: Keerthi Publishing House, 1983).

Dhavan, Rajeev. "Introduction", in Rajeev Dhavan and Paul Thomas (Eds.), *Nehru and the Constitution* (New Delhi: Indian Law Institute, 1975).

——. *The Supreme Court of India: A Socio-legal Critique of its Juristic Technique* (Bombay: N.M. Tripathi, 1977).

——. *The Amendment: Conspiracy or Revolution?* (Allahabad: Wheeler, 1978).

——. *President's Rule in the States* (New Delhi: Indian Law Institute, 1979).

Dibona, Joseph E. *Change and Conflict in the Indian University* (USA: Duke University, 1969).

Dicey, A.V. *Introduction to the Study of the Law of the Constitution* (London: Macmillan, 10th Ed., 1959).

Divatia, Kumud. *The Nature of Inter-relations of Government of India in the 20th Century* (Bombay: Popular Book Depot, 1957).

Dogra, P.D. and R.C. Dhiman (Eds.). *Forestry Research Education in India* (New Delhi: Indian National Science Academy, 1994).

Dore, R.P. *The Education in Tokugawa Japan* (London: Routledge, 1965).

Drèze, Jean and Amartya Sen. *India: Economic Development and Social Opportunity* (New Delhi: Oxford University Press, 1985).

——. *India: Development and Participation* (New Delhi: Oxford University Press, 2002).

Dror, Yehezkol. *Public Policy Making Re-examined* (New Brunswick, USA: Transaction Publishers, 3rd Printing 1983, 1st Ed., 1968).

Dua, B.D. "The Prime Minister and Federal System", in James Manor (Ed.), *Nehru to the Nineties* (London: Hurst and Company, 1994).

Dua, B.D. and M.P. Singh (Eds.), *Indian Federalism and the New Millennium* (New Delhi: Manohar, 2004).

Dua, Hans R. *Hegemony of English: Future of Developing Languages in the Third World* (Mysore: Yashoda Publications, 1994).

——. *Science Policy, Education and National Planning* (Mysore: Yashoda Publications, 2001).

Duchacek, Ivo D. *Comparative Federalism: The Territorial Dimension of Politics* (New York: Holt, Rinehart and Winston, 1970).

Eisenstein, Elizabeth. *The Printing Press as an Agent of Change*, 2 Vols. (Cambridge: Cambridge University Press, 1978).

Elazar, Daniel J. "Federalism", in David L. Sills (Ed.), *International Encyclopedia of Social Sciences*, Vol. 5 (London: Macmillan and Co., 1968), pp. 353–67.

——. *Exploring Federalism* (Albama: The University of Alabama Press, 1987).

Embling, Jack. *A Fresh Look at Higher Education: European Implications of the Carnegie Commission Reports* (Amsterdam: Elsevier Publishing Co., 1974).

Fisher, Julie. *Non-Governments: NGOs and the Political Development of the Third World* (Jaipur/New Delhi: Rawat Publications, 2003).

Flexner, Abraham. *Medical Education in the US and Canada: A Report to the Carnegie Foundation for the Advancement of Teaching* (New York, Bulletin No. 4, 1910).

——. *Medical Education in Europe: A Report to the Carnegie Foundation for the Advancement of Teaching* (New York, Bulletin No. 6, 1912).

Franda, Marcus. *West Bengal and the Federalizing Process in India* (Princeton: Princeton University Press, 1968).

——. *Small is Politics: Organizational Alternatives to India's Rural Development* (New Delhi: Wiley Eastern, 1979).

Frankel, Francine. *Political Economy of India 1947–2004* (New Delhi: Oxford University Press, 2004).

Freire, Paul. *The Pedagogy of the Oppressed* (London: Penguin, 1972).

Friedrich, Carl J. *Trends in Federalism in Theory and Practice* (London: Pall-Mall Press, 1968).

Fuller, Oliver. "Higher Education Governance in UK: Change and Continuity", in Alberto Amaral et al. (Eds.), *Governing Higher Education* (Dordrecht, Netherlands: Kluwer Academic Publishers, 2002), pp. 187–211.

Gadkari, S.S. and M.R. Kolhatkar (Eds.). *Innovations in Public Administration* (Bombay: Allied Publishers, 2002).

Gadgil, Madhav and Ramchandra Guha. *Ecology and Equity* (London: Routledge, 1990).

Gandhi, K.L. *The Problem of Official Language in India* (New Delhi: Arya Book Depot, 1984).

Garg, B.R. *Policy Documents in Indian Education* (Ambala Cantonment: Associated Publishers, 2001).

Gehlot, M.S. *The Office of the Governor: Its Constitutional Image and Reality* (Allahabad: Chugh Publications, 1977).

Ghosal, Sumantra et al. (Eds.). *World Class in India* (New Delhi: Penguin India, 2001).

Ghosh, Suresh Chandra. *The History of Education in Modern India 1757–1986* (New Delhi: Orient Longman, 1995).

Gnanam, A., David Bradbury and Antony Stella (Eds.). *Benchmarking Quality of Higher Education: The Indo-UK Perspectives* (New Delhi: Sterling Publishers, 2003).

Gopal, S. *The Vice-Royalty of Lord Irwin* (New Delhi: Oxford University Press, 1971).

——. (Ed.). *Jawaharlal Nehru: An Anthology* (New Delhi: Oxford University Press, 1980).

Grant, Harman P. "Inter-governmental Relations in Federal Systems", in Mary *Hawkesworth* and Maurice Kogan (Eds.), *Encyclopedia of Government and Politics*, Vol. I (London: Routledge, 1992).

——. *Federal Intervention in American Education: Past, Present and Future* (Melbourne: Georgia House, 1987).

Guha, Ramachandra. *India after Gandhi* (New Delhi: Macmillan, 2008).

——. "Crucibles of Modernity", in Ira Pande (Ed.), *Beyond Degrees: Finding Success in Higher Education* (New Delhi: Harper Collins, 2008), pp. 2–11.

Gupta, Atulchandra (Ed.). *Studies in Bengal Renaissance* (Jadavpur: National Council of Education, 1958).

Gupta, R.S. et al. (Eds.). *Language and the State: Perspectives on the Eighth Schedule* (New Delhi: Creative Books, 1995).

Gwyer, Maurice and A. Appadorai (Eds.). *Speeches and Documents on the Indian Constitution*, Vol. I (Bombay: Oxford University Press, 1957).

Hanson, A.H. *The Process of Planning: A Study of India's Five Year Plans 1950–1964* (London: Oxford University Press, 1966).

Hasan, Zoya, E. Sridharan and R. Sudarshan (Eds.). *India's Living Constitution: Ideas, Practices, Controversies* (New Delhi: Permanent Black, 2004).

Haq, Mahbub-ul. *Reflections on Human Development* (London: Oxford University Press, 1995).

Henry, Nicholas. *Public Administration and Public Affairs* (New Delhi: Prentice Hall of India, 2001).

Holdford John. *International Perspectives on Life-long Learning* (London, Kogan Page, 1999).

Honig, Stanley. *Modernizing Britain: Central, Devolved, Federal?* (London: Federation Trust, 2002).

Isaac, T.M. Thomas with Richard N. Franke. *Local Democracy and Development: People's Campaign for Decentralized Planning in Kerala* (New Delhi: Leftword, August 2000).

Indiresan, Jayalaxmi. "Quest for Quality: Intervention versus Impact", in Suma Chitnis and Philip Altbach (Eds.), *Higher Education Reforms in India: Experience and Perspectives* (New Delhi: Sage, 1993), pp. 309–33.

Indiresan, P.V. and N.C. Nigam. "The Indian Institutes of Technology: Excellence in Peril", in Suma Chitnis and Philip G. Altbach (Eds.), *Higher Education Reforms in India: Experience and Perspectives* (New Delhi: Sage Publications, 1993), pp. 334–364.

Irene, A. Gilbert. "The Organization of Academic Profession in India: The IES (1864–1974)", in Susanne H. Rudolph and Lloyd I. Rudolph (Eds.), *Education and Politics in India: Studies in Organization, Society and Polity* (Bombay: Oxford University Press, 1972), pp. 319–42.

Irvine, John (Ed.). *Equipping Science for the 21st Century* (Cheltenham, UK: Edgar Elgar, 1997).

Jacob, Alice. "Centre-State Governmental Relations in the Federal System", in S.N. Jain et al. (Eds.), *The Centre and the States* (New Delhi: National Publishing Co., 1972).

Jaggi, O.P. *Western Medicine: Indian Medical Education and Research* (Delhi/Lucknow: Atmaram & Sons, 1970).

Jain, M.P. *Outlines of Indian Legal History* (Bombay: N.M. Tripathi & Sons, 5th Ed., 1990).

——. "Some Reflections on the Research Progress of the Indian Law Institute", in S.N. Jain et al. (Eds.), *Legal Research and Methodology* (Mumbai: N.M. Tripathi & Sons, 2nd Ed., 2001), pp. 138–83.

——. *Indian Constitutional Law*, Vols. I and II (Nagpur: Wadhwa & Co., 5th Ed., 2003).

Jayaram, N. "The Language Question in Higher Education: Trends and Issues", in Suma Chitnis and Philip Altbach (Eds.), *Higher Education Reforms in India: Experience and Perspectives* (New Delhi: Sage, 1993), pp. 84–114.

——. "The Fall of the Guru: The Decline of the Academic Profession in India", in Philip Altbach (Ed.), *The Academic Profession in the Developing and the Middle Eastern Countries* (New York: Boston College Press, 2000).

Jeffries, Charles. *Illiteracy: A World Problem* (London: Pall-Mall Press, 1967).

Joshi, K.L. *Problems of Higher Education in India: An Approach to Structural Analysis and Reorganization* (Mumbai: Popular Prakashan, 1979).

——. *Higher Education: Historical and Other Problems* (Bombay: Popular Prakashan, 1981).

Kamat, A.R. *Educational Situation and Other Essays on Education* (New Delhi: Peoples' Publishing House, 1973).

Karve, R.P. *History of Government Law College, Bombay* (Bombay, 1938).

Kashyap, Anirban. *Governor's Role in Indian Constitution* (New Delhi: Lancer's Book, 1993).

Kashyap, Subhash C. (Ed.). *Union-State Relations in India* (New Delhi: Institute of Constitutional and Parliamentary Studies, 1969).

——. (Ed.). *National Policy Studies* (New Delhi: Tata McGraw Hill Publishing for Lok Sabha Secretariat, 1990).

Kaul, J.N. *Governance of Universities: Autonomy of the University Community* (New Delhi: Abhinav Publications, 1988).

Kaul, Rekha. *Caste, Class and Education* (New Delhi: Sage, 1993).

Kejariwal, O.P. *The Asiatic Society of Bengal: The Discovery of India's Past 1784–1838* (New Delhi: Oxford University Press, 1988).

Kelly, Gail P. "Setting the Boundaries of Debate about Education", in Philip G. Altbach (Ed.), *Excellence in Education* (New York: Prometheus Books, 1985), pp. 35–42.

Kennedy, Gerald Studdert. *Province and the Raj* (New Delhi: Sage, 1998).

Kesavan, B.S. *History of Printing and Publishing in India: A Story of Cultural Re-awakening,* Vol. I: *South Indian Origins of Printing and Its Efflorescence in Bengal,* Vol. II: *Origins of Printing and Publishing in Karnataka, Andhra Pradesh and Kerala*, Vol. III: *Origins of Printing and Publishing in the Hindi Heartland* (New Delhi: National Book Trust, 1985, 1988, 1993).

Khan, Rasheeduddin. *Federal India: A Design for Change* (New Delhi: Vikas, 1992).

Khanna, D.D. and G. Kueck (Eds.). *Principles, Power and Politics* (New Delhi: Macmillan India Ltd., 1999).

Khera, S.S. *Government in Business* (New Delhi: National Publishers, 1997).

Khilnani, Sunil. *The Idea of India* (New Delhi: Penguin Books, 1997).

Kincaid, John. "American Experience in the Theory and Practice of Fiscal Federalism", in Balveer Arora and Douglas Verney (Eds.), *Multiple Identities in a Single State: Indian Federalism in Comparative Perspective* (New Delhi: Konark, 1995), pp. 324–38.

King, Preston. *Federalism and Federations* (London: Croom Helm, 1982).

Kirpal, B.N. et al. (Eds.). *Supreme but not Infallible* (New Delhi: Oxford University Press, 2000).

Kohli, Atul (Ed.). *The Success of India's Democracy* (Cambridge: Cambridge University Press 2001, South Asia Ed., 2002).

Kolhatkar, D.D. *Commentary on the University Laws in India* (Indore: The Lawyers' Haven, 1978).

Kolhatkar, M.R. "Globalization and Higher Education Sector in India: A Policy Deficit", in S.C. Behar (Ed.), *Globalizing Education: Perception and Processes* (Pune: Indian Institute of Education, March 2005), pp. 205–16.

——. Educational Planning and National Development (New Delhi: M.D. Publications, 1997).

Kopf, David. *British Orientalism and the Bengal Renaissance: The Dynamics of Indian Modernization 1773–1835* (Berkeley: University of California Press, 1969).

——. *The Brahmo Samaj and the Shaping of the Modern Indian Mind* (Princeton: Princeton University Press, 1979).

Kothari, Rajani. "The Congress 'System' in India", in Hasan Zoya (Ed.), *Parties and Party Politics in India* (Oxford: Oxford University Press, 2002) (Originally published in *Asian Survey* in 1963).

Koundinya, R.K. and M.R. Kolhatkar. "District Planning and the Role of Panchayati Raj Institutions", in S.S. Gadkari and M.R. Kolhatkar (Eds.), *Innovations in Public Administration* (New Delhi: Allied Publishers, 2000).

Kripal, Viney and Meenakshi Gupta (Eds.). *Equality through Reservations* (Jaipur/New Delhi: Rawat Publications, 1999).

Kulandaiswamy, V.C. "National Educational Policies vis-à-vis Distance Education", in Suresh Garg et al. (Eds.), *Four Decades of Distance Education in India: Reflections on Policy and Practice* (New Delhi: Viva Books, 2004), pp. 24–38.

Kumar, Dharma. "The Fiscal System", in Dharma Kumar (Ed.), *Cambridge Economic History of India*, Vol. II (New Delhi: Orient Longman, 1992).

Lahoti, R.C. *Preamble: The Spirit and the Background of the Constitution of India* (Lucknow: Frontier Book Co., 2004).

Laska, John A. *Planning and Educational Development in India* (New York: Teachers' College Press, 1968).

Laubach, Frank. *India Shall be Literate* (Nagpur: National Christian Council of India, 1940).

Lewis, John P. *India's Political Economy: Governance and Reform* (New Delhi: Oxford University Press, 1995).

Lewis, Michael. *Inventing Global Ecology: Tracking the Biodiversity Ideas in India* (New Delhi: Orient Longman, 2003).

Louis, Prakash (Compiler). *Policy Documents of the Government of India* (New Delhi: Indian Social Institute, 2003).

Low, David. *Britain and Indian Nationalism* (Cambridge: Cambridge University Press, 1997).

MacMohan, Arthur W. (Ed.). *Federalism: Mature and Emergent* (Garden City, New York: Doubleday & Co., 1955).

Madan, T.N. *Doctors and Society: Three Asian Case Studies: India, Malaysia and Sri Lanka* (New Delhi: Vikas, 1980).

Madan, T.N. and B.G. Halbar. "Caste and Communities in the Private and Public Education of Mysore State", in Susanne H. Rudolph and Lloyd I. Rudolph (Eds.), *Education and Politics in India* (Delhi: Oxford University Press, 1972), pp. 121–47.

Maheshwari, S.R. *Government through Consultation: Advisory Committees for Independent Administration* (New Delhi: IIPA, July 1972).

Maheshwari, Shriram. *Problems and Issues in Administrative Federalism* (New Delhi: Allied, 1992).

——. *The Machinery of Governance in India* (New Delhi: Macmillan India, 2004).

Majumdar, A.K. *The Problems of Hindi: A Study* (Bombay: Bharatiya Vidya Bhavan, 1965).

——. *British Paramountcy and Indian Renaissance* (Bombay: Bharatiya Vidya Bhavan, 2nd Ed., 1981: a volume in the Bhavan's History of India Series).

Majumdar, Srilekha. "Infrastructure and Educational Administration", in Marmar Mukhopadhyaya and M. Parikh (Eds.), *Education in India: The Fifty Years* (New Delhi: Vikas, 1999), pp. 229–43.

Manor, James. "The Presidency", in Devesh Kapur and Pratap Bhanu Mehta (Eds.), *Public Institutions in India: Performance and Design* (New Delhi: Oxford University Press, 2005).

Masani, M.R. *India's Constitution at Work* (Bombay: Allied Publishers, 1940).

Mathew, A. *Ministry of Education: An Organizational History* (New Delhi: NIEPA, 1990).

Mathew, George. "The Federal Principle in Local Government", in Nirmal Mukarji and Balveer Arora (Eds.), *Federalism in India: Origin and Development* (New Delhi: Vikas, 1992).

——. *Panchayati Raj: From Legislation to Movement* (New Delhi: Concept, 1994).

Mathur, M.V., Ramesh K. Arora and Meena Sogani (Eds.). *Indian University System: Revitalization and Reform* (New Delhi: Wiley Eastern Ltd., 1994).

Mathur, P.L. *Role of Governor in Non-Congress States* (Jaipur: Rawat Publications, 1988).

McCully, Bruce T. *English Education and the Origin of Indian Nationalism* (New York: Columbia University Press, 1940).

Mehta, Pratap Bhanu. "India's Judiciary – The Promised Uncertainty", in Devesh Kapur and Pratap Bhanu Mehta (Eds.), *Public Institutions in India: Performance and Design* (New Delhi: Oxford University Press, 2005), pp. 158–93.

——. "The Inner Conflict of Constitutionalism: Judicial Review and the Basic Structure", in Zoya Hasan et al. (Eds.), *India's Living Constitution: Ideas, Practices and Controversies* (Delhi: Permanent Black, 2002), pp. 179–206.

Mehta, S.L. and B.N. Mathur (Eds.). *Fifty Years of Agricultural Education in India* (New Delhi: ICAR, 2000).

Menon, Nivedita and Aditya Nigam. *Power and Contestation: India since 1989* (Hyderabad: Orient Longman, 2008).

Menon, V.P. *Montague-Chelmsford Reforms* (Bombay: Bharatiya Vidya Bhavan, 1965).

Metcalfe, Barbara. *Colonial Contestations* (New Delhi: Sage, 2003).

Misra, B.B. *The Indian Middle Class* (Delhi: Oxford University Press, 1978, First Ed., 1961).

Mohanty, Nivedita. *Orissa Nationalism: Quest for United Orissa 1866–1936* (Delhi: Manohar, 1982).

Moore, R.J. "The Making of India's Paper Federation", in C.H. Phillips and Mary Wainwright (Eds.), *The Partition of India: Policies and Perspectives* (London: George Allen & Unwin, 1970).

Morris-Jones, W.H. *The Government and Politics of India* (UK: Eothen Press, 1970, Indian Reprint by Universal Book Stall, New Delhi, 1996).

Mugridge, Ian (Ed.). *Founding the Open Universities: Essays in Memory of G. Ram Reddy* (New Delhi: Sterling Publishers, 1997).

Mukarji, Nirmal and Balveer Arora. *Federalism in India: Origin and Development* (New Delhi: Vikas, 1992).

Mukherjee, Meenakshi. *Realism and Reality: The Novel and Society in India* (New Delhi: Oxford University Press, 1985).

——. *The Perishable Empire: Essays in Indian Writing in English* (New Delhi: Oxford University Press, 2003).

Mukherji, P. *Indian Constitutional Documents (1600–1918),* Vol. II (Calcutta/Shimla: Thacker Spink & Co., 1918).

Muthanna, D.M. *History of Modern Karnataka* (Delhi: Sterling, 1980).

Nagraj, M.V. "Legal Education through Distance Learning: Role of BCI", in A.K. Kaul and V.K. Ahuja (Eds.), *Legal Education in India in the 21st Century* (New Delhi: All-India Law Teachers' Congress, Faculty of Law, University of Delhi, 1999), pp. 304–05.

Naik, J.P. *Role of Central Government in Education* (New Delhi: Ministry of Education, 1961) (subsequently a chapter of 1965 Publication infra.).

——. *Educational Planning in India* (Bombay: Allied Publishers, 1965).

——. *Education in the Fourth Plan* (Bombay: Nachiketa Publications, 1968).

——. *Equality, Quality and Quantity: The Elusive Triangle in Indian Education* (Bombay: Allied Publishers, 1975).

——. *Education Commission and After* (New Delhi: Allied Publishers, 1983, Reprinted by APH Publishing Co., New Delhi, 1997).

Naik, J.P. and Syed Nurullah. *A Students' History of Education in India* (Bombay: Macmillan, Sixth Edition, 1974).

Naidu, N. Chandrababu with Shevanti Ninan. *Plain Speaking* (Bombay: Viking, Penguin, 2000).

Nand, P.K. "Cultural Construction and Professionalization: Nursing in India", in Giriraj Gupta (Ed.), *Social and Cultural Context of Education in India* (New Delhi: Vikas, 1980).

Nanda, B.R. *Gokhale: The Indian Moderates and the British Raj* (Delhi: Oxford University Press, 1977).

Nandy, Ashis. "Federalism, the Ideology of the State and Cultural Pluralism", in Nirmal Mukarji and Balveer Arora (Eds.), *Federalism in India: Origin and Development* (New Delhi: Vikas, 1992), pp. 27–40.

Natarajan, J. History of Indian Journalism: Part II of the Report of the Press Commission (New Delhi: Publication Division, Ministry of Information and Broadcasting, August 1955).

Nayyar, Baldev Raj. *National Communication and Language Policy in India* (New York: Frederick A. Praeger, 1968).

Nehru, Jawaharlal. *Autobiography* (London: Oxford University Press, 1st Ed., 1936, Epilogue added in 1940).

——. *The Unity of India* (London: Lindsay Drummond, 1941).

Nice, David C. *Federalism: The Politics of Inter-governmental Relations* (New York: St. Martin Inc., 1987).

Nurulla, Syed and J.P. Naik. *A History of Education in India during the British Times* (Bombay: Macmillan, 1st Ed., 1943, 2nd Ed., 1951).

Oommen, T.K. *Citizenship, Nationality and Ethnicity* (Oxford: Polity Press, 1976, Indian Reprint 2001).

Padda, Darshan S. and N.L. Maurya. "Accreditation of Higher Agricultural Education in India", in S.L. Mehta and B.N. Mathur (Eds.), *Fifty Years of Agricultural Education in India* (New Delhi: ICAR, 2000), pp. 125–39.

Page, G. Terry and J.B. Thomas (Eds.). *International Dictionary of Education* (London: Kegan Paul, 1977).

Pal, Chandra. *Centre-State Relations and Cooperative Federalism* (New Delhi: Deep & Deep Publishers, 1993).

Panchamukhi, P.R. (Ed.). *Studies in Educational Reforms in India*, Vols. I, II, III, IV and V. (Bombay: Himalaya Publishing, 1989).

Panikkar, K.M. *Working of Dyarchy in India: 1919–1927* (Bombay: D.B. Taraporevala Sons & Co., 1928).

Paranjape, H.K. *The Reorganised Planning Commission* (New Delhi: IIPA, September 1970).

Pateman, Carol. *Participation and Democratic Theory* (Cambridge: Cambridge University Press, 1970).

Pathan, S.N. *Quality Improvement Programme in Higher Education through NAAC* (Bhopal: Intellectual Book Bureau, 2005).

Patil, S.H. *Changing Bases of Federal Units in India*, Vols. I and II (New Delhi: Mohit Publications, 2006).

Pattison, Robert. *On Literacy: The Politics of the Word from Homer to the Age of Rock* (New York: Oxford University Press, 1982).

Pennycock, Alastar. *The Cultural Politics of Education as an International Language* (London: Longman, 1984).

——. *English and Discourse of Colonialism* (London: Routledge, 1998).

Phadke, Y.D. *Politics and Language* (Bombay: Himalaya Publishers, 1979).

Philipson, Robert. *Linguistic Imperialism* (Oxford: Oxford University Press, 1992).

Phukon, G. *Assam's Attitude to Federalism* (New Delhi: Sterling, 1984).

Pinto, David Antony and Marina Pinto. *Municipal Corporation of Greater Mumbai and the Ward Administration* (New Delhi: Konark Publishers, 2005).

Pinto, Marina R. *Federalism and Higher Education: The Indian Experience* (Bombay: Orient Longman, 1982).

——. *Public Policy and Delivery System in Higher Education* (Unpublished Report of a UGC Sponsored Minor Research Project – Typescript, Mumbai 1991)

——. "Coping with Federal Tension: Spotlight on the Governor", in T.P. Sankaran Kutty Nair (Ed.), *Contemporary India: Opportunities and Challenges* (Cochin: M.V. Pylee Foundation, 1993), pp. 56–70.

Prakash, Amit. *Jharkhand: The Politics of Development and Identity* (New Delhi: Orient Longman, 2001).

Prasad, Anirudh. *Centre-State Powers under Indian Federalism* (New Delhi: Deep & Deep Publishers, 1987).

——. *University Education, Administration and the Law* (New Delhi: Deep & Deep Publishers, 2000).

Psacharopoulos, George and Maureen Woodhall. *Education for Development: An Analysis of Investment Choices* (New York: Oxford University Press, 1985).

Putnam, Robert D. *Making Democracy Work: Civic Traditions in Modern Italy* (Princeton: Princeton University Press, 1993).

Pylee, M.V. *The Federal Court of India* (Bombay: Manaktalas, 1966).

Ramchandran, Raju. "The Supreme Court and the Basic Structure Doctrine", in B.N. Kirpal et al. (Eds.), *Supreme but not Infallible* (New Delhi: Oxford University Press, 2000), pp. 107–33.

Randhawa, M.S. *A History of ICAR* (New Delhi: ICAR, 1979).

Rao, K. Sudha. *Institutions Deemed to be Universities: Contribution to Higher and Professional Education and Research* (Rajasthan: Banasthali Vidyapeeth, 2003).

Rao, M. Govind. "Indian Fiscal Federalism from a Comparative Perspective", in Balveer Arora and Douglas Verney (Eds.), *Multiple Identities in a Single State: Indian Federalism in Comparative Perspective* (New Delhi: Konark Publishers, 1995).

Rao, K.V. Narayan. *The Emergence of Andhra Pradesh* (Bombay: Popular Prakashan, 1973).

Rao, V. Venkat. "North-Eastern Council and Union–State Relations", in N. Sanajaoba (Ed.), *Basic Issues in Union–State Relations* (New Delhi: Thomson Publications, 1985).

Raza, Moonis. *Higher Education in India: Retrospect and Prospect* (New Delhi: Association of Indian Universities, 1991).

Renold, Leah. *A Hindu Education: Early Years of Banaras Hindu University* (New Delhi: Oxford University Press, 2005).

Riker, William H. "Federalism", in Fred I. Greenstein and Nelson W. Polsby (Eds.), *Handbook of Political Science*, Vol. 5 (Reading, Mass.: Addison-Wesley Publishing Co., 1975).

Riker, William H. *The Development of American Federalism* (Boston: Kluwer Academic Publishers, 1987).

Rosen, George. *Western Economists and Eastern Societies: Aspects of Change in South Asia (1950–1970)* (New Delhi: Oxford University Press, 1985).

Rosenthal, Donald B. *The Expansive Elite: District Politics and State Policy-making in India* (Berkeley and Los Angeles: The University of California Press, 1977).

Rozenzweig, R.M. *Federal Intervention in Higher Education* (New York, McGraw-Hill, 1962).

Rudolph, Lloyd I. and Susanne H. Rudolph. *The Modernity of Tradition: Political Development in India* (Chicago: University of Chicago Press, 1967).

——. *In Pursuit of Lakshmi: The Political Economy of the Indian State* (Chicago: University of Chicago Press, 1987).

Rudolph, Susanne H. and Lloyd I. Rudolph (Ed.) *Education and Politics in India: Studies in Organisation, Society and Policy* (Delhi: Oxford University Press, 1974).

Saez, Lawrence. *Federalism without Centre* (New Delhi: Sage Publications, 2002).

Saha, S.N. "National Academy of Agricultural Research Management, Hyderabad", in S.L. Mehta and B.N. Mathur (Eds.), *Fifty Years of Agricultural Education in India* (New Delhi: ICAR, 2000).

Said, Edward. *Orientalism* (London: Penguin, 1978).

Saigal, K. "Federal Democracy and Pluralism in the North-East", in Nirmal Mukarji and Balveer Arora (Eds.), *Federalism in India: Origin and Development* (New Delhi: Vikas, 1992), pp. 213–37.

Saraswathi, L.S. "The Medium of Instruction in Tamil Nadu", in P.R. Panchamukhi (Ed.), *Studies in Educational Reforms in India,* Vol. IV (Bombay: Himalaya Publishing, 1989), pp. 1–89.

Sarangpani, Padma M. "The Open Class Room and its Critics", in Preet Rustagi (Ed.), *Concerns, Conflicts and Cohesion: Universalization of Elementary Education in India* (New Delhi: Oxford University Press, 2009), pp. 191–209.

Sathe, S.P. *Judicial Activism* (New Delhi: Oxford University Press, 2002).

——. "Nehru and Federalism", in Rajeev Dhavan and Paul Thomas (Eds.), *Nehru and the Constitution* (New Delhi: Indian Law Institute, 1975).

——. "Post Graduate Teaching and Research in Law", in S.K. Agrawal (Ed.), *Legal Education in India: Problems and Perspectives* (Bombay: N.M. Tripathi & Sons, 1983).

——. "Universities and the Law", in Amrik Sigh and G.D. Sharma (Eds.), *Higher Education in India: The Social Context* (New Delhi: Konark Publishers, 1988).

Sawer, Geoffrey. *Modern Federalism* (London: C.A. Watts & Co., 1969).

Saxena, Rekha. "Role of Inter-Governmental Agencies in Federal India", in B.D. Dua and M.P. Singh (Eds.), *Indian Federalism in the New Millennium* (New Delhi: Manohar, 2003).

——. *Situating Federalism: Mechanisms of Intergovernmental Relations in Canada and India* (New Delhi: Manohar, 2006).

Seal, Anil. *The Emergence of Indian Nationalism: The Competition and Collaboration in the Late 19th Century* (Cambridge: Cambridge University Press, 1968).

Seervai, H.M. *Constitutional Law of India*, Vols. I, II and III (Bombay: N.M. Tripathi & Sons, 4th Ed., 1991, 1993, 1996).

Setalvad, M.C. *Union and State Relations under the Indian Constitution* (Calcutta: Eastern Law House, 1974).

Shah, K.T. *The Report of the National Planning Committee* (Bombay: Vora & Company, 1948).

Sharma, G.D. "NIEPA: Instrumentality of Change", in P.R. Panchmukhi (Ed.), *Studies in Educational Reforms in India*, Vol. II (Bombay: Himalaya Publishing, 1989), pp. 506–62.

Sharma, Kavita A. *Fifty Years of UGC* (New Delhi: UGC, 2003).

Shattock, Michael. *The UGC and the Management of British Universities* (Buckingham: SRHE/Open University Press, 1994).

Shils, Edward A. "Toward a Modern Intellectual Community in New States", in James S. Coleman (Ed.), *Education and Political Development* (Princeton, NJ: Princeton University Press, 1967).

Shiv, Rao B. (Ed.). *The Framing of India's Constitution*, Vols. I to V (New Delhi: IIPA, 1968).

Shourie, Arun. *Eminent Historians: Their Technology, Their Line, Their Fraud* (New Delhi: ASA Publications, 1998).

——. *Governance and the Sclerosis that has set in* (New Delhi: ASA/Rupa & Co., 2004).

Shukla, J.D. *Indianization of All-India Services* (New Delhi: Allied Publications, 1982).

——. *Towards the New Pattern of Education in India* (New Delhi: Sterling Publishers, 1976).

——. "Central Board of Secondary Education", in P.R. Panchmukhi (Ed.), *Studies in Educational Reforms in India*, Vol. II (Bombay: Himalaya Publishing, 1989), pp. 411–49.

Shultz, T.W. "Education and Economic Growth", in N.B. Henry (Ed.), *Social Forces Influencing American Education* (Chicago: National Society for the Study of Education, University of Chicago Press, 1961).

Simeon, Richard. *Federal Provincial Diplomacy: The Making of Recent Policy in Canada* (Toronto: University of Toronto Press, 1972).

Singh, M.P. "Towards a More Federalized Parliamentary System in India: Exploring Functional Change", pp. 187–204 and "The Impact of Global and Regional Integration", in B.D. Dua and M.P. Singh (Eds.), *Indian Federalism in the New Millennium* (New Delhi: Manohar, 2003), pp. 370–435.

Singh, S.P. *Centre-State Relations in Agricultural Development* (New Delhi: Vikas, 1973).

Smiley, Donald V. *The Federal Condition in Canada* (Toronto: McGraw Hill Press Ltd., 1987).

Social Science Research Council. *Social Science Research Capacity in South Asia* (New York, 2002).

Sorabjee, Soli S. et al. (Eds.). *The Governor: Sage or Saboteur?* (New Delhi: Roli Book International, 1985).

Spolsky, Bernard. *Language Policy* (Cambridge: Cambridge University Press, 2004).

Sprott, P. *DMK in Power* (Bombay: Nachiketa Publications, 1970).

Stabbing, P. *Forestry in India*, Vols. I, II, III and IV (London: Kegan Paul, different years in 1920s).

Stepan, Alfred. "Federalism, Multinational Societies and Negotiating a Democratic State Nation", in K. Shankar Bajpai (Ed.), *Democracy and Diversity* (New Delhi: Oxford University Press, 2007), pp. 225–61.

Stokes, Eric. *The English Utilitarians and India* (London: Oxford University Press, 1959, Indian Reprint 1982).

Streeten, Paul and Michael Lipton (Eds.). *The Crisis of Indian Planning: Economic Planning in the 1960's* (London: Oxford University Press, 1968).

Studdert-Kennedy, Gerald. *Providence and the Raj* (New Delhi: Sage, 1998).

Styler, W.E. *Adult Education in India* (Oxford: Oxford University Press, 1966).

Supreme Court of India. *The Supreme Court of India: Sentinel of Freedom* (New Delhi, 2000).

Taylor, David. *The Territories and States of India* (London: Europa Publications, 2002).

Teaford, John. *The Rise of the States: The Evolution of American States* (Baltimore: Johns Hopkins University Press, 2002).

Tilak, J.B.G. (Ed.). *Financing of Secondary Education in India* (New Delhi: Shipra Publications, 2008).

Toole, Lawrence J.O. (Ed.). *American Inter-governmental Relations* (Washington DC: CQ Press, 2000).

Tooley, James. *The Beautiful Tree: A Personal Journey into How the World's Poorest People are Educating Themselves¿* (New Delhi: Penguin-Viking, 2009).

Trautmann, Thomas R. *Aryans and British India* (Berkeley: University of California Press, 1997).

——. *Languages and Nations: The Dravidian Proof of Colonial Madras* (Berkeley and Los Angeles: The University of California Press, 2006).

Trevelyan, C.E. *On the Education of the People of India* (London: Longman, Orme, Brown, Green, 1838).

Ulrik, Stark. *An Empire of Books: The Naval Kishore Press and the Diffusion of the Printed Word in Colonial India* (New Delhi: Permanent Black, 2007).

Varma, L.R., P.K. Khosla and R.N. Sahgal. "Status of Forestry Education and Training in India", in S.L. Mehta and B.N. Mathur (Eds.), *Fifty Years of Agricultural Education in India* (New Delhi: ICAR, 2000).

Venkatarangiya, M. *Competitive and Cooperative Trends in Federalism* (Poona: Gokhale Institute of Politics & Economics, 1951).

Venkatarangiya, M. and M. Pattabhiram (Eds.). *Local Government in India* (Select Readings), (Bombay: Allied Publishers, 1969).

Venkatarangiya, M. and M. Shiviah. *Indian Federalism* (New Delhi: Arnold Heineman, 1975).

Verney, Douglas. "Are all Federations Federal? The US, Canada and India", in Balveer Arora and Douglas Verney (Eds.), *Multiple Identities in Single States: Indian Federalism in Comparative Perspective* (New Delhi: Konark Publishers, 1995).

——. "India in Search of a New Regime", in Francine R. Frankel et al. (Eds.), *Transforming India: Social and Political Dynamics of Democracy* (New Delhi: Oxford University Press, 2000).

Vernon, R.V. and N. Mansergh (Eds.). *Advisory Bodies: A Study of Their Uses in Relation to Central Government (1919–1939)* (London: George Unwin, 1940).

Vishwanathan, Gauri. "English in a Literate Society", in Rajeshwari Sundar Rajan (Ed.), *The Lie of the Land: English Literary Studies in India* (New Delhi: Oxford University Press, 1992).

——. *The Masks of Conquest* (New York: The Columbia University Press, 1989).

Vishwanathan, Shiv. *Organization for Science: The Making of an Industrial Research Laboratory* (New Delhi: Oxford University Press, 1985).

Warikoo, K. "Language and Politics in Jammu and Kashmir: Issues and Perspectives", in Asha Sarangi (Ed.), *Language and Politics in India* (New Delhi: Oxford University Press, 2009).

Watts, R.L. *New Federations: Experiments in the Commonwealth* (Oxford: Clarendon Press, 1966).

Watts, Ronald L. "An Introduction to the themes of the 4th International Conference" in Anwar Shah et al. (Eds.), *Conference Reader of the Fourth International Conference on Federalism* (New Delhi: Inter-State Council, 2007).

Weiner, Myron. *The Child and the State in India* (New Delhi: Oxford University Press, 1999).

——. *The Politics of Scarcity* (Bombay: Asia Publishing, 1963).

Weller, Patrick. "The Establishment of Schools Commission: A Case-Study in the Politics of Education", in I.K.F. Birch and B. Smart (Eds.), *The Commonwealth Governance and Education 1964–1976* Richmond (Victoria, Australia: Drummond, 1973).

Wheare, K.C. *The Federal Government* (London: Oxford University Press, Fourth Ed., 1963).

Wolfenden, Sir John F. "Great Britain", in James A. Perkins (Ed.), *Higher Education: From Autonomy to Systems* (Washington DC, Voice of America: Forum Series, 1973).

Yadav, M.S. and Santosh Panda. "Open and Distance Higher Education: Policy and Development", in Santosh Panda (Ed.), *Open and Distance Education* (New Delhi: Arvalli Books International, 1999).

Zastoupil, Lynn and Martin Moir (Eds.). *The Great Education Debate* (London: Curzon Press, 1999).

III. Articles

Ambedkar, B.R. "Thoughts on the Reforms of Legal Education in the Bombay Presidency", *Government Law College Magazine*, Vol. VII, No. 1, January 1936, pp. 6–17.

Anonymous. "Proposed Amendments to Medical Council of India Act", *Freedom First*, Mumbai, October-December 2005, pp. 25–26.

Awasthi, A.K. "Legal Education: Role of BCI, Judicial Intervention and Suggestions", *Indian Bar Review*, Vol. XXIX, Nos. 3 & 4, 2002, pp. 9–30.

——. "Powerlessness of BCI to Improve Standards in Legal Education", *Journal of Indian Law Institute*, January-March 2004, pp. 55–78.

Chowdhary, T.H. "Do we need the AICTE¿", *Economic and Political Weekly* (*EPW*), 17th February, 2001, pp. 595–96.

Deshpande, J.V. "AICTE as Politicians' Handmaiden", *EPW*, 2nd December, 2000, pp. 4302–08.

——. "Education as Business", *EPW*, 15th July, 2002, pp. 2506–08.

Fazal, M.A. "Subsidiarity Principle in European Unions", *Journal of the Indian Law Institute,* July-September 1996, pp. 311–30.

Gopalkrishnan, R. and A. Sharma. "Education Guarantee Scheme in Madhya Pradesh", *EPW*, Vol. 33, No. 37, 26th September, 1998.

Gopalan, K. "On the Working of the National Council for Teacher Education (NCTE)", *University News*, Vol. 40, No. 30, 29th July, 2002, pp. 6–8.

Habib Irfan, Arjun Dev, Anil Sadgopal, Shamim Akhtar, K.M. Srimali, K.N. Ganesh, Romila Thapar and Anubhuti Maurya. "Debating Education" (Articles on NCF 2005), *Social Scientist*, Vol. 33, Nos. 9–10, September/October 2005, pp. 1–64.

Hulshorf, Karin. "Follow the Learning Curve", *Times of India,* 1st April, 2010.

India Today, 6th October, 2008, pp. 51–57.

Jha, B.K. "Technical Education in UP", *EPW*, 29th May, 2004, pp. 2207–08.

Kumar, Krishna. "Agriculture, Modernization and Education: Contours of a Departure", *EPW*, Vol. 31, 1996, pp. 2267–74.

Kolhatkar, M.R. "Second Chamber in States: Role in the Three Tier Federalism", *Journal of Constitutional and Parliamentary Studies*, January-June 2007, pp. 89–98.

——. "Yashpal Committee Report: A Lost Opportunity", *Samaj Prabodhan Patrika*, Belgaon, July-December 2009 (Marathi). "Learning about Learning", *Economic Times*, Mumbai, 4th February, 2010.

Menon, Madhav. "Convocation Address at Jadavpur University", 2001, *University News*, Vol. 40, No. 3, 21st January, 2002.

Munck, Ronald. "Globalization and Democracy", *Annals of American Academy of Political and Social Science*, May 2002, pp. 10–21.

Powar, K.B. "Deemed to be Universities: Their Genesis and History: Present Status and Future Prospects", *University News*, Vol. 43, No. 13, 29th March, 2004.

Qadeer, Imrana and K. Nayar. "Politics of Pedagogy in Public Health", *Social Scientist*, Vol. 34, No. 2, January-February 2005, pp. 47–75.

Report of the Supreme Court Committee on Reforms of Legal Education, *Indian Bar Review*, Vol. XXII, No. 4, 1995, pp. 7–34.

Sen, Amartya. "Child Report on West Bengal", I & II, *Hindu*, 19th/20th December, 2009.

Tilak, J.B.G. "Centre State Relations in the Financing of Education in India", *Comparative Educational Review*, Vol. 33, No. 4, November 1987, pp. 450–80.

——. "Knowledge Commission and Higher Education", *University News*, 26th November to 21st December, 2007, pp. 59–62.

——. "The Proposed NCHE: A Solution worse than the Disease¿", *EPW*, 1st May, 2010, pp. 11–13.

——. "Budget 2010: Neither Vision nor Policy for Education", *EPW*, 27th March, 2010, pp. 60–64.

——. "The Foreign Educational Institutions Bill: A Critique", *EPW*, May 8–14, 2010, pp. 12–15.

Zoya Robert, Gobind Nankani and Indermit Gill. "Rethinking Growth", *Finance and Development*, Washington DC, March 2006, pp. 7–11.

List of Cases Cited

- *Ashok Kumar Thakur vs. Union of India,* 2008.
- *Aruna Roy vs. Union of India,* 2003.
- *Atibari Tea Co. vs. Assam* (1961) 1 SCR 869.
- *Automobile Transport (Rajasthan) Ltd. vs. Rajasthan* (1963) 1 SCR 491.
- *J.P. Unnikrishnan vs. State of Andhra Pradesh,* (1993) 1 SCC 645.
- *Kiran Babu vs. State of Andhra Pradesh* (AIR 1986 AP 275).
- *Kuldip Nayar vs. Union of India* (2006) SCW 4408.
- *Manek Gandhi vs. Union of India* (1978) 2 SCR 621.
- *Mohini Jain vs. State of Karnataka,* (1992) 2 SCC 645.
- *Mohini Jain vs. State of Karnataka,* (1992) 3 SCC 666.
- *O.N. Mahendru vs. Bar Council,* AIR 1968 SC 888.
- *Osmania University Teachers' Association vs. State of AP,* AIR 1987 SC 2034.
- *Pradeep Jain vs. Union of India* (AIR 1984 SC 1420).
- *Shamsher Singh vs. State of Punjab* (AIR 1974 SC 2192).
- *S.R. Bommai vs. Union of India* (1994) 3 SCC 1919.
- *State of Karnataka vs. Union of India* (1973) 4 SCC 304.
- *State of Rajasthan vs. Union of India* (1977) 3 SCC 572.
- *TMA Pai Foundation vs. State of Karnataka* (2002) 6 SCC 481.

Index